THE
FINAL OVER

THE CRICKETERS
OF SUMMER 1914

CHRISTOPHER SANDFORD

To Sefton Sandford

1925–2012

Cover illustrations
Front: top: Hampshire County Cricket Club 1914 line-up. (Hampshire CCC, courtesy of Dave Allen)
Back: British troops arrive at Le Harve.

First published 2014
by Spellmount, an imprint of The History Press
The Mill, Brimscombe Port
Stroud, Gloucestershire, GL5 2QG
www.thehistorypress.co.uk

Reprinted 2014
This paperback edition published 2015

British Library Cataloguing in Publication Data.
A catalogue record for this book is available from the British Library.

ISBN 978 0 7509 6298 8

Typesetting and origination by The History Press
Printed and bound in Great Britain by TJ International Ltd

CONTENTS

Preface   7

1   Golden Age   11
2   Spring   32
3   Early Summer   51
4   Midsummer   76
5   High Summer   102
6   Blood-red Sunset over the Thames   124
7   To Arms   144
8   '16 Dead Englishmen'   170
9   Endgame   201

Appendix: Roll of Honour   234

Bibliography   245
Sources and Chapter Notes   246
Index   252

PREFACE

A few years ago I was watching my local cricket club in action when a man of about middle age, coated in designer stubble and with several bits of metal puncturing his face, clad only in voluminous army-surplus shorts, came by to chat. I should mention that the club is in Seattle, USA. After watching the game for a few minutes with an increasingly bemused expression, he asked the inevitable question: could I please explain the attraction? I made the usual not very successful attempt by an Englishman to decipher the game of cricket to an American. The man left, rocked to his core that one batsman could score as many as 20 or 30 in a single game and, I think, also muttering something about a contest that can last five days and end in a draw not immediately conforming to American-spectator standards of entertainment. It was only later, giving the matter some more thought, that I realised the answer to the question was in fact *security*. With one or two rare exceptions, I've always felt completely and contentedly safe while at a cricket match: not only physically safe, but safe from the faintly nagging feeling that something, somewhere, is about to happen to my ultimate detriment. For me, it's a sort of holiday from the real world. So long as I'm at the back of a stand at Lord's or the Oval, or sprawled under the boundary trees in Seattle, nothing can go seriously wrong.

All of which is fine as far as it goes. Perhaps one needs to be mildly paranoid about the outside world in the first place in order to find a sanctuary in cricket. It is worth mentioning only because of the very obvious contrast to the players and spectators of the game in England exactly a hundred years ago; for many of them, life could hardly have been less safe or secure as the clock wound down inexorably to the first week of August. It only adds to the poignancy of the story to see how few of them had any inkling of disaster until almost the last instant. Four out of five adults in Britain, according to one study, actually and consciously disbelieved that there would be a general war right up until the moment on the bank holiday Friday of 31 July 1914 when the Stock Exchange closed down early for the first time in its 113-year modern history. 'If the bankers were worried, so should we be', said Harold Wright, an opening batsman at Leicestershire. Just over a year later, Wright was mown down in the sustained and ultimately futile Allied offensive at Gallipoli. He was 31.

The Final Over is not a statistical, or necessarily a chronological, record of every first-class cricket match played in England that season. There are other books, notably *Wisden*, that do the job admirably. It does, however, take the view that cricket is a reflection of life, and that by and large cricketers reacted to the crisis in exactly the same way as everyone else, no better and no worse. The records show that they volunteered at broadly the same rate as other young men, and that they died, too, in proportion: in coldly statistical terms, roughly one in nine of those who fought did not return alive. This book follows some of those individuals and their families on and off the cricket field, and ultimately onto the bloody beaches of Gallipoli, or into the trenches of Flanders that had been churned into a sea of mud and rubble.

The Final Over attempts to shed light on the 'golden age' of English cricket; to demonstrate what it meant to be an 'amateur' or a 'professional' player a hundred years ago; and to show again the arbitrary nature of war, where one man could fall and the man next to him come home and live to be 90.

And there were other casualties. The outbreak of war weighed heavily on some of the recently retired greats of cricket, many of them already struggling to cope with what Andrew Stoddart, the former England captain, called 'life after death'. As we'll see, the implications for several of these men would be devastating. The notion of an industry or profession jettisoning some of its most distinguished practitioners in their early middle age may also have a certain resonance today.

Finally, this is neither a political nor a military history of the First World War. There is no shortage of published work on the subject, and a very few suggestions can be found in the bibliography at the end of the book. I should also make clear that it is not a comprehensive list of all worldwide cricketers in some way affected by the war, and no slight is intended on any name omitted. My own main interest is the narrower but hopefully timely one of showing how certain British public figures, particularly sportsmen, reacted to the events of that summer. During the two years I was writing the book, I sometimes thought back to an earlier work I did on Arthur Conan Doyle and Harry Houdini, a relationship that at first prospered and then imploded spectacularly in the 1920s. Of his kind, Conan Doyle (a keen cricketer) was perhaps typical of the sort of instinctive patriot whose conceptions of war were shaped more by the past than by premonitions of the future. In the period from November 1914 to November 1918, he lost eleven of his immediate family members, including his eldest son, to combat or disease. Doyle, it seems to me, embodied some of the paradoxes brought about by the First World War; the creator of English literature's most famous human calculating machine, he spent the rest of his life attempting to contact dead people. I mention it just to show how the broad events treated in this book made some men and broke so many others. If nothing else, I have tried to portray the individuals seen here in the context of how they viewed the partly ludicrous, partly horrific acts of that summer, and not necessarily as we see them today. Although I hesitate to use the word 'enjoyable', it was a strangely absorbing book to write – rather more so, I admit, than my recent biography of the Rolling Stones, a group of undoubted charm, whose essential effect on their audience could surely be reproduced by stewards walking up and down the aisles jolting random concert-goers with cattle prods. I only wish I could blame someone listed below for the shortcomings of the text. They are mine alone.

For archive material, input or advice I should thank, institutionally: The *American Conservative*, Blackheath RFC, Bookcase, *Bright Lights*, the British Library, the British Museum, Cambridge University Library, CBS News, *Chronicles*, Cricket Australia, CricInfo, the Cricket Society, *Daily Mail*, *Daily Telegraph*, ECB, Essex CCC, General Register Office, Gethsemane Lutheran Church, Hampshire CCC, HMS *Protector* Association, the Imperial War Museum, Kent CCC, the MCC Library, Middlesex CCC, the *Missoulian*, National Army Museum, *Navy News*, Pip, Public Records Office, Radley College, Renton Library, Rugby School, St Peter and Paul Church Tonbridge, Seattle Cricket Club, Seattle Mariners, Seattle Public Library, Somerset CCC, South Africa Cricket Association, Sportspages, Surrey CCC, Surrey History Centre, *Taki's Magazine*, UK National Archives, USA Cricket Association, Warwickshire CCC, Yorkshire CCC.

Professionally: Wendy Adams, Christina Alder, Dave Allen, Jeffrey Archer, Stanley Booth, Paul Bradley, Phil Britt, Paul Brooke, Susan Carey, Dan Chernow, Kathryn Churchouse, Allan Clarke, Paul Clements, the Cricket Writers' Club, Robert Curphey, Curtis Brown, Paul Darlow, Alan Deane, Tony Debenham, Andrew Dellow, Mike Dent, Michael Dorr, Lauren Dwyer, Alan Edwards, the late Godfrey Evans, Rex Evans, Mike Fargo, Tom Finn, Judy Flanders, Tom Fleming, John Fraser, Bill Furmedge, Ann Gammie, Jim Geller, Tony Gill, Freddy Gray, Ryan Grice, the late Reg Hayter, Michael Heath, Andrew Hignell, Jim Hoven, Emily Hunt, the late Len Hutton, Neil Jenkinson, Mike Jones, Edith Keep, David Kelly, Imran Khan, Max King, Alan Lane, Barbara Levy, Cindy Link, John Major, Robert Mann, Ian Marshall, the late Christopher Martin-Jenkins, Dave Mason, Colin Midson, Jo Miller, Nicola Nye, Maureen O'Donnell, Orbis, Michael Owen-Smith, Max Paley, Palgrave Macmillan, David Pracy, Katharina Rae, Neil Rand, Andrew Renshaw, Jim Repard, Mike Richards, Scott P. Richert, David Robertson, Neil Robinson, Peter

Robinson, Jane Rosen, Malcolm Rowley, Stephen Saunders, Paul Shelley, Don Short, Ron Simms, Ben Slight, A.C. Smith, Peter Smith, Andrew Stuart, Janet Tayler, Don Taylor, Andrew Trigg, Charles Vann, Suzanne Walker, Carol Ward, Simon Ware, Adele Warlow, Alan Weyer, Mark White, Jo Whitford, Aaron Wolf, Tom Wolfe, David Wood, Martin Wood, Tony Yeo.

Personally: Ann Allsop, Arvid Anderson, Maynard Atik, the Banners, Pete Barnes, Alison Bent, Hilary and Robert Bruce, Jon Burke, John Bush, Lincoln Callaghan, Don Carson, Pat Champion, Hunter Chatriand, Cocina, Common Ground, John Cottrell-Dormer, Tim Cox, Celia Culpan, Deb K. Das, the Davenport, the Deanes, Mark Demos, Monty Dennison, the Dowdall family, Emerald Downs, John and Barbara Dungee, Bob Dylan, Rev. Joanne Engquist, John Engstrom, Explorer West, Malcolm Galfe, the Gay Hussar, Colleen Graffy, Tom Graveney, Jeff Griffin, Grumbles, Masood Halim, the late Marvin Hamlisch, *Hemispheres*, the late Judy Hentz, Alastair Hignell, Charles Hillman, the late Amy Hofstetter, Alex Holmes, Hotel Vancouver, Jo Jacobius, the Jamiesons, Lincoln Kamell, the Keelings, Aslam Khan, Scott Kramer, KSA, Terry Lambert, Belinda Lawson, the late Borghild Lee, Todd Linse, Cherry Liu, the Lorimers, Rusty MacLean, the Macris, George Madsen, Lee Mattson, Chip Maxson, Les McBride, Jim and Rana Meyersahm, Missoula Doubletree, Sheila Mohn, Bertie Morgan, the Morgans, John and Colleen Murray, Jonathan Naumann, Chuck Ogmund, Larry Olsen, Phil Oppenheim, Pacific Rim Hotel Vancouver, Valya Page, Michael Palmer, Robin Parish, Peter Perchard, Greg Phillips, Chris Pickrell, PNB, Roman Polanski, the Prins family, Renton Coin Shop, Dean Richardson, Ailsa Rushbrooke, Debbie Saks, Sam, my father the late Sefton Sandford, Sue Sandford, Peter Scaramanga, Seattle Symphony, John Shepherd, the Sheriff family, the late Cat Sinclair, Fred and Cindy Smith, Rev. and Mrs Harry Smith, Debbie Standish, Lill Stanley, my friend the late Ted Stanley, Thaddeus Stuart, Jack Surendranath, the Taylors, TEW, Mandolyna Theodoracopulos, Diana Turner, Ben and Mary Tyvand, William Underhill, Diana Villar, Ross Viner, Tony Vinter, Lisbeth Vogl, John and Mary Wainwright, Neill Warfield, the late Chris West, Richard Wigmore, Willis Fleming family, Rusty Zainoulline.

And, as always, a low bow to Karen and Nicholas Sandford.

C.S.

2014

1

GOLDEN AGE

MCC's seventh tour of South Africa started like an elaborate costume drama. The teams took the field on Saturday 8 November 1913 at the then haphazardly rustic Newlands ground in Cape Town accompanied by a brass band, a welcoming speech by the city's mayor, and a crowd of 3,000 spectators in 'loud stripes and voluminous summer dresses'. The local *Weekend Argus* generously described the visitors as being 'as good a side as ever left England'. Nine of the fourteen tourists were veterans of the successful campaign to Australia of 1911/12, also led by the boxing cricketer Johnny Douglas of Essex, and they completed their strength with the young Surrey amateur Morice Bird, notable for having once scored two hundreds for Harrow in their annual clash at Lord's against Eton; Lionel Tennyson, the poet's grandson, who appeared for Eton in the same tie, if with rather less success; the Norfolk and Sussex all-rounder Albert Relf, a sound man in a crisis; and the Yorkshireman Major Booth, good enough to have scored over 1,000 runs and taken 158 wickets in the previous English summer, whose forename was to prove somewhat confusing when he went on to join the army as a 2nd lieutenant. According to the *Argus*, 'the Englishmen as a whole appeared robust to the point of invincible on the Cape', whereas the home team had struck a lean period 'with a host of run-getters, but not much to offer in the field'. After a lacklustre opening performance at Cape Town, the tourists duly won all three of the first four Tests that were completed, before appearing for the final international game at Port Elizabeth which ran from 27 February to 3 March 1914. In the event, it was to be the last Test match involving England's cricketers for nearly seven years.

They won comfortably there, too. It has been rated as good an all-round England side as would appear anywhere again until the 1950s, and is worth giving in batting order: J.B. Hobbs, W. Rhodes, H. Strudwick (wkt), J.W. Hearne, C.P. Mead, F.E. Woolley, J.W.H.T. Douglas (capt), L.H. Tennyson, M.C. Bird, M.W. Booth, A.C. Relf. Major Booth got his chance only because the great fast-medium bowler and contrarian Sydney Barnes, who was 37, pulled out due to a financial disagreement. He would not represent England again. In the four Tests he did play in South Africa Barnes took 49 wickets, which was only one fewer than all the eight other England bowlers used in the series. Despite the tourists' victory at Port Elizabeth, the *Argus* reported that the last day's crowd was 'convivial', watching the comings and goings of their batsmen with equanimity, and 'filling the blanks in the play with their own human-ity … there was frequent laughter around the refreshment tent when a spectator there scored a repartee'. When South Africa's Reggie Hands, one of three cricket-playing brothers and a former England rugby international, got a wide long-hop from Douglas, he stepped back and shaped to make a full-blooded shot for a certain four to square leg. But not so. Somehow Hands completely misjudged the line of the ball, lost his balance, and fell to earth flat on his chest. Strudwick, the England keeper, made about 5 yards in a shallow dive worthy of the Olympic pool, and still had time to right himself and remove the bails while the batsman remained *hors de combat*. This 'brought a fresh round of satiri-cal comment from among the crowd', wrote the *Argus*. 'They accepted the inevitable, and fast ensuing, loss of the Test in excellent heart.'

There was an equally happy informality about the party later that evening for both sets of players and their guests. Before dinner, the cricketers mingled with the state prime minister Louis Botha. Grasping the England captain by the arm and alluding to his former career as an Olympic middleweight boxing champion, the premier said, 'Well, it's another knockout blow, Mr Douglas. I heartily congratulate you. The only difference is that your victims here can at least walk away unassisted.' Douglas remembered being charmed by the humour and generosity of this little exchange, and of his South African hosts in general. 'It was the tour of everybody who played in it', he wrote. 'Victor and vanquished emerged with equal honour; and the chief laurel crowned the game of cricket itself.'

It is worth dwelling on that particular Test at Port Elizabeth for a moment, if only to see what happened to some of its participants over the next five years. Within a month of the outbreak of war in August 1914, three of England's batsmen, Hobbs, Rhodes and Strudwick, were employed full- or part-time in munitions factories; Hearne and Woolley both served in civilian posts and continued to play cricket in the Bradford League, where they would occasionally encounter Sydney Barnes, who would appear there well into his sixties; Charles 'Phil' Mead was apparently excused active duty, suffering from varicose veins and other medical issues; and Morice Bird fought bravely at Gallipoli, where he contracted amoebic dysentery, later emerging after the war as coach of Harrow, his old school, before his early death at the age of 45.

Moving down the England batting order, some of the players fared better than others. One or two of their lives, much like the times, often proved unhappy, macabre, turbulent, impoverished and plain bleak. On 23 July 1914, 24-year-old Lionel Tennyson was part of the Hampshire side starting a three-day match against Surrey at the United Services ground in Portsmouth. It was a day of 'listless inactivity', both on and off the field, the city's *Evening News* reported. Surrey, the County Championship leaders, eventually won the match by 8 wickets with two sessions to spare. Tennyson, a serving soldier, elected not to appear in his side's next match, against Essex at Leyton, which ended in a draw on the evening of Saturday 1 August. Heavy rain then set in. Two nights later, on the bank holiday Monday, Tennyson went to bed in his London flat and dreamed he was scoring a match-winning century for his county. 'Although I acknowledged the applause in the orthodox fashion,' he wrote, 'it refused to stop.' Gradually Tennyson realised that his dream was over and that the noise he heard was that of the night porter banging on the door, announcing he had a telegram to deliver. It was from his regiment, urgently recalling him to base 'in light of the current situation'. Tennyson left his flat and reported back to barracks in Colchester at eight o'clock that morning. Three weeks later he was in the bloody retreat from Mons; twice Mentioned in Dispatches and three times wounded, he survived the war and eventually returned to captain Hampshire and England.

Major Booth, the sometimes brilliant batsman and wily swing bowler who took 4-49 to finish off the South African batting in the Test at Port Elizabeth, immediately joined the army on the outbreak of war. After serving as a sergeant with the West Yorkshire regiment in the Egyptian campaign, he was commissioned as a 2nd lieutenant and sent to the Western Front. He was killed by shell fire on 1 July 1916, at the age of 29, after going over the top on the first day of the Somme offensive.

Johnny Douglas, the England captain in South Africa, also volunteered on the outbreak of war. Behind his muscular and occasionally arrogant presence on the cricket field it was thought that there lay a more complex, often misunderstood character. 'Johnny never spared himself and did everything for the team', his colleague Percy Fender once said. 'Any problems arose because he seldom appreciated that others weren't necessarily as physically or mentally hard as he was.' Douglas survived the war and returned to civilian life to play another eleven Tests. On 19 December 1930 he drowned when the SS *Oberon*, on which he and some of his family were travelling, collided with another ship in heavy fog off the coast of Denmark. According to evidence given at the enquiry, Douglas perished while trying to save his elderly father.

Perhaps the most poignant fate of any of Douglas's pre-war team was that of the veteran all-rounder Albert Relf, who was good enough to take 1,897 first-class wickets and score 22,238 runs in a 16-year career for Sussex and England. As a batsman, Relf may not have been the most dynamic of stroke-players, but this was offset by his stout defence, his determination, and his ability to improvise in tight situations. 'No one seeing him for the first time would suppose him capable of getting his hundred in top company', said *Wisden*. 'He has a way of letting the ball hit the bat that is certainly not impressive to the eye. Still, the fact remains that season after season he makes as many runs as men who look twice as good as he is.' After the war, this seemingly unflappable character took a job as cricket coach at Wellington College. Apparently depressed about money and the state of his wife's health following a gallstone operation, Relf walked out to the school's First XI pavilion on a stormy Good Friday morning in March 1937, locked the door, braced a shotgun against his heart and pulled the trigger. His wife later made a full recovery and came in to a considerable inheritance. Relf was 62 years old.

III

In March 1921, the British War Office published 'final and corrected' figures listing a total of 573,507 UK servicemen killed in action from 4 August 1914 to 30 September 1919; 254,176 were classified as 'missing' in the same period, less 154,308 released prisoners, for a net total of 673,375 dead or unaccounted for. There were 1,643,469 individuals described as 'wounded or otherwise affected' in the same report. Other estimates have suggested that there were some 744,700 British combat deaths, out of roughly 6,211,500 total enlistments. The real number will never be accurately known.

By averaging the above sets of statistics, it is possible to say that the chance of a British serviceman losing his life during the First World War was between 10.8 per cent and 11.9 per cent, or roughly one in nine. Although less catastrophic than sometimes thought, these are sobering figures: it's widely agreed, for instance, that the UK suffered some 383,000 and 67,000 military and civilian deaths respectively in the Second World War, which lasted nearly six years. In purely statistical terms, the loss of Major Booth at the Somme might be said to show that the England cricket team suffered broadly the same casualty rate as for the British armed forces as a whole. If Lionel Tennyson had also died of his wounds, someone might be theorising that Test cricketers were twice as badly affected as the norm and would thus write about the tendency of red-blooded sportsmen to throw themselves in harm's way when the situation arose. It is surely enough to repeat that cricket is a reflection of life, and that the mixed motives and varying fortunes of Johnny Douglas's last pre-war side show that his players had their share of humanising contradictions, just like the rest of us. Clearly there were those who enlisted out of high-minded duty, and others who welcomed the call to arms for more personal reasons. To some, at least, the armed forces represented a refuge where the failed, felonious or fed up could simply go to disappear. Lionel Tennyson seemed to allude to this trend when he later wrote of the droves of 'poor, smashed-up, timid little men' queuing outside the door of a London recruiting station. A cricketer-soldier named Ian Hay said that 'war is hell, and all that, but it has a good deal to recommend it. It wipes out all the small nuisances of peace-time'. Personal ambition was just as much the animating spirit of those young volunteers as of the sportsman judging the fine balance of his own performance against that of the team. The role of cricket in war makes such a fitting study precisely because most cricketers met the challenge the same as everyone else did, no better and no worse. There were fierce attachments to the patriotic cause, and there was also a good deal of bemused indignation that the country had somehow got itself in this mess in the first place.

Before leaving the world of cold statistics, we might also note that when England resumed playing international cricket in December 1920, against Australia, their team contained no fewer than six of the men who had appeared in that final pre-war game at Port Elizabeth, which would be to confer a flattering degree of consistency if applied to a modern English representative side. More significantly, three of the South African XI in that last Test also died in the war. The all-rounder Claude Newberry fell in the Somme campaign on 1 August 1916, aged 27; the seam bowler Eric 'Bill' Lundie was killed at Passchendaele in September 1917, aged 29, having played his first and only Test in Port Elizabeth; and the double-international Reginald Hands succumbed to wounds suffered on the Western Front in April 1918, also aged 29. Reggie Schwarz, another cricket-rugby international, played for South Africa twenty times between 1905 and 1912. He served in the King's Royal Rifle Corps throughout the war, winning the Military Cross, and survived the trenches only to fall victim to the worldwide Spanish flu epidemic on 18 November 1918, just a week after the Armistice, aged 43.

III

When the historians and sociologists came to look back on the events of August 1914, some of them made a rather tenuous case about the self-destructive nature of British culture, or society as a whole, as if the nation had somehow been engaged in a headlong communal death wish. Without going overboard, we can perhaps say that it was one of those eras when a precociously talented artistic elite seeks to subvert the consensus mood and disconcert its audience. By June 1914, for example, the touring Imperial Russian Ballet was all the rage at London's Covent

Garden. The company's latest production, *Légende de Joseph*, took place on a set decked out in pink marble, with towering pineapple-shaped gold columns and a cast dressed largely in yellow silk, attended by a host of sparsely clad Moorish slaves and two Russian wolfhounds in sparkling diamante collars. As a result, a certain theatricality began to creep into London society dress and furnishings. For the more rhythmically minded, meanwhile, there was *Hullo Rag-time!*, a song-and-dance revue that ran for nearly 500 performances in 1913–14. Essentially, this was an excuse for wailing young women to high-kick in dresses of a singularly sparing cut, while a line of bongo drummers went into a syncopated frenzy. Some saw it all as a profound indictment of cultural vacuity – others found vacuity in the performance itself. To the 19-year-old cricket-playing author J.B. Priestley, the show was all about 'progressiveness and dislocation' in British society.

For those who like to see some higher societal meaning in the arts, there was also Vorticism, an aggressively modernist movement under the loose direction of the 29-year-old painter and author Wyndham Lewis, headquartered at the unambiguously named Rebel Art Centre in central London. *The Times* described the work displayed there as 'not so much pictures as theories illustrated in paint'. In July 1914, the Vorticists provoked an unusually heated critical debate when they staged an exhibition of 'angular abstractions'. At what proved to be the show's opening and closing night, there were reports of fist fights both among the audience, and between the audience and the police, and one well-dressed patron is said to have climbed an avant-garde rendering of the Statue of Liberty and then swung, ape-like, from a black chandelier. In later years, Lewis insisted that he had repeatedly flicked the gallery's lights on and off in a strobe-like effect, hoping this would put a stop to the fracas. The accounts are as varied and confused as the scenes they claim to describe, and the only certainty is that the Vorticists disbanded shortly afterwards, and that Lewis himself went on to serve with distinction on the Western Front as an artillery officer and war artist.

Disillusion with the past and an apparent impatience to destroy the last vestiges of Victorianism were not the only background factors said to have set British society on the road to war: 'roar[ing] for its own death,' in one contemporary account. Others have claimed that there was something about English sport in general, and cricket in particular, that lent itself to the fatally jingoistic mood of August 1914. In most teams, Priestley theorised, there was a certain 'dogged and implacable devotion to the higher cause … a disinclination to upend authority'. 'We were all romantics', said Ulric Nisbet, a 17-year-old member of the Marlborough XI, who went off to war instead of finishing his last year at school. 'With us the attitude was "Theirs not to reason why." There was no tennis at Marlborough, for example. That was too individual: the public school was a team.' The diaries and letters of many first-class cricketers who served at the front speak of 'the great game', the 'wonderful feeling of fellowship', the 'exhilaration' of fighting alongside one's friends and comrades. At the beginning of the war, many enlisted in groups in order to form their own cricketing sub-battalions. A widow named Judith Flanders looked out on a dusty field in Carshalton, Surrey, one morning in September 1914 and saw rows of men marching off to camp in 'blazers, straw hats and striped caps, some of them swinging a bat over their shoulders. They were singing and joking all the way.' Cricketer psychologists such as Mike Brearley have speculated that the game's essential structure of long periods of tedium, punctuated by sudden bursts of drama or controlled chaos (and, for the departed batsman, oblivion), might serve as a metaphor of some sort for military life.

Of course it is just as likely that the roughly 4,000 cricketers and officials of all standards around the world who signed up and died for their country in the First World War did so for the same quietly heroic reasons as everyone else. Sergeant Colin 'Charlie' Blythe, of Kent and England, was 38 when he was killed by shell fire on the railway line outside Passchendaele on 8 November 1917. A fellow serviceman who survived the war wrote: 'we remember his cheerfulness, his keen sense of joy and devotion, even in the most arduous circumstances, and the brave deeds he performed daily without any hesitation or comment on his part.' Despite his epilepsy, Blythe both played the violin and perhaps more importantly took 2,503 first-class wickets, 100 of them in Tests, with his slow-to-medium left-arm spin. Some opposing batsmen also attributed his success to a marked volatility and aggression. C.B. Fry thought him to be 'the classic case of a fast bowler's mind trapped inside a slow bowler's body'. A monument erected to Blythe and other Kent players at the entrance to the St Lawrence ground in Canterbury says: 'He was unsurpassed among the famous bowlers of the period and beloved by his fellow cricketers.'

Shortly after arriving with his unit at Passchendaele, Blythe remarked on the once-idyllic landscape which had been beaten into a sea of mud and rubble torn up by the German artillery. 'There is no part of the human body I haven't seen damaged or blown to pieces', he wrote. To add a personal sense of loss, his younger brother Sidney had been killed in the fighting at the Somme just over a year earlier. At one time in October 1917, Blythe and his battalion had passed over the spot of Sidney's death. That was 'bad enough', he admitted, and soon hunger added to the men's misery. By early November, they had outrun their supply lines which were disrupted by German air attacks and were effectively living off the land, such as it was. The older Blythe seems to have had no illusions about the nature of war. His commanding officer later wrote that 'he did not think it was a glorious affair, or that the English inevitably won. For him, there was nothing romantic about suffering, as there was for some of the society-warriors, but he maintained a buoyant note. What he most wanted was to do his job and to serve his fellow brothers-in-arms.' Like most front-line soldiers, Colin Blythe looked at the war from the narrow circle of his own unit. In his letters authority is portrayed as stubborn or obtuse, while all around him were 'the finest stock', 'the best fighters in the world', with 'no swank or bounce' about them – 'the men you would lay down your life for'.

III

It is often said the outbreak of the First World War brought an end to a golden age of English cricket. Even professional matches had a certain country-house flavour to them that was conspicuously gone by 1919. A modern county cricketer would hardly recognise the packed grounds on which his counterpart played a hundred years ago, seemingly as part of an extended Georgian garden party, with gaudily clad spectators, and often their servants and pets, too, camped out around the boundary. A finely tuned social etiquette prevailed among the little groups who darted to and fro between overs, like shoals of tropical fish. In general terms, the game combined a colourful splash of summer pastels with an intensity of support that worried the anonymous correspondent of *Cricket* magazine: 'I do think sometimes that the Kent crowd is just a little *too* much wrapped up in Kent's doings', he wrote.

Technically, of course, cricket had its shortcomings. With a few notable exceptions, the batting tended to be rustic, the man who could 'bowl a bit' was in vogue, the fielding wasn't great, and many county pitches were rudimentary at best. 'The sport is, like the music-hall, truly an all-round entertainment', a *Times* critic wrote in 1914. 'There is a peculiar fascination about watching the many-striped stars gently exercise among rolling green fields and bucolic extras.' Some rural grounds were all but indistinguishable from the neighbouring farms. At Taunton, a stray pig quite often wandered out from the ring of spectators to visit the square. But it would be wrong to portray the pre-war County Championship as merely a case of effete young men in cravats behaving as if they had stepped out of the pages of a P.G. Wodehouse book. There was little of the Corinthian spirit about Colin Blythe, for one. Born in Deptford in 1879, Blythe left school at 12 and applied for a county trial largely as a way to avoid working alongside his father as a fitter. He took a wicket with his first ball in first-class cricket, and resolved then and there to make it his career. As he began an over, the thin and lantern-jawed Blythe would sometimes work himself into a state approaching hatred for the batsman he was about to bowl to. If they watched closely enough, his teammates could hear him muttering to himself and see him clenching his jaw. There was once some protracted controversy when C.B. Fry, batting for Hampshire, objected to Blythe deliberately bowling full-tosses to him in such a way that the ball was completely lost in the sun. This was a rare occasion when the batsman complained about the light being too good. Blythe's story is not one of schoolboy romance but of a professional sportsman who asked, and gave, no quarter.*

On the morning of 6 May 1914 the Hampshire players took the field for their opening match of the season, against Leicestershire at Southampton. Reporting on the match, *The Times* was rhapsodic: 'it [was] all a voyage of the most joyous anticipation, played out among lush hills, blue skies and glistening fresh paint upon the pavilion railings.' However often stated, there is a poignancy to the idea of so many young men going straight from the pastoral world of English cricket to the horrific scenes of carnage that awaited them on the battlegrounds of northern France. Three months later, fourteen of the twenty-two players at Southampton would actively participate in the war. Hampshire's demon fast bowler Arthur Jaques, one of the few first-class cricketers born in China, fell at the Battle of Loos in September 1915. Leicestershire's opening batsman Harold Wright divided his time between playing cricket and managing his family's elastic webbing factory in Quorn. In July 1914 Wright was commissioned as a captain with the 6th Loyal North Lancashires, and twelve months later took part in the sustained attack at Gallipoli, where he was severely wounded. Refusing medical treatment, he continued to fire at the enemy lines until eventually losing consciousness. Evacuated back to England, Harold Wright died there from his wounds on 14 September 1915, at the age of 31. Several of his letters home write of the 'adventure' of war, and of a zeal for the 'good fight' as a whole. This quality of enthusiasm might seem eccentric to our more cynical age. Wright's generation was the first to fly, to travel in cars, to see films and to hear disembodied voices coming to them over the radio. Perhaps it is not surprising so many of them retained a sense of wonder even in the most trying circumstances.

At around the time the young Harold Wright was setting new batting records at Mill Hill school, a boyish and still only modestly successful middle-aged Scottish author named James Barrie was assembling his own touring cricket side. Born in 1860, the short and moustachioed Barrie would go on to some acclaim with *Peter Pan*, but was chiefly known at the time for a series of locally popular novels of parochial

---

* Colin Blythe was only one of several distinguished English slow left-arm bowlers to show a healthy (some might say bloody-minded) competitive streak over the years. The list would also include Hedley Verity, Johnny Wardle, Tony Lock, Phil Edmonds, Phil Tufnell and Monty Panesar, among many others. Someone should write a book about this strange connection between cricket's most gentle and cultivated specialist skill and the hostility of its leading practitioners.

Scotland, as well as a play about the eighteenth-century poet Richard Savage which had closed after one matinee performance. As soon as he announced he was raising a team, Barrie was deluged with applications by players not only from Britain but all over Europe. The side's first fixture did not bode well for this cosmopolitan line-up: one French playwright turned up wearing pyjamas, a colleague extended the idea by falling asleep in the outfield, while a third man, a Belgian, thought that the game had finished every time the umpire called 'Over'. Barrie's men managed a total of just 11 runs on that occasion. The writers Arthur Conan Doyle, Willie Hornung, A.A. Milne and P.G. Wodehouse, of Sherlock Holmes, Raffles, Winnie the Pooh and Jeeves fame respectively, all turned out for the side over the years. Since Barrie himself went on to produce *The Admirable Crichton*, members of his eleven would be responsible for creating English fiction's two most famous valets. Conan Doyle once achieved the unusual distinction of managing to set himself on fire when batting. A ball struck him on the outside of the thigh and ignited the box of matches he kept in his pocket. After experimenting with various alliterative nicknames – Jingo Jim's, Bards and Barbarians, the Tartan Terrors and so on – the team eventually called themselves the 'Allahakbarries', which they translated as 'God help us.'

When the war came, the Allahakbarries suffered as much as everyone else. Guy du Maurier, a soldier-author who wrote a patriotic play called *An Englishman's Home*, fell at the Battle of Neuve Chapelle in March 1915. Barrie added the graphic detail that his friend had 'wandered around the battlefield for half-an-hour with his stomach hanging out, begging somebody to finish him off'. Following the death of their parents, du Maurier had become the co-guardian of his five Llewelyn Davies nephews, who served as the inspiration for *Peter Pan*. Barrie wrote to George Llewelyn Davies, who was in France with the Rifle Brigade, to inform him of Guy's death; by the time Barrie received his reply, George himself had been killed; he was 21. George's younger brother Peter fought at the Somme, and was invalided home after six weeks suffering from shell-shock. He later returned to the front and won the Military Cross. Four regular members of the Allahakbarries side, including Conan Doyle, lost a son in the war. The emotional scars affected Barrie for the rest of his life. 'The war has done at least one big thing', he said early in 1919, 'it has taken spring out of the year.' The Allahakbarries never played as a team again, though there was a brief but poignant revival in 1922 when Barrie, in a tweed suit and homburg, picked up a cricket ball and bowled it to Field Marshal Haig, the British commander at the Somme, who faced it in full military uniform. The author bowled him out. Barrie died in 1937 and Peter Llewelyn Davies committed suicide in 1960, aged 63.

III

Over the August bank holiday of 1914, coastal England teemed with men and women sporting a variety of decorous bloomers and modest dark-toned stockings who still bathed in separate preserves; couples parading on the front arm-in-arm was the limit of a public show of affection. Brighton and the other resorts had rarely been as full as they were that weekend. Elsewhere in England, there was a busy programme of summer sport. The annual Henley Regatta had wound up on 5 July, with record crowds enjoying the 'grilling hot' days of Renoir-like display, though its general mood of ostentation lingered: thanks to the Anglo-American Exposition, there were an estimated 80,000 tourists from across the Atlantic in London, which saw a full-scale baseball game played at Holland Park and nightly fireworks over Westminster. According to the *Daily Mirror*, American women preferred 'white canvas boots and suits of fine blue serge', and were easily recognisable by the battery-operated fans many carried while en route to their dates at 'the air-cooled Cecil Hotel, or the new-fangled soda-fountain in the Strand'. Among those the crowds had come to see at Henley was the chisel-jawed Australian Frederick Kelly. By all accounts, this 'beautifully rugged specimen', as *The Lady* called him, was one of those Renaissance men to whom nature runs riot in its gifts. Having won a chestful of medals as an oarsman, he turned to the running-track, 'where he was as fleet as a greyhound', and also played competitive tennis, golf and polo. Away from the sports field, Kelly was an accomplished classical pianist and composer, and once conducted a programme of his work to a full house at London's Wigmore Hall. He immediately joined a detachment of the Marines on the outbreak of war, won the Distinguished Service Cross (DSC), and died in November 1916, aged 35, while leading an attack on a German machine-gun emplacement at the Somme.

Meanwhile, the Jersey golfer Harry Vardon won the sixth and last of his British Open championships, amid scenes which again contained as much blazered pageantry as raw sport. Vardon volunteered to fight on the outbreak of war, when he was 44, but was found to be suffering from tuberculosis. North of the border, the Hearts football team finished the Scottish season in some style, with a run of eight successive wins. On the same day at the end of the season, every member of the side joined the British army. Three of the eleven, Harry Wattie, Duncan Currie and Ernie Ellis, were killed on the first morning of the Somme offensive. A colleague, Paddy Crossan, survived the war but later died, aged 39, his lungs all but destroyed by poison gas.

At Wimbledon, Norman Brookes of Australia won the men's singles final against New Zealand's Tony Wilding, holder of the title for the previous four years. Wilding had also appeared as an all-rounder in first-class cricket for Canterbury. On the outbreak of war he joined the Royal Marines, and was killed during an attack on enemy sniper positions at Neuve Chapelle in May 1915 at the age of 31. The popular German champion Otto Froitzheim went straight from Wimbledon to take part in an international challenge cup in the United States. War was declared halfway through his first match. Froitzheim sailed home to enlist, but his boat was detained by a Royal Navy patrol and he was taken into custody in Gibraltar. As the war continued, many of the non-combatant German POWs were transferred to England. As a result, Froitzheim spent the next four years in an internment camp at Leigh-on-Sea, where he was regularly seen strolling on the front clad in a German tennis blazer and that town's only pair of cerise trousers, chatting affably with the locals. Released in January 1919, he was briefly engaged to the filmmaker Leni Riefenstahl, and died in 1962, aged 78.

In cricket, everything changed and everything stayed the same. On the bank holiday Monday of 3 August, there was a crowd of 15,000 at the Oval to watch Jack Hobbs score 226 in just over four hours for Surrey against Nottinghamshire. Due to the weather, the match was drawn. Hobbs notes the event serenely in his autobiography: 'I made [the runs], with never a thought of war.' Late the following afternoon, as the British government delivered its note to Germany, signs were pasted up announcing that the Oval would be 'commandeered for military pur-poses' at the close of the match. On Wednesday morning, 5 August, the players and spectators returned to the ground to find themselves at war. It was raining. According to *Wisden*, the mood in the stands reflected a 'notably less convivial' atmosphere than had prevailed a day earlier. 'After Surrey's innings had been fin-ished off, [Nottinghamshire's] Gunn and Hardstaff stayed together for two hours. So bad was the "barracking" at times that several of the offenders were removed by the police.'

Canterbury cricket week opened to bright sunshine, and capacity crowds, with a hard-fought match between Kent and Sussex. Colin Blythe returned figures of 6-107 and 4-39, but by the time Sussex came to win with just twelve minutes left, said *Wisden*, the event was 'shorn of most of its social functions'. Hospitality tents reserved for the East Kent regiment and other army units had been hurriedly deserted. At Old Trafford, the 37-year-old Lancashire captain Albert Hornby, son of the great 'Monkey' Hornby, was called from the field on the first morning of the annual Roses match against Yorkshire and rushed south to join his regiment. Although Hornby survived the war, his younger brothers John and Walter were wounded and killed respectively. Three of Hornby senior's four sons predeceased him. Yorkshire's captain in the match, Sir Archibald White, also left the field early in order to report to the War Office. Reggie Spooner, of Lancashire and England, soon followed them into the colours. Spooner was another of those prodigiously talented athletes, good enough to have played both rugby and cricket at international level. He cut a dashing figure. Six feet 2in tall and superbly lithe, he wore immaculately tailored suits and gave one royal admirer 'the appearance of strutting even when sitting down'. It was said that no one played the cover drive better than he did until Walter Hammond appeared on the scene. Captain Spooner saw action with the Lincolnshire regiment, but was invalided home after being wounded at Mons. He played only a few more times after the war, though he lived to be 80. Both Pelham Warner and Arthur Carr, captain of Middlesex and Notts respectively, abandoned cricket after being called away by the authorities.

III

Early death is frequently seen as a sort of martyrdom. Individual deaths are often depicted that way, with whole news broadcasts devoted to covering the funeral of, say, a self-destructive, middle-aged showbusiness celebrity, and it is possible much the same thing applies to an era that ends abruptly or violently. So it might be best to approach the 'golden age' of cricket with caution. The 1890–1914 period certainly contained its fair share of acknowledged giants of the game such as Grace, Trumper, Hobbs, Barnes, Ranjitsinhji, Woolley and Foster. During the same era, Test cricket and representative tours both acquired something close to their modern structure. England and Australia played each other in fifteen series during those years, with England narrowly winning eight series to seven. Although it offered few of today's limited-overs batting fireworks or terrier-like fielding (and as late as 1913 the MCC side was accompanied to South Africa by all of two pressmen, one an expert on bowls), the hard-fought and animated game of around the turn of the century was enormously popular with crowds in Britain and overseas. Stately-home cricket was at its peak and the public-school game enjoyed no fewer than eighty-four closely typed pages of coverage in the 1915 *Wisden*, which is roughly eighty-one more than it does today. The annual Oxford-Cambridge match at Lord's remained one of the highlights of the London social season. Add a thriving series of northern leagues, a network of increasingly well-organised clubs and villages, and private teams such as Barrie's travelling the length and breadth of the country each weekend, and it is clear cricket was not only the dominant English sport, but one of the nation's defining themes.

Of course, it is also possible that we tend to idealise the age precisely because it finished as suddenly and brutally as it did. Even after a second great conflict loomed and the Great War had become known as the First World War, the events of 1914–18 were seen as the end of an age of innocence, the end of a way of life identified with the nineteenth century, and a transition to the age of modernity. For decades, the phrase *before the war* meant 'before 1914', and the words carried echoes of a time that was lost forever. Defining social eras is always a risky business, and often owes more to nostalgia than to dry historical facts. The cricket writer David Frith alludes to this when he talks of the 'soft, romantic shafts of museum lighting' that can retrospectively colour our judgement of certain periods of the game. It's difficult to write objectively of a group of young sportsmen knowing that so many of them will go on to die in action, be wounded, or come home with mental scars that will never heal. The war gave a whole generation deep and well-justified reasons to be sceptical about the wisdom of political and social leadership, and that scepticism of authority spilled over even into cricket, which never quite regained its air of magnificently feudal charm on its return to England in May 1919.

Although the war and its aftermath necessarily chastened the cricket world, not everything about the pre-1914 game was of utopian innocence, or everything post-1918 of cynical self-interest. Just to put some perspective on it, we find the great Victorian W.G. Grace, in 1895, concerned that cricket had become 'too much of a business like football' – perhaps ironically, from a man as famous for his robust financial negotiating as for his batting. When Grace agreed to captain the MCC side to Australia in 1891/92, he did so only after securing a personal fee of £3,000 (a county professional – or 'professor' – of the day might earn as much as £150 a year, but he did so without job security or a pension, and in the knowledge that he faced a likely ignominious exit in his mid-thirties, which was not quite the same thing). Grace's successor as England captain, Andrew Stoddart, angrily withdrew from a home Test against Australia in 1896 after the *Morning Leader* ran an editorial attack on him for his practice of demanding 'extortionate' performance bonuses. No fewer than five England players in the same match threatened to take strike action unless they were paid twice their normal fee. Clearly, too, not everything was relentless swashbuckling on the field of play. One correspondent's recollection of the Nottingham Test that year was of 'hour after hour of the backward-defensive stroke, of cricket as dour and grey as the smoke going up straight from the chimneys beside the Trent'.

The idea that Britain itself was an unmitigated social paradise in the years before 1914 also needs correction. Apart from the Irish Question, the trade unions were up in arms, conditions in many factories had changed little from Dickens's day, and for large numbers of working-class children malnutrition was the rule and adequate food and shelter the exception. In one Birmingham suburb, it was reported, the local state school 'did not satisfy the most basic educational or even sanitary requirements', while even in more affluent mid-Sussex the *Express* newspaper deplored the number of 'stunted-looking youths with some debility, and the pallor of anemia'. The life expectancy for a British male was 46. These facts do not exactly suggest a Garden of Eden before the Fall. Meanwhile, the suffragette movement was beginning to make itself heard by the smashing of shop windows, the holding of rallies, and the periodic invasion of golf tournaments and race meetings. One correspondent of *Cricket* magazine was worried that the 'vandals' would desecrate the most hallowed turf of all:

> Are the authorities at Lord's taking heed of the latest aspect of the 'monstrous regiment of women', with a view to protecting their sacred charges? After the golf greens, surely the cricket grounds in their due season? And that will be a matter of vastly larger import to the main body of the community.

Still, for a cricketer it was a good life while it lasted. A professional like Colin Blythe, who was married with several dependent relatives, must have enjoyed the opportunity to escape a hard and monotonous career in a factory and instead be paid for doing what he loved, earning not only a fixed salary but a cash bonus of 2 guineas for each first-class wicket he took over a total of 80. He managed 167 in the 1913 season and 159 in 1914. As well as county and Test cricket, Blythe was invited to regular country-house matches, like the one he played at Old Buckenham Hall in Norfolk in September 1913, where the owner, a socially ambitious Australian mining tycoon named Robinson, presented each of the players with a bag of six gold sovereigns, an engraved cigar case and a bottle of 'dynamite-strength' liqueur before leading them in to an elaborate banquet – 'a marathon event with six courses, and topped off by an Australian brandy of such potency it was considered unwise to smoke in the same vicinity'. Blythe was also asked to play in the annual Gentlemen *v*. Players fixture at Scarborough at the beginning of a week-long festival, and finally in a 'Kent and Yorkshire against The Rest' match at the Oval, where he took only one wicket but enjoyed another 'long and well-provisioned beano' at London's Strand Palace Hotel after stumps were drawn on 17 September. According to another of the players, Major Booth, everything went well enough at the dinner until someone asked someone else to pass the soup 'and he airlined it'. Booth then went under the table, where he found George Hirst of Yorkshire and England. Someone bowled a series of bread rolls down the tile floor. Gilbert Jessop hit at least one of them with a hard-backed menu. Two policemen turned up, one of them a former MCC player named Rawson, whereupon 'they proceeded to remove his helmet and use it as a receptacle'. A great deal of beer was also poured over Hirst's head, and he remembered experiencing a 'wavy feeling' when rattling up in the train the next morning to Leeds. Shortly after all this, Blythe was able to enjoy a brief winter holiday in Chamonix in the French Alps, where he mingled with the likes of Arthur Conan Doyle, Count Betrand de Lesseps – son of the canal builder – and a resting German opera diva 'among other prominent figures of the Arts', before moving around France and various small towns on the Italian Riviera, eventually reporting back to Canterbury on 12 April 1914.

It was also an era when many first-class cricketers excelled at more than one sport. Andrew Stoddart was probably the leading English example of the Renaissance man who played Test cricket and international rugby, as well as being a founding member of what became both the British Lions and the Barbarians. He was the son of a Durham colliery owner who made himself into the beau ideal of a southern gentleman cricketer, and later used his considerable charm to help win (and then lose) large sums as a City stockbroker. Long before their 1914 'crisis of Europe' tableau, Stoddart had his own waxwork effigy at Madame Tussaud's. There were numerous other cases of the performer popularly acclaimed at two or more sports, including among others George Vernon, Reginald Hands, 'Monkey' Hornby, Sammy Woods, Richard Young, Cuthbert 'Pinky' Burnup, Reggie Schwarz and Frank Mitchell. Mitchell achieved the unusual distinction of winning a triple blue at Cambridge, before going on to play rugby for England and Test cricket for England and South Africa. An all-rounder in the fullest sense, Major Robert Poore played cricket for South Africa, Natal and Hampshire, interrupting his career only to serve with distinction on the away side in the Boer War. He also excelled at polo, golf, tennis, fencing and the blunderbuss. A genuine eccentric, in hot weather Poore fielded in a solar topee and once advised a terrified young colleague that the best way to play Harold Larwood was to 'fix yer bayonets and charge 'im'.

Another versatile character was Lieutenant Cecil Abercrombie, who combined a brief but distinguished naval career with playing cricket for Hampshire, for whom he scored four centuries in his first and only full season, including one on his county debut, and rugby for the United Services and Scotland. Abercrombie 'flashed his bat like a cavalry sword', said the *Gazette*, rather mixing its armed forces. It was widely said that he hit the ball as hard as anyone in the history of cricket to then. On the outbreak of war, Lieutenant Abercrombie immediately rejoined his squadron at Portsmouth. On 31 May 1916 at 5.30 p.m. he was on the bridge of the armoured cruiser HMS *Defence*, sailing about 3 miles in advance of the main British fleet off Jutland. Emerging from the mist, a German battlecruiser and four dreadnoughts opened fire from a distance of 7,000 yards. The *Defence* was hit by two salvoes from the enemy ships that caused her aft magazine to explode. Within two minutes, the resulting fire had spread by way of the ammunition passages to the ship's main magazines, which detonated in turn. There were no survivors among the 900-strong crew. Cecil Abercrombie had just celebrated his 30th birthday.

Abercrombie largely learned his cricket in the nets at Portsmouth, where he often practised with his friend Lionel Tennyson when both men were making their way into the Hampshire side. Because of injuries and military commitments they rarely had the chance actually to play together, and we can only speculate on how they might possibly have found themselves appearing alongside one another in the post-war England team, when they would have been in their early thirties. Tennyson missed much of the 1913 season largely because of army duties, but always remembered the Friday afternoon when he went to the county ground at Southampton to watch the cricket prior to driving 'Uncle Cec' up to London for a weekend house party.

The match was Hampshire *v.* Sussex in mid-August, and it was as good an example as any of the 'quaint idyll' ideal of cricket's golden age. It began on one of those perfect late-summer mornings, with the local *Gazette* reporting that 'thousands stood wilting under the heat to pay their admission of ninepence at the turnstiles, which clicked away busily'. Immediately next to the report of the match, the paper noted that the German Kaiser had spoken to journalists that week about settling his territorial ambitions with 'blood and iron'. The visitors won the toss, batted, and made exactly 300. The opener Joe Vine hit a lightning-fast 75, often profitably exploring the aerial route over extra cover, and Vallance Jupp, coming in at number seven, added 50 not out. The Sussex side contained no fewer than three Relf brothers, as well as the 20-year-old Percy Fender, in his last season with the county before moving to Surrey. On this occasion, Fender, a mercurially talented and often eccentric cricketer whom a later critic felt had 'prefigured Peter Sellers playing the part of Inspector Clouseau', departed for a second-ball duck. The *Gazette* remarked that 'the refreshment tent, which had emptied when "PGF" strode out to the crease, soon filled to capacity again'. Hampshire went in late on the first evening and scored 420, with Phil Mead contributing 100 at a run a minute. The bowling Relf brothers all came in for grief, though the youngest of the three, Ernest, eventually finished with creditable figures of 2-26. Fifty years later, Fender could still remember the subtle efforts of the Sussex bowlers not to catch their captain's eye and become the next victim. Cecil Abercrombie then chipped in with what the paper called an 'exquisite cameo' of 37. At one stage, Fender himself bowled him what he remembered as a 'really good fast-medium yorker on his leg stump'; Abercrombie killed the ball with a forward prod, 'then looked up, courteously touched his cap and grinned: "Well bowled, Master".' Fender thought to himself, 'He won't expect another one', so he repeated the performance. This time, Abercrombie took a half-step forward and deposited the ball over long-on, where it eventually landed in a mobile whelk stall. 'He was a joy to watch unless you happened to be bowling to him', said Fender, ruefully.

Sussex came out to bat a second time. Vine outdid himself with an innings of 104 in just over two hours. He began his stay quietly enough, clipping a four or two against the seam attack of Arthur Jaques and George Brown. But with the arrival of the spinners came one of the most ferocious onslaughts on any type of bowling which can ever have been inflicted in Southampton's 115-year history as a county cricket ground. Vine erupted, smashing 65 off 7 overs before Hampshire called for drinks, including a huge pull for six off McDonell which cleared the crowd and disappeared over Northlands Road in the direction of the Old Cemetery, and then brought up his century with two consecutive clattering straight drives for four. Vine's innings was all the more remarkable for being carried off in virtual isolation. The Sussex captain Herbert Chaplin made 53 and Robert Relf hit 11 in an over before he ran himself out, but that was about it from the visitors. Hampshire were left needing 135 to win, and got home with just less than an hour and 5 wickets to spare. Abercrombie contributed another characteristically brief but pugnacious knock of 33, peppering the old wooden scorebox-cum-groundsman's hut with fours. Following that, it was reported, 'Mr George Brown dispatched the third ball he faced for six, but off the fourth was smartly stumped by the Sussex custodian Arthur Lang.' Whether alluding to international events or just in celebration of the match, the crowd then broke into a spirited version of 'Rule, Britannia!'. After stumps were drawn, Abercrombie and Tennyson climbed into the latter's borrowed two-seater Sunbeam Tonneau and headed for Mayfair. History does not record the details of their subsequent house party, although just to give it some general context it is known that not long before this Tennyson had enlivened a period of overnight guard duty at the Tower of London by inviting some friends, including the entire female cast of the Gaiety chorus, to share his vigil.

III

The whole concept of premature or violent death was one that was quite familiar to a generation of Englishmen in the early years of the twentieth century. It sometimes seems almost surprising that anyone got out of the so-called golden age in one piece. In the space of less than a decade the world staggered from the Russo-Japanese War to the bloody and sustained upheaval in Morocco, from revolts in Bosnia, and both internal and external revolution in Mexico, to a wholesale crisis in the Balkans. And those were just the set-piece conflicts. The sinking of the *Titanic* in April 1912 was only one, if the most vividly reported, of the individual human tragedies of the era, 'and not one without its uplifting features', Lionel Tennyson noted. 'There were many cases of outstanding decency and sacrifice.' Above all, the loss of the *Titanic* showed how Englishmen could die, the newspapers told their readers. Others took cheer from the stirring words of Captain Robert Scott's diary when, seven months later, it was discovered next to his frozen body and that of his companions in the Antarctic ice. As a whole, Britons were expected to be phlegmatic about death, and they often were. Not wholly untypical was the case of Commander Frederick Greville Egerton, Royal Navy. A brilliant schoolboy cricketer, he is remembered by the *Globe* as 'a dashing bat who, against a very fine eleven of I Zingari, made some phenomenal hits towards the sea at Scarborough'. On 2 November 1899, the 31-year-old Egerton was mortally wounded by an enemy shell while directing the fire of HMS *Powerful*'s guns at Ladysmith. Both his legs were blown away from his body. 'That puts a stop to my cricket', he's said to have remarked, before pausing to light a cigarette. Despite emergency surgery, Commander Egerton died in a field hospital later that night.

As we have seen, some commentators have inferred from the frequently passive and on occasion heroic way in which many British men met their end that Britons of all ages, and at all levels of society, were embarked on a collective suicide mission in the period immediately before August 1914. Life, it is said, was significantly cheaper in an era when a fatal mining collapse or the latest train derailment to kill dozens of ordinary citizens was such a staple of the daily press. The poet and soldier Osbert Sitwell was not the only one who looked back on the sinking of the *Titanic* and saw 'a symbol of the approaching fate of western civilisation'. The call to arms, so the theory goes, was no more than the logical result of several years of churning social upheaval, the bloody but inescapable expression of what J.B. Priestley called the 'underlying despair' of the era.

Compelling as it may be on a sociological level, Priestley's death-wish theory isn't always supported by hard facts. A reading of the British daily press up to late July 1914 – let alone the testimony of scores of ordinary Britons – does not seem to show a nation in a fit of mass depression. For weeks at a time, nothing was said in the newspapers' financial sections about inflation or unemployment, for instance. All market signs pointed upward. In July 1914 domestic iron and steel prices were the highest they had been since the Boer War, and the Chancellor faced the pleasant prospect of deciding what to do with a trade surplus. The upper levels of English society continued to operate in their full Edwardian pomp. On 16 July 2,300 guests waltzed the night away in the last pre-war Court Ball at Buckingham Palace. Contemporary diaries are full of lyrical descriptions of six-course meals, or of the gastronomic and other pleasures of Henley and Lord's. Returning home one evening from the cricket through the apple orchards of Kent, the young Siegfried Sassoon would tell his diary that he felt 'all the goodness of being alive'.

Although British society as a whole was relatively stable, there was no shortage of individual examples where someone was prepared to put his reckless love of adventure ahead of his own welfare. The country wasn't then troubled, as it was later, by health and safety officials, so there was ample scope for the intrepid or merely obsessive thrill-seeker to indulge himself. There was the case, for instance, of Captain Samuel Cody. Born Franklin Cowdery in Davenport, Iowa, as a young man Cody had played the same roulette tables in Dodge City as Wyatt Earp, and competed with Annie Oakley at sharp-shooting before moving to England around 1900 to begin carrying out experiments with kites, hot-air balloons and eventually a series of 60hp biplanes. When on the ground, he adapted an old cowboy habit by hitching his aircraft to a tree. In October 1908, Cody recorded the first official powered flight: a length of 463 yards, which ended in a crash. The following year, he set a world record by carrying the first female air passenger, a woman he introduced as 'Madame Sophistros', but who was actually his common-law wife Ena.

On 7 August 1913, Cody was killed when his prototype seaplane broke up 500ft in the air above southern England. The funeral procession at Aldershot Military Cemetery drew an estimated crowd of 100,000. Cody's story is worth mentioning here chiefly because at the time of his last flight he was carrying a passenger: W.H.B. 'Bill' Evans, a former cricket captain of Oxford University, Worcestershire and Hampshire. Evans was 30 when he met his death at Cody's side. He was another of those full-service British sportsmen who was equally proficient at all ball games. A swashbuckling batsman, it was said of Evans that 'there was something in his nature that eschewed the easy path in life, and gave rein to adventure. When he opened his shoulders at the crease, the next parish or the roof of the pavilion knew about it.' In his final first-class match against Middlesex at Lord's, Evans hit 9 in 3 balls in the first innings before running himself out, while in the second innings his stay was even briefer: after depositing the first ball he faced from the Australian seamer Frank Tarrant into the Tavern, he 'smashed at the second with his bat held at an angle of 90, and, after flailing the air, turned round to see his stumps representing the majority of the remaining angles' (clean bowled, in our language). As he strode off, Evans briefly detoured across the square to shake hands with the bowler. 'The drinks are on you, Frank', he said, before continuing on his way to the pavilion. *The*

Sportsman said that 'the ground cheered him to the rafters'. Somewhere in Evans's fundamental outlook on life lies the key of why so many Britons jumped at the chance to enlist when the time came to do so.

The *Wisden* of 1915, chronicling as usual the deaths of the year before, makes the following entry:

CAPT. DANIEL GEORGE HAROLD AUCKINLECK, of the Royal Inniskilling Fusiliers, was killed in action on 21 October. He was born on 18 September 1877, and was in the Winchester XI in 1894 and 1895 when, in his two matches against Eton, he scored 23 and 28 not out, 14 and 0. He was a useful batsman and a fair bowler.

Although not the most lavish tribute ever paid to a cricketer in print, Captain Auckinleck does have one melancholy distinction: his *Wisden* obituary was the first, alphabetically, to commemorate those who died in the First World War. There would be another 1,684 such names before it all ended.

2

SPRING

There is a certain appeal to the idea that the spring of 1914 was the final gasp of a golden era in British life. There were still no returning wounded soldiers in their blue suits and scarlet ties on the city streets, no daily casualty lists in the morning press, and no incendiary Zeppelin raids in the skies at night. 'A lovely season was bringing ripeness to the kindly fruits of England', wrote the poet and historian Reginald Pound, with just a touch of hyperbole. 'Gorse blazed like solar flares on the hills. Down and wold and moor rolled towards horizons that were never more enticing. Daily the sun went down out of cloudless skies that were wine-coloured at dusk and at night a carnival of stars.' Statistically, May and early June were generally warm, but in fact much of the later summer was depressingly wet. At the time Johnny Douglas's MCC side returned from their tour of South Africa – a 'wonderfully convivial' voyage, but for 'the nearly total dearth of ladies' – the papers' front pages were dominated, in the marvellously flat words of *The Times*, by 'the distasteful news from the National Gallery', where the suffragette Mary Richardson had succeeded in slashing the *Rokeby Venus* with a meat-cleaver smuggled in under her skirt. 'Until the public ceases to countenance the abuse of women', she announced, 'the stones cast against me for the destruction of this picture are each an evidence against them of artistic as well as moral and political humbug and hypocrisy.' Excessive self-doubt was not a notable characteristic of this particular campaigner, who went on to become a senior officer in the British Union of Fascists.

On 21 March, the great Victorian amateur cricketer Joseph Makinson died, aged 77. Popularly known as 'Lofty' (he was 5ft 5in tall) – though 'Sir' to the professionals – he was not only a tidy seam bowler for Cambridge University and Lancashire but also a batsman of unusually athletic technique. In its obituary, *Wisden* spoke of his 'dancing out of his ground to hit in a way quite foreign to the style of modern players'. W.G. Grace was more explicitly enthusiastic, recalling how in 1877 Makinson had 'battered 104 runs of stunning skill and agility' for the Gentlemen of Lancashire against the South. 'The sheer energy expended was astonishing, but he kept fresh to the end.' In later years, Makinson had served as a stipendiary magistrate at Salford, where he is said to have combined 'mild legal acumen with a certain idiosyncrasy in personal manner and style', not least in his habit of keeping a cricket bat on the judge's bench. He was especially proud of the fact that over the course of a long career none of his decisions were overturned on appeal. In retrospect, Makinson's death was another small sign that the golden age, with its sense both of hierarchy and individuality, was giving way to one of comparative egalitarianism and uniformity. A further hint that an old world was on its way out and a new one on its way in came just three weeks later, on 11 April 1914, when George Bernard Shaw's play *Pygmalion* opened to a stormy reception at His Majesty's Theatre, London. For days beforehand, the newspapers speculated feverishly on whether or not the show's leading lady Stella Campbell would dare utter the line 'Not bloody likely!', as written for her by Shaw. In general the press were as simultaneously shocked and thrilled by the prospect as they were fifty-five years later when confronted with full-frontal nudity on the stage in *Oh! Calcutta!* The *Daily Sketch* editorialised that 'if the censor does not forbid it then anything might happen!' When Campbell did announce the 'incarnadine adverb' (as the *Daily Mail* fastidiously put it), the audience laughed for a full ninety seconds. Appalled by the shallow response, Shaw stormed off.

The next morning, England's 259 registered first-class cricketers began reporting back to their counties to prepare for the 1914 season. It was the last day of the long Easter weekend, which the London *Globe* reported had witnessed a 'carnival of rainbow-striped dresses and lace collars' at one end of society and 'chaotic scenes more akin to Bombay' at the other. On the Saturday morning long queues formed at Victoria station in a stampede to leave the capital for resorts in the south, with hundreds of passengers waiting for up to five hours. The day before, people had started to line up at 6.45 a.m. for the afternoon train to Brighton. When it finally arrived the crowd rushed the barrier, and police had the 'gravest trouble' controlling them. Babies were handed over heads to female railway staff, who took care of them until their mothers got through. Several children became lost, and a teenage girl died in the crush. On 24 April, in rather more refined conditions, King George and Queen Mary returned to Victoria from a state visit to France, which the press judged a success. Having crossed the Channel to Cherbourg on the royal yacht, the party were received in Paris and presented with a parchment recording 'the undying bonds of goodwill and affection uniting our two peoples'. The *Globe* was especially struck by the fact that 'there was a great departure from tradition, as, making use of a solid-gold pen, Queen Mary signed the document as well as the King, and Madame Poincaré as well as the President'. The paper added that 'in further deference to Her Majesty, the first English Consort to be received officially in Paris, the municipal council outdid itself in the organisation of lavish and artistic entertainment'. With the king and queen now safely back in London, both the social season and the cricket season could begin.

It may not always have been sunlight and parasols, but the summer of 1913 had been warm, dry and full of runs, and at the end of it Lord Hawke, the former Yorkshire and England batsman and MCC president-elect, announced that the domestic game at all levels had 'now attained its supreme lustre' and 'become a truly formidable piece of the national fabric'. In cold statistical terms, the season's 217 first-class matches attracted slightly fewer than 2 million paying customers, who were entertained by a full programme of county cricket and gala events like the Oxford v. Cambridge and Gentlemen v. Players matches, but not a single Test or one-day cup final – figures today's cricket administrators could only dream of. At the age of 43, Surrey's Tom Hayward joined W.G. Grace as the only two batsmen yet to have scored a hundred first-class hundreds. Players such as Lionel Tennyson and Phil Mead of Hampshire, George Gunn of Nottinghamshire, Frank Woolley of Kent and John Hearne of Middlesex formed an impressive satellite-ring of batsmen around the acknowledged stars, Surrey's Jack Hobbs and Yorkshire's Wilfred Rhodes. Colin Blythe did most sustained damage with the ball, though for sheer volume his aggregate of 167 first-class wickets at 16.34 apiece was beaten by Yorkshire's Major Booth with 181 and Surrey's Bill Hitch with 174. *Wisden* named Booth, Hitch, Gunn, Tennyson and Albert Relf its five cricketers of the year. Kent took the County Championship ahead of Yorkshire and Surrey. The season ended and the MCC team under Johnny Douglas set out on their extended South African tour. Their triumphant return six months later gave English cricket lovers no serious grounds to suppose the golden age would be drawing to a close anytime soon.

At that winter's meeting of the MCC Committee at the Junior Carlton Club in London, Lord Hawke and his colleagues considered the usual routine housekeeping matters. There was some discussion of the 1914 fixture list and of various relatively minor points involving salaries and rents. It was unanimously agreed that the committee should write and congratulate the Treasurer of the Club on his birthday. The only hint of the darkening European situation came in a short note in the minutes: 'in the case of any member who has served or is serving in His Majesty's Forces during any portion of the year, his subscription shall be returned on application to the Secretary'. These gestures were necessary at moments of 'some national trial', Lord Hawke later noted.

III

There is nothing quite like the gathering of players, officials and press on the first day's gentle exercise before the beginning of a new English cricket season. The start-of-term atmosphere, with its ambient smell of linseed oil and embrocation, is often enlivened by tropical rain or even snow falling on the newly cut playing area. It has been necessary more than once for the ground staff at Worcester to swim for the pavilion on these occasions. By contrast, April 1914 was unusually warm and dry (prior to a sharp cold snap in early May), and Phil Mead wrote of 'a morning of awakening blue, all varnish and high hopes', as he reported back to the freshly painted county ground in Southampton. It seemed as if the new season would pick up where the old one had left off, with rock-hard pitches, ice-fast outfields and packed public stands where shirtsleeves and straw hats were in order.

While the county players prepared for the first-class season, much of the early action took place at the club and village level. At Rottingdean, an old smugglers' cove just along the clifftop from Brighton, a 42-year-old barber named Jack Beck walked out to the crease at 1.35 p.m. one hot Saturday, and left it again shortly before 3 p.m. with a score of 138, retired. The ground at Rottingdean was then a rough, rather randomly mown field, with a stiff sea breeze sometimes knocking over deckchairs and sending dust and newspapers eddying around as if the old *Brighton Belle* had just passed by the platform; but it served. Thistles abounded in the outfield, which was grazed by sheep; brambled hedges invited lost balls on two sides, and a long, steep slope leading down to the square gave the bowler from that end a brisk push-off to his run. When you added a timbered pavilion and a back-drop of lush, gently rolling hills, you had one of those flawed but agreeable grounds that give rural English cricket its special charm. The *Argus* wrote:

> Anyone who was fielding that [April] afternoon deserved the pity of all charitable persons. Mr Beck gave a demonstration of hitting of unsurpassed ferocity. He hit a ball more than once clean out of the playing area, and struck the clock on the front of the pavilion, somehow without breaking it.

When Beck later left the crease, to rueful applause from the fielding side, it was reported that 'he quit modestly, with no sign he considered himself to have done anything exceptional'. Later in the afternoon, after the change of innings, one of the umpires fell ill. Beck was quickly asked to take his place, and 'did so conscientiously, without the least suspicion of favouring his teammates in their appeals'.

While club and village cricket got down to business, Britain's universities also began their necessarily brief season. There were particularly high hopes at Oxford, whose 1914 team boasted two brilliant and audacious stroke-players. Donald

Knight, just up from Malvern but already noted by Surrey, was said to be 'as flashy, mercurial and inconsistent as an April day'. Miles Howell was an opener more in the Geoffrey Boycott mould: 'as a rule, he began soberly, but launched gradually into his full range of shots', wrote the *Globe*. Much was expected, too, of the South African-born leg spinner Basil Melle, who had taken 55 wickets in just eight games the previous year. According to *Wisden* 'he was the crack bowler. Unfortunately, Melle broke one of his fingers soon after the season began, and as a result [was] not even a shadow of his former self. It is not too much to say that his falling off crippled the side.'

Apart from the university match, the highlight of Oxford's season that year came at Old Buckenham Hall, in Norfolk, where they played out a draw with Lionel Robinson's select XI. On a perfect morning, the students batted first and scored 339, with Knight and Howell furnishing a century opening stand. True to form, Howell began slowly, but it was said his last 25 runs were made in quarter of an hour 'by a bewildering mixture and variety of the drive, the cut, the hook and the pull, [with] the extravagant prod his weapon of choice against the turn.' In reply, Robinson's XI could manage just 147. Ninety of those runs came from 52-year-old Sir Tim O'Brien, who had made his first-class debut for Middlesex in 1881, and gone on to play five Tests for England. *Wisden* was effusive:

> This was a big performance. I happen to know that O'Brien has a poor opinion of most modern bowlers, contending that in their craze for the swerve they have lost much in spin and accuracy of length. At Buckenham, he gave the swervers and slingers of the Oxford eleven a good deal to think about.

Three months later, O'Brien would officially top the season's first-class batting table with the impressive average of 100.50, although against that it is only fair to note that he scored some 2,400 fewer total runs than Hobbs, who was second in the list.

Needing 192 to make Oxford bat again, Robinson's side began with a flurry of strokes that soon dispelled the gloomy memory of their first innings. Once again, the man of the hour was O'Brien. He scored 111 in three hours, with fourteen fours, while several of his skilfully placed ones and twos were warmly applauded by spectators in the refreshment tent, rumoured to hold 2,000 pints of beer. The Oxford bowler William Boswell wryly remarked, 'I put them where I liked, and he put them where he liked.' Robinson's men reached 200 and erased the deficit for the loss of only 2 wickets. After O'Brien, Lieutenant Kenelm McCloughlin of the Indian army and Jack MacBryan, a stockbroker and soldier, shared a stand said to have 'swung between dour competence and flashing aggression against the bad ball', taking the score to 257–3. Fifth in was Bernard Bosanquet, inventor of the googly but seen here to better effect with the bat; after a stay of just less than an hour, with his score on 59, he strolled down the wicket and was stumped by half a pitch-length by the Oxford keeper Edward Shaw. According to the local paper, 'Umpire Pilch's ready acceptance of the appeal was good-naturedly endorsed by the crowd on the third-man boundary'. Shortly after Bosanquet's dismissal, rain began to fall. Wearing a voluminous crested overcoat, Robinson walked to the middle to confer with the officials, a butler in livery holding an umbrella over his head as he did so. Shortly after that the match was declared a draw, with the home team on 311–7. Some 400 runs had been scored on an abbreviated final day, and both sets of players were cheered as they appeared for a prize-giving ceremony in front of the pavilion, 'Sir Timothy O'Brien being particularly feted in a vocally robust, if not musical, ovation'.

Six of the twenty-two players died in, or immediately following, the war. Oxford's William Boswell and Edward Shaw fell in the summer of 1916 in fighting around the Somme, both aged 24. Their teammate Donald Johnston had the cruel fate of surviving more than four years' overseas duty, only to die in the final attack on the German lines around St Quentin in September 1918. He was 23. Of Robinson's side, Kenelm McCloughlin was cut down at the age of 31 during the Allied infantry advance on Loos, where Lionel Tennyson also fought, in September 1915. The military historian Walter Reid quoted a German eyewitness to this action.

[We] stood up, and some stood even on the parapet of the trench, and fired into the approaching wave of infantrymen as they advanced over open ground. Never had machine-guns had such straightforward work to do … with barrels becoming hot and swimming in oil, they traversed to and fro along the enemy's ranks. One machine-gun alone fired 12,500 rounds that afternoon. The effect was devastating. Men could be seen falling literally in hundreds, but they continued their march in good order and without interruption.

Arthur Lang, the Cambridge and Sussex wicketkeeper, died in the bloody and futile scramble in the mud before the German trenches near Messines in January 1915. He was 24. Batting with him for Robinson's XI in Norfolk was the cricket and rugby double international Reggie Schwarz. As we've seen, Schwarz, having been twice wounded, won the Military Cross (MC) and survived the combat only to die in the flu pandemic, aged 43, just a week after the armistice. Tim O'Brien volunteered for duty on the outbreak of war and served as an honorary major with the Remounts until January 1919, by which time he was 57. His teammate Jack MacBryan went to France in August 1914 as a 2nd lieutenant with the Prince

Albert's Light Infantry. Wounded and taken prisoner in the first month of fighting, he spent the next four years in a series of German internment camps. Though not one to dwell on his ordeal, he remarked at a dinner held at the Taunton county ground in May 1919 that his first few nights in captivity had 'not been pleasant – I felt they must have taken twenty years off my life expectancy'. MacBryan went on to win a gold medal as part of the British hockey team at the 1920 Olympics. Britain clinched the title by the unusual means of a walkover in the final against France, whose team was officially described as 'indisposed' – a euphemism, it is said, for the Frenchmen being unable to perform thanks to overdoing it at a premature celebration party the night before. MacBryan also played competitive rugby, fives and golf, and was something of a pioneer at alpine tobogganing. In July 1924 he was chosen to play as an amateur for England in the fourth Test against South Africa at Old Trafford. It was a three-day match, and rain ruined most of it. MacBryan neither batted nor bowled. His wet two hours in the field on the first morning proved to be his only experience of international cricket. *The Times* remembered him as 'sound and keen, rather than menacing' as a batsman, 'with a fierce cut, but a range of full-flowing strokes otherwise limited by his war injury'. He lived to be 90.

MacBryan was playing at Old Trafford in the first place only because the committee had omitted Jack Hobbs, who was then 41 but still well on his way to an aggregate of 2,094 first-class runs for the season. Hobbs's offence was to have declined an offer to tour Australia with MCC that winter, 'being unwilling to leave my business unattended for the duration', he said. He was another of the great stalwarts of the English national game who struggled to make a living from it. In 1914, Hobbs was approaching the pinnacle of his fame, and fast becoming as powerful an international sporting legend in his own way as W.G. Grace had been in his. He earned around £375 that season in basic fees and bonuses. Though much better off than his groundsman father had been at the same age, this was only in the lower reaches of a typical middle-class income. Later that year, Hobbs and his wife Ada were able to put down £150 deposit on their first home. Product endorsements, ghostwritten articles and investments brought in perhaps another £300 to the family's budget, but Hobbs's benefit match in August 1914 was a severe disappointment. The army's confiscation of the Oval meant that the fixture was hurriedly moved to Lord's – which the Surrey committee felt 'might prove to be disadvantageous owing to that ground's restrictions on collecting boxes, and other factors'. They were right. Hobbs earned just £337 from the two-day fixture against Kent, which was more than some other beneficiaries but considerably less than he would have hoped for. By then, the German army was well on its way to overrunning Belgium, and four British army divisions containing 80,000 men and 30,000 horses had embarked for Rouen and the French channel ports. Although well attended, the press reported, 'Hobbs's match necessarily went forward in a strained atmosphere … It rained almost throughout'. Surrey won by 8 wickets, although Colin Blythe took 9-97 in one of his last matches before signing up.

The Surrey captain that season was Cyril Anstruther Wilkinson, a keen schoolboy cricketer at Blundell's who struggled at county level. In an eleven-year first-class career, interrupted by war service, he scored just 1,773 runs at an average of 25. An amateur, Wilkinson went on to qualify at the Bar and eventually to become the registrar of the Probate and Divorce Division for twenty-four years. Talented at several other sports, he appeared alongside Jack MacBryan in the victorious British hockey team at the post-war Olympics. Much like Mike Brearley some sixty years later, Wilkinson was seen less as a technically dazzling batsman and more as a firm, astute leader. It was said in the Surrey yearbook that he had 'a galvanic effect driv[ing] his tired bowlers to one more supreme effort'. As a rule, when the county team travelled, Wilkinson and his fellow amateur Percy Fender made their own arrangements, sometimes staying in a different hotel to their nine colleagues, frequently sharing a taxi to the ground, and once there often enjoying the use of their own dressing room. Neither one was a wealthy man. Wilkinson had only recently qualified, and Fender just about held down a sales job with a firm of wholesale stationers and paper-bag manufacturers in south London (it may have helped, he admitted, that his father was the company's managing director). Over the years, Fender grew used to juggling business meetings to fit the needs of the cricket fixture list. On summer mornings, he was regularly to be found at his desk at 7 a.m., working out ways to promote his firm's range of patented waterproof bags or absorbent paper towels, before reporting for duty at the Oval three hours later. Towards the end of his long life, Fender placidly noted that an MCC tour of Australia had cost him about £400, since 'your hand was never out of your pocket in paying for cabs, meals and other incidentals not covered by the Club … we had to approach the committee for livable terms'. When Fender married, the press made much of the fact that his wife Ruth was one of the few young women in Britain to sport a monocle. It was a gift to the caricaturists. Despite the claims of the *Tatler* and others, this wasn't so much a social affectation on her part, but because of a drooping eyelid. Later, on an MCC tour of South Africa, Fender was able to avoid bankruptcy only by the expedient of joining in several late-night poker games organised by wealthy businessmen. He also befriended a Cape Town stockbroker and practising medium named Ashton Jonson, under whose guidance he 'actively explored the occult, though no spirits returned to offer me tips about share prices'.

Fender told me about all this not to complain, but to illustrate the widespread modern misapprehension of what it meant to be a gentleman cricketer around the time of the First World War. 'By and large, we were broke but happy', he said. 'Of course, there were perks …' Alluding to this same theme, Lionel Tennyson always fondly remembered the eve-of-departure dinner thrown by the South African board for the MCC at the Mount Nelson hotel, Cape Town, in March 1914. Thirty years later, he could still list the exact bill of fare: 'an enormous pig, with all the trimmings, including new potatoes, fresh corn, chicken dumplings, apple pie, shaved ice, liqueurs and coffee'. At some stage, Johnny Douglas made a gracious speech in which he remarked that after their eventual retirement most of his players could only have two possible occupations. One was to run 'thirst emporiums', that is, bars, as they were 'already proficient in that area'; the other was to be 'professional travelers or tourists of some kind', as that would allow them to revisit the charming country where they had spent so enjoyable a winter. A musical program then followed, with festivities ended by 'a troupe of native dancers wearing costumes of the most scanty cut', after which the boys gave three cheers for the girls. When the Englishmen's ship docked at Southampton nineteen days later, Douglas and his fellow amateurs Tennyson and Bird came down the gangway to be led off to a waiting car, while the ten professionals disembarked to a more leisurely reception by customs officers before being reunited with their families.

Major Booth was one of those whose homecoming was what he called 'a muted affair' after so long and successful a tour. A few scraps of newsreel footage exist, and show a tall young man in a grey suit and straw hat apparently struggling with an overladen luggage-trolley. Booth had two inside pockets in his jacket: his father James's picture was in the left-hand one, his mother Louise's in the other. He had been born in that rich breeding ground for cricketers, Pudsey, Yorkshire, twenty-seven years earlier and like the then prime minister, Herbert Asquith, had been educated at the Moravian Church boarding school at Fulneck, near Leeds. At 17, Booth had moved to the small South Yorkshire mining town of Wath-upon-Dearne, where he signed up as a colliery electrician. Twelve-hour days working both overground and underground for meagre wages, with digs of a small, gaslit room, were a 'harsh introduction to the real world', he wrote, 'and one that did me a lot of good'. Like Colin Blythe in Kent, he leapt at the chance of a county trial. A fluent batsman and a medium-fast bowler who could also turn an off-break, Booth began to appear for Yorkshire in June 1908, slowly improving from a poor start. Over the next five seasons he was to take 557 wickets at 19 apiece, and score 4,244 runs at an average of 22.69. Although inconsistent, his batting was often flamboyant, and the *Globe* reported 'he hit at every ball that was off the wicket, and a great many that were straight'. Lionel Tennyson said of Booth that he could be 'plain-spoken', but that 'he was never in his life sly or disloyal. Time was too valuable, life too short, and to have acted unfaithfully would have gone against his Christian and Moravian principles'. *Wisden's* summary of the man read, 'tall of stature, good-looking, and of engaging address, Booth was a very popular figure both on and off the field'.

The 1914 Yorkshire season started with an away win by an innings and 156 runs over Northamptonshire. Booth characteristically threw his bat at the second delivery he faced and was out for a duck, but showed his best form with the ball: his 3-42 off 22 overs and 1-15 off 6 was said to have 'ripped out the Northants top tier' and brought weighty plaudits from *The Times*, who called him 'a Colossus among men'. From there Yorkshire travelled to Lord's to play an MCC side captained by Neville Tufnell of Cambridge University and, briefly, England. The visitors again won by an innings. The bowling honours were shared by Booth and the left-arm medium-pacer Alonzo Drake. Drake was another one of those cricketers to play a second sport competitively, with appearances for Sheffield United (24 goals in the First Division) and five other football clubs. His 11 wickets in the match cost him only 42 runs. *The Times* also mentioned the batting of the left-handed Roy Kilner, late of the Mitchell Main colliery team, 'with one straight six disturbing patrons in the lower pavilion balcony'. Kilner's unprepossessing appearance and awkward stance at the wicket had initially led several opposition bowlers to underestimate him on his arrival in county cricket. This turned out to be a grave mistake. 'Somewhat square of build', as the press put it, Kilner was soon affectionately known to colleagues and supporters alike as the 'Friar Tuck' of Yorkshire cricket. Although illness had recently reduced his weight by two stone, it was reported in April 1914 that his stamina was 'as gargantuan as his appetite', and that he remained 'a most solid performer, in every sense of the word'. The Yorkshire committee was also full of praise for their wicketkeeper at Lord's, Arthur Dolphin. His stumping of the MCC batsman Peter Clarke 'off a genuinely fast ball from Drake, nearly defied belief in point of swiftness of eye and hand'. Like his friend Kilner, Dolphin was a solidly built customer who was seemingly impervious to injury. In the course of a seventeen-year career, he was badly hurt on only one occasion, when, waking up from a nap, he fell out of a dressing room chair and broke his wrist.

In early September 1914, Major Booth, Roy Kilner and Arthur Dolphin were among the founding recruits of the 15th (Service) Battalion, the West Yorkshire Regiment, known as the 'Leeds Pals'. Alonzo Drake had tried to volunteer, but was refused on medical grounds. While on embarkation leave in November 1914, Lance-Corporal Kilner married his childhood sweetheart Annie Campbelljohn at Wombwell parish church; Sergeant (later 2nd Lieutenant) Booth was best man. As we will see, Booth died in the most pitiful circumstances in the opening hours of the Somme offensive in 1916. Kilner was wounded by shrapnel in the same action. After recovering in a military hospital near Blackpool, he returned to the front and remained there as a mechanic-soldier until January 1919. Roy and Annie Kilner named their second son Major. After the war Kilner (sometimes appearing under the alias 'Smith') played football for Preston North End and resumed his cricket career at Yorkshire, winning nine Test caps between 1924 and 1926. He died in April 1928 of enteric fever, contracted on a coaching trip to India, at the age of 37. Arthur Dolphin survived the Egyptian front and later became a popular first-class umpire, renowned for his practice of never wearing a hat even on the hottest day. He attributed this habit to his searing experience of desert warfare, 'the cruellest of all tests, which I pray no Englishman of my time will ever see again'. Dolphin died at his home in Yorkshire on 23 October 1942, which was the first day of the Battle of El Alamein; he was 56. Alonzo Drake took 5 wickets in an innings 29 times in his five-year first-class career. Playing him on a damp or drying wicket was likened by Pelham Warner to 'stumbling around in a dark room trying to hit a marble as it bounced on the floor'. He died of a heart attack in February 1919, aged 34.

III

MCC put a weak side into the field under Neville Tufnell for their second match of the season, against Kent, and paid the price by being beaten by an innings and 19 runs just after lunch on the second day. MCC's first innings lasted only two and a half hours, in large part due to Colin Blythe's 4-55 off 20 overs. After tea, play was suspended by what was either a particularly intense storm, or one of the few authentic hurricanes ever to have hit St John's Wood. The *Morning Post* wrote that 'without warning a fierce wind appeared from the east and rain fell with such force that from the stands the players quickly dissolved from view'. After slumping to 26-3 on the resumption, Kent rallied to make 276, thanks to a sparkling 94 by Woolley. It rained again overnight. Neville Tufnell was sufficiently wary of Colin Blythe's bowling in those conditions to mutter 'the bugger's done us' when Blythe duly took his first wicket of the innings, which can only have been disheartening to the next batsman in, who happened to be sitting next to him on the dressing room balcony at the time. The only resistance came from a Captain Nigel Haig, nephew of Lord Harris and a cousin of the general, who also played top-class tennis, racquets, squash and golf, apart from his all-round prowess on the cricket field. Haig, who won the Military Cross in the war, scored 42 in the MCC second innings; Kent concluded their victory after just eight hours' play. 'No bowler could have shown to greater advantage than C. Blythe', said the paper.

Sitting in the pavilion seats during the sunnier intervals at Lord's was a rather care-worn and heavyset, moustachioed figure who was then 51 but might have passed for his mid-sixties. He was Andrew Stoddart, who, as a younger, immaculately tailored man-about-town, his dark hair worn *en brosse*, had been the object of cult worship by admirers around the world, many of them female, and was more especially famous in the last years of the nineteenth century as a dashing England cricket and rugby double international captain. In the winter of 1894–95 he had led the Englishmen on a triumphant tour of Australia, on which he scored 870 first-class runs at an average of 51. In the second innings of the Melbourne Test, which England won, Stoddart made 173, which was 98 more than his entire side managed in the first innings. *Punch* celebrated the occasion with a poem which contained the lines:

> Then wrote the queen of England
> Whose hand is blessed by God
> I must do something handsome
> For my dear victorious Stod.

Although formal honours eluded him, Stoddart was widely feted in song and verse, and his new wax model was the talk of the summer 1895 season at Madame Tussaud's. Three years later, England surrendered the Ashes four Tests to one, and Stoddart returned home to a more muted welcome. His parting comments about the 'ill-bred' barracking of some of the Australian crowds produced considerable heat in the press. *Wisden* wrote 'to speak the plain truth, there has not for a very long time been anything so disappointing in connection with English cricket as the tour of Mr Stoddart's team'. After that, Stoddart played only one more full first-class season for Middlesex, bowing out with a final score for his county of 221, although he continued to appear in club cricket until 1907, when he was 44.

By the spring of 1914, Stoddart had prematurely become senile. As an old rugby colleague named Robert Sheriff said:

> He looked very heavy and very tired … he said he could still always sleep well, eat well and especially drink well! but that he no longer jumped out of bed the way he used to, and felt as if he would be quite content to spend the whole day in bed. I'd never yet heard him admit that he was beginning to fail.

He would speak of conversations with Stoddart in which 'his eyes would shift focus from you to the window and he would fall silent – to all intents and purposes, he had departed the room'.

In October 1906, Stoddart had married for the first time at the age of 43. His wife was an Australian widow, Ethel Luckham, who was said to be 35, although some reports put her only in her late twenties. Marriage at Stoddart's age and to a much younger wife (he had first met her while on tour nineteen years earlier, when she can only have been a teenager) was not unusual in those days and his circles. Though childless, the couple initially seem to have been reasonably happy. In 1911, the Stoddarts moved to a large Victorian house at 115 Clifton Hill, about a ten-minute walk from Lord's. It was said to be haunted by the ghost of a maid who had died there. Some time later Stoddart lost his job as secretary of Queen's Club, which had paid him £300 a year and allowed a reasonably high expense account. It's thought that his marriage came to be one based more on mutual tolerance rather than any grand passion. Increasingly irritable and worried about his finances, Stoddart told various cricketing friends that he regretted retiring from the game as early as he had. For one who had achieved such professional success as he had, who had been as acclaimed on the sports field and as popular in society drawing rooms, few would have predicted a middle age of almost unrelieved anguish. In the delicate words of Stoddart's biographer David Frith, 'by now he was reduced to playing the occasional foursome at bowls, with whisky and soda the stakes'.

By April 1914, Stoddart had not only lost control of events but had the greatest difficulty in even summoning the willpower to leave his home and walk the short distance to Lord's. He no longer responded to the greetings of well-wishers on his way into the ground, and once there preferred to sit in isolation, a hunched figure in a tight black suit and invariably carrying a furled umbrella, of whom C.B. Fry fairly said, 'you didn't feel like going and putting your arm round his shoulder'. It was later suggested that he was suffering from chronic pneumonia, and had become even more short-tempered as a result. Compounding Stoddart's black mood, his elder brother Harry, the one man he consistently admired, died late that June after a stroke. It happened to be the same day on which the schoolboy terrorist Gavrilo Princip shot the Archduke Franz Ferdinand at Sarajevo; a confluence of local and global disaster. Early in July, a well-known England cricket administrator was at Lord's one afternoon and took the opportunity to ask the 'grey-faced old gentleman' sitting alone in the members' seats if he planned to attend the ground's centenary dinner scheduled to take place later that month at London's Cecil Hotel. After a long pause, Stoddart finally said, 'we will have to wait and see what the situation is', before concluding the conversation with the remark: 'it is impossible to follow the cricket with all these distractions'.

The final scenes of Stoddart's life were played out in the Clifton Hill house, into which he had moved, so he said, to 'get some peace', as even the slightest noise of someone coughing or rustling a newspaper now got on his nerves. The war had then been on for eight months, and had already fallen into the stalemate of the trenches. Conditions at the front were appalling. An Allied offensive that spring at Neuve Chapelle gained some ground, but could not be exploited because of a shortage of reserves and ammunition and poor weather. The British lost over 13,000 men as a result. The following week, the Germans deployed the first chemical-gas attack of the war, with dense greenish-yellow clouds of chlorine rolling over the Allied lines near Langemark in west Flanders. The first the troops in the rear knew about it was from seeing a unit of French African Territorials run past, pointing at their throats and crying out incoherently.

These were not events to lighten Andrew Stoddart's mood at home in Clifton Hill. It was said 'his temper became shorter, his demands more impossible, his decisions more arbitrary' in the early weeks of 1915. For Stoddart, the global situation was overshadowed by what would now surely be diagnosed as clinical depression. It is known that he suffered from nightmares. Perhaps memories of the past, of his days flying down the touchline as an England three-quarter, or scoring a Test-winning century, began to haunt him. The final crisis came on the night of Easter Saturday, after he had quietly told his wife, 'life is not worth living'. *The Times* reported only that he was 'in financial straits [and] had lost all his money through events in Europe'. Many of Stoddart's admirers were convinced that he was as much a victim of the terrible first year of the war as the men who fought and died in the trenches. Over the next six months the cricket world would go on to suffer the loss from natural causes both of Victor Trumper, aged only 37, and W.G. Grace himself, aged 67. Grace had said he could not bear the thought of so many young friends being 'mowed down' in battle, and just before the end had complained bitterly of the nightly Zeppelin raids over London. Trying to cheer him up, a cricketing colleague had asked him how he could be worried by distant aircraft when he had so fearlessly dominated the world's fastest bowlers. 'I could see those beggars,' Grace replied, 'I can't see these.'

III

In his biography of Jack Hobbs, the cricket historian Ronald Mason wrote that 'the dry bright summer of 1914 is compact of all the ironies', before speaking of the 'parallelism that links the sunny spring of that golden year with the high deceptive waves of gay secure complacency on which Europe sailed to the brink in those last years and months'. We can perhaps take Mason's point, even if his purple patch tortures the analogy: as noted, the weather at least through the first half of the season was initially warm, but then cool and unsettled. It may only be in long perspective that the sun shone so brightly. But there were certainly 'ironies' to savour. One of them was the Anglo-American Peace Ball, held one midnight at the Albert Hall to celebrate the centenary of the signing of the Treaty of Ghent, which formally closed the war of 1812. 'In honouring the occasion,' the programme notes read, 'the countries that have given birth to Shakespeare and Lincoln, Milton and Penn … are setting a magnificent example to the rest of the civilised world for whom armed conflict is surely extinct.' On the same night as the curtain rose on a parade of forty-eight ladies, each dressed as an individual US state (followed by Boudicca in an imaginative froth of chain-mail and peacock feathers), the British army was issuing its 'precautionary period' orders to prepare for full mobilisation. According to the *Post*, there were 'some bellicose noises' to be heard among the Albert Hall crowd, and a climactic pro-peace speech by the real-estate heiress and *Titanic* survivor Madeleine Astor, clad as Rhode Island, was not only unwisely long, but so oblivious to the true European state of affairs that even some of her fellow presenters fell asleep. Mrs Astor's legendary self-confidence was not, however, impaired: she recorded in her diary, 'I think my points well received.'

The crisis that shook many Britons out of their apathy was not the assassination of the Austrian archduke and his wife Sophie, but the delivery of an ultimatum three weeks later by Austria-Hungary to Serbia. Few Britons thought that the archduke's death would lead to war. None of Europe's major military or political figures thought it a significant enough event to attend the funeral or to cancel their summer holiday plans. The Habsburg emperor himself didn't bother to attend his nephew's burial. The Viennese demarche, however, at once set unprecedentedly harsh conditions against Serbia, affronted Russia, Serbia's self-anointed protector, and brought into play the rigid requirements of Germany's Schlieffen Plan, inexorable as a ticking bomb. On passing through Berlin, the *Express* correspondent Alan Easton found excited mobs gathered in front of the royal palace, where the Kaiser appeared to announce that 'the sword has been forced into our hand'. On the whole, these were not events that exuded the same sense of communal goodwill, or mawkish sentimentality, that was on show at the Albert Hall.

With a war coming, many English public schools stepped up their young students' preparedness; as the historian Michael Moynihan recalls, 'marching on church parade through the streets of the town to the sound of bugle and drum and the sergeant-major's growl, "Put some *swank* into it".' Although there was no official MCC directive, Lord Harris let it be known that he personally favoured the institution of military drills alongside 'the more traditional coaching of our young players' in 1914. The idea was to provide an example in 'athletic good cheer' and

46

'such motivating forces as patriotism, sense of duty, cleanliness and discipline' to the rest of the nation. By the time the schools' season closed in late July, it would no longer be a question of preparedness but of mobilisation to fight a war for which an estimated 370,000 recent school-leavers had volunteered by the end of September.

For many people, the horror of the trenches remains forever and inescapably associated with the soldier-poets and more particularly with the doomed figure of Rupert Brooke. For years, every British schoolchild could quote Brooke's opening lines from 'The Soldier'. They have perhaps suffered from over-familiarity as a result. Over time Brooke's poetry managed to insinuate itself as among the most durable propaganda for both pro- and anti-war factions. His own feeling of joy and gratitude that 'a reckoning ha[d] come at last' in 1914 was echoed in Germany. The war meant 'purification, liberation', said Thomas Mann, from the 'toxic comfort of peace'.

Critics still debate whether Brooke's poems are among the few supreme utterances of English patriotism, or full of hollow if wildly popular bombast. The answer, perhaps, is a bit of both. Less well known is the fact that in 1905 Brooke followed Pelham Warner into the XI at Rugby school, where he headed the bowling averages and was something of a trailblazer in his habit of wearing sunglasses in the field. The school annual lists him as 'a slow man who at times kept a good length and puzzled the batsmen', surely analogous to his later career.

Cricket had begun at Rugby in the early 1820s, and in 1855 the school played its first two-day match with Marlborough, an annual event that would be staged at Lord's for most of the next hundred years. Convinced that muscular Christianity was the key to both national progress and personal advancement, Rugby's headmaster from 1909–21, Rev. Albert David, was one of those to introduce physical education into the curriculum, and specifically to support military drills for the school's sports sides. David, a future Bishop of Liverpool, wrote an exasperated report to one cricket-playing boy: 'surely you can see for yourself that your idleness and refusal to do any little task that is in the slightest degree irksome renders you totally unfit to serve the greater team of your God and country?'

In 1914, the Rugby XI was dominated by the left-handed batsman John Bryan and two slow bowlers, John Poole and Eric Champion. *Wisden* wrote of the last, 'he bowls very slow, and tosses the ball up very far. [This delivery] is often effective, as it gives nervous batsmen time to think on the stroke.' Champion took 4-17 with his high lobs in the Marlborough tie that year. Rugby won easily, though both sides displayed some tigerish fielding. The catch with which Marlborough's Ernest Paul dismissed Champion was said to be one of the most brilliant ever seen at that level. The batsman was on 29, and had already taken fours off the first 2 balls of an over before aiming a mighty heave at the third. Everyone looked down the ground to see where the shot had landed, and the spectators began to open a space on the boundary, but the ball never reached them. Paul made a dozen yards' ground from his position at mid-on, dived headlong, met the ball with his left hand, and held it. Pelham Warner was there at the close, and particularly remembered that both sides had put on a 'show of excellence, both of play and of character, that so distinguishes our great schools'.

Three of the young Marlborough XI fell in the war. Second Lieutenant Ernest Paul, having won the Military Cross, succumbed to his wounds sustained in fighting around Amiens in April 1918, at the age of 20. His colleagues Cecil Heal and Sydney Clarke both died in action, aged 18 and 20 respectively. On the Rugby side, 2nd Lieutenant Eric Champion, of the South Lancashires, fell at Messines on 11 June 1917; he was 21. Lieutenant John Poole of the 4th Rifle Corps was reported killed in action around Ypres on 15 May 1915, aged 19. The public and private tributes to Poole were substantial and generous, but also premature. In fact, he had been wounded and taken prisoner in the shambles of battle, but escaped from captivity the following year. Poole was later awarded the Distinguished Service Order (DSO), MC and OBE, Mentioned in Dispatches three times, and ended his life as an ostrich farmer in Rhodesia. *Wisden* said that 'he was brilliant in the field and a good slow left-hand bowler', while the *Globe* called him 'the best attacking young cricketer of his age'. In August 1914, Rugby began the practice of ringing its 3¼-ton Boomer bell each day at noon during the war. In all, the school lost 682 of its former students among the dead.

III

In the spring of 1914, about 3 miles to the north-west of Lord's, a stout figure dressed in a funereally dark suit and carpet slippers, with a blanket sometimes thrown round his shoulders for warmth, could often be seen shuffling up and down Willesden Lane between his lodgings at one end and his regular pub, The Crown, at the other. Although only 41, he looked twenty years older. Of late his face had taken on a ghastly hue, the skin hanging around his once jowly cheeks, in grotesque contrast to his bloated lower body and swollen feet, the product of what would now be called edema and was then diagnosed as dropsy. His name was Albert Trott. A few years earlier he had been widely acknowledged as the finest all-round cricketer in the world. Trott had played his last match for MCC as recently as June 1911, when he was out for a pair against Cambridge University at Lord's. It was a poignant end to a career that had reached a peak in the 1899 and 1900 seasons, in both of which he scored over 1,000 runs and took more than 200 wickets. In July 1899, batting for MCC and Ground against the Australians, Trott hit a ball that bounced off the top of the

Lord's pavilion and into the garden of a nearby home belonging to the Club's dressing room attendant. After retiring from first-class cricket he had appeared briefly as an umpire, until burgeoning weight and other problems had sapped his inner strength, 'pushing him beyond the realm of good judgement', as *Wisden* later noted. Preferring to self-medicate his illness, the once ebullient Trott wondered aloud whether Germany's Princess Sophie, disappointed in love and suffering a variety of health concerns, might not have done the right thing in committing suicide at the age of 25 in a sensationally reported case that year. 'Where's anybody who cares about me?', he is said to have lamented on one occasion at the pub. 'Where are they? The world's lousy ... no good.' They were words that might equally have been uttered by Andrew Stoddart, in his seclusion only a few miles away.

Trott was born in Australia in 1873, and burst onto the Test scene against Stoddart's touring Englishmen in 1894/95. In his international debut at Adelaide, going in at number ten, he scored 38 and 72, both times not out, and took 8-43 in the England second innings. Trott finished the series with a batting average of 102 and a bowling average of 21. For some unknown reason he was not chosen for the Australian team that toured England in 1896, which was captained by his elder brother Harry. Having been overlooked by the national selectors, Trott made his way to London under his own steam and eventually qualified to play for Middlesex. He took 102 wickets for the county in 1898, despite missing more than a month's cricket through injury. A certain no-nonsense pragmatism allied to technical versatility was a Trott hallmark. As a bowler, he could turn the ball in either direction, or send it down medium-fast with a whirling, javelin-thrower's action. As a batsman he tended to eschew the defensive and favour the big hit, especially at Lord's, where he became as popular as any player would be until Denis Compton's heyday two generations later. Neville Cardus wrote of a Middlesex match against Yorkshire, in which Trott once hit the ball to an enormous height. Deep on the midwicket boundary, Yorkshire's Walker Wainwright ran to and fro, gazing upwards, apparently readying himself for the eventual catch. But when the moment came at last, he stood by and let the ball drop at his feet. 'Lord Hawke, his captain, came dashing across to see why he had refused it, but had to laugh at Wainwright's excuse that it was simply "too 'igh, your Lordship".' In the field, the Middlesex captain, acting on the crowd's behalf, often advised Trott to be dramatic, which meant that he had only to act naturally. Plainly spoken and affirming strong Australian values, Trott in some ways seemed an unlikely recruit to the most socially refined of English county sides. But in those years no one doubted the sheer enthusiasm or all-round prowess of his cricket. In some nine full seasons he took 452 catches, frequently pocketing the ball virtually off the face of the bat and then throwing in a somersault or two for good measure.

By 1907, Trott's popularity with the crowd was assured, and it was said 'he enjoyed regular ales with spectators while visiting the deep'. Unfortunately, his actual cricket was in decline. As Trott's weight increased his effectiveness began to decrease, and his modest salary for Middlesex stretched only so far in providing the tailored clothes, expensive dinners and constantly replenished female companions whom he had first shown off with all the pride of a self-made entrepreneur. By May of that year he was desperately in need of funds, and so went into his three-day benefit match against Somerset at Lord's with hopes of a substantial payday. In a tragicomic turn of events, Trott himself sabotaged the occasion by performing the hat-trick twice in the Somerset second innings, thus bringing the game to a close nearly a day early. These were self-destructive skills of a high order. 'It was a great achievement,' Philip Trevor wrote in *The Times*, 'but had the cricket lasted long[er], as at one time seemed probable, there would certainly have been a large attendance of the public, and the Beneficiary would have been the financial gainer thereby.' Neville Cardus echoed the thought by writing 'Trott bowled himself into the bankruptcy court'.

This was the background to the impoverished existence of the middle-aged man hobbling painfully up and down his north London high street. Relatively little is known of Trott's last few weeks, although he was at Lord's in late May to watch his old county win a match against Worcestershire, the last time he was definitely seen at the ground. A spectator named McCord remembered watching this 'pugnaciously gentle man' stop and briefly debate with a gatekeeper his right to free entry before, his point made, going on to 'pass anonymously into the public stand'. The visit may have been an exercise in nostalgia for Trott, or he may simply have welcomed the chance to escape for a few hours from his daily routine. It's possible he might have brushed shoulders in the crowd that day with Andrew Stoddart, both an adversary and a colleague all those years earlier. Whatever his motives, for that one afternoon he was back at the scene of his greatest triumphs, where he had not only famously hit the ball on the bounce over the pavilion but gone on the following year to score 22 (2 4 4 4 4) off an over, and, according to report, 'put one ball among the seats on the top roof, and another on to the portico balcony', among other feats of sustained aerial bombardment. Or perhaps Trott wanted to recapture the moment when, batting for Middlesex against Yorkshire, he had suddenly cut loose after a slow start and scored 137 runs in just eighty-eight minutes, including a straight drive that hit the pavilion railings so hard it ricocheted back, first bounce, into the bowler's hand. Even the fielding side had applauded it. Now, in the spring of 1914, Trott was largely forgotten and in great pain from edema. The news of his sad fate that summer has struck many observers as a symbol of the coming end of the golden age. Cricket was quickly engulfed by the cataclysm of war five days later.

EARLY SUMMER

If any cricketer of the era rivalled Albert Trott for batting fireworks it was Gilbert Jessop of Gloucestershire and England. Born in Cheltenham in 1874, Jessop, a good enough seam bowler to take 873 career first-class wickets, exploded on to the scene while studying for the priesthood at Cambridge in the mid-1890s. In his first Varsity Match at Lord's, opening the bowling and batting at number eight, his brief but crisp innings of 19 against a strong Oxford attack was seen as 'promising … it seemed there was a dasher bursting to come out of him'. He followed it with a flurry of big scores, often made by way of an initial spring off the back foot and a snap of the wrists. In 1897 Jessop did the double, with 1,219 first-class runs and 116 wickets, and went on to become one of *Wisden*'s five cricketers of the year. After making an uncharacteristically quiet Test debut against the Australians, his *annus mirabilis* came in 1900 when he was appointed captain and secretary of Gloucestershire. Despite his additional duties, Jessop scored 2,210 sulphurous runs and took 104 wickets, including a career-best 8-29 against Essex. His two innings in the county match with Yorkshire at Bradford each featured a century before lunch. Neville Cardus wrote that bowling to Jessop in this mood was like 'dwelling on the slopes of Vesuvius, [as] slow fires were likely to break out without warning into a mighty eruption'.

In August 1902, Jessop came to the crease with England at 48-5 while chasing 263 to win against Australia at the Oval. Seventy-seven minutes later he was caught Noble, bowled Armstrong for 104, which included seventeen fours and an all-run five – and it should be remembered, as with Trott's innings, that in those days a ball had to go out of the ground to score six. Jessop made his hundred off just 76 deliveries, and England won by one wicket, in what Ronald Mason calls 'one of the last great enchantments of the Victorian age'. The following June, Jessop was to prove equally busy in making 286, with 42 fours, in 175 minutes for Gloucestershire against Sussex. *Wisden* reported that he scored the runs with 'splendid driving and hitting on the leg side' of which a few vestiges remained with him to the end of his playing days. 'Gloucester had a doleful and disastrous season,' the almanack wrote of the summer of 1914, 'when Jessop only found time for nine matches. However, he scored one truly brilliant innings of 78.'

For all his resolute approach to batting, *The Times* spoke for many when it insisted that Jessop was 'no mere agricultural swiper', but was rather a 'scientific quick scorer' with a 'full arsenal of strokes'. Right up to the outbreak of war, when he was 40, he enjoyed 'an absolute command of all the shots, [with] exceptional co-ordinative powers of eye, hand and, particularly, feet'. A stocky man, Jessop positioned himself at the crease in a shallow crouch, with his legs wide apart, knees slightly bent, the bat held away from his body. Despite this ungainly stance, he was able to react to the ball the instant it left the bowler's hand. Cardus said, 'if he sensed it was short-pitched he was back on his stumps in a flash, if he saw it fuller in the early flight he was yards down the track to meet it; whatever the ball was, he was on it'. Over some twenty years, Jessop's best innings consistently gave the impression of being both thrillingly fast and yet quite unhurried. Among his fifty-three centuries were five scores of more than 200. Playing for Gloucestershire against a strong West Indies side at Bristol in June 1900, Jessop scored 157 between 3.30 p.m. and 4.30 p.m. on the first day. Appearing for the Gentlemen of the South against the Players at Hastings in 1907, he hit 191 in ninety minutes, and took just forty-two minutes over his first hundred. Having tripped himself up on his way down the pitch, Jessop executed one leg-side four while lying flat on the ground and scything, rather than hitting, the ball to the boundary.

Jessop combined all this with a range of other competitive sports, a versatility shared by many other top cricketers of the time. He was adept at football, hockey and rugby, and, *Wisden* said, 'would have played billiards for Cambridge against Oxford, but was gated and could not take part. In one week he made two breaks over 150'. As a young man, Jessop could run the 100 yards in 10.2 seconds. In 1914 he took part in the British amateur golf championship, and *The Times* reported that he 'tempered his all-round hitting ability with uncommon patience and technique on the greens'.

Jessop was in every sense one of the Renaissance men of the day. Initially a schoolteacher, he later enjoyed some success as a journalist and author, and was canny enough both to have made a small fortune on the stock market and then to have sold out shortly before the Wall Street Crash of October 1929. In 1902 he married a young Australian woman whom he met when returning on the boat from an England cricket tour. Prior to that he had enjoyed a somewhat raffish social life, and it was a testament to his charm that on the whole the late-Victorian public were amused rather than censorious. Jessop served with the Lincolnshire Regiment

throughout the First World War. While home on leave in 1916, he took the opportunity of a day's rest cure at a spa in Bath. At one stage in the session he was locked
into a wooden steam-box, which overheated before the attendant returned to free
him. As an added challenge, his legs had been stretched out immobile in front of
him in a pair of metal stirrups in order to bring relief to a painful back. Jessop later
remarked that his efforts to escape while struggling to remain conscious from this
confinement had been the most terrifying thirty minutes of his life. Anyone familiar with the James Bond film *Thunderball* has only to think of the scene in which
Bond nearly dies while undergoing a similar torture, but without the subsequent
consolation of a buxom nurse, to get a flavour of the ordeal. Jessop suffered permanent damage to his heart as a result. In 1918 he was invalided out of the army, and
for the next twenty years made his living as a writer and secretary of the Edgware
golf club. He died in May 1955, aged 80. Jessop had abandoned his own plans to be
ordained on leaving Cambridge, but his son Gilbert (like him, named in honour
of W.G. Grace) went on to take holy orders and to play cricket for MCC, Dorset
and Hampshire. In a Minor Counties match against Cornwall in August 1939, the
younger Jessop scored a run-a-minute 69 not out, with what the yearbook calls a
'battery of fours and one flat six that cleared the bowler's head and skimmed low
all the way into the cow field. His father, who was present, would have approved.'

When it came to assessing other players in his journalism or books, Jessop took an
approach that was much like his batting. It was to cut through trivia to the essential,
to sum up a man in a few broad brushstrokes, and above all to keep it simple. In
June 1907, he wrote in an open letter to Colin Blythe:

> I remember well your first appearance against Gloucester, when you looked just
> sixteen. You displayed a peculiar run up and delivery. It was a gentle amble followed
> by a last final hop. Of modern bowlers you are certainly the greatest. The [Test] side
> can hardly take to the field without you. You have a great reputation with the horses
> to the benefit of yourself and of your friends. Your popularity has been raised with
> both song and violin. I trust it will be many a year before that hop, skip and jump is
> no longer familiar to us, and that you will claim one or even two hundred wickets a
> season. However, I pray I may be spared from becoming one of them.

The charm and generosity of this little sketch are typical of Jessop's newspaper
articles, which were generally shrewd and prescient, if sometimes a bit oracular.
'Circumstance', he wrote elsewhere, 'is the greatest leveller'. In a cricket world 'of
some predictability, where records by season and career belong only to the greatest players, any maverick person in white flannels may produce one unforgettable

feat' – a truism that certainly applied to Colin Blythe's third match of the 1914 season, for Kent against Oxford University at the Parks. Early expectation at Oxford ran high that year, prompting the *Sporting Life* to comment that the county champions had 'a stiff task ahead of them' on the cloudy Whitsun morning of 25 May. The students' middle order trio of Donald Knight, Robert Boddington and Geoff Colman 'all came to the party with a big reputation' while their number six, Fred Knott, 'gave promise of being one of the great English batsmen of his time'.

In the event, Knight, Boddington and Colman contributed just 3 runs between them in the Oxford first innings of 337, though Knott made 49. The man of the hour was 19-year-old freshman Miles Howell, who scored 123, with fourteen fours, in 200 minutes. If not quite in the Jessop class, it was a remarkable feat of controlled hitting. *Sporting Life* reported that Howell 'imposed terrible savagery' on the Kent attack, though Blythe got him, caught off a 'high-bouncing twister of a ball', in the end. The Oxford fast bowler Philip Havelock-Davies, coming in at number ten, then flung the bat for a career-best score of 55. Davies went on to do the hat-trick later in the season, and played once for Sussex, for whom he took 2-26 and scored no runs. In the county yearbook he is listed as a 'good bowler, if not inclined to linger with the bat'.

In the first over of the Kent reply at the Parks, Harold 'Wally' Hardinge hit Davies straight back over his head for four. To the *Oxford Times*, 'this rather set the tone for the procession that followed'. After Hardinge departed, James Seymour and Lionel Troughton both made centuries as part of a Kent score of 571. Following this there was another swing of fortune. *Wisden* wrote that 'Oxford saved the game in capital style on the last day, but owed much to their opponents' mistakes', with seven dropped catches and what another critic called 'amateur standards of chasing in the field, where some of the players appeared to be moving with their bootlaces tied together'. It is possible that by then Kent's heart wasn't fully in the fight, which ended in a rainy draw. Oxford scored 323-5 in their second innings, with Knight making 63. Colin Blythe had match figures of 4-59 in 25 overs and 0-38 in 27, a model of tactical acumen, patience and endurance. For long stretches of the game he bowled in tandem with a young leg-spinner named Alfred or 'Tich' Freeman, who was making his first-class debut.

Miles Howell left Oxford at the end of the summer term of 1914, joined the army and served through the war on the Western Front, where he was twice wounded. He returned to captain Oxford at both cricket and football. Always batting in glasses, he was good enough to play for Surrey intermittently from 1920 to 1925. In August 1922 he appeared for the Oxford and Cambridge side against Glamorgan at Cardiff under the alias 'W.G. Osbourne'. 'The identity of Osbourne remained a mystery for many years, and it was never explained why he used the pseudonym', said *Wisden*. The initials are suggestive.

Howell's Oxford teammate and close friend Philip Havelock-Davies served with the Royal Tank Corps on the Western Front, won the MC, and was wounded by the projection of boiling-oil cans and containers of gas into the British 'rest' positions around Cambrai in November 1917. Although he returned to play for a variety of teams including the Army, Hong Kong and the Free Foresters from 1919 to 1927, Davies never fully recovered his health. He died in an army hospital in January 1930, aged 36.

Wally Hardinge of Kent was another of those men to represent his country at more than one sport, albeit briefly and without, perhaps, showing to his best. In April 1910, he played a single football international for England against Scotland at Glasgow, and replaced Jack Hobbs in the England side for the third Test against Australia at Leeds in July 1921 when Hobbs came down with appendicitis. Hardinge scored 25 and 5, and was not picked again. Between these two events, he served as a chief petty officer in the Royal Navy and saw action at Jutland. After retiring as a player, Hardinge went on to coach several professional cricket and football teams, including Tottenham Hotspur. He died in 1965, aged 79.

James Seymour is largely forgotten today, but almost every long-serving English cricketer owes him a debt of gratitude. In July 1920, Kent awarded him a benefit match against Hampshire at Canterbury. As usual in those days, the county kept the money, reported to have been £939, until Seymour was able to convince them he had what the Committee called a 'sober enough project' (a fruit farm) to invest it in. Soon afterwards, the Inland Revenue took an interest in the matter. In May 1923, they took Seymour to court, claiming that the funds were a 'taxable profit' and that with subsequent interest and penalties he owed the Crown £3,752, a sum larger than his net assets. In time the High Court ruled in Seymour's favour, but their decision was then unanimously overturned by the Court of Appeal. It appeared to even the most seasoned financial experts, like the business correspondent of *The Times*, that that concluded the affair. Such observers underestimated Seymour's obstinacy and resilience. In 1927 the House of Lords ruled that he could keep his money after all. Announcing their decision, Lord Phillimore said: 'I do not feel compelled by any of the authorities to hold that an employer cannot make a solitary gift to his employee without rendering the gift liable to taxation', a principle that prominent English cricketers still apply today, every time they bank £400,000 or £500,000 from a benefit season. Seymour himself died in 1930, aged 50, having at least lived long enough to have his day in court.

Tich Freeman went on to take 3,776 career first-class wickets with a combination of leg spin and its variants, including a phenomenal 304 wickets in the dry summer of 1928. It seems a logical, chronological progression that he should have played his first season for Kent just as Colin Blythe played his last.

Blythe himself took a second-class seat on the train from Oxford on the night of 27 May, changed stations in London, and got back to Tonbridge, to a supper 'not so much cold as it was positively icy' shortly after midnight. Home was a detached house with a small front garden and hedge, gas lighting, and a zinc bath his family placed on the kitchen floor every Saturday night. Although officially called Killarney, they whimsically referred to the place as Emohruo, or 'Our home' backwards. Blythe left again at 8 a.m. the next morning to make his way to the old Private Banks ground on Canadian Avenue in Catford. It was a rickety little place even by the standards of the wooden facilities of the time. First used for occasional county matches in 1874, the cricket field was essentially a roped-off corner of a large public sports ground and park. There was a modest pavilion on one side and a jerry-built tier of benches on the other, where people could sit for 6d or 1s, depending on the importance of the game being played. The Catford pitch left much to be desired. Blythe remarked that his main concern when appearing there was to 'not vanish into one of the pot-holes on the wicket'. The other amenities were equally basic, with a pervasive smell of cabbage and other, more noxious odours that 'rose pungently and with increasing effect from the direction of the pavilion onto the playing area'. The Kent dressing room was then the only one in the place, inasmuch as visitors put on their whites at their hotels or struggled into them behind a nearby tree. Perhaps unsurprisingly, Blythe seemed to strain for his best form in the match against Leicestershire which began there on the morning of 28 May. A sparse crowd watched in miserable weather as the batsmen generally had the best of the bowlers. *Wisden* wrote that on the final day 'the light became so defective that nothing could be done after half-past three', and the game was abandoned as a draw. Although wicketless for once, Blythe was consistent, with figures of 0–18 off 11 overs in both Leicestershire innings.

Five miles away, in the slightly more rarefied atmosphere of the Kennington Oval, Surrey began a three-day match that week with Warwickshire. In the course of it they suddenly emerged as the free-scoring and generally formidable unit they would remain for the rest of the season. Surrey came abruptly into form on the Friday morning of 29 May; beginning the first session on 47–2, by teatime they had advanced to 541. It was the first of five occasions that year when they passed 500 runs, as well as the three when they hit 400 or more. According to *Wisden*, 'it was said at the Oval quite early in the season that, by reason of their batting alone, Surrey would suffer very few defeats, and this impression, formed in May, was abundantly confirmed by all the subsequent cricket'.

Hobbs, who earlier that week had made 100 in seventy-five minutes against Yorkshire at Bradford, outdid that here by scoring 183 out of 224 from the bat in two hours fifty minutes. His innings included twenty-one fours, two sixes and a five. It was only 43 runs less than the entire Warwickshire team had managed on the first day. Batting at number seven for Surrey, Percy Fender chipped in with a typically brisk 140 in two hours. 'He ran every kind of risk with obvious cheerfulness', one report said. Unusually, Fender moved from 94 to 100 with an all-run six. Surrey's William Abel, a medium-fast and leg-break bowler, not known for his sustained hitting, then turned the screw with a chanceless knock of 87, and Andrew Ducat casually added 50. Insofar as there were any Warwickshire bowling honours they belonged to the seamer Percy Jeeves, who took 3-109 in 29 overs, and would have had more if the slips had done their job. Writing in November 1913, *Cricket* described this player as 'clean cut, standing about 5 feet eight inches, only about 10½ stone, but well knit and athletic in build … he has a nice run up to the wicket, a very loose arm, and a beautiful body swing, and makes the ball go away very quickly with his arm'. The shy, fastidiously tidy and reserved Jeeves, relatively abstemious and totally uninterested in food, was in some ways a fish out of water among the roisterers of the Warwickshire professionals' dressing room. Early in July 1914, Jeeves would be picked for the Players against the Gentlemen at the Oval and was 'splendid', *Cricket* said. 'Some of the Gentlemen went all to pieces against him.' *Wisden* called Jeeves, who was 26, 'perhaps one of the great bowlers of the future'.

In the Warwickshire follow-on against Surrey, Fender and Abel showed their all-round prowess by taking 9 wickets between them. After an opening partnership of 58, the visitors lost their remaining batsmen for 60 runs. Surrey duly won by an innings, went to the top of the Championship table, and shared the front page with the Home Rule crisis in all the London evening papers.

A few weeks later, after the outbreak of war, Percy Jeeves joined the 15th Battalion, Royal Warwickshire Regiment. On 22 July 1916 he was killed in action on the Somme. In September of that year, P.G. Wodehouse's immortal valet made his debut in a story published in the *Saturday Evening Post*. Nearly a century on, Wodehouse scholars still debate the exact genesis of the character. To review the books, lectures, tours, films and other, more ad hoc projects inspired by the fictional Jeeves today is not to note a revival of interest, but simply to let down a bucket into a bottomless well. It is agreed at least that in August 1913 the 31-year-old Wodehouse was at the College Ground, Cheltenham, to see Gloucestershire beat Warwickshire, and that Jeeves played, if not with much luck. Described in the local press as 'effete and pallid', he took just 0-43 and 1-12 and scored 1 run in the match. Jeeves's all-round performance was comfortably eclipsed by that of men like Edward Dennett,

Alf Dipper and Bill Quaife, but apparently none of these names impressed themselves on the author in quite the same way. Private Percy Jeeves, who was 28 at the time of his death, left an estate valued at £223. The *Birmingham Post* called him 'one of the finest specimens of the clean-living young cricketers that ever donned flannels – a true sportsman through and through, with a heart too big for defeat and a temperament too free from conceit for success to spoil'.

Andrew Ducat of Surrey was another one of those athletes good enough to compete at representative level in more than one sport. Between 1910 and 1920 he played six football internationals, and, like Wally Hardinge, won a single Test cap as a free-styled middle-order batsman against Australia at Leeds in July 1921. In July 1942, Ducat collapsed at the wicket while batting for the Surrey Home Guard in a match at Lord's. A few minutes later he was pronounced dead of an apparent heart attack. The match was immediately abandoned, and Pelham Warner wrote: 'such an event had never happened at Lord's before, and the sudden tragic passing of this very popular cricketer and famous footballer, apparently full of health and vigour, was a severe shock to those present.' Andrew Ducat was 56.

According to the county yearbook, 'there were times in 1914 when Surrey's bowling looked ordinary: at others it looked top notch'. The hero of the first day against Warwickshire at the Oval was Bill Hitch, a right-arm fast bowler, who dismissed Ernest 'Tiger' Smith, Percy Jeeves and William Hands with successive balls and finished the innings with figures of 6-74. From a short, hopping run-up and whippy action, accompanied by a climactic grunt, Hitch could let slip a genuinely quick ball, especially if it was a bouncer, and at 27, but in only his third full season at that level, he possessed impressive control of pace and movement. In 1914, he took 147 first-class wickets, and was a good enough batsman to once crack 51 in forty minutes for England against Australia. Hitch survived the war, but was never quite the same player again.

Hobbs, of course, stood alone: as *Wisden* – abandoning its note of critical reserve – said, he was 'pre-eminently the batsman, and man, of the year'. Following his 183 against Warwickshire, he went on to make 215 not out against Essex at Leyton, in a Surrey innings where the next highest score was 27. In the next match, Hobbs came out to bat after a hailstorm at the Oval against Hampshire and put up 163 in 200 minutes with seventeen fours, 'and was quite free from serious blemish', in *Wisden's* measured words. He then had a rare failure in the derby match against Middlesex, but soon atoned for this with knocks of 64 and 142 against Lancashire, 122 against Kent and 226 against Nottinghamshire, 'making runs all round the wicket in masterly fashion and giving no chance'. Nottingham's veteran all-rounder Jim Iremonger was so depressed with his figures of 1-107 that he decided there and then to finish with professional cricket at the end of the year – and this was a hardened county pro who not only played international football but, more pertinently, had just set a world record at the age of 38 by bowling 66 consecutive overs at medium-fast pace in a match against Hampshire. 'He was not one to surrender the fight', *The Times* remarked. But Iremonger went home that night and told his younger brother Albert, like him a cricketing footballer, 'that bugger was hitting them through the covers like spotlight [tracer] bullets. You've never seen anything like it.'

Like W.G. Grace before him, Hobbs had clearly transcended cricket, and become familiar to tens of thousands of ordinary Britons who never went near Lord's or the Oval. Besides Herbert Asquith, one paper editorialised, he was England's 'first citizen', a man who had studiously applied himself and 'succeeded so well that he has passed out of the ranks of sport into one of the great men of the Empire'. To his biographer Ronald Mason, Hobbs was almost a god among men, 'with [his] delicate features and prominent contemplative eyes … his modest grace and adventurous brilliance that retained through the dizziest triumphs a quality of self-effacing decorum and quietness'. In plain terms, Hobbs was the bridge between the gentlemanly off-side play of Victorian batsmen in beards and top hats and the concentration and discipline of recognisably 'modern' greats like Hammond, Bradman and Hutton. Jim Iremonger spoke for many bowlers when in August 1914 he asked with some heat 'how does anyone ever get him out?' Hobbs finished that season with 2,697 first-class runs at an average of just under 60. About the worst that could be said of him as a cricketer was that he sometimes seemed to lack the killer touch. Amid the triumphs there was often a vague sense of unease: of batting suicides, opportunities not taken. Dangerous though it is to use the word 'only' in relation to double centuries, on a comparative basis it has to be applied to Hobbs's career record of scoring 16 innings of 200 or more, which is 21 fewer than Bradman managed, and roughly on a par with the likes of Mark Ramprakash and Graeme Hick. Despite everything, Hobbs was never merely a run-making machine, and there were clearly times when Surrey or England were well set and he felt that his work at the crease was done. As a man he had a natural modesty and a certain equanimity to events in general that was much admired and that tended to assert itself in even the darkest situation. Possibly it was this quality that led Hobbs to remark blandly that he had not initially volunteered for the army because, in the thick of the desperate fighting of September 1914, he had not realised 'how serious the war would be'.

Misunderstandings could hardly go further. Just as Hobbs was taking a relatively restrained 64 off Lancashire that summer, events in Europe were assuming a newly irresistible momentum. On 5 July, Germany pledged its support – the famous 'blank cheque' – for whatever punitive action the Austro-Hungarian empire might care to take against Serbia. The Austrian note to Serbia followed eighteen days later. In England, a mark of the gravity of the situation came when the king announced his decision not to attend the races at Goodwood, due to the 'serious turn of affairs' on the Continent. The London stock market shut down, and there were long lines of anxious depositors at the front doors of high street banks, clamouring to withdraw their funds. Within a few more weeks, Lord's had been commandeered by the Territorial Artillery, while the pavilion witnessed the unusual spectacle of dozens of War Office employees and civilian volunteers sitting at long workbenches, engaged in making hay-nets for horses, part of the widespread official delusion that the war would be about epic cavalry charges, rather than about aircraft and poison gas. 'Some 18,000 of these nets were completed and sent to Woolwich', Pelham Warner wrote with satisfaction.

The tension of the summer and the fitful weather continued to depress attendances at some first-class cricket matches. *Wisden* reported that:

> Financially, Hampshire were hit very hard; receipts from the August games being so much affected that the season's work resulted in a deficit of over £700 ... Kent had a bitter experience of the effect of the War on cricket finance – profits dropped to the extent of £1,000, and the matches transferred from Dover to Canterbury raised little support ... at Lancashire there was a loss on the season of £1,314 ... Sussex deserved vastly better support than was accorded by the lukewarm public of Brighton ... financially, Northamptonshire had a disastrous year ... it was a calamitous time at Somerset. At a special meeting in October it was decided to make efforts to improve the position so that the club might be carried on under more favourable auspices.

On 6 May 1914 MCC held its annual general meeting at Lord's. One of the most notable, and cheering, aspects of the summer's events was that in general the cricket establishment carried on its business as usual. 'In a tone of mild regret, [but] the utmost calm', club treasurer Sir Spencer Ponsonby-Fane stated that 124,621 spectators had paid at the Lord's turnstiles in 1913 as against 211,389 in 1912, although he confidently hoped this trend would be reversed in the new season. Fortunately, outside income from investments and rents remained adequate for the club's needs. The price of an annual seat at the ground was fixed at £1. There were some notable exceptions to the attendance rule, however, and in early July the Gentlemen *v.* Players fixture drew a crowd of around 28,000, spread over three days, to the Oval, where there were also several full houses even for midweek county games. On the cloudy Monday morning of a three-day match at Lord's in high June between an MCC South African XI and the Rest of England about 12,000 people, exclusive of members, paid to see the Rest's Ted 'Punter' Humphreys, of Kent, score 111 in three hours. It says something for the popularity of cricket at the time that *Wisden* wrote only that 'the match, without proving a great attraction, was well patronised'. A week later, the same ground was packed to the rafters for the Varsity match, while for the Eton *v.* Harrow tie that followed, 'in the course of the two days over 23,000 people paid for admission, the full attendances being estimated at over 38,000. As the weather from start to finish was perfect, there was nothing to interfere with the enjoyment of the cricket'; and on the second day the Foreign Secretary himself was there to watch the play and take tea in the committee room before leaving on another long, country-house weekend, all part of the Edwardian twilight of British politics.

Given the fact that English sporting life and English society in general seemed so serenely tranquil in the early summer of 1914, it is fair to ask how there could be such an apparently contagious excitement for war just a few weeks later. In fact, several well-organised and highly vocal groups and individuals stood aside from the consensus. Some expressed their reservations in terms of a patriotic duty, while others protested the war with unnuanced anger and revulsion. The Labour politician Keir Hardie spoke of the 'obscenity of picking a quarrel with our German comrades'. His words were echoed by groups like the Women's Social & Political Union and Sylvia Pankhurst's newspaper *Workers' Dreadnought*, whose editorials impatiently awaited the class war that would end the war of nations. Alas, when Hardie and Pankhurst later visited the valleys of South Wales to denounce the outbreak of hostilities to what they assumed would be a receptive audience, they were drowned out by miners singing 'Rule, Britannia!'. During the weekend before the war, the *Guardian* published a front-page letter from the welfare campaigner Emily Hobhouse remarking that 'few English people have seen war in its nakedness ... they know nothing of the poverty, destruction, disease, pain, misery and mortality which follow in its train. I have seen all of this and more.'

Many people were prepared to believe that the war would be over within a matter of weeks. Several prominent British public figures, including Jack Hobbs, spoke of military intervention in Europe as being 'a means to the end of a negotiation' with Germany, a sort of 'short, sharp shock' that would restore affairs to their rightful Edwardian order. In August 1914 the new British War Minister, Lord Kitchener, astonished the Cabinet by predicting that the fighting might last 'three years or more ... a nation like Germany, after having forced the issue, will only give in after it is beaten to the ground. That will take a very long time. We cannot know how long.' Few others in authority were inclined to plan ahead for a war that would last for more than six months. Many of those who enlisted were fearful not of being killed, but of not getting a chance to fight before it was all over. The cricketer and novelist Alec Waugh, who was then 16, spoke for at least some of his generation when he said, 'we did not want the war to end before we had reached the trenches. We dreaded having to sit silent after the war when men only a few months older than ourselves compared front-line experiences.'* A bedrock belief, and surely one of the reasons so many young men volunteered so eagerly, was that what Hobbs called the 'active entanglement of the armies' would be over by Christmas. The same essentially willing spirit was found in all the combatant nations. In Germany, the Kaiser was even more optimistic: 'you will be home before the leaves turn', he told the marching troops in August.

III

All this still lay in the future when in late May Middlesex played host to Hampshire in a Championship match at Lord's. In front of a Saturday morning crowd of around 11,000, the visitors batted first and scored 269. Earlier in the season, Lionel Tennyson's commanding officer in the Rifle Brigade had written of the challenges of his combining military and sporting careers:

> I am afraid there is no possibility of [Tennyson] being able to soldier and play first-class cricket at the same time. He was given a lot of leave last year as he did not really start playing until the earlier or most important part of the training was over. This year, however, we shall be doing company training and musketry for 6 weeks from this date, and there is no chance of his being able to get away while they are going on.

Tennyson was, however, available to play for Hampshire at Lord's, if not at his very best: he scored 32 and 1, did not bowl, and, in the *Globe*'s account, was said to have 'lumbered amiably around the outfield'.

In reply, Middlesex were 79-6 before going on to add 248 runs for their last 4 wickets. Coming in at number nine, Nigel Haig scored 60 and at number ten the former lightweight boxer, recently qualified doctor and amateur cricketer Arthur Littlejohn hit 66 not out. Up the order, Pelham Warner batted two and three-quarter hours for his 38.

While Middlesex began badly and improved, it was the reverse story in the Hampshire second innings. Going in 59 runs in arrears they made 37 of them

---

* Waugh duly went to the Western Front. After seeing action at Passchendaele he was captured by the Germans and spent the final year of the war in an enemy work camp.

before a wicket fell, but then managed to be all out for 91. The Australian left-armer Frank Tarrant and the leg-spinning all-rounder 'Young Jack' Hearne, cousin of J.T. Hearne, took 9 wickets between them. Batting at number 10, Arthur Jaques hit the first ball he faced over Tarrant's head, and off the second ball Tarrant clean-bowled him. Middlesex won by 9 wickets, and along with Surrey now began to draw away from the field at the top of the Championship.

Eleven weeks later, Lionel Tennyson sailed with his battalion to Le Havre, where, he wrote in his diary:

We were met by crowds of Frenchmen on the wharves shouting, 'Are we down-hearted – No!' and 'It's a long way to Tipperary', etc. As we steamed in to the wharf we were to land at everything seemed pretty quiet except the bustle of a sea port. We unloaded ship and finished at 4.30 p.m., being very tired and hot. Had some coffee, and about 8.30 p.m. started to march to a camp at Harfleur, 8 miles from Havre, up a terribly steep hill … Reached there sweating like anything about 10.30, [then] issued with three days' rations and told to march down hill at once to the station and push off to the front as fast as we could, as the English had had a severe defeat and heavy casualties and we were wanted in the firing line as soon as possible.

Barely five years before he wrote these words, Tennyson had been a schoolboy at Eton. Less than four weeks before he wrote them, he was playing cricket for Hampshire. As we have seen, Tennyson survived the war; his county colleague Arthur Jaques, who took 117 first-class wickets in 1914, virtually inventing what became known as 'leg-theory' in the process, died in action with the West Yorkshire Regiment in September 1915; he was 27.

Frank Tarrant spent much of the war in India, where he had some success playing cricket for a variety of invitation teams. Appearing for the Europeans against the Muslims at the Gymkhana ground, Pune, in September 1915, he had bowling figures of 5-6 and 5-9. The club report mentions that Tarrant was presented with a silver loving-cup to mark the occasion. After the war he went native and made a career in India, where he often proved unplayable on matting wickets against weak batting. Tarrant's Middlesex teammate 'Young Jack' Hearne played twenty-four times for England and, seemingly like so many cricketing war veterans, died in 1965; he was 74. Nigel Haig served in France with the Royal Field Artillery, won the MC, was wounded at the Somme, but survived to be 78. Their mutual colleague Dr Arthur Littlejohn went to the United States on the outbreak of war to supervise food supplies for the troops in Europe. While in New York Littlejohn contracted tuberculosis, eventually returned to London, and died there in December 1919, aged 39. 'His connection with first-class cricket did not last long,' *Wisden* wrote, 'but he made a very distinct mark. Indeed, when he first played for Middlesex, his bowling caused something approaching a sensation.'

Watching Hampshire go down at Lord's against Middlesex were two cricketers, one still an active player, both among the great English sports polymaths of their time. One of their names is largely forgotten today, while the other remains one of the most iconic of the twentieth century, even though he played his last first-class match in 1922, long before most cricket lovers alive today were born, and his Test match batting average of 32.18 is only about half that of a Jacques Kallis. Yet if his overall statistics, in a sport obsessed with statistical nuance, seem less sublime than they once did, his reputation as the greatest of cricketing all-rounders persists for a legion of writers, commentators and ordinary fans who could never have seen him in action.

The first of the two men was a 27-year-old qualifying solicitor named Robert Wilfred Jesson, 'Wilf' to his friends. Born in Southampton in 1886, he had played in the Sherborne XI from 1903 to 1905, taking 40 wickets in his last year, before going up to Oxford. As a student he is remembered in his Merton College annual as a 'hard-hitting bat [and] a leg-spinner whose high arm, poise of stride and extreme accuracy make him in every respect a classic bowler of his type'. Jesson appeared intermittently for Hampshire between 1907 and 1910. He made a sensational county debut when he took 5-42 in the first morning's play against Warwickshire at Southampton, sufficient for the crowd to call him onto the balcony for a sustained ovation at the lunch interval. 'It seemed too good to be true', the *Evening News* wrote, and in fact it was; in Jesson's fourteen remaining matches for Hampshire, he took just 15 more wickets. By common agreement, he was a model of the old amateur school, gracious and self-effacing and yet hard as flint when the situation demanded: few batsmen can claim to have withstood the four-man Surrey attack of Hitch, Lees, Hayes and 'Razor' Smith as he did in a county game at Southampton in July 1907. On what was reported as 'a trampoline' of a pitch, Jesson top-scored with 38, typical of a batsman whom *The Times* called 'solid and direct, [who] by determination and courage and keeping sensibly within his own limitations, played many useful innings'.

In the summer of 1914, Jesson was articled to a firm of solicitors in Southampton called Hepherd and Winstanley. It is not known how far he might have gone in the law, although it's a matter of record both that he took only a third-class degree at Oxford and that in general he preferred the outdoor life. Jesson was unmarried, though reputedly fond of the ladies, and seems to have occasionally taken rooms in Vincent Square, Westminster, while visiting London. Between his career and his social life he still found time for regular club cricket, hockey and rugby, and was good enough at the last to play on the wing for Rosslyn Park. Jesson was of medium build, compact, balanced and light on his feet. He spoke in a level, class-less voice and is remembered for a dry and often self-deprecating wit. On 6 August 1914 he joined the Inns of Court Officer Training Corps, and just a fortnight later was gazetted as a 2nd lieutenant with the 5th Battalion, Wiltshire Regiment. Jesson served at Gallipoli, where in 1915 he was wounded, twice Mentioned in Dispatches and eventually invalided home, suffering from frostbite. Six months later, at his own insistence, he returned to the front, where we will meet him again.

The other watching cricketer at Lord's was Charles 'C.B.' Fry, who was then 42 and whom John Arlott later described as 'autocratic, angry and self-willed; he was also magnanimous, extravagant, generous, elegant, brilliant and fun. Fry was prob-ably the most variously gifted Englishman of any age. He might have been wafted down from Olympus.'

In fact, Fry was born in Croydon in 1872, the son of a civil servant, and was thought of as a solid, and somewhat moody, rather than exceptional, figure at Repton and Oxford, where he left with a fourth-class degree. It has been argued that he suffered from some sort of personality disorder, or even manic depression, while a student. A precociously talented all-round athlete, he played football for Southampton, with whom he reached the 1902 FA Cup Final, turned out for the Oxford, Blackheath and Barbarians rugby teams, was considered the best rifle shot in England, and at one stage equalled the then world long-jump record. In his seventies he was still able to perform his party-piece of jumping backwards onto a mantelpiece from a standing start. Among other things, Fry was also a schoolteacher, unsuccessful Liberal par-liamentary candidate, magazine editor, novelist and broadcaster, and for forty years the captain superintendent of the training ship *Mercury* on the River Hamble. In later life, he attempted to persuade Joachim von Ribbentrop, when ambassador to Britain, that Nazi Germany should take up cricket at international level. *Vanity Fair* once commented, 'he is sometimes known as "CB", but it has lately been suggested that he should be called "Charles III".' To other commentators, he was simply 'the Almighty'. The common sentiment, shared by Fry himself, was that nobody else did quite as many things quite as brilliantly well as he did.

In cricket, Fry began life as that comparative rarity, a Surrey player with a birth qualification. After scoring 3 and 0 on his debut for the county in 1891, he was to move on successively to Oxford University, Sussex and Hampshire. He played the first of his twenty-six Tests for England as one of Lord Hawke's touring side against South Africa at Port Elizabeth in February 1896, where in a low-scoring match he hit 43 and 15. In general a textbook right-handed bat, Fry was also a great improviser who, to protect his ribs against the fast bowler, sometimes leapt in the air to come down on the ball and eliminate catches to the in-fielders. The first few times he did it, the patrons at Port Elizabeth laughed, as did the South Africans; but by the end of the Test series Fry appeared to have made his point with an average of 40.66. In 1901, he scored six successive first-class centuries, a record since equalled by only two other batsmen. The purple patch continued into June of the next season, when Fry smashed 122 in just over two hours for Sussex against Middlesex at Lord's. Over the course of a twenty-five-year career he made 30,886 runs, with ninety-four centuries, at an average of over 50. In earlier life, Fry had been an enthusiastic quick bowler, although after being called for throwing in 1898 he tended to let this side of his game lapse. In all he took 166 first-class wickets, and bowled 10 balls for England without success. Add to this the fact that Fry possessed Grecian good looks, with a clipped, cavalryman's moustache, moved as easily in the drawing rooms of Mayfair and Chelsea as he did on the games field, and entertained not entirely fanciful hopes of becoming a Hollywood star, and one can see why he was so widely thought to exemplify an Edwardian male ideal. He was a dilettante in the best sense of the word. Fry's imagination was as uninhibited as his batting, and gave rise to several colourful myths about him that persist to this day. The story that he was offered the throne of Albania while attending a post-war meeting of the League of Nations is almost certainly apocryphal. In later life, Fry suffered a series of mental breakdowns, which among other things saw him develop a dread of Indians, including his one-time county colleague and friend Ranjitsinhji. He died in September 1956, aged 84.

By late May 1914, Fry had been out of first-class cricket for almost two years. After leading England in the Triangular Tests in 1912 and publishing his book *Batsmanship*, he had increasingly turned to his work with the sea cadets, and was eventually awarded the rank of Captain in the Royal Naval Reserve. He loved the ceremonial aspects of this particular job. From time to time, Fry would put out on the Hamble in a tiny gunboat, flying an ensign of his own design showing crossed cricket bats. The *Globe* wrote that 'he would stride about in his uniform, looking every inch like six admirals'. But after watching Hampshire lose to Middlesex at Lord's, Fry casually mentioned to his county's new captain, Edward Sprot, that he might be persuaded to return for a limited number of matches. Sprot relayed this significant news to his President, who issued the necessary invitation. The result was that on the morning of 4 June Fry went out to open the batting for Hampshire against Gloucestershire at Portsmouth. He scored 41 in the first innings and 112 in the second. 'Fry played faultless cricket, driving in quite his best form', said *Wisden*. It was the beginning of a long Indian summer for Fry, split by the war, that lasted over ten seasons. In 1921 he was invited to captain England again at the age of 49, but declined the honour. Fry took his cricket seriously enough, as the statistics show, and was as keen as anyone to win. But, as he wrote, 'I never forgot that it was a game, and as such I enjoyed it myself and did all I could to see that others enjoyed it too, including the spectators'.

III

Few more disastrous starts to a Championship season can have been made than that achieved by Essex in 1914. They began with four successive heavy defeats, the third of which came against Yorkshire at Leyton. 'This was a most disappointing performance', *Wisden* noted with some restraint. Essex batted first for 259, with Major Booth taking 6-96. In reply Yorkshire scored 441. Their veteran opening batsman Benjamin Wilson made 106 in something around four hours. 'He seldom drove, and took few risks', *Wisden* reported. There was perhaps an early hint of Geoff Boycott about this player, whom the almanack praised for his 'great technique' but chided for 'the over-cautious game of which he is so fond'. On the outbreak of war, Wilson, who was 34, volunteered for infantry duty and in time saw action at the Somme. In 1914 he was considered a good enough player to help keep Jack Wilson (no relation) out of the Yorkshire side. The latter had first come into the team in 1911, when he was 21, although most of his cricket was to be played on the country-house scene, in particular for the Free Foresters. Jack Wilson's war career reads like something out of a *Biggles* novel. Commissioned into the Royal Naval Air Service, in the pre-dawn hours of 7 April 1915 he and a fellow officer went up in a bright-yellow Sopwith Strutter biplane and, according to the Admiralty report, 'observed two submarines lying alongside the Mole at Zeebrugge and [under] fire attacked them, it was believed with successful results'. These were not to be Major Wilson's only acts of valour. On a later occasion, he took off, in his own spare words 'at 0400, down a paraffin flare path and accomplished our mission over enemy lines, which was undertaken in mediocre weather and to some distinctly unappreciative response by the German guns'. On return, Wilson's aircraft was found to have sustained 136 bullet holes. His first words on landing were to enquire about the score of a current Yorkshire league match. Wilson was later awarded the DSO and the Belgian Order of the Crown. Meanwhile, Yorkshire won by an innings at Leyton; Major Booth took 14 wickets in the match.

Essex fared even worse in their next fixture, against Middlesex, who eventually declared their first innings at 464-1 and did not have to bat again, with Frank Tarrant scoring an unbeaten 250. This time it was 'Young Jack' Hearne who took 14 wickets in the match, and only a timely thunderstorm took the proceedings into a third day.

Wisden was left to conclude that 'enterprise cost Douglas, the Essex captain, dearly', and that no decision to send the opposition in that ends with them scoring some 500 runs for the loss of 1 wicket 'can be considered entirely satisfactory'.

But after a wretched start, Essex underwent what *Wisden* called 'a sudden twist of fortune, which brought about an astonishing change in the play of the side'. Strangely enough, the turning-point came in an away match with Surrey, 'whose bad days were few, and their good days many', as *Wisden* said of that winning season. The visitors seemed to begin on a familiar note by losing half their batsmen for 45 runs on the first morning, but ultimately recovered to 264. Surrey in turn managed just half that total, with Johnny Douglas and his fellow seamer Bert Tremlin bowling unchanged to take 6-60 and 4-68 respectively. Essex batted again, in steady rain and to some satirical handclapping, and eventually reached 277-3 declared. In the midst of what was called 'a generally dogged rather than spectacular' performance, their wicketkeeper, Rev. Frank Gillingham, hit an unbeaten 121 in three hours, with four-teen fours. Chasing 410, Surrey soon found themselves at 22-5 and were all out for 86; Douglas and Tremlin, again bowling unrelieved, took 5 wickets each. Accurate and businesslike off his spry, clipped run, Douglas, in particular, was full of variation, control and hostility. At 31 he remained one of England's leading fast bowlers, as well as strengthening his claims to a place among the top all-rounders. Bowling tightly and holding their catches, Essex fully deserved to win on a flag-strewn spring bank holiday ground which *The Times* said at the end was looking 'groomed like a high-born lady, finally bathed in sunshine and packed to capacity'.

Frank Gillingham was born in 1875; unusually for a first-class cricketer, in Tokyo. A tall, muscular right-handed bat, he was good enough to score 9,942 career runs at an average of just over 30, including an innings of 201 against Middlesex at Lord's in 1904. Ordained into the Church of England in 1899, he served as a curate at Leyton, where he was remembered both as a tireless community worker and a model of busi-ness efficiency. The *Church Times* correspondent called him 'a clean-desk man. When he arrives for work at six each morning, he prepares a schedule for the day. He likes to draw a line through each appointment as it ends.' Gillingham volunteered to serve as a chaplain attached to the Royal Army Medical Corps, based at Ypres, in August 1914. Another reporter called Gillingham's speaking style 'wonderfully effusive on matters spiritual', with overflow crowds of front-line troops regularly attending his services held amongst the ruins of a battlefield. The reporter was deeply impressed by Gillingham's oratory, if not by his knowledge of more military matters, on which:

> The Rev was cheerfully ignorant, although very eloquent. He generally con-
> formed to a tried and tested formula. There was the opening joke, then some

telling Biblical observation, all done in a dry and compelling manner through which there ticked away an impression of unfeigned personal humility and an equally irresistible sense of humour.

After the war, Gillingham was appointed chaplain to the king. He played his final first-class match in July 1928, when he was nearly 53.

Like James Seymour and his victory over the taxman, Gillingham was also to have a wider claim to fame than his mere statistics on the field. At Leyton in May 1927, for a county match against the touring New Zealanders, he became the BBC's first ball-by-ball commentator. According to his Essex colleague T.N. Pearce, Gillingham was asked to do the job because he was 'a terrific preacher', who was 'as perfectly at ease in a Cathedral as in the meanest jerry-built shack provided to the press in those days'. 'The Reverend spoke gaily and with perfect poise', the *Globe* agreed. Instead of talking exclusively about the cricket, Gillingham's inaugural commentary 'dwelled upon matters such as the number of passing birds, and the variety of interesting hats to be seen in the ladies' stand', surely another precedent for much of today's radio coverage. It has been said that Gillingham continued to provide occasional match reports 'until he infuriated Lord Reith, the BBC's overlord and a stickler for a complete absence of anything commercial, when he filled in time during a rain break at the Oval by reading the various advertisements round the ground'. Married with a son, who was also ordained, Gillingham died suddenly while on a visit to the casino in Monaco in 1953; he was 77. Pelham Warner wrote of him in the *Cricketer*, 'he was a man with a charming individuality, who exerted a powerful and beneficial influence over people of various types and characteristics. No one ever came to him in trouble without going away comforted. His friends and admirers were numerous indeed.'

III

County cricket enjoyed some of its greatest pre-war days in the early season of 1914, at least when the weather allowed. Although the ball generally dominated the bat, there were many individual treats like Frank Woolley's innings of 147 out of 210 in a shade over two hours for Kent against Leicestershire, or Hobbs's controlled early knock of 86 for Surrey against Somerset, in which he batted like a compact new sports car being run in. Certainly few of those who came to the grounds that May can have suspected that the clock was already winding down on a golden era. On 9 May Derbyshire began a three-day match at home to Worcestershire. For the visitors, Maurice Foster scored a brief but robust 13, and as a result of this and his lively fielding was said to have been 'the star of a popular, well mannered side which did its best to entertain the crowd in between the downpours'. On the day after the match, Foster's older brother Reginald, or 'Tip', one of seven siblings who all played for the county, died after a struggle with diabetes; he was 36.

Over some ten seasons at the turn of the century, Tip Foster stroked 9,076 generally immaculate first-class runs, including a score of 287 for England against Australia at Sydney in 1903. Like C.B. Fry, he was precociously gifted at most ball games, played ferociously competitive tennis, racquets and golf, and scored twice for England in a football international against Ireland; he remains the only man to have captained England at both football and cricket. In later years, Foster's time was increasingly taken up with business commitments, his charitable works on behalf of sick children and a place on the MCC Committee. *Wisden* wrote that:

> It was characteristic of Mr Foster that [he] could at any time return to first-class cricket and play as well as if he had been in full practice all the season. A case in point occurred in 1910. He only played once for Worcestershire that year, but he scored 133 against Yorkshire.

With hindsight, Foster's early death was a muted sign that English cricket's old guard was passing on.

III

Wars by their nature tend to be idle butchers. They generally rouse themselves to kill only when the victim is very young – 17, in many combat cases – and even then often fail to give the *coup de grâce*. When in May 1914 Oxford University drew their home match with Kent, the students included a fourth-year man named William Camac Wilkinson at number six. Wilkinson's potential was seen when he made 129, 92 of which came in boundaries, for Oxford against MCC in May 1913. In 1914 he had a relatively poor season and failed to appear in that year's Varsity match. Immediately after going down from the university in July, he joined the army on the unattached list of the Territorials and was commissioned in the Coldstream Guards that November. While on duty in France Wilkinson was shot through the right hand and narrowly avoided amputation. Despite this, he promptly applied, or rather demanded, to return to the front, and was awarded the MC for his action at Ypres in September 1917. The citation read:

> Lt. William Wilkinson: For conspicuous gallantry and devotion to duty in commanding his company with the utmost fearlessness and ability after his company

commander had become a casualty. Having led them in the attack, he walked up and down during consolidation, regardless of the fact that enemy snipers were firing at very close range, urging his men to greater efforts so that they should get quickly under cover. Later in the evening, he made a personal reconnaissance of a strong point, made his dispositions before dark, and subsequently led his company forward and captured it with the greatest dash and gallantry.

When the war ended, Wilkinson, now 25, remained in the army. His wound had frozen and grotesquely shrunk his hand, and left him with only limited movement of his wrist and lower forearm. Despite what he called this 'footling matter' Wilkinson soon returned to cricket, improvising a new batting grip, and played seventy-four more first-class matches until his eventual retirement in 1939. Opening the innings for the Army against Cambridge University in June 1922, he scored 104 in eighty-five minutes; the late-cut four with which he reached his century was said to have been 'imperial', while other blows 'reverberated off the boundary-boards and spectator seating straight back to the middle'. 'He was not a slow scorer', *Wisden* noted, perhaps superfluously. 'Almost as remarkable as his batting was his fielding. Though much of his work on his right side had to be done back-handed by his left hand, he was never reckoned a liability in the field.'

Recalled to the army at the start of the Second World War when he was 47, Wilkinson soon added the George Medal to his insignia for his action in walking unaccompanied into an enemy minefield to carry out a wounded soldier. The DSO followed in May 1944, when, during the final stages of the Battle of Monte Cassino, he 'proceeded to cross [a] bridge, under heavy mortar and small arms fire, and then unhurriedly lay down smoke cannisters' to provide cover for a subsequent assault, which he led. With the end of hostilities, Wilkinson was appointed to the military government in the British Zone in Austria from 1945 to 1947. It is said that Trevor Howard put something of him into his role as Major Calloway in *The Third Man*, a character notable for his shrewdness, bravery and procedural competence who does not confuse those attributes with personal charm. In later years, Wilkinson often appeared at Lord's, notably flush of face, and was not shy in remarking on some deficiency in the turnout of the ground or its spectators when compared to his exacting standards. *Wisden* wrote:

A legendary character whose outspokenness knew no close season, he was no respecter of persons; yet he is seldom mentioned by anyone who knew him without genuine affection ... even after the second War he continued to make runs in club cricket and he himself believed that the century which he made in his last innings was the 100th of his career. In any case it was a fitting finale to the life of a brave and determined man.

William Wilkinson died in September 1983, aged 90.

Another young cricketer coming to prominence in 1914 was Trevor Molony, then 17 and regarded as a star all-rounder at Repton. From 1916 to 1918 he served overseas with the Royal Flying Corps, returning to take a place at Cambridge University. It should be mentioned here that Molony performed as an under-arm lob bowler. In May 1921, aged 23, he was selected to play for Surrey against Nottinghamshire at Trent Bridge. Bowling with eight men on the leg side, Molony took 3-11 in 7 overs. According to the *Cricketer*, he was accurate, varied his flight and bowled 'exceedingly good full-tosses at awkward height ... the attempts of the last few batsmen in the Notts side to play him were ludicrous and evinced much laughter from the crowd'. The county appear to have tired of the experiment after that, and Molony's remaining cricket was to be confined to the Incogniti and Repton Pilgrims. He served as a station commander in the RAF during the Second World War. The last county cricketer to be picked solely for his lob bowling, Trevor Molony died in 1962, aged 65.

Then there was Arthur Donald Denton, the youngest of three batting brothers who divided their time between the family boot-making business and playing for Northamptonshire either side of the First World War. If not quite on a par with the Fosters at Worcester or the Tyldesleys of Lancashire, this was a dynasty the county yearbook said was 'not only consistently effective, but wonderfully versatile in their utterly different styles – one could imagine the three of them, fortified by a fast bowler and a wicketkeeper, giving a game to most sides'. Don Denton made his debut for Northants against Sussex in July 1914 and scored 51 not out, after his elder twin brothers had put on 145 for the first wicket. He played three more matches that summer and, said *Wisden*, 'batted in such form as to suggest great things in the future'.

Don Denton joined the army immediately on the outbreak of war, when he was 18. Commissioned as a 2nd lieutenant in the 2nd Battalion, Northamptonshire Regiment, he was wounded in fighting around Artois in September 1915 and eventually lost his left leg above the knee. In a further cruel twist, his elder brothers Jack and Billy were officially reported missing in action, presumed dead, though a postcard later arrived at their parents' home announcing they were German prisoners-of-war. All three brothers were reunited in the Northamptonshire XI against Leicestershire at Northampton in June 1919. Don Denton went in to bat at number eight, with his brother Jack as a runner. The Leicestershire captain Cecil Wood, approached for his permission, sent a note back to the home dressing room: 'if any fellow has been to the war and has had his leg off and wants to play, he is good enough for me and can have twenty runners'. Don Denton scored 29 not out and 8 in the match. He played just twice more for his county, finishing with 276 first-class runs at an average of 25. His last game, like his first, was against Sussex. *The Times* said that he 'played fine cricket on his swansong, [and] one can only sigh and wonder what he might have done but for his handicap'.

III

One of the most striking features of the summer of 1914, in cricket administration as well as the wider world, is that right up until the last moment everything appeared so normal. Beneath the surface, events were teeming with sometimes furious, invisible activity. In Germany, the Kaiser was to express privately his view in June that a 'limited' or 'localised' war against France could be launched through Belgium. His confidence on this score was due in part to his belief that 'the Belgians have no heart for the fight' and that 'the very finger of God points now to Paris', as he remarked to the Italian ambassador. He followed this announcement by assuring his guest 'with the clarity of insight possessed by the Teutonic intellect' that Italy herself would be well advised to consider her position in the coming struggle. 'We are ready and the sooner the better for us', the Kaiser concluded, twisting the monocle several times in his eye. In Russia, the Grand Duke Nicholas, the tsar's cousin and commander-in-chief of the army, had recently been to France to co-ordinate joint operations, and was said to have remarked that only if Germany 'were crushed once and all and divided up again into little states' could Europe expect to live in peace. In Austria-Hungary, the improvisation of the Dual Monarchy was an increasingly precarious affair; in the words of the historian David Fromkin, 'maintaining its formal ranking as a Great Power in good part by courtesy of the others'. A large and aggressive element in Austrian life, not least her ruling elite, openly called for the suppression of what the foreign minister Leopold von Berchtold termed her 'deviant sub-states' and in particular for a 'final and fundamental reckoning' with Serbia.

In the midst of this, life was relatively untroubled for many middle- and upper-class Britons. To the extent that most followed affairs in Europe, it was in the belief that economic realities would keep the great powers from waging war on one another. In some fundamental ways, life was also freer and fuller than it is today. According to the historian A.J.P. Taylor, 'until August 1914 a sensible, law-abiding Englishman could cheerfully grow old and hardly notice the existence of the state'. Within the limits of your bank account, you could live anywhere you wanted and travel anywhere in the world without anyone's permission. Rupert Brooke made a leisurely tour of North

America in the year before the war with only his personal calling-card as identification, and would have been appalled by the idea of anything so vulgar as owning a passport. When the 20-year-old Harold Macmillan travelled around Europe, cycling back and forth over the scene of what would become some of the war's bloodiest battles, where he himself would be wounded, he was 'waved through international borders with as little fuss as if passing between Sussex and Hampshire'.

Nowhere was this fundamental equanimity to events better seen than in English domestic cricket. In mid-May 1914, the French general staff had finalised their arrangements to meet and repulse an attack by Germany – the so-called Plan 17 – and the Germans were completing their widening of the Kiel Canal, allowing their largest battleships direct access from the North Sea to the Baltic, and a key strategic step on the road to war. On the 18th of the month, the Middlesex cricket committee in turn met at Lord's. They reported that the club showed a healthy balance of £475 7s 10d on deposit at the London & South Western Bank, with another £301 19s 4d in investments. In other business, 'Mr P.F. Warner was invited to attend a Secretaries' Meeting on behalf of the county', and a Fred Burton was to be 'nominated as club professional on the staff for 1915–16', an appointment postponed indefinitely by events. The only mild note of contention came in a discussion about 'whether or not the proposed Sat and Weds starts for first-class matches should be universal'. Although the matter was deferred, a later 'informal exchange' between Warner and his fellow county captains achieved 'insight and understanding of each others' policies' on the issue, which was to have come into effect in May 1915.

Among the other talking points at Lord's that month were the preparations to celebrate the ground's centenary in June. Two 'most attractive and fashionable gala matches' were scheduled, with an intervening dinner arranged at a London hotel. There was only a faint hint of unpleasantness at the MCC's own general meeting that month, in the committee's veiled reference that:

> In case the conduct of any member either within or out of the Club shall, in the opinion of the Committee or of any 20 members of the Club … be injurious to the character and interest of the Club, the Committee shall be empowered to recommend, in writing, such member to resign.

On a happier note that week, 47-year-old 'Old Jack' Hearne became the first bowler to take 3,000 first-class wickets when, appearing for MCC, he dismissed Kent's Wally Hardinge on the first afternoon of a rain-soaked game at Lord's. Hearne was to finish his career only in 1924 when, approaching his 60th birthday, he retired with a haul of 3,061 victims.

Meanwhile, Middlesex and Surrey, the London rivals, battled it out at the top of the Championship table, with Kent, Yorkshire and Sussex leading the rest of the field. Essex continued their steady improvement, and went on to beat Lancashire by 156 runs at Old Trafford in the last week of May. In another rain-affected game, Johnny Douglas scored 63 and 25 and took 11 wickets. His chief batting partner was 38-year-old Percy 'Peter' Perrin, who hit a typically robust 60 in the Essex first innings. A north London publican, property developer and Rolls-Royce owner, Perrin would go on to play more first-class matches as an amateur – 496 – than any other English cricketer. Since he also wrote a profuse number of articles and coaching texts, single-handedly ran an inner-London playing fields organisation, sat on the board of several other charities and served ten years as a Test selector, he was probably to be kept as busy as any other British public figure. He had some of C.B. Fry's extrovert style and booming self-confidence, with the added charm of a cockney accent. Recalling the period from 1896, the year of his debut for Essex, to 1939, Perrin wrote, 'I did once manage to plan a two-day holiday with my wife to the south coast, but I crashed the Rolls the night before and broke my head.'

Opening the batting for Lancashire against Essex was a 35-year-old amateur named Alfred Hartley. Like Perrin, he enjoyed a varied career outside of cricket; born in New Orleans in 1879, he had successively worked as a lifeguard and cane-planter in the West Indies, writer, businessman and soldier. 'He could not be classified among the greatest of Lancashire batsmen,' *Wisden* wrote:

> But during his few seasons for the county he was invaluable ... having found a place in first-class cricket he improved from year to year ... scoring 234 against Somerset at Manchester, 126 not out against Somerset at Bath, and 168 against Leicestershire at Leicester. On the strength of his fine cricket he was deservedly chosen for the Gentlemen against Players.

Alfred Hartley was not to develop the potential he had shown as a late-maturing batsman in his mid-thirties. He was commissioned in the Royal Garrison Artillery on the outbreak of war and served almost four years in France, which included seeing action at the Somme. On 9 October 1918 he was mortally wounded by enemy shelling at Maissemy, near St Quentin. At that stage the war was a month away from its end and Hartley himself had not quite turned 40.

MIDSUMMER

One of the concluding passages of the long speech made by Lord Hawke at the MCC annual meeting in May 1914 had focused on the bright prospects for cricket's future. In particular, there were grounds for 'high optimism' on the school and university fronts, where 'we are sowing the seeds of the first-class cricket of the future, [and] we regard this to be a cardinal development'. Even in the event of war, he continued:

> I think it would be a pity to deny the ardour of boys … we, on our part, shall fulfill our annual fixtures with the Public Schools, and in addition to this an encouraging fact has been the Easter classes for boys. The work done at these, and the sound nature of the tuition given, is of great benefit [and] the improvement shown has been remarkable … one of the most notable features of the policy of your committee of late years has been the encouragement of Public School and other boy cricket, [and] this is one of the great achievements which has been possible in recent times.

While Hawke himself was to remain in office throughout the war, in *Wisden*'s view 'the greatest help in giving wise counsel' in a fraught situation, it is not known exactly how many of the estimated 750,000 British military deaths in the same period were young cricketers of one sort or another, although the cadet corps in the public schools and universities made a disproportionate sacrifice. By the summer of 1919 almost every pavilion at college, school and village level had its own Honour Roll of the fallen. Based on a study of individual matches, it is possible to say that, with notable exceptions, an average of two to three members of each organised school team in the summer of 1914 died or were wounded in combat, giving cricket an unwanted place towards the very top of the mortality table.

What *The Times* called 'some anxious Continental rumblings' had taken place by the middle of June 1914 – including the holding of Anglo-Russian naval talks 'to prepare mutual marine defence arrangements' in the careful words of the communiqué – so Lord Hawke's rhetoric of optimism was, in the wider context, already questionable. But the immediate prospects for English cricket seemed very fair, and the weather now began to improve steadily, with 265 hours of sunshine recorded in London during the month. Attendances were also on the rise, with over 10,000 spectators at Lord's to see the opening day's play between the Old Etonians and the Old Harrovians – the first such clash in twenty-two years. Lionel Tennyson, at 24 the baby of the Eton side, scored a hurricane-fast 43, 'with one of two sixes he hit landing in the shrubbery behind the Tavern'. A casual observer could have been forgiven for thinking that all was well in England in that generally sunny and dry month. On 9 June, 55-year-old Edward House – Colonel House, to give him his honorary Texas title – arrived in London to report back on 'the European situation and its possible amelioration by wise American counsel' to his boss, President Woodrow Wilson. It did not prove an easy commission. Many of Britain's leading political figures were not immediately available, although Edward Grey, the Foreign Secretary, eventually gave his visitor lunch. House wrote to Wilson: 'I find here everything cluttered up with social affairs and it is impossible to work quickly. Here they have thoughts on Lord's, garden parties, etc, etc.'

One of the curiosities of the sporting calendar that June was a two-day fixture at Lord's pitting MCC against Egypt and the Soudan. It was as close to a full-scale international match as the summer of 1914 came. It's somehow tempting to agree with the non-cricketing correspondent of *Tatler* and think of the visitors as 'exotically clad representatives [of] a still extensive Empire of 13 million square miles of land, on which the sun never sets ... natives of some dusty, far-flung colonial outpost which hidden among its chaotic souks and bazaars boasts an immaculate cricket field', where, perhaps served by white-coated attendants in ruby sashes, 'men in Fezes can unwind with a refreshing glass of *qasab* sugar-juice at the close of play'.

In reality, ten of the eleven Egyptian players had been born in Britain and gone overseas to work as civil servants, doctors, engineers and the like. Two of them had been teenaged apprentices at Lord's. The visitors' star all-rounder, Gustavus Brander, had been born in Hampshire in 1881 and enjoyed some success with Suffolk in the Minor Counties championship before emigrating in 1907. Egypt's renowned opening bat, Richard More, had played for Oxford University and Middlesex in the early years of the century. The other opener, Percy Organ, originally from Oakley in Buckinghamshire, went on to be a mainstay of Cornwall cricket in the 1920s.

The tourists arrived at Lord's in a hired charabanc, and there was a convivial supper that night at the Café Royal followed by a visit to the Alhambra music hall in Leicester Square, 'during which many old associations were revived', to quote one report.

Unfortunately, the match itself did not always live up to the success of the social arrangements. Batting first, Egypt and the Soudan managed just 79 all out off 27 overs in their first innings. With the visitors unable to cope for any length of time with the MCC fast bowlers, and in particular with Arthur Newman of Wiltshire and the West of England, all 10 wickets fell before lunch on the first day. The game lasted as long as it did only because of some leisurely home batting and an interruption for bad light on the second morning.

Of MCC's reply of 270, Rupert Anson, of Middlesex, scored 55 and Scotland's Mark McKenzie, lately of Oxford University, 47, adding 101 for the second wicket. After the interruption, Egypt batted again and made an altogether more competitive 204. This time around, their batting was said to have 'allied grim determination to a laudable desire to entertain', if without ever seriously putting the outcome in doubt. Left needing 14 runs for victory, MCC required only 2 overs. The winning shot was by Hackney-born Ted Cuthbertson, recently down from Cambridge, a cut for four that thundered through the off side; 'a "not a man move" shot', as *The Times* called it. MCC won by 10 wickets a game 'that was played with great enthusiasm, although in the end logic prevailed over romance', the paper added.

Lieutenant Edward Cuthbertson of the Royal Warwickshire Regiment was born in December 1889, and was a batting prodigy at Malvern. He appeared five times for Cambridge University without getting his blue, and also played student football. He had had hopes of becoming a lawyer. When the war came, 'everything else seem[ed] minor and petty, and a distraction from the true realities', he wrote to his teammate Rupert Anson. Lieutenant Cuthbertson fell in action at Amara, Mesopotamia, on 24 July 1917, at the age of 27.

Lieutenant Mark Kincaid McKenzie of the King's Royal Rifle Corps was born in Edinburgh in August 1888. Educated at Winchester and Oxford, he appeared for the university against Kent in 1910, clean-bowling the county captain Ted Dillon with his first ball, but, like Edward Cuthbertson, missed out on a blue. Lieutenant McKenzie was killed in the bloody and protracted fighting at Soissons, near the Marne, in September 1914. He was 26.

The captain of the MCC side against the Egyptians was Lord Bernard Gordon-Lennox, one of a large clan of talented amateur sportsmen. It has been said that, when selecting the man to lead the typical English cricket team of 1914, a titled connection, however distant, was universally accepted as the last word. Gordon-Lennox himself could boast only a modest first-class record. Appearing in a single match for Middlesex in May 1903, he scored no runs and took no wickets. For all that, he was a prolific run-getter at Sandhurst, for whom he hit 80 against Woolwich in 1897, and subsequently went on tour with I Zingari, scoring 119 against All Egypt at Alexandria. His overall career as a soldier-cricketer would be spectacular, both statistically and socially, and he was also, in Lionel Tennyson's words, 'incomparable company' on tour. Commissioned into the Grenadier Guards, the 36-year-old Major Gordon-Lennox was killed in action near Ypres on 10 November 1914.

On the Egyptian side, there was Joseph Ruscombe Sandford. Born in March 1881 in Devon, he played in the Malvern XI in 1898, where he 'rendered valuable assistance to the established batsmen', finishing with an average of 10. After appearing in Minor Counties cricket, and winning one rugby union cap for England, Sandford resigned a mastership at Harrow to join the Sudan Civil Service. For three years he was in charge of Omdurman and was described in *The Times* as 'one of the best and most capable of officials', a man 'whose integrity and sporting instincts survived the severest test'. He died of what is recorded only as 'disease' in the civic hospital, Khartoum, in July 1916, aged 35.

III

When *Wisden* came to review the 1914 season, it found a word of approval for most of the sixteen sides contesting the County Championship. Somerset, who came in fifteenth, 'underwent some changes', the almanack allowed, but 'notwithstanding the gloom that prevailed in August, the matches at [Weston-super-Mare] were well attended, [and] in happier circumstances would have been a great success ... White bowled with deadly effect ... A.E. Newton showed remarkable form behind the wickets for a man approaching the age of fifty-two', while even for last-place Gloucestershire, whose mounting debts raised fears that the club would have to be wound up, there were high marks for 'the bowling of Dennett and the batting of Sewell. Jessop at his best could hardly have scored at a greater pace ... As regards the other batsmen, C.S. Barnett showed marked skill on more than one occasion, and Langdon was much the same as in 1913.'

Not quite every team, however, was granted this same modicum of praise. For some, it was not a question of their being either good or bad, just rather boring. Tucked away towards the end of *Wisden's* round-up of the 1914 Championship is this melancholy little note: 'There is no getting away from the fact that Notts had an uninteresting season. The batting was strong enough to meet all reasonable requirements, and the long-sought fast bowler was found in F. Barratt, but the team lacked the match-winning faculty.' Although by no means the worst or least warranted of

Wisden's capsule reviews, it may be among the most depressing. 'Taking the season as a whole,' the unknown critic adds, 'the results, having regard to the Notts team, should certainly have been better.'

Nottinghamshire did, however, feature in more than one entertaining match that season, even if it was as the losing side. In mid-June they narrowly went down to Middlesex at Trent Bridge, when the visitors managed to score the winning runs, in poor light, with half an hour left to play. There were also two hard-fought meetings with Surrey, in one of which Hobbs hit his 226, and an enjoyably fluid game with Kent later in July. 'There was a remarkable finish to this match,' *Wisden* noted:

> Notts, after holding the upper hand for two days, had to admit defeat by 47 runs. When on Tuesday afternoon rain stopped play, Kent looked set to be beaten in a single innings. On [Wednesday] evening, Notts had only 101 to make to win, but this was obviously a somewhat formidable task against Blythe and Woolley on a drying pitch. They were soon eight wickets down for 39.

For both entertainment and morbid interest, meanwhile, there was the county's fixture against Hampshire at Southampton in early June. Charles Fry, in the second match of his comeback, scored 27, including his 30,000th first-class run, in the Hampshire first innings of 246. The bowling laurels went to 20-year-old Fred Barratt, who took 7-109 with his right-arm seam. Barratt had made a sensational debut in professional cricket only a month earlier when, appearing for Notts against MCC at Lord's, he took 8-91 in the first innings. He followed that with 5-58 in his first County Championship match. From a mining background, and robustly fit – his party trick was to tear a pack of playing cards in half with his banana-size fingers – he was also a good enough footballer to turn out for Aston Villa and Sheffield Wednesday. Although Barratt survived the war, it was said by the county yearbook that 'he was slow in finding his old form with the ball' in the 1920s. However, he improved steadily as a batsman. In 1928, his benefit year, Barratt made 1,167 runs at an average of 30. This included an unbeaten innings of 139 against Warwickshire which contained seven sixes and eighteen fours, and another of 110 against Glamorgan, which the annual said involved 'some mighty hitting', including five sixes. His story was not only one of success but, in Neville Cardus's eyes, a romantic one: 'called forth to serve, this unassuming man of the soil fought with gallantry for his country, adorned the summer game, and then all too quickly was gone'. Barratt eventually played five Tests for England and took 1,224 first-class wickets in a fourteen-year career interrupted by the war. He died in January 1947, aged 52.

In their reply at Southampton, Nottinghamshire managed just 143, with their captain and number nine Arthur Jones making a polished 33: 'even the Hampshire men were drawn to smile in admiration at one straight blow for four', *The Times* wrote. In only his twenty-sixth match, Arthur Jaques took his 100th first-class wicket. There was a moment of comedy in the Hampshire second innings when the two Charles, Fry and Mead, found themselves standing at the same end while the Notts mid-on, Willis Walker, somehow missed both the stumps and all ten of his colleagues with his throw. 'The smiles on the batsmen's faces were wide', it was reported. Mead's subsequent 69 in an hour was a swashbuckler's innings containing a six and nine fours. Compounding a rather wretched performance, Walker, normally an accomplished middle-order bat, scored a pair. He later good-naturedly said that that particular match 'took a year off my life'. Set an improbable 352 to win, Notts finished at 244-5. Their opener George Gunn made 96, a 'masterly innings, batting with great restraint so long as his side stood in danger, and afterwards hitting brilliantly'. Willis Walker lived to be 99.

Arthur Jones, the Nottinghamshire captain, was born in 1872 and educated at Bedford Modern school and Cambridge. Regarded as a brilliant, sometimes impetuous right-handed batsman, occasional leg-spin bowler and fearless close-field, he was named a *Wisden* cricketer of the year in 1900. Burly with a luxuriant black moustache, he captained Notts for the next fourteen seasons. In 1907/08, Jones led England on tour of Australia, but played in only two matches because of illness. In all he won twelve Test caps and scored some 23,000 first-class runs. Off the cricket field he was described by George Gunn as 'a man of intense personal charm and complete selflessness, who did everything for young people', never happier than when refereeing a boys' rugby match.

When reviewing Nottinghamshire's generally dismal performance in the 1914 season, *Wisden* allowed:

No doubt the unhappy loss of A.O. Jones as captain brought about to a large extent the sort of lassitude that came over the side. Nothing could replace the captain's contagious energy and enthusiasm. Jones started playing at the beginning of the year, but it was plain to all his friends that he would not be able to go on for long. Sadly wasted and looking wretchedly ill, he was a mere shadow of his old self.

Nottinghamshire's match against Hampshire would prove to be Jones's last appearance in any form of cricket. Civilian life did not have much appeal and three months later he applied forlornly for an army commission, 'as I can still at least make myself heard over great distances'. It was not to be. Suffering from tuberculosis, Arthur Jones died at his brother's home in Bedford on 21 December 1914, aged 42.

Wisden took a dim view of Nottinghamshire's next match immediately following Jones's retirement, against Lancashire at Trent Bridge. 'Not only did Notts take two hours before lunch on Thursday to make 45 runs,' it chided, 'but on Saturday, when standing 99 ahead with nine wickets in hand, they occupied three hours and fifty minutes in adding 175 runs. This absurdly unenterprising play necessarily led to the match being drawn.' The reader may wish to compare these scoring rates to today's County Championship matches. In the Notts second innings, the opener Joe Hardstaff scored 106 not out in four hours. When Lancashire went in again on the final afternoon they needed 275 to win in two and a quarter hours, which would have been close to double the run-rate in the match up until then. In the event, they were to fall some way short, at 141-3. Harold Garnett, Lancashire's wicketkeeping opener, scored 100 in two hours, although not without blemish: 'he gave two chances in the slips, and the cricket towards the close was not very serious', said *Wisden*. Garnett may be one of the few men to have played representative sport for both Lancashire and Argentina, where he amassed a fortune in mining and commodity trading in the early part of the century. He sacrificed his business career to become a soldier in August 1914. Commissioned as a captain in the South Wales Borderers, Garnett fell in action near Cambrai on 3 December 1917; he was 38.

Like Reginald Foster's, the death of the Lancashire and England all-rounder Allan Gibson Steel that month was another sign that English cricket's old guard was changing. Born in 1858, Steel, also like Foster one of seven cricketing brothers, was a schoolboy prodigy at Marlborough who went on to dazzle at Cambridge. As a freshman in 1878, he topped the bowling averages for the whole of England. Steel played in the first-ever Test on home soil, in 1880, and even at that level was said to be an 'effortlessly businesslike and productive scorer with all the shots in his locker, and never left a ball alone unless it cleared his head'. All of his thirteen Tests were played against Australia. Steel's name is commemorated in the poem inscribed on the side of the urn with the original Ashes that was presented to the England team at Melbourne in January 1883; on that tour he topped both the batting and the bowling averages. In terms of technique, if not of personal flamboyance, the aptly named Steel was reckoned by many in his day to be the equal of W.G. Grace. From different social strata, the two men were not close. In 1895, Steel, a successful barrister of private means, remarked of Grace's fundraising activities that with 'the flood of shillings pouring in, one can not but feel a little alarm for the dignity of our great game'. Many modern cricket historians have doubts about the records of the late nineteenth century, an era when there were no regulations governing the minimum time for a first-class match, and contemporary opinion often trumped hard facts. Steel's career Test and first-class totals of 600 and 7,000 runs respectively have struck at least some of the game's less romantically minded statisticians as suspiciously rounded. As with Grace, there have been various attempts over the years to change, quite significantly, the accepted figures. But even allowing for any quirks of late-Victorian scorekeeping, it is agreed that Steel retired, after fifteen years, to almost universal acclaim, even then a rare thing for an England Test captain. He went on to be President of MCC, and played a key role in the perennial debate about changing the LBW law, cricket's own Schleswig-Holstein Question. He died on 15 June 1914, aged 55.

Steel's eldest son Allan Ivo, also an all-rounder, played five first-class matches for Middlesex and MCC. Declining the offer of a place at Cambridge, he set off in May 1914 on a mining expedition to Kashmir. Legend insists that while there he unearthed a diamond worth many millions of pounds, and could have retired to a life of colossal luxury. Instead, he sailed home immediately war was declared, and received a commission in the Coldstream Guards. Allan Ivo Steel fell in action near Langemark in Belgium on 8 October 1917, aged 25. A younger brother, Jack, a lieutenant in the Royal Navy, was swept away while serving on HMS *Munster* the following April. Yet another brother of great promise died in the trenches. The boys' mother Georgina Steel lost her husband, all three sons, and nine other immediate family members in the four years from June 1914.

Two days after the Egyptian cricket team took its leave of England, a party from Haverford College, near Philadelphia, arrived to play a series of ten club and school matches. Although unusual, it was by no means the most exotic tour that year, which also saw visiting sides from Scotland, Ireland and China, and the Americans acquitted themselves well, with a close victory over Eton in mid-July. A final record of five losses to three wins, with two draws, was not a massive defeat considering the known difference in strength between the tourists and most of their opponents.

Haverford's first fixture, even so, a single-innings game against Shrewsbury, ended poorly when they were shot out for 68. The home bowling honours went to Tom Onslow, who took 4-42 with a mixture of leg-breaks and googlies, 'which the Americans treated with awe', *Cricket* reported. Being strikingly good-looking, with a lock of unruly dark hair falling over his forehead, one contemporary diary spoke of Onslow's 'dark eyes, beautiful voice [and] natural gift for generosity and warmth'. *Wisden* confidently said of him that 'he will be in the 1915 side'. Instead, he joined the army at the age of 17, won a commission with the King's Shropshire Light Infantry, and, as 2nd Lieutenant Onslow, fell in action near Calais in January 1917 at the age of 19. Onslow's schoolfriend Basil Ellis, who opened the Shrewsbury batting against Haverford, fought alongside him in the same battalion. The *Globe* described Ellis as a 'steady and sound' batsman who 'never claimed to be a stylist, but was supremely effective'. It was said that as a teenager he was 'comfortable and charming, [and] few of his contemporaries' sisters were immune to his fresh good looks'. As Lieutenant Ellis, he fell in action in Belgium on 16 June 1915, aged 18.

Reviewing the performance of the Haverford side as a whole on tour, *Wisden* wrote: 'W.C. Brinton bowled at times with great effect.' A locksmith by trade, who had occasional professional dealings with Houdini, Brinton volunteered for overseas service with the Religious Society of Friends immediately following the United States' entry into the war in April 1917. It was said that as a schoolboy 'he already had the gift of complete selflessness and empathy for others'. Walter Brinton died of influenza in December of the following year, while engaged in reconstruction work in northern France. He was 24.

III

Along with shell-manufacturing shortages and other technical deficiencies, the British would long struggle with recruitment and organisational problems with all branches of their armed services. Well into the war there were debates over whether an all-volunteer force would suffice, or if some form of draft were needed. Although the eventual decision was cobbled together as a legislative compromise and exempted not only 'multifarious trades and occupations' but the whole of Ireland, it produced a tenfold expansion in the size of the British army, with seventy divisions under arms. These remedial measures came about only after quite significant voluntary efforts had been made. On the outbreak of war, the British regular army consisted of 247,432 troops and some 420,000 reserves. In the period 5–31 August, 310,000 young Britons signed up to fight, and another 450,000, or 500 battalions' worth, had volunteered by the end of September. Recruitment held steady at around 70,000 a month during the remainder of 1914 and 1915. Fully a third of those who came forward, often in groups of friends, clubs or teams, were aged 19 or younger.

Among English schoolboys who played cricket in the summer of 1914 and subsequently fell in action were: Geoffrey Butler and Ken Davies of Haileybury, who died in the same week of May 1917; Charles Wooler and Frank Roseveare of Sedbergh; Archibald Lindsay and Stephen Walter of Wellington; Herbert Wait and Jack Dewar of Oakham; Alfred Fawdry of King Edward's, Birmingham; Ron Chester of Merchant Taylors; Frank Dalziel of Leys; Alfred Schiff of Dulwich; Donald James of

Clifton; Dean West of Oundle; John Brice-Smith of Cranleigh; Osborne Tancock of Bedford Grammar; Arthur Carey of Malvern; and Cecil Thompson of the Forest School and Essex: all cut down before their 21st birthdays. George Whitehead, opening bat and captain of the Clifton side in 1914, died in action with the Royal Flying Corps. Epsom lost Thomas Lucas and their hard-hitting batsman Archie Paxton, the latter mown down in the first few minutes of fighting at the Somme. The Dulwich all-rounder Laurence Chidson was reckoned by *Cricket* 'the brightest prospect by far' in a team led by the future England Test player Arthur Gilligan. As Captain Chidson, MC, of the King's Royal Rifles, he fell in action in April 1917. George Marsden-Smedley captained Harrow in their closely fought game with Eton at Lord's in July 1914. 'He keeps a straight bat', *Wisden* remarked. On 18 August 1916, as 2nd Lieutenant Marsden of the Royal Rifles, he fell in fighting around the Somme, aged 21. His body was never found. Twenty-year-old John Howell of the King's Royal Corps was killed in Flanders, on his first day of action, in September 1915. Barely a year earlier, he had scored two double centuries and a century for Repton. 'Among all the young cricketers who have fallen in the War, not one of brighter promise can be named', *Wisden* said. There was a particularly hard toll at Radley, which lost Geoffrey Adams, Ernest Wood, George Coote and Thomas Irwin from their regular XI of 1914; a fifth man, Richard Bucknall, survived only to fall in the Battle of Singapore in February 1942. Christ's Hospital were reckoned to have had the best young opening bowling pair in England in Paul Stevenson and Arthur Creese: Stevenson fell in action in 1915, and Creese three years later. Their teammate Edmund Blunden served at the front and later wrote about the experience in his collection *The Waggoner*, among other poems. A lesser literary talent, but a greater sacrifice, was Private Ernest Allen, Scots Guards, who left his job as a trainee on the Cricket Reporting Agency to go to war. *Wisden* reports that 'he was shot through the head during the night action at Cuinchy' on 1 January 1915. He was 19.

The above list is far from exhaustive. Nearly a century later, we are still learning the names of cricketers of all types who gave their lives in the First World War. The 2012 edition of *Wisden* has the story by Andrew Renshaw of Niel Fagan, a Rugby schoolboy who joined the Rifle Brigade, went to France in July 1915, and fell a year later at the Somme. After lying badly wounded in no-man's-land for a day and a night, Fagan was able to crawl back to his lines. He died in hospital some two weeks later, aged 20.

Another cricketer who volunteered was John Henry Parsons, who played for Warwickshire from 1910 to 1914 as a professional. Born in 1890, he was a useful member of the side which dramatically won the Championship in 1911, finishing with 568 first-class runs at an average of 23. After a setback in the wet summer of

1912, he got 1,258 runs at 32 in 1913 and in 1914 was picked for the Players at the Oval. But his shining hour that season came in Warwickshire's bruising defeat of Worcestershire at Dudley. The visitors were required to bat only once: they scored 645-7 declared, of which Frank Foster contributed an unbeaten 305, including a five and forty-four fours, and Parsons 102, with a relatively modest dozen boundaries. According to *Wisden*, 'the match was then brought to a startling conclusion, Field going on to bowl when Worcestershire had scored 85 for the loss of four batsmen, and taking the six outstanding wickets at a cost of only two runs. Warwickshire won by an innings and 321 runs.'

Commissioned into the army, John Parsons fought both on the Western Front and in the Middle East, was often wounded, twice Mentioned in Dispatches, and won the MC. Lean and moustachioed, he looked the part of the dashing cavalry officer he was, being one of the few survivors of the British mounted attack against German and Turkish machine-guns at Huj, near Gaza, in November 1917, an action that bears some comparison with the Charge of the Light Brigade. As Captain J.H. Parsons he eventually resumed his professional career, and in 1926/27 toured with the MCC side in India, not then a Test country, where he had an average of 50. On the first morning at the Somme, Parsons had walked towards the German trenches, apparently inviting himself to be shot, methodically firing a revolver in each hand. Perhaps unsurprisingly, little about his subsequent experiences on the cricket field seemed to disturb him.

In 1928, Parsons was ordained into the Church of England. From then until his retirement in 1936, he played on as an amateur for Warwickshire. In 1930 Parsons was selected to represent the Gentlemen at Lord's, thus achieving the unusual feat of having appeared for both sides in the fixture. The *Cricketer* called him 'a superb driver of fast bowling, which he believed in attacking', who but for the war might well have played for England. In his final county match, Warwickshire, under his captaincy, beat Yorkshire by 1 wicket at Scarborough. Parsons, who was then in his mid-forties, hit 94 out of 121, with four sixes and twelve fours, in the last evening's run-chase. Yorkshire did not make it easy for him. Anyone wishing to know what the term 'muscular Christianity' means in practice could do worse than study his life. One of his fellow officers remembered the horrific moment when, in the blood and smoke of Huj, 'Jack Parsons had the sword dashed from his hand, which was badly cut in the process. From the corner of my eye I saw him calmly retrieve his weapon, re-mount, and charge once more. He never gave up.'

III

In Kent, 35-year-old Colin Blythe had made the most of the wet early season, with more than 30 wickets by the end of May. One of the local newsagency reporters who followed the side was a young south Londoner named Hugh Sidey. Not long out of school, and a would-be county cricketer, he later said of himself that he had been 'bumptious' and 'quite often, a pain in the neck' at the time he took up his duties. 'I wanted to make a name for myself', he noted. Early in June, Sidey filed a story which, in so many words, suggested that Blythe, while still a fine bowler, was now drawing to the end of his long career.

> Charlie was not pleased. He became angry about my coverage, and then defiant. When I asked him in the players' dressing-room if he was thinking about retirement, his jaw tightened and he said, 'You can write what you want, son. Come September, I'll still have my 150 wickets.' Then he looked straight at me and said firmly, 'I'm *not* going to quit'.

Blythe's stubbornness and determination emerged in such moments, providing a glimpse of the steel beneath the placid exterior. When he got into his stride, he was a loud and sometimes volatile talker, and not one burdened by undue doubt. Usually, however, the ambition was concealed by Blythe's amiable disposition. John Major has written of him in his book *More Than a Game* as a 'sensitive, delicate man, blessed with the gift of truly great left-arm spin', a verdict echoed by that of *Sporting Life* ninety years before: 'he remained simple and unassuming, [with] a tendency to play down his abilities on the few occasions he was persuaded to talk of them. His wonderful career never spoiled the man.'

Most of Blythe's Kent teammates did not know him well, but they considered him a cheerful sort and easy enough to be around. According to Sidey, there was some occasional good-natured chafing about his violin and his tendency to practise it in the dressing room, which he took without offence. But it would be wrong to portray Blythe as invariably laid-back or indifferent to his own interests. Like almost every professional cricketer of the time, he harboured certain reservations about the terms and conditions of his playing contract. These amounted to him being 'a slave to [Kent's treasurer] Mr Furley and his fellow gods', he once remarked, with some asperity. The county committee had already irked Blythe over the winter of 1912–13, when he had repeatedly asked them to release £500 of the roughly £1,500 held back from the proceeds of his benefit year, which he needed for 'repairs, taxation and mortgage' on the family's modest detached home in Goldsmid Road, Tonbridge. The funds were extracted only after 'heated' correspondence, he complained – and even then 'Furley explained that some of the investments of my money "had not done as well as expected"'. Blythe was to remark on his lack of faith in the Committee's business judgement at regular intervals during the rest of his life. His wife Gertrude said, 'we had to resort to extreme measures just to get by', which apparently included her taking on washing work at home (Blythe, even so, as we have seen, had scraped together the funds for a recent winter break in the French Alps). There were several other such domestic indignities. A recurrent problem with the gas board in the early weeks of 1914 made the Blythes fair game for nasty letters threatening to have their debt turned over to a collection agency. It was a depressingly familiar state of affairs for a county cricketer, if one that was especially poignant in this case. While Blythe was continuing to revolutionise the whole art of slow bowling, and be feted by *The Times* as 'the great man of our national sport' he and his wife were worrying about their utility bills. Although only 26, it was remembered that Gertrude was 'no longer quite so doll-like or care-free, [and] instead become stooped and grey' after seven years of marriage. Hugh Sidey remarked on the austerity of Blythe's daily life in 1914. 'Charlie was a cheap man to feed. You could keep him happy quite a long time, just supplying him with apples.' Although he was endlessly keen and willing on the cricket field, Blythe also suffered badly from nerves on the big occasion, which may help to explain why he played only nineteen Tests.

On the Monday morning of 15 June 1914, Blythe walked the short distance from his home, through the timbered centre of Tonbridge, to the town's Angel Ground,* where he had first come to notice as a young cricketer at the end of the nineteenth century. It was raining. The small pavilion was flag-strewn and the public stands were newly painted. Despite the weather, a crowd of some 4,000 was on hand to see the first day's play between Kent and Hampshire. It was the opening match of Tonbridge Week, and it was reported that the 'fresh atmosphere of the town had raised a velvety turf on a ground surrounded by trees and rivers on every side'. The *Globe* also complimented the pitch, but complained about the amount of smoking that went on, in the presence of ladies, in the grandstand. By 11 a.m. the rain that was lingering after breakfast had blown away, and Kent's Arthur Fielder bowled the first over under a sky that was patchily blue. The visitors were soon in trouble, at 54-5. 'But they retrieved a wretched start,' said *Wisden*, 'when Mead and Sprot came together and added 149. Lucky with some of his strokes, Sprot neverthe-less drove and pulled in great form.' In turn, Kent were 64-6, and all out for 152.

---

* A much-loved cricket and football venue, and a nursery to the likes of Blythe, James Seymour and Frank Woolley, the ground was eventually closed and, following a lengthy High Court battle, sold for redevelopment in 1980. Today, the site is occupied by the Angel Shopping Centre, several supermarkets and discount shops, and their car parks.

Runs in general were hard to come by; when his time came, Blythe, three short-legs brazenly close, played much of the bowling with his pads, but still finished with a creditable 25. He wore mud-stained flannels, a broad black belt and a sardonic smile. Kent easily failed to score 302 to win. For once, Blythe was only modestly successful with the ball, taking 1-33 and 3-30 – but was a 'capable and popular star guest in the marquee at the close of play', the *Globe* reported. Hampshire, though without the services of Charles Fry and Lionel Tennyson, won by 133 runs.

Kent persevered with the same eleven men for the match that began the following morning against Yorkshire, but to a very different outcome. The visitors made a good start: 114-2 at lunch on the first day, they were then all out for 227 by tea. Blythe took 4-42, including his 50th wicket of the season. Despite the collapse, the Yorkshiremen would still have been moderately pleased with their total on a pitch of increasingly variable bounce and movement, which the early Kent batsmen found equally hard to master. But, after a slow start, an innings of calculated savagery by Woolley, who hit 96, changed the balance of power of the game and laid the foundation for a significant home score, 493. *Wisden* was not impressed by the Yorkshire reply: 'the visitors, batting deplorably, were all out in two hours'. Kent won by an innings and 149 runs.

As Tonbridge Week continued, 50 miles to the north the final preparations were under way for the first-ever county match to be played at the Castle Park ground in Colchester. Although it suffered from various drainage problems over the years, the pitch 'looked capital' on the sunny morning of 18 June, when Essex hosted Worcestershire. 'Watched by about 2,000 people each day,' *Wisden* said, 'the match proved a success.' Because of the choice of venue, there was more than usual interest in a game being played by two middle-ranking Championship sides, both at the national and local levels. Bright red-lettered playbills announcing the fixture adorned the windows of almost every nearby shop, with a large county flag flying from the tower of Colchester Castle serving as a backdrop for the cricket.

Batting first, Essex recovered from an unfortunate start to make 440, with Captain Walter Turner, Royal Artillery, hitting 84 in an hour. Worcestershire scored fast, but not enough, and Essex, preferring to bat again though 224 ahead, were able to set the visitors a target of 408, which they comfortably failed to reach. The home team's slow-bowling amateur Geoffrey Davies, just down from Cambridge, took 6-51 on the third afternoon, which included the 100th wicket of his short career. After going in at number ten and scoring a brisk 24, this represented 'especially good all-round work on his part', *The Times* noted.

Born at Poplar in October 1892, Davies was a versatile young athlete who won schoolboy prizes for swimming, racquets and tennis. Tall and lean, with wavy fair hair, it is remembered that he 'walked with a graceful, loose-jointed stride', and possessed 'formidable quantities of energy'. While waiting for his opponent to serve on the tennis court, Davies 'rapidly twisted the racket, bounced from foot to foot, and swayed his body, always ready to spring to either side. Walking back to his College or off to the bathing pool, he often swung the racket at an imaginary ball'. 'Among the Cambridge bowlers [of 1914] he stood alone,' *Wisden* added, 'combining a high delivery with good length and plenty of headwork, he deserved all his success.' Davies took 45 wickets for the University that summer term, including 5 in the match against Oxford at Lord's. Following this success, Cambridge named him their secretary for 1915, which was to have been his last year as a student before going on to a career in finance.

In his final cricket match, Geoffrey Davies made 118 and took 4-18 as Essex beat Somerset at Weston-super-Mare on the evening of 1 September 1914. By then the Allies were already in full retreat at Mons, and Paris, deserted by the government and about a million of its people, was threatened by five German armies. Davies immediately volunteered, and was commissioned in the Essex Regiment. After a couple of months' training, his battalion was sent to the front, just missing the carnage at Ypres, but in time for the Battle of Neuve Chapelle in March 1915. For the majority the actual experience of the horrors of war destroyed their initial enthusiasm, but not in Davies's case. According to a fellow officer named Eric Seal, 'he remained as calm and affable as in civilian life … never complaining of the hardships and dangers', and soon rising to the rank of captain. There are few details known about Davies's military duties that summer (when he should have been in his last term at Cambridge), except that he served in a newly reinforced unit stationed in the trenches between Arras and the Somme. His last recorded act was to remove his gas mask and place it over the face of a British soldier who was lying wounded and without equipment, when a poison attack was thought imminent in the line south of Dunkirk. For this and other actions, he was posthumously Mentioned in Dispatches. Geoffrey Davies was killed at Hulloch, near Calais, on 26 September 1915, at the age of 22. *Wisden* considered that 'there can be little doubt that, but for the war, he would have developed into an England player'.

III

Just a mile or two south of the Castle Park ground, Colchester, the army's Meeanee Barracks was now the centrepiece of a sprawling complex of drab brick buildings and wooden huts recently enlarged to house the 30,000 men of the Eastern District forces. Among them was Lionel Tennyson. It says something about the youth policy of the army's command at the time that Tennyson's immediate superior, Captain Prittie, wrote of him in April 1914:

He is a very useful company officer, knows his work well and is energetic and handles his men excellently ... But I am afraid that he is hopelessly handicapped by his age as regards eventually getting command of a battalion. There are several younger officers senior to him and he has no chance of getting in front of them.

Tennyson was then 24 years old. Solidly built, with dark, slicked-back hair, he was an occasional poet, a marksman, a pipe-smoker, a drinker and a lover of fast horses and faster women. He spoke in a high, ringing voice, which was sometimes prone to a mild attack of rhotacism, as in: 'that *wuddy* man'. He was very proud of his ancestry, which he could trace back for many generations (and frequently did), and claimed to remember vividly attending the funeral of his famous grandfather in Westminster Abbey, 'walking up the aisle in a little white frock', at which time he was not yet 3 years old.

Tennyson's daily regimen in June 1914, though hardly relaxed, was 'very far from disagreeable', he later remarked. Things 'tended to start poorly', with a 6 a.m. reveille and a full morning's list of activities, which included map-making, small-arms, military history, and, inevitably, 'endless square-bashing and PT'. Lunch, however, was 'often an enjoyably protracted affair', after which there might be a lecture, and several hours devoted to sport. Tennyson also remembered, perhaps with a touch of hyperbole, that he was 'stood drinks continually by one's brother officer from 12 noon until eleven pm'. Dinner was taken in the mess, a 'splendidly formal' meal of several courses, served by the white-coated stewards who were 'always at one's elbow', often a traditional roast, though in summer 'a cold bill might prevail – lobster, fresh salmon, game, birds, hams and salads'. Afterwards came 'several rounds' of vintage port, drunk out of regimental silver goblets. 'It was all a great deal more lavish than High Table at Cambridge, but otherwise quite like it.'

While Lionel Tennyson was soldiering, his friend Robert Jesson was, like his father before him, practising law in Southampton. At 27, his county cricket days were already behind him. Although no scorecards have come to light, Jesson appears to have occasionally turned out that summer for the Inns of Court team, at least once on the ground opposite his London rooms in Vincent Square. Tennyson himself thought the young all-rounder had been 'a very real prospect for Hampshire ... [I could not] help feeling an error was made when he slipped out of the side'. It is likely that a number of the county's supporters would have echoed the sentiment. Jesson, in conference with two other young lawyers in the week of 29 June, like many people 'struggled to comprehend' the events of the previous Sunday in Sarajevo, and the subsequent remarks of the German government that,

in the stark words of her foreign minister, now saw the opportunity of a 'final settling of accounts' with Serbia. It's remembered that Jesson also spoke quietly of his
fear of a general conflict whose 'destructive capacity will quite shock the world',
a feat of prediction beyond most British statesmen of the time. On the following Thursday, 2 July, Yorkshire began a three-day match with Hampshire at Hull.
The home and visitors' bowling was opened by Major Booth and Arthur Jaques
respectively, Alonzo Drake took 8-62 in the match, and the arctic conditions on the
first day saw the frequent appearance on the field of the Hampshire twelfth man,
a 21-year-old all-rounder from Frimley named Herbert Rogers – who went on
to join the Seaforth Highlanders – bearing extra sweaters and hot drinks, some of
them fortified by rum. The visitors collapsed to 79-7 in their second innings, but
escaped with a draw. Of the six cricketers listed above, only Lionel Tennyson would
be alive five years later.

In that same week in June, Middlesex and Surrey, standing neck to neck in the
Championship, played each other at the Oval. For once Hobbs failed, caught for 4
in the opening overs, and then sat watching for the rest of the day while Hayward,
Hayes, Ducat, Wilkinson and Fender pounded 544 off a strong Middlesex attack.
Despite following on, the visitors held out for a draw, thanks largely to an unbeaten
innings of 191 by 'Young Jack' Hearne. At Edgbaston, meanwhile, Percy Jeeves took
5-75 for Warwickshire against Lancashire, but the visitors escaped defeat when,
with nine men out and 192 runs behind, a thunderstorm burst over the ground
on the third afternoon and play was abandoned. To the north, the sun shone at
Chesterfield long enough for Derbyshire to dispose of Somerset in just two days.
Wisden's account was harsh. 'After making 233 in their second innings, Derby put
Somerset in with 255 to get, but the latter failed so utterly dismally that another
seventy-five minutes saw the end.' Batting number eight for the home team,
20-year-old Geoffrey Jackson scored 7 and 9 in his first and only appearance in
the Championship that season. The son of the managing director of a Cheshire
colliery, Jackson went to Harrow and Balliol College, Oxford, where he was twelfth
man for the university XI. In seven first-class matches he would score 150 runs
at an average of 12.50, and take 10 wickets with his occasional seam bowling. He
is remembered for his 'loud laughter, energy, intelligence and undying optimism,
whatever the circumstances', which made him talked-about in the dressing room,
as did his habit of reading aloud from a series of schoolboy adventure stories such
as P.C. Wren's *The Snake and the Sword* or Conan Doyle's *The Valley of Fear*, which
he carried around in his cricket bag. On the outbreak of war Jackson volunteered
and received a commission in the Rifle Brigade. He went to France in October
1914 and was invalided home in May of the following year, after the Second Battle

of Ypres, suffering from gas poisoning. There were 60,000 British and 36,000 German casualties in the action. At his own request, Jackson returned to the front in December 1915, and served there continuously for the next sixteen months. He was Mentioned in Dispatches on New Year's Day 1916. On 9 April 1917, the 23-year-old Jackson was wounded by shell fire after advancing with his unit some 5,000 yards into the enemy positions at Arras, Belgium, and died before he could be carried to the dressing station.

III

One of the several enjoyably eccentric highlights of the 1914 season was a one-day match between MCC and the Royal Academy of Arts at Lord's. The following year's *Wisden* tucks the game away in three short lines, which contain only the team scores and none of the individual players' names. More than likely, the report would have been slid over by nine readers out of ten, without engaging more than a moment's attention; but in its own way the match was a classic among pre-war English sporting curiosities, to be lost to the fixture list after 1918, as well as a last salute to some brave cricketers.

MCC batted first, and scored 376-6 declared off 71 overs. Again for purposes of comparison, these took just over three hours. In the tactful words of the *Morning Post*, 'the artists' bowling was put under strain by a *tour de force* innings from C.H. Chaldecott, who hit up 132 in swift time'. Little more is known of Chaldecott, who returned from the war to play once more for MCC, against Hampstead at Lord's in July 1922, and then to fade from the record books. One of his batting partners against the Artists was the tall, saturnine figure of Gordon Guggisberg, who scored an unbeaten 32. Although largely forgotten today, he was something of a national icon in the inter-war years. Born in Ontario in 1869, Guggisberg had come to England as a 10-year-old, set several records for athletics at schoolboy level, and finished his education at the Royal Military Academy, Woolwich, before being commissioned into the Royal Engineers. He was to rejoin the army in August 1914, at the age of 45, after which he was a front-line commander at the Somme, twice wounded, Mentioned in Dispatches five times, and awarded the DSO. Guggisberg's first-class cricket career was on the whole modest: he played a single three-day match for MCC against Derbyshire at Lord's in 1905, scoring no runs and taking no wickets. However, after the war he went on to serve as successively Governor of the Gold Coast and of British Guiana, to found the renowned Achimota boarding school in modern Ghana, and to write widely on everything from the future of tropical Africa to a pamphlet called 'Chapters on

Batting & Bowling Etiquette when in the Colonies'. Tall and thin, with a sallow, moustachioed face somewhat reminiscent of Boris Karloff's, Guggisberg retired full of honours to Bexhill-on-Sea, and died there in 1930. Joining him in the MCC side against the Royal Academy was 30-year-old William Bates, who also appeared for his native Yorkshire between 1907 and 1914, as well as playing football for Bolton and Leeds United, before qualifying for Glamorgan after the war. His son Ted, also a footballer, became the manager of Southampton.

There was a large crowd on hand at Lord's, particularly vocal around the Tavern, to see the Artists' turn at bat shortly after 3 p.m. It was reported that there was some 'spirited repartee' in that part of the ground, with an 'alert air even about the more demure members in the pavilion, as of those who expect amusement in the near future'.

They were not disappointed. The Academy's opening batsman, George Swinstead, a popular painter of landscapes and coastal scenes, lasted just 1 ball. His partner Henry Justice Ford, an illustrator of children's stories, with a lucrative sideline in 'found art' composed largely of seaweed, shells and funguses, managed to score a run-a-minute 18, including a huge pull for six far back into the grandstand. But then just as suddenly the visitors were 25-4, en route to a total of 135. The sculptor Charles Jackson was bowled for 3, and his colleague Maurice Gray, a friend of Gropius and a pioneer of modernist typography, departed first ball. After that there were to be some flailed cameo performances in the late middle-order, which at least gave what the *Post* called 'the Chelsea contingent among the house' something to cheer. The number eight batsman Francis FitzJohn Crisp, winner of an Academy gold medal, hit a brisk 42 not out, and the designer Hugh Benson, the last man, chipped in with 16. Despite the spirited rearguard action, MCC won by 241 runs. 'The game came to a sudden termination', said one report, 'owing to Sir Frederick Gordon Guggisberg removing all three of H.C. Benson's stumps', following which 'a tremendous roar went up in the Tavern, succeeded by the sound and sight of several parties there collapsing prone over the boundary fence'.

On the outbreak of war, Francis Crisp volunteered for the Artists' Battalion, and was later gazetted as a 2nd lieutenant in the Grenadier Guards. He was killed in fighting around Soissons on 5 January 1915, aged 33. The *New York Times* said of Crisp that he was 'an artist of rare promise, whose exhibition of oil paintings and water colors attracted wide attention here two years ago'. Maurice Gray also enlisted, and was commissioned on 25 August 1914. As Captain Gray of the 2nd Dragoon Guards he was to fall in action at Beaucourt-en-Santerre, near the Somme, on 8 August 1918, at the age of 28. Hugh Benson, a private infantry soldier, was killed at Ypres on 22 June 1915, aged 30.

Exactly a year before the death of Private Benson, on a cool and misty but dry midsummer morning at Lord's, the MCC side which had toured South Africa under Johnny Douglas began their gala three-day match with the Rest of England. *The Times* rather precisely said that the game was 'nicely patronised, [with] 10,458 customers present' on the first morning. An atmosphere that combined sport with a society set-piece prevailed. 'There were many extravagant hats and vividly blazered figures … On Tuesday His Majesty honoured the ground with his presence, being accompanied by the Prince of Wales and Prince Albert' (this presented the bonus of three successive kings of England). 'The captains of the two elevens, Mr Douglas and Mr Fry, were presented to him in full view of the crowd.' Unfortunately, the cricket never quite lived up to the undoubted glamour of the social arrangements, with the Rest recording a 'truly colossal' win by an innings and 189 runs, delayed until the third day only because heavy rain fell immediately after the royal visit.

In honour of the centenary of their tenure at Lord's, MCC held a banquet on the second evening of the match at the Cecil Hotel, on the Thames Embankment near the Savoy. The venue, which sported a Moorish façade, carved marble columns, velvet pile carpeting and an Indian-style smoking room, was the last word in opulence. In retrospect, the sumptuous meal that ensued shares some of the same morbid allure of the last sitting at the captain's table on the *Titanic* before she struck the iceberg; in both cases, the paradisical world the events symbolised soon lay in ruins (as literally true of the Cecil as of the *Titanic* – in 1930, the hotel was unceremoniously flattened to make way for Shell Mex House). *Wisden* reported of the dinner, 'it [was] the most memorable affair of the season … nothing could have represented more forcibly the greatness of cricket. On every hand were men whose names are familiar wherever the English language is spoken.'

In the chair – his features composed behind the famous moustache in an expression 'alert even to the point of severity' – sat Lord Hawke, the President of MCC. On his right was Prince Albert of Schleswig-Holstein, the grandson of Queen Victoria, who proposed the loyal toast to his cousin the present king, 'among other very gracious tributes to His Majesty and His subjects'. The British-educated Prince Albert was then aged 45, and considerably above average as a cricketer; it was said that he 'could astonish even professional players' with his high-tossed leg-breaks. Six weeks later, the prince was to return hurriedly to Germany and take up a commission in the Prussian army, quickly reaching the rank of lieutenant colonel in the 3rd Uhlans of the Guard. Punctilious to the last, on the day of his departure the *Morning Post* reported that 'Albert of Schleswig-Holstein has communicated with the secretary of the Marylebone Cricket Club, indicating that he has resigned his membership thereof'. Excused front-line service by the Kaiser, the prince spent the war in Berlin and eventually died there in 1931.

'Never, perhaps, have so many famous cricketers, young and old, been gathered together', *Wisden* remarked of the centenary dinner. 'To mention only the best known names, the company included Lord Harris, The Hon F.S. Jackson, Mr A.C. MacLaren, Mr R.H. Spooner, Canon Edward Lyttelton, Sir T.C. O'Brien, Mr G. McGregor, Mr John Shuter, Mr A.J. Webbe, Mr H.K. Foster and the members of the two elevens taking part in the match at Lord's', along with some 300 lesser mortals. Lord Hawke expressed a warmly applauded belief that MCC would continue to thrive no matter what kind of world it found itself in a hundred years hence. The club president then read out a letter from Ranjitsinhji, now the Jam Sahib of Nawanagar, and in some difficulty with the British tax authorities, conveying his regrets for being unavoidably absent. W.G. Grace was there, and his speech received an ovation 'worthy of a prince'. Now 65, the grand old man of cricket had become a stooped, grey-bearded figure, of whom one witness said, 'he shuffled in … his illness showed in his face, I thought, and from the side his skin had the yellowish-grey look you find on dead men'. But when Grace stood to speak about the robust state of county cricket, 'he seemed to take on another appearance; the pallor and signs of sickness left him and all at once you were sitting with a vigorous, commanding, strong man whose mind was so clear, so well-organised, so quick that you suddenly became aware of the sheer force of his presence'. Charles Green of Cambridge University and Middlesex, a former President of MCC and Master of the Essex Foxhounds, was 'rapturously hear-heared' when he later remarked, 'Dr Grace is, as you all know, the greatest cricketer that ever lived or ever will live.' 'The dinner was in every way a memorable gathering,' *Wisden* concluded.

Cricket, and so much else, may have been living on borrowed time, but in late June 1914 there was no obvious sign that its 'last flickering embers would be snuffed out', as Edmund Blunden wrote of the war years, less than two months later. The generally sunny mood was reflected by everything from the large crowds flocking to Lord's and the other grounds – with 17,000 at the Oval on the last Saturday in the month to see Surrey score 502-6 against Middlesex – to the minutes of the three successive Monday morning meetings of the MCC Committee.

On 15 June, the Club's first order of business was to confirm arrangements for the list of those to propose toasts at the centenary dinner, followed by the draw for its annual real-tennis tournament and other housekeeping matters. 'The question of a telephone upstairs [in the pavilion] was referred to the Property and Works Sub-Committee', Lord Hawke recorded. On 22 June the Finance Sub-Committee was able to report a healthy balance of £2,774 10s 2d at Glyn's Bank, which among other things allowed the Club to entertain a request to contribute to the cost of repairs to the pavilion at the Parks ground in Oxford. Meanwhile, the catering was in hand for the visit of the king to Lord's the following day, private detectives had been hired, and the acting secretary reported on 'the provisions that had been made with respect to tea for guests during the Navy and Army Match in the garden of No. 2 Grove End Road'. On 29 June, the day after the assassinations in Bosnia, the Committee met to report that its assets had risen to £2,908. Amid general congratulations on the success of the centenary dinner, it was voted that a 'good meal' should be arranged for the Lord's ground staff, and individual employees rewarded for their recent service. 'A special grant of £1 to Cannon and 15s to Twelftree for extra work in connection with the centenary celebrations was approved', the minutes noted. Despite Edmund Blunden's later claim that 'a terrible and palpable foreboding [had] hung over the season from its second month', the general tone of MCC's meetings as a whole would not seem to have been that of a governing body that saw itself as being on the edge of a precipice.

There was a crowd of some 13,000 on the final day at Lord's to see the Navy's Robert Cunliffe, an aggressive batsman with some pretensions to leg-spin, help his side clinch victory over the Army by 170 runs. Nineteen of the 22 players would see combat during the war. Grotesque as it is to use the word 'only' about casualties, on a relative basis it might fairly be applied here. Each side lost a man in action, which was less than the case for most organised sports teams in 1914. The Army's William Parker enjoyed the best analysis of his brief cricket career in the match, with returns of 3-64 and 1-17. As Captain Parker of the 8th Battalion, Rifle Brigade, he was killed in fighting around Hooge in Belgium on 30 July 1915, aged 28. Lieutenant Fred Trumble, Royal Navy, played his first and only first-class match at Lord's. On 5 May 1918, aged 24, he fell on the deck of HMS *Warwick* as she attempted to blockade the port of Ostend and exchanged fire with the defending guns. In one of those perverse twists of war, Trumble's old colleague Robert Cunliffe, widely known as a dashing character whom *The Times* called 'brazenly reckless of his own safety', lived to be 95.

In an unrelated development, thousands of miles away, the great Australian batsman Victor Trumper announced his retirement due to ill-health in June 1914. C.B. Fry said of him that 'he defied all orthodox rules, yet every stroke he played satisfied the ultimate criterion of style – the minimum of effort, the maximum of effect'. Trumper would succumb to Bright's Disease just a year later, aged 37. Twenty thousand mourners lined the route of his funeral procession in Sydney. His death, coming on the first anniversary of the Sarajevo assassination, marks another milestone in the passing of cricket's golden age.

III

Just as the Army and Navy players walked out onto the field at Lord's on the Thursday morning of 25 June, a meeting was starting in Vienna between the Habsburg-Austrian finance minister, Leon von Bilinski, and the Serb ambassador Ljuba Jovanovic. Even by the standards of the thicket of Slav politics of 1914 it was a tangled affair. Jovanovic apparently decided to soften the message his government had told him to deliver – that Belgrade had definite information of a plot to kill the Austrian archduke – and instead to speak only in general terms of the volatile mood in Sarajevo as a whole, and to warn that 'any official visits thereto might best be arranged on a more sparing basis'. The envoy had sought the interview with Bilinski in the first place only because he was currently not on speaking terms with the Habsburg foreign minister Count von Berchtold, whom he might otherwise have been expected to brief. Bilinski, in turn, was said to have received the news of a potential threat against the heir presumptive of the old emperor in a 'cool and phlegmatic manner ... he replied that he was confident in the security planning of his subordinate, General Oskar Potiorek', governor of the provinces, who had assured him the visit would proceed 'untroubled by the sort of restiveness' that had seen the assassination of roughly one head of state, including the presidents of France, Mexico and the United States, the prime ministers of Egypt, Greece and Spain (twice), the kings of Italy and Serbia, and the shah of Persia, each year from 1894 to 1914. Compounding the many sub-plots to the meeting, the ambitious Jovanovic was known to be politically friendly with Dragutin Apis, head of the sinister group known as the Black Hand, which continued to oppose the 1908 Habsburg annexation of Bosnia-Herzegovina, and thus may not have been unduly worried about what might happen to the royal party. In turn, Bilinski was then feuding with his deputy Potiorek, who was the nominee to replace him. 'If things went wrong on the visit, it would not be I who was culpable', he later wrote. It was in this looking-glass world that a feckless but dedicated 19-year-old, with a wiry moustache said to 'make him look a bit like an organ grinder', was able to fire the shots heard around the globe.

III

On 25 June, as events were unfolding in central Europe, a three-day cricket match began at the tree-lined Spa ground in Gloucester. The visiting Lancashire team won a decisive victory by an innings and 33 runs. It would have been hard to recognise the bucolic setting, with its modest crowd of men in formal double-breasted suits and women in full dresses, holding parasols, promenading between the perfectly spaced oaks and terraced flower beds, as part of the same Continent playing host to the Black Hand, with its manifesto of 'a speedy bringing about of revolution ... by all means including executions, overturning of trams and buses, explosions in public buildings and other direct action'. Never in the very top flight of sports arenas, the Spa ground simply presented 'the pleasant vista of a prolonged tea party to a gentle backdrop of play', *Cricket* said.

On a 'perfect and flat' wicket, Gloucestershire managed scores of just 155 and 206. Other than the opening pair of Langdon and Dipper, most of the side played below form and Gilbert Jessop scored a pair. In their first innings, the home team's last 5 wickets went down for 6 runs. 'As in so many of their matches, the Gloucester batting lacked consistency', was *Wisden*'s measured view. Lancashire, by contrast, 'found run-getting a comparatively simple matter'. Their win left them seventh in the Championship table, behind Surrey, Middlesex, Kent, Yorkshire, Hampshire and Sussex, with Gloucestershire a distant sixteenth.

Three players in the match lost their lives in the war. Gloucestershire's young batsman John Nason had had a glittering early career before joining the county. He had once opened the innings for the University School against Hastings; after half an hour, the scorecard read: 'J.W.W. Nason b. Cox, 97; L. Inskipp, not out, 1; bye, 1; Total (1 wkt) 99.' The *Globe* remembered him for a 'dignity and composure at the wicket ... He never scrambled for a run, but dispatched the ball with the merest turn of the wrist'. As Captain Nason of the Royal Flying Corps, he was killed on Boxing Day 1916, aged 27. As we have seen, the Lancashire team lost both their wicketkeeper Harold Garnett and their all-rounder William Tyldesley, one of four cricketing brothers, who as a lieutenant in the Loyal North Lancashires fell near Ypres during the final German push of April 1918. He was 30.

In that same week in June 1914, Leicestershire hosted at Ashby-de-la-Zouch an in-form Kent, for whom Frank Woolley scored 117 in just over two hours. On a green, seamer's wicket, Colin Blythe had to be content with figures of 1-30 and 3-69. It was enough: Kent won by 134 runs. 'Watched by good crowds, the match was quite a success', *Wisden* commented. Leicester's bespectacled opening bowler Alec Skelding made good use of the conditions to take 5-58 on the first morning. Possessed of deadpan humour, Skelding survived to return to cricket, and seemed to actually become faster as he got older. In one account, 'the thickest pads were needed by the batsman to defend his shins from Skelding's express yorker'. In his benefit year of 1927, when he was 40, he took 102 wickets at an average of 20.81. Skelding went on to become one of the game's great umpires from 1931 to 1959, his habitually thin, fixed smile and glinting spectacles giving one departing batsman a 'slightly sinister impression – you could see him standing in a black overcoat'; he died less than a year after his retirement, aged 73.

Leicester's next home game after their loss to Kent was played in scorching heat against Worcestershire at Coalville. Although the visitors lost, their 19-year-old batsman Frank Chester scored 93 at a run a minute on the first day. Skelding later remarked that his glasses had repeatedly steamed up with the exertion of bowling at him: 'I went on hearing only and appealed twice an over,' he explained. Chester had made a sensational debut in the 1912 season, when he scored 703 runs, including three centuries, and took 44 wickets with his occasional off-spin. *Wisden* said of him that year: 'Nothing stood out more prominently than the remarkable development of Chester, the youngest professional regularly engaged in first-class cricket ... very few players in the history of cricket have shown such form at just seventeen and a half.' Chester volunteered on the outbreak of war, and joined the Royal Field Artillery in a battery commanded by 58-year-old Major Frederic Allsopp, captain of the Worcestershire Second XI. (Allsopp, who appears to have been economical when giving the army his age, had taken his only two first-class wickets with what the *Globe* called his 'unassuming, round-arm lobs' in the year 1884.) In July 1917, at Salonika, Chester was hit in the right shoulder by shrapnel. After gangrene set in, surgeons removed the arm just below the elbow. He was then 22, and his active cricket career was over. After the war Chester turned to umpiring, using an artificial arm to make the necessary signals, and stood with distinction (and 'occasional irascibility', his *Wisden* obituary notes) at first-class and Test level for the next thirty-five years. E. W. Swanton called him 'as nearly infallible as a man could be in his profession'. Alongside Alec Skelding, Chester was said to have 'raised umpiring to a higher art than had ever been known in the history of cricket'. Like Skelding, he died almost immediately following his retirement, aged 62.

On the Saturday morning of 27 June 1914, 20-year-old Geoffrey Jackson made one of his few first-class appearances for Derbyshire between his coming down from Oxford and going to the war. In those days, a flavour of West Country eccentricity was rarely absent from the county's opponents, Somerset, whose team included seven amateurs, among them two pairs of brothers, as well as an opening bowler who was 43 years old, another whose extremely slow deliveries, sent down from a great height, 'often got batsmen in two minds and caused an impulse to hit which overcame all discretion', and a wicketkeeper approaching the age of 52. The match was scheduled for three days, but Derbyshire completed their win in two. On the rest day in between, Gavrilo Princip succeeded at the second attempt in murdering the visiting archduke and his wife. In London, *The Times* reported that 'the principal victim of the outrage was wearing a sky-blue tunic and a helmet with green peacock feathers'. The event made the British front pages for a few days, until the press went back to their blanket coverage of the Irish Question, Wimbledon and Henley. Before being seized by the crowd, Princip swallowed a cyanide capsule; it was either too old or too weak to work, and its only effect was to make him vomit. He died of tuberculosis in April 1918, while in captivity; he was 23.

Bismarck reportedly said in 1884 that it would be 'some damned fool thing in the Balkans' that would eventually ignite a world war. Thirty years later Princip's tragi-comic actions at Sarajevo, enough to start a vicious circle of military preparation and intensified national hatreds, fulfilled the prediction. The frenzied outpouring of emotion may have been most shrill in Berlin and Vienna, but many others were ready for war when it came. Rupert Brooke was not just speaking for himself when he wrote, 'Now, God be thanked Who has matched us with His hour.' The calcula-tions and miscalculations that followed over the next five weeks are for others to debate; but as a direct result, the young Derbyshire cricketer Geoffrey Jackson, with his love of dressing room jokes and schoolboy adventure stories, was to become one of around 17 million servicemen and civilians to lose their lives.

HIGH SUMMER

Although the folk memory of the summer of 1914 remains one of idyllic blue skies and uninterrupted sunshine right up to the outbreak of war, this was not the case around central Manchester in the first week of July. When Lancashire began their match with Surrey at Old Trafford on the 4th of the month, it was reported locally that 'rain, rain and more rain' had flooded whole sections of the outfield, necessitating 'shoring up of the boundaries with sandbags against encroaching mud and water deluging the lower stands'. That play started on time on the Saturday morning and was cut short only by poor light was a baffling achievement to the visiting players who had witnessed the ground the previous evening, when it resembled nothing so much as a boating lake. As it was, *Wisden* reported, 'as the turf had not fully recovered Hornby, on winning the toss for Lancashire, put Surrey in first. Disastrous consequences attended this policy, Surrey winning by an innings and 2 runs.'

Hobbs, currently leading the batting averages with an average 18 ahead of the next man, was content here with 64, while his colleague Ernie Hayes added 103 in a shade under three hours. Faced with a total of 393, Lancashire managed innings of just 216 and 175. In the *Guardian*'s diplomatic phrase, 'there were numerous batting failures, and even Mr Hornby achieved little numerically' – a euphemism for scores of 4 and 0. The match was played for the benefit of Lancashire's veteran off-spinner Bill Huddleston, who rose to the occasion with figures of 6-98 off 50 overs. Precise details of his takings were not given in the press, but his testimonial year as a whole raised £896, 'which the Committee paid out in tiny sums, and pretty much at their own convenience,' he later noted. In time, the phlegmatic Huddleston returned from the war but not to first-class cricket. Surrey's Ernie Hayes, sourly handsome with brilliantined dark hair and a pantomime-villain's moustache, volunteered for the army in October 1914, when he was 38. Commissioned into the Sportsman's Battalion, wounded at the Somme and later awarded the MBE, he returned to briefly play as an amateur after the war. In 1926, just short of his 50th birthday, he made a comeback for Leicestershire and was run out for 99 in his first match.

That same wet week in July 1914, Glamorgan played out a draw in a friendly with Northamptonshire at the St Helen's ground, Swansea. The home team's opener, a dentist named Norman Riches, scored 95, while his partner 'Jock' Tait was said to have had cover-point 'wringing his hands, if not groping in vain for the ball' with his own brief but potent knock of 40. Unusually for a Welsh sportsman, Tait was born in the Shetland Islands, having come south to try his hand in an insurance business based around the Cardiff docks. In addition to cricket, he played rugby for Swansea and football for Cardiff Corinthians and Newport, going on to win a Welsh amateur international cap against England. The team's next man in after him, Tom Whittington, was also Glamorgan's long-time secretary and as such largely responsible for securing the county's first-class status in 1921. Although none of the home side in that particular match fell in action, it could be said that at least one of them lost his life as a result of the war. Glamorgan's middle-order batsman and treasurer Dyson Williams served as a lieutenant colonel with the Welsh Regiment from 1914–18, and was awarded both the MC and DSO. His obituary notes that 'following his experiences at the front, which left him mentally and physically scarred, [he] took up gambling, and lost a vast amount of his accrued money in the process'. Williams played his first and only Championship game in August 1921, when he captained Glamorgan against Hampshire at Cardiff. Eight months later, he committed suicide in his London office; he was 44.

As a symbol of England's golden age both in cricket and elsewhere, it would be hard to top the annual Varsity Match at Lord's. The Test batsman-turned-author Albert Knight saw 'everything fine in the country' epitomised by this parade of its gilded youth. 'The game is in so many ways the most interesting episode of each recurring year', Knight wrote in his characteristically graceful, if at times flowery, style in *The Complete Cricketer*:

> The social aspect of it is that most calculated to impress the ordinary observer. The miles-long line of cabs and motors which stretch adown and around the neighbourhood of St John's Wood, roughly indicates what wealth and power, what fashion and influence, still interest themselves in a game which town slum and village green alike love … The Varsity match manifests what, in practice at least, seems an 'impossible loyalty' to the glow and glory of pure sport.

What this meant in practice was that Oxford comfortably won a match played under mainly grey skies but to packed crowds, who towards the end 'kept up one long crescendo of thunderous and partisan applause'. On the middle day, when the sun briefly shone, there were thought to have been around 17,000 people in the ground. *Wisden* said that 'there was no lack of talent on either side, [but] the cricket scarcely rose above a respectable mediocrity', for which the wretched weather 'that turned the famous panorama into a quagmire' was largely responsible.

As we have seen, Oxford lost their players William Boswell and Edward Shaw, who fell only two years later at the Somme, both aged 24. Cambridge also made a heavy sacrifice to the war. Much had been expected of their opening bat Alban Arnold, who had come up with a big reputation from Malvern, and who hit 89 against MCC at Lord's just a week before the Varsity game. He also played eleven matches for Hampshire in the latter part of the 1914 season, and was said to have 'rendered the county capital service'. He fell fighting with the Royal Fusiliers at Ovillers-la-Boisselle in France in July 1916, aged 23. Although Arnold's body was never recovered, he is commemorated on the Thiepval Memorial to the missing of the Somme. *Wisden* believed 'he would probably have developed into a cricketer of very high class'.

Ken Woodroffe of Cambridge, a seam bowler, met with startling success when appearing for Sussex against Surrey at the Oval later that July. The presumptive county champions began the last day's play needing 149 to win with all 10 wickets intact. Hobbs and company then played so wildly that when the last man came in 4 runs were still wanted. Although Surrey scrambled home, Woodroffe had figures of 6-43 and, it was reported, 'put the fear of God in the batsmen ... shortly before tea a wonderful match was over. The scene of enthusiasm at the finish was quite indescribable. Smiling shyly, Woodroffe was thunderously applauded from all sides.'

Just nine months after these events, 2nd Lieutenant Woodroffe of the 6th Battalion, Rifle Brigade, fell in action at Ypres; he was 22. He remained characteristically cheerful to the end. 'I should like a quiet day or two to catch up on correspondence', he noted, mildly, shortly before his death. 'But the guns still pound away. All are quite confident, though both sides are clearly paying a terrible price. I want to get into the German trenches very much.' Woodroffe's cricketing brother Sidney, of the 8th Rifle Brigade, was killed two months later while showing such bravery that he was awarded the Victoria Cross. He was 19.

Of the twenty-two young men who played in the 1914 Varsity game, five died in action and fourteen others served in the armed forces at some point before November 1918, many with great distinction. As just one example, there was the dashing Cambridge all-rounder the Hon. Freddy Calthorpe, who took 5-43 with his 'corkscrew-like' seam bowling in the second innings at Lord's, but more to the point joined the Royal Flying Corps immediately war was declared. After some cursory training around Norwich, he spent the next two years dealing with Zeppelin raids on London, and two more after that flying low-level reconnaissance missions over the Western Front. Calthorpe survived the war and in 1919 returned to Cambridge, where *Wisden* reports he would have captained the university XI 'if the letter of invitation had not miscarried'. Although stereotypically upper-class to look at and to listen to – his voice could have shattered glass – he was capable of some rueful half-lights when writing about the changing post-war world. Calthorpe later played for Warwickshire and England, whom he captained in his only four Test matches. The heir to the family estates in London and Norfolk, he was the son of the 8th Baron Calthorpe, but died in November 1935, aged 43, predeceasing his father. His nephew is the cricket commentator Henry Blofeld.

In the more austere atmosphere of Bramall Lane, Sheffield, meanwhile, Yorkshire lost to Kent for the second time in a fortnight. Rain prevented play on the first morning, 'kicking up a sooty fog' over the cutlery town, and all but ruined the match thereafter. The home side managed just 101 in their first innings, and by lunch the next day Kent were in the relatively comfortable position of 106-5. Major Booth bowled at this point, and in his first over had Woolley caught in the outfield as the batsman tried to pull a long-hop. From there Kent folded to 126 all out, Booth taking 5-43. The Yorkshire reply lasted just an hour and three-quarters. It contained 100 runs, and featured two notable events: the bowling of Colin Blythe, who took 8-55, and a show of obduracy by Booth typical of the unyielding spirit of Yorkshire cricket, as *The Times* reported:

> Enterprise and initiative are one thing, but this seemed to go too far ... [Booth], upon being given out for treading on his wicket, vigorously protested that he had finished his stroke when the bail was dislodged. In time, the Yorkshire captain [Sir Archibald White] came out to investigate and consult with his batsman, who had declined to leave the arena.

Although Booth then departed, signing himself off by smashing the stumps, *Wisden* reported that 'the umpire was subjected to considerable hooting'. Booth and Blythe took 10 wickets apiece in the match, which Kent won by 5 wickets. As we've seen, both these hardy competitors, as well as Kent's David Jennings, who in August 1918 succumbed to an illness *Wisden* blamed on 'shell-shock and gas', aged 29, would die in the war.

Over those same three days in July, Warwickshire beat Hampshire by 6 wickets at Edgbaston, and briefly rose to fifth in the Championship table as a result. According to the local *Evening Mail*, 'the ball consistently slid around in the damp, and there were several heaven-shaking shouts and wild gesticulations on the part of both sets of fast men'. One of the besieged umpires was none other than the former Lancashire stalwart opener Dick Barlow, now aged 63. Although a model professional, he might be thought an unlikely muse for Francis Thompson's celebrated lines about his being a 'run-stealer, flicker[ing] to and fro', having once scored 5 in 150 minutes for Lancashire, and 42 in almost four hours for England against Australia at Sydney, eliciting a satirical poem in *Punch*. Both the primary 'fast men' in the Edgbaston match, Arthur Jaques and Percy Jeeves, would perish in the war.

In London the following day, the spats-wearing, anglophile German ambassador Prince Karl Lichnowsky met Sir Edward Grey to discuss the aftermath of Sarajevo. He reported that Grey 'was in a thoroughly confident mood, and declared that he saw no reason for taking a pessimistic view of the situation'. The Eton and Harrow match began at Lord's the next morning, for once in perfect weather. Among the 22,000 spectators on the second day was Randall Davidson, the Archbishop of Canterbury, an Old Harrovian but seen to be dozing under a parasol impartially fringed with tassels in the colours of both schools. Although it was close, Eton won the tie for the fifth year running. There was a grand ball that night at Earl's Court for some 2,000 of the players' families and friends, 'with Hindoo fakirs, sideshows and dancing to the Coldstream Guards band ... [There] was much high-spirited grappling around the water fountains and helter-skelter'. Eton's Charles Vane-Tempest, 20, Richard Crossman, 20, Basil Christy, 19, and Frederick Johnstone, 19, all fell in the coming war, as did Harrow's Richard Chancellor, 20, George Smedley, 19, and Harry Renton, 19. Robert Makant of Harrow fought in France with the Loyal North Lancashire Regiment, winning the MC, but was later lured to a rendezvous and murdered by brigands in the Bazyan Pass in Kurdistan. He was 25.

On 11 July, Derbyshire began a three-day home match with Lancashire, who were captained in Hornby's absence by 21-year-old Robert Boddington, 'an Oxford man of great charm, who batted right-hand and occasionally kept wicket to a fair standard, if without brilliancy'. Leading his men on in bright sunshine, he wore a striped silk belt and a Rugby school cap, tilted back at a rakish angle with a strap under the chin. In the event it was to be Boddington's only county match of the season, although he returned to play for Lancashire on a casual basis until 1924, retiring with a batting average of 12.

Derbyshire made themselves safe with their batting on the first day, when they ran up a total of 431-8, and eventually came away with a draw – a good result, given that they lost all four of their other Championship matches in July. *The Times* said there was 'ringing applause' for the home keeper Joe Humphries who, going in tenth, played the more aggressive counterfoil in a stout last-wicket partnership with the

Gibraltar-like Jim Horsley, before going on to make 4 catches and a stumping. Humphries was then 38, and had first played for his county in 1899. He was one of the many players who volunteered in August 1914 and returned from the war, but not to first-class cricket. By the end of the season Derbyshire had pulled themselves off the foot of the Championship table and finished twelfth, an improvement of one place on 1913. Bucking the trend of even some of the wealthiest counties, *Wisden* said that:

> Derby's gates [were] always fairly good, and the membership increased consider-
> ably, with the result that there were no financial embarrassments in working the
> club. This is the more noteworthy when it is considered that owing to the out-
> break of the War the attendances in August naturally showed a falling-off.

On the warm Monday morning of 13 July, a crowd of some 6,000 was packed into the Nevill Ground, Tunbridge Wells, to see third-placed Kent play Essex. The visitors were captained for the occasion by their 40-year-old amateur batsman Frederick Fane, who in 1906 had become the first Irish-born player to score a century for England, but finished his Test career shortly afterwards with a modest average of 25. The field at Tunbridge Wells was a classic monument to organised rural cricket, with just that touch of the haphazard to it: there were flag-strewn tents and low, wooden stands, with a tiny press box clamped to the side of a hill behind the third-man boundary, of which Ray Robinson once wrote in the *Morning Post*: 'the architect who designed this perch had a poor idea of angles. From the seat occupied by your correspondent, four fieldsmen, one batsman and one umpire were in view – a quorum, perhaps, but hardly satisfying to the eager critic.' In 1914, both sets of players democratically changed and dined in a temporary hut erected at the Railway End, since militant suffragettes had burnt down the ground's timber pavilion the previous year.

The match itself was one-sided. 'Dismissed on a capital wicket in little more than two hours, Essex quite failed to retrieve the ground lost by this poor performance, and on the second evening found themselves beaten by an innings', wrote *Wisden*. For Kent, David Jennings scored 106, which was to be the highest score of his career, and Colin Blythe took 5-40; neither man survived the war. Their teammate Eric Hatfield, an all-rounder, had taken 12 wickets for Eton against Harrow at Lord's in July 1903, when he was barely 15, and gone on to Oxford, where he may possibly have been a youthful recruit to the Secret Intelligence Service, as he sometimes hinted. In 1914, he played for Kent whenever required, but 'though always an enthu-siastic and popular cricketer, was not good enough to secure a regular place in the county team'. As Captain Hatfeild of the East Kent Regiment, or 'Buffs', he was awarded the MC for his role in repulsing the last German attack on the Marne in July 1918, 'fighting with fanatical ardour, despite being grievously fatigued and ravaged by influenza'. Two months after this action, Hatfeild fell while leading his men in their climactic assault on the German lines at Cambrai; he was 31.

Frederick Fane of Essex also served on the Western Front, and won the MC. Returning from the war, carrying a leg wound but ready, as he put it, for 'another loop around the circuit', he played his last first-class match in July 1924, thirty years after his debut. In 1954, he was able to enjoy the unusual experience of reading his own obituary when *Wisden* wrongly reported his death; the man concerned was a cousin with a similar name. Fred Fane lived to be 85, dying in November 1960.

Cricket was not immune from the effects of the build-up to war, and the first pre-mobilisation notices in early July had sent soldier-sportsmen, like Hornby of Lancashire and White of Yorkshire, heading south to rejoin their regiments, a reinforcing element in the overall momentum of the conflict. In the Meeanee Barracks, Colchester, Lionel Tennyson was able to combine his 'endless square-bashing and PT' with appearances in the Green Jackets team against other army units. By 17 July sandbags had already appeared piled up against the outer wall of the Oval, though it was initially unclear if these were to help repel a possible attack from foreign guns, or as a defence against the day when the Irish would rebel and the barricades be manned against 'the thunder of hooves and mutinous terror in the streets of London', as the *Globe* chillingly put it later that week. On 23 July, the prime minister cancelled a visit to the theatre, as he had to see the king about Ulster. Irish Guards on sentry duty cheered Irish leaders entering Buckingham Palace. England seemed to be on the brink of a civil war.

While the London papers were given over to frenzied rumours of phantom saboteurs and bombs, the chancelleries of Europe were sleepwalking into a real-life holocaust. By the end of July, the *Globe* said that the 'principal threat' to peace had taken one of those bewildering turns that constitute the basic story of the summer, and 'once again swung to the continent'. The letters of players such as Arthur Jaques and Colin Blythe spoke of the practical implications for them and their families of going off to war, with a concern about matters like the storage of their equipment and the possible ration of coal and food, as though these would be the worst of the privations ahead. On 31 July, the day before the bank holiday weekend, *The Times*'s front page warned of 'Russian Military Concentration' and 'German Mobilisation Imminent'. Before long, questions were being asked about the propriety of playing sport while tens of thousands of other civilians made for their nearest recruiting station, and in time a number of county committees added their own call to duty by docking the pay of any of their unmarried professionals who failed to sign up.

In the face of all this, the MCC maintained its essential calm toward outside events as reflected in the minutes of the club's weekly meetings. On 6 July, at Lord's, 'it was agreed that the Dinner to the Staff in commemoration of the Centenary year should take place in October; that the female employees of the Refreshment Department should be invited, and that champagne be provided. It was also agreed that suitable musical artistes should be engaged.' In addition, there was to be the 'usual outing of the Refreshment Department [at] an outlay not exceeding £20'. In other business, two seats were to be provided 'for the son of the Sultan of Jehore for the Eton & Harrow match', and permission was granted 'to the Southern Ladies' Lacrosse Club to commence their practices at Lord's on October the 14th'. Seemingly the one reference to the latent Irish problem was in the committee's curt note, 'request for admission for the Bishop of Armagh to the Lord's pavilion was not entertained', though it is not known if this reflected disapproval of the primate's role in the Ulster crisis, or some more local concern. The only other hint of trouble lay in the entry: 'some report having reached the Committee respecting Tarrant's conduct at Eton during the MCC and Eton College match, the acting secretary was instructed to communicate with Mr Wells and to ask if he had any complaint to make as to Tarrant's behaviour.'

On 13 July, the committee spent some time discussing the sanitary facilities at Lord's, with the ultimate decision that 'a rule of the Club should be that only members who are taking part in a match, or practising, or playing tennis or racquets be entitled to the use of baths'. There was no further mention of Frank Tarrant and his alleged indecorum at Eton, though in a separate incident 'the acting secretary reported that owing to misunderstanding on the part of the MCC Manager, the last two matches of the Warwickshire Tour had to be scratched. Letters of regret having been sent and accepted, the matter was now closed'.

On 20 July, MCC advanced the arrangements for its staff dinner to be held on 16 October, and approved 'the suggested memento for each employee of a small medallion together with copies of the MCC Souvenirs'. A motion was passed 'to present a silver-mounted ball to Mr J.W.H.T. Douglas for his bowling in the Gentlemen against Players match', in which the Essex captain had taken 9-105 and 4-67. On a more sombre note, 'respecting visit to South Africa with MCC Team, the request by S.F. Barnes for reimbursement of out of pocket expenses was not entertained'. There is also a sadly terse reference to Andrew Stoddart, against whose name are scratched the words: 'regret reinstatement impossible'. Although Stoddart had bowed out for Middlesex with a double century in September 1900, and was still scoring heavily in club cricket seven years later, he had since all but disappeared from view. He lived his retired, impoverished life, came out for public moments like the Centenary dinner, then went back again to the bowls and the solitaire and a steadily escalating diet of large whiskys. After his brother's death in June 1914, Stoddart seemed to close down entirely. He either resigned, or was asked to leave his position as secretary of Queen's Club, and then fell into arrears with his MCC subscription. Stoddart talked at some length of visiting Australia that winter following a long bout of flu, but in the end cancelled, speaking of his need to be on hand in London should 'Lord's' choose to contact him with the offer of a job. That call never came. Instead, Stoddart, who was 51, bowled, reminisced, read the newspaper, and drank.

On 27 July, the MCC Committee's regular Monday meeting discussed the refurbishment of the squash and tennis courts at Lord's. It was moved to present bats to six young players who had scored centuries, and that in future the MCC v. Minor Counties fixture should be played over three days and not two. The only note of discord came in a debate about the request of a member named Lieutenant Colonel FitzGerald to transfer his membership to a friend, since he himself was returning to active service – 'the appeal was not entertained, the Committee having no power to grant such a thing'.

During this same period, in Vienna, Count Berchtold continued his unhurried drafting of the Austro-Hungarian protest to Serbia. When colleagues in the government questioned whether the use of the word 'ultimatum' in the text might be counterproductive, Berchtold readily offered a compromise. The document would be a 'note with a time limit', not an ultimatum. Its eventual delivery by the Habsburg ambassador, Giesl von Gieslingen, on the evening of Thursday 23 July proved to be tragicomic. The Serbian prime minister had left Belgrade on an electioneering trip, and so the terms were read out to his Foreign Secretary, who spoke neither German nor French and thus needed the services of an interpreter, who proved just barely equal to the job. When von Gieslingen finished his recitation, he said that no response other than unconditional acceptance would be satisfactory, and that this was required within two days. Overnight, the Russian foreign minister, the irascible Sergei Sazonov, announced that Austria could only have had the temerity to send such a note with the knowledge and support of Germany, and that both countries were plotting to drive Russia out of the Balkans. On 26 July, Berchtold and his colleagues rejected the Serbian reply; on 28 July they declared war; and on 29 July their troops began shelling Belgrade. Later that day Russia mobilised along her Austrian border. On 31 July, Germany issued a double ultimatum to France and Russia, asking the former for a declaration of neutrality and warning the latter to demobilise within twelve hours 'and make us a distinct declaration to that effect'. A final flurry of 'Nicky–Willy' telegrams between Moscow and Berlin proved too little and too late. The tsar rather morbidly noted that he would have accepted his own crucifixion if it could somehow have averted the crisis, and in the end that is what he got, although it was a long and slow one.

III

Proving again that cricket is better than life, there were 4,329 spectators present on what turned out to be a glorious summer day in mid-July to see an all-Ireland team, reported as consisting of 'five Roman Catholics, five Protestants [and] one equivocal' take on an Anglo-Scottish side at the Observatory Lane ground, Dublin. Many others watched from the roofs and windows of the trim red-bricked cottages lining the boundary wall. With a gabled wooden pavilion, two men in shirtsleeves scoring under a large elm, and a scrum of local youths somewhat haphazardly working the telegraph, it was a scene of classic British rustic charm, far removed from the bitter political squabbling centred around Dublin Castle just a mile or two to the north.

To the local *Freeman's Journal* correspondent, a 'fabulously keen and good' match ensued, unprecedented as one 'wherein the fortunes swung with such utter rapidity from one side to the other'. Over three days, there were 'several Irish innings of personality and lustre', and the strong visiting team 'did not emerge without anxiety'. Eventually set 182 to win in a little over three hours, Ireland fell 11 runs short. The hero of the day was 31-year-old Scotsman Henry Nicoll – 'a vast figure in graying flannels, tartan cravat and cap' – well known in Angus as a bank manager and Liberal councillor, who in his first and only first-class cricket match took 7-64 with an assortment of 'high lobs and wrist-spin [that was] a closed book to our men'. Afterwards, 'the bunting, the speeches, the many toasts proposed from the players' balcony, and the fireworks' all entertained the crowd until night drew in. The *Journal* remarked: 'of course it was all only a game, but it was also a tribute to the best mood of goodwill man can create'.

Three of the visiting team at Dublin lost their lives in the war. Walter Greive and William Stuart both fell in fighting around Arras in April 1917, aged 25 and 27 respectively. Their colleague David Kennedy was 'shot down with a bullet through the brain' during the opening minutes of the Somme offensive of July 1916; he was 25. The Irish all-round athlete and occasional poet Arthur Bateman had qualified as a doctor in June 1914, shortly before representing his country at cricket. Two months later he volunteered for duty with the Royal Army Medical Corps, and went to France as a Captain attached to the 7th Cameron Highlanders early in 1915. In March 1918 he was declared missing presumed dead, after a shell landed on the dressing-station where he was working near the line at Arras. He was 27, and one of four members of the 1914 Dublin University XI to die in action.

On 18 July 1914, while the politicians continued to debate Irish home rule and the nationalist author Erskine Childers took direct action and ran a consignment of 1,500 German guns into Dublin harbour, Surrey scored 402 under a sweltering sky against Lancashire at the Oval. Jack Hobbs and Tom Hayward essentially used the first session for batting practice, hammering 71 in an hour: 'making every allowance, a most disappointing display by the visitors', *Wisden* thought. Hobbs was out shortly after lunch for 142. Henry Harrison then added 97, and lower in the order there were runs from Andrew Ducat and Percy Fender. It was a scorching day, the *Globe* said, with the 'flowery bonnets and straw hats pressed together like a huge, coloured quilt' at the Vauxhall end. Heavy rain fell overnight and Lancashire, caught on a sticky dog, were shot out for scores of 108 and 136. Hayward's protégé Bill Hitch, cutting his pace but moving the ball both ways, took 5-36 in the second innings. Aged 42, Archie MacLaren returned for Lancashire after a long absence, but, *Wisden* was left to remark, 'met with no success'.

Later that week at Leeds, the weather also played a part in Yorkshire's win over Nottinghamshire. On a slow, damp pitch, the home side managed just 75 in their first innings. After another two days of alternating sunshine and showers, Notts, needing to score 201 to win, were all out for 103. According to the Yorkshire yearbook, 'It was an astonishing victory, and a player or players threw the stumps in the air in their jubilation', later the subject of a disapproving note by the county committee. In another show of the robust side of northern cricket, Alonzo Drake – not a stereotypical Yorkshire player, at least to look at, with his jade-smooth skin and sallow cheeks – in the second innings drove a ball back to the bowler, who dropping it as he went to lob it up, claimed that he had held it long enough to complete the catch. Drake stood his ground. 'The umpire decided in favour of the batsman,' said *Wisden*, 'the Notts players strongly protesting.'

On Friday 24 July, the Royal Artillery and Royal Engineers teams began a two-day match at Lord's. The Artillery won by an innings and 163 runs. It seems almost a relief to say that only two of the players died in the war itself: Arthur Collins, who fell at Ypres in November 1914, aged 29; and Neville Wells-Cole, killed in almost the same area four years later, aged 26. As a 13-year-old Clifton College boy, Collins had scored an innings of 628 not out in a house match spread over five weekday afternoons in June 1899. As if not a sufficient contribution, he also took 11 wickets. He had been married just five months at the time of his death. Collins's brother officer Harold Willcocks took 6-38 in the Engineers' first innings, and was judged by *Cricket* an 'excellent change bowler and catcher, with a first-class career his for the asking'. He too served at the front, and was awarded the Croix de Chevalier of the Légion d'honneur for his actions at the Marne in September

1914, barely six weeks after being chaired off in triumph by his teammates at Lord's. Major Willcocks was eventually invalided home to the Royal Herbert Hospital, Woolwich, suffering from shrapnel wounds and gas poisoning. He died there on 7 May 1919, aged 28.

Though the summer was unfolding in such a way as to give future historians the impression of an unbroken, golden season of vogue events like the Henley regatta and the Varsity match, by late July many ordinary Britons were well aware that the clock was already counting down to the moment when Russia's foreign minister and Germany's ambassador to Russia would fall weeping into each other's arms, and Britain herself finally mobilised for war. As the details of the Austrian ultimatum became known, events seemed to flow with what the *Globe* called 'irresistible rapidity'. Almost exactly forty-eight hours after the 'note with a time limit' was delivered, Serbia's response to it led the Habsburg ambassador to Belgrade to pack his bags and leave for home. In London, Edward Grey wrote, 'I do not consider that public opinion would or ought to sanction our going to war over a Serbian quarrel. If, however, war does take place, the development of other issues may draw us into it, and I am therefore anxious to avoid it.' Grey's concern did not, however, prevent him from leaving for a scheduled weekend of fly-fishing in the country. On 26 July the newspapers were full of the crisis. *The Times* reported 'a general feeling of anxiety', heightened later in the week by a rise in the bank rate from 4 to 9 per cent. Between the headlines, and the king's absence at Goodwood, and the first sightings of young recruits marching by on the streets to the tune of *Tipperary*, it was clear that war preparations, if 'preliminary', were far from trivial. In Tonbridge, Colin Blythe remarked that 'the family all spoke of it. Cricket suddenly seemed to us very insignificant … we talked it through, wondering what on earth would happen.'

On that note, on 23 July Nottinghamshire began a three-day match against Gloucestershire at Trent Bridge. Just a week earlier, the Gentlemen *v.* Players game at Lord's had begun in what *Wisden* called 'almost tropical' heat, with the morning sunshine bouncing off a bleached-looking wicket, and 'tall drinks called for' throughout the later sessions. These were significantly different conditions to those at Nottingham, where the game began in a fresh wind and deteriorated from there: 'so showery was the weather at the end that, following upon an hour and three-quarters of actual cricket, much interrupted by the rain, the contest was abandoned as a draw two hours before time', *Wisden* said. A county tie like this between two of the Championship's lower-order sides naturally lacked some of the social frisson of the Gentlemen *v.* Players fixture, but even so the crowd of just 871 spectators on hand at the end was a sorry reflection both of 'the miserable scene and also, perhaps, of larger concerns', *The Times* correspondent wrote.

In between the stoppages, Nottinghamshire scored 299, reportedly 'in large part due to the folly of their opponents, more than half-a-dozen chances being missed'. In the visitors' reply, Jessop hit 78 out of a partnership of 82 in an hour. Before play was finally abandoned on the Saturday afternoon, there was time for John Gunn of Notts to score 73, with just one blemish: on 55, he gave a hard chance with a shot that 'left the bat at high speed and fell towards the man on the mid-wicket horizon', who dropped it. Ironically, the fielder in question, William St Clair Grant, was a Scottish international rugby back known for his safe pair of hands. He was to play only four first-class cricket matches, of which this was the third. Grant enlisted in the army on his 20th birthday in September 1914, and went to France the following spring. Many would have been discouraged by this turn of events, 'but he positively thrived there', a fellow officer named Hersh recalled. 'I never knew anyone so full of life.' As Captain Grant of the Cameron Highlanders, he won the MC and the Croix de Guerre Belge; wounded in fighting around Passchendaele in the last weeks of the war, he died in a field hospital on 26 September 1918, at the age of 24.

Given the rapidly darkening turn of events in late July 1914, it seems mildly ironic that the army would now choose to release Lionel Tennyson to play cricket. He returned to the Hampshire side alongside C.B. Fry in a soggy draw against Sussex at Southampton, staged for Alec Bowell's benefit. Tennyson scored 35 and 9, 'looking graceful in the drive and assured on the leg side', if later 'somewhat inert in the field'. The Hampshire treasurer, a local JP and former club cricketer named Bernard Harfield, would remember handing Tennyson his travel expenses with some misgiving – 'the Lieutenant roared through each day as if it were his last, and one could but rue some of the chosen investments of his funds', he later remarked.

Tennyson, unleashed from his summer of 'endless square-bashing' in Colchester, was a perpetual holidaymaker on the prowl. He found the Southampton casino and the then thriving Tweseldown racecourse, near Aldershot, especially tempting. Tennyson always had a tip on a horse, a 'sure thing' that would make everyone wealthy. A year earlier, he had managed to lose £12,000 in the course of a week at the races. His father had had to pay off the debt. Tennyson himself owned five horses, some of which he rode in point-to-point events, and another of which, in an attempt to recoup his losses, he once entered in the Regulation Plate at Newbury. It finished last. Bernard Harfield recalled that:

He had no regard for money, none. The first full summer he was with us he lost more money at the casino tables and the races than a professional player would make all year. That's a fact. Not that it was only him. Edward Sprot captained the Hampshire team when I first came to Southampton. He was a fanatic all-round sportsman, with a lot of beautiful equipment. He had to sell an antique billiards table once just to get out of Tweseldown. That's how much money he lost.

On 23 July, Tennyson was in the Hampshire team to play Surrey at Portsmouth. It was the match when Andrew Ducat scored 108 and, curiously enough, Hobbs took over an hour to make 16. The visitors won by 8 wickets. Over the same three-day period, Leicestershire played out an unusually fast-paced draw with Warwickshire at Hinckley. Percy Jeeves opened the visitors' bowling, and Alec Skelding took his 50th wicket of the season for Leicester. Both made good use of a pitch that started damp, and then deteriorated from there. The batting honours went to Warwickshire's 42-year-old opener Septimus Kinneir, with a century later said by *Wisden* to have been 'graceful, and yet without any of the exaggeration of pull that so often marks a left-hander'. Kinneir, a professional who also excelled at sports as diverse as bocce, snooker and archery ('nothing too strenuous', as he once noted) had come up through the ranks of Wiltshire cricket, and found the first-class game congenial enough. When Warwickshire won the County Championship in 1911, he had the highest aggregate, 1,418 runs (averaging 44), and went on tour to Australia with MCC that winter. Despite his age, Kinneir volunteered for active service in 1914, and survived nearly two years' continuous infantry duty in France. He returned safely to England, but not to first-class cricket. On 16 October 1928 he died after crashing his motorcycle on his way home from playing golf. He was 57.

That same week in July 1914, Yorkshire played a three-day game with Lancashire at the Circle ground, Hull; not an official Roses Match, or even part of the County Championship, but an extra fixture arranged around the town's annual 'parade of flowers' summer festival. It says something for the popularity of northern cricket that there were 6,000 spectators in the park on the first morning, when it was blowing a gale. According to *Wisden*, 'apart from Sharp and Huddleston, the Lancashire men batted in rather laborious fashion, taking more than four hours and a half on the opening day to score 233-7. Yorkshire's cricket on Friday was marked by more vigour than had characterised that of their opponents, but the home side, in making 312-6, owed much to blunders in the field.' Despite the rain, it was a 'jolly scene', the *York Star* reported, 'and laughter unconstrained rendered many an otherwise dull innings a choice morsel to mull over with an ale'. The Circle had the enviable reputation of being at the same time one of the most attractive out-grounds in England, and of having usually one of the very best wickets. It was bordered on one side by West Park Lake, over the years a popular target for big hitters like Gilbert Jessop, and a twice-daily steam-train ran up and down a branch-line just to the south. Inside the ground there was a timbered pavilion, low stands, and a row of stables used by a polo club that shared the premises. Off to one side, the Hull Brewing tent was well known locally as 'Critics' Corner'. Situated 'amidst lovely environs, with a fine view of the game everywhere obtainable', in Jessop's phrase, the Circle was demolished in 2000 to make way for the KC Stadium complex, the home to various football and rugby league teams, as well as to rock concerts by the likes of Elton John.

In the one Yorkshire innings possible that festival weekend, 36-year-old Wilfred Rhodes, then the holder of 47 England caps, hit an unbeaten 105. Although the *Star* felt 'it would be flattering to claim he was still at his best', Rhodes's last Test appearance would come only long after the war, when he was 52. In turn, the visitors relied heavily on their seamer and occasional batsman Ralph Whitehead – a man with 'bowed legs and a baleful look' – who once genially told the sporting press that he thought of his own bowling as 'no more than a joke'. If so, it was a singularly practical one, as he dismissed three batsmen here for 6 runs, while on his way to figures of 8-77. Whitehead had made a sensational first-class debut when, in June 1908, he came in to bat at number nine for Lancashire against Notts at Old Trafford. According to *Wisden*, 'he put on 188 with his captain A.H. Hornby and, when the last wicket fell, was left unbeaten on 131 after only 3 hours batting. Hornby gave him his county cap between innings and, perhaps assuming he was on infallible form, brought him on to bowl immediately. Then everything went wrong.' Whitehead was called for throwing four times in his first 5 balls, and taken out of the attack shortly afterwards. He survived in cricket, though rarely again making an impact, and finished his career in August 1914 with 300 first-class wickets. Later that winter, the *Oldham Standard* reported that 'Lance-Corporal Ralph Whitehead, who is attached to the 10th Reserve Battalion Manchester regiment, has secured his first-class championship and second-class medals for bomb-throwing, given by the Aldershot Command Athletic Association. His delivery action was impeccable.'

As Yorkshire finally abandoned their 'parade of flowers' gala match in the rain at Hull, 200 miles away the Grove Park club hosted a one-day game against Eltham on a field in Hounslow near the present-day Heathrow Airport. The tie holds a lasting place in cricket history if only because it was to be the last ever visit to the crease for the visitors' number five batsman: W.G. Grace, who had celebrated his 66th birthday the week before. Grace's team were in some bother at 31-4, but in a fitting valete he hit an unbeaten 69 out of an eventual total of 155-6 declared. According to the *Eltham and District Times*, '"WG" batted admirably … he got his runs all round the wicket, being especially strong on the off side. His chief hits included one five, six fours, and seven twos.' Having made his first-class debut in 1865, the year of General Sherman's climactic march in the American Civil War and Lewis Carroll's publication of *Alice's Adventures in Wonderland*, Grace had lived to see an age where armed aircraft and submarines, like poison gas and the machine-gun, had become an essential element of every modern nation's arsenal. Eltham could not quite force the win: Grove Park finished on 99-8, and Grace is said to have returned to the dressing room, packed his bag and said firmly: 'There. I shan't play any more.'

In fact he did play once more. On 8 August, Grace turned out for Eltham against Northbrook, in front of a 'thin but vocal audience' at the old Footscray Road ground. It was another draw. Grace himself neither batted nor bowled. By then the first wave of the British Expeditionary Force (BEF) had landed in France, and the Germans were busy reducing Belgium's fortress-towns to rubble. Cricket's patriarchal figure bowed out after fifty-seven consecutive seasons of competitive play. Just over a fortnight later, Grace would write to *The Sportsman*, noting presciently that 'the fighting will probably be prolonged', and calling for cricketers to put bat and ball away 'and come to the help of their country without delay in its hour of need'. *The Times* later said that Grace's letter 'came as a far greater shock to many thousands of ordinary Britons' than the official declaration of war.

During this period Surrey and Middlesex continued to play a game of leapfrog at the top of the Championship table, and the south Londoners went first again when they completed their win against Hampshire at Portsmouth. Sussex suffered only their second defeat of the summer when they went down by an innings to Essex at Southend, Johnny Douglas taking 6-18 to shoot the visitors out for 47 in their second innings. Meanwhile, Warwickshire won their away tie with Lancashire, and temporarily went to fourth place. There was still a lot of rain about, and in the next match at Old Trafford the groundsman hurriedly had to prepare a new pitch after the start had been delayed when the original one was found to be what the *News* called 'a swamp'. While the work went on, the paper added, the spectators 'shivered with the chill'.

There were more sympathetic conditions in Kent, where the fruit-pickers made their annual appearance in July, and in a little over a week Colin Blythe's side hosted successive matches against Middlesex and Surrey. The games pitted the three strongest teams in England against each other, and were crucial to settling the eventual championship table – the cricket was dotted with miniature replicas of that summer's classic moments. The meeting with Middlesex at Mote Park, Maidstone, produced 10 wickets for Blythe, and 'at least six palpable chances missed' when the visitors were in the field. Eight thousand spectators, a record for the ground, were there to see Kent win by an innings. On the night the match finished, a young housemaid named Bessie Ellis wrote of the now 'sweltering Kent heat' and of the arrival of 'many hundreds' of day-labourers from the east end of London. 'They came for two or three weeks', she said later. 'It was their yearly holiday. They had bonfires in the open fields and cooked on a big fire. They went to the pub drinking and had enormous sing-songs in the evening. They used to chase us and we got frightened. There was never a swede or a cabbage left when they were around, let alone a damson or a plum.'

The following week, at Blackheath, Surrey at least put up a good fight when trying to win a match on Kent soil for the first time in seventeen years. An over-all summary in *Wisden* said that 'circumstances generally combined to invest the game with exceptional interest, Surrey at the moment standing at the head of the counties, and Kent running Middlesex a close race for second'. Bill Hitch took 5 wickets in the Kent first innings, and it was said 'in bowling Mr A.P. Day, sent a bail 48 yards'. Surrey then stayed in all day and made 509. Hobbs and Hayward hit up 122 apiece, leading Colin Blythe to remark drily, 'at least we know now when the buggers are vulnerable'. As it was, rain again set in on the third day, and Surrey had to settle for a draw. There's a certain economy to *Wisden*'s final word on the match: 'Carr bowled with so little of his customary skill that he did not assist Kent again.' Born in 1872, Douglas Carr had come into the county XI only in 1909, when his leg-break and googly bowling claimed no fewer than 42 wickets in his first six games. On this form he was chosen to represent England against Australia at the Oval, becoming the first man ever to play Test cricket in his first year in the county game. Although Carr took 7 wickets in the match, he never appeared for his country again. Between then and his playing for Kent against Surrey, his bowl-ing had proved only fitfully brilliant, while his batting became legendary for its ineptitude: in 1913, he scored only 95 runs in 18 completed innings. After taking 0-134 at Blackheath, Carr asked to be excused from appearing for the county again that season, which effectively meant forever. Like many others, he returned from the war but not to cricket.

At Leyton that week, Lionel Tennyson left himself out of the Hampshire side to play Essex, so Alban Arnold, just down from Cambridge, batted in his place. Essex generally had the better of another rain-soaked draw, their opener Colin McIver scoring 113. Born in 1881 in Hong Kong, McIver had won Cambridge blues at cricket and football, played for the England amateur team who beat France in Paris by fifteen goals to nil, and was another one of those effortlessly talented all-round athletes who were so profuse in 1914. In the first weeks of the war, the Essex club would proudly publish a list of sixty-two current or former players serv-ing in the armed forces. Captain McIver of the Queen's West Surrey Regiment is shown as 'Wounded', although he survived to play first-class cricket until 1934, when he was 53. Six other members of the Essex XI of July 1914 are named on active duty and one, Captain Davies, had already fallen in action. Rifleman Paul

Hilleard, 12th London Regiment, comfortably topped the county's Second XI batting averages in 1914. *Wisden* considered him a 'great prospect'. He died at Ypres in April 1915, aged 21. A player named Harold Mead, a private in the Essex Regiment, is also given as 'Wounded'. Invalided home, he died in April 1921, aged 25. Mead's father Walter, known as the Essex Treasure, had taken 1,916 first-class wickets in a twenty-year career, which included one Test for England, bowling a variety of brisk-paced spin. In 1900, Mead senior was awarded a benefit, but, in an exceptionally wet summer, it realised only £137. Then his wife and infant child died, and he asked the Essex county chairman Charles Green, a shipowner, for a small increase in his winter wage. Green refused, accusing him of 'a grasping and unpatriotic attitude'. Mead missed two seasons' cricket as a result, but was eventually reinstated after writing his committee a letter of apology. He played on for Essex long enough to see his son join him in the side. After the war he lived in a small house at North Weald with his two surviving children, mother and widowed sister-in-law. Walter Mead died in 1954, aged 85, within a few days of his friend Colin McIver. As we have seen, Alban Arnold fell in action at the Somme. He was 23.

III

At the end of July 1914, bottom-placed Gloucestershire went up to Old Trafford for their regulation defeat by Lancashire. 'Gloucester practically lost the match on the first day as, in the face of a home total of 238, they had six of their best [*sic*] batsmen out for 66. From this disastrous start no recovery could be made', *Wisden* wrote. Much of the damage was done by Lancashire's medium-pacer Cecil 'Ciss' Parkin – another classic northern cricketer of his kind, being hawk-faced and possessing a certain earthy frankness. He was also a great entertainer when the mood struck him, and was known to perform conjuring tricks at otherwise dull moments in the outfield. As a 19-year-old, Parkin had played once for Yorkshire before it was discovered he had been born at Eaglescliffe, 50 yards outside the county boundary. He spent the next eight seasons atoning for the scandal in league and minor county cricket. Parkin made a belated but sensational debut for Lancashire against Leicestershire in July 1914, taking 14 wickets in the match. He finished the season top of the county bowling averages, but then lost what might have been his four best years to front-line infantry duty in the war. It was not until 1920, when he was 34, that Parkin finally became a full-time professional cricketer. He soon played ten Tests, but both his Lancashire and England careers ended abruptly when he publicly criticised their respective selection committees and the 'pitiful' wages they paid. After that, Parkin returned to the leagues.

Lancashire cricket as a whole was especially hard hit by the war. As well as first-team players like William Tyldesley, Harold Garnett and Alfred Hartley, the county club lost both its groundsman and his assistant, three other staff members and at least eight former employees. Old Trafford itself was taken over by the Red Cross, and over three years a hospital ward in the pavilion treated 2,867 patients. The local league sides were not exempt from the sacrifice. On 20 June 1914, the Nelson club proudly opened a new pavilion in the interval of their derby match against Colne. At least two of the party of nine visiting dignitaries and five of the twenty-two cricketers fell in the fighting in France. In September of that year, the press reported that the War Office had accepted an offer made by the mayor of Accrington, Captain John Harwood, to raise a complete battalion. When recruitment began, 104 men were accepted in the first two hours, and 'these included many of the best-known Lancastrian sporting names'. Two years later, it was reported that out of 720 'Accrington Pals' who took part in the first Somme offensive of July 1916, 584 were killed, wounded or missing. In January of the following year, a Lancashire and Durham club cricketer and miner named Peter Goggins was one of three British soldiers executed by firing squad for desertion. The chaplain who prayed with the condemned soldiers before their deaths remarked that he had never met three braver men. Goggins, of the Durham Light Infantry, was 23 years old.

But perhaps the most poignant cricket-related story locally was that of Gilbert Mackereth, a young insurance broker in 1914 who played as a flamboyant opening bat for several sides around his native Salford, and was commended for a 'spectacular ariel shot that rattled the tiles' on the new Nelson pavilion roof in a game early in August. Just a month later, he enlisted as a private with the Royal Fusiliers, also known as the Public Schools Battalion, before being commissioned in the Lancashire Fusiliers. In June 1917, Mackereth was awarded the MC for his action in rescuing a group of soldiers stranded under heavy fire during the Allied attack on Gricourt. He was later severely wounded in fighting at Cambrai, but asked to remain at the front rather than be sent home to England. After the war, Mackereth joined the diplomatic corps and eventually became British ambassador to Colombia from 1947 to 1953, being knighted for his services. He never lost his love of cricket and in retirement, in Spain, would 'start his day with a leisurely reading of the sports pages of the *Daily Telegraph*, and trawl backwards through the paper from there'. Mackereth died in San Sebastian in 1962, aged 69. Some forty-five years later, the local authorities placed a notice of eviction on his grave, claiming that the equivalent of £280 in back tax was owed on it. After a campaign by family and friends in Salford, Sir Gilbert's remains were brought home and buried in a garden of remembrance at the Fusilier Museum in Greater Manchester. He is thought to be the first veteran of the First World War to be repatriated to England since the burial of the Unknown Soldier at Westminster Abbey in 1920.

III

While the screw of events turned tighter in the last days of July 1914, organised cricket carried on even as the first players began hurriedly leaving their clubs to report to their local reserve units or other military posts. Pelham Warner and Frank Mann at Middlesex, Lionel Tennyson at Hampshire and Aubrey Sharp at Leicester were among the first of those to be listed as 'Absent' in their county scorebooks. But championship play continued. The rain saved Sussex from almost certain doom in a match against Northamptonshire at Hove, where the visitors' Denton twins scored 145 for the first wicket and their captain Sydney Smith added 177 in only three and a half hours. The Trinidadian-born Smith was unique in playing representative cricket for England, the West Indies and New Zealand. An early prototype of Garry Sobers, it was said 'it was hard to set a field for him, such was his genius for collecting runs', while he could also bowl, field and captain equally well, and to the manner born. Playing away against Warwickshire in July 1914, he took 4 wickets in 4 balls with a variety of left-arm spin fast enough to include a regular bouncer. When the war came, Smith moved with his family to Auckland, where he continued to appear in first-class cricket and lived to be 82.

As the Royal Artillery and Royal Engineers teams were playing at Lord's, a mile or two to the north the endgame was now starting for Albert Trott. Trott, whom we last saw hobbling in his slippers up and down the streets of Willesden, had been the golden all-round man of cricket only a decade earlier. Just a few career highlights seem to make the case that he was the Ian Botham of his day, the most ebullient of men, if sadly denied the sort of commercial opportunities to be available to Botham and a few others in the 1980s. Early in the 1894/95 series with England, the Australian captain George Giffen 'was commiserating with Harry Trott, who was at the time doing nothing. He replied, "Don't mind me, but keep an eye on that young brother of mine. You'll find him a good one before the season is over".' Before long, Giffen duly found himself sizing up a powerfully built, dark-haired 21-year-old whose square shoulders were matched by the determined set of his jaw. In his Test debut at Adelaide, Albert Trott scored 38 and 72, both times not out, and took 8 cheap wickets with his slinging, round-arm action in the England second innings, effectively lighting the touchpaper on a professional career that took him from Australia to London, where Pelham Warner's view was that he was 'the best all-round player alive now; the head of my profession'. It has to be said that Trott's early promise was only fitfully realised, but in full cry he could be quite devastating. In the English season of 1899, he stood on top of the cricketing world like no one else since Grace. In one glorious patch that midsummer, Trott took 12 wickets and scored innings of 123 and 35 not out for Middlesex against Sussex at Lord's; took 8 wickets in the next match against Kent; 13 wickets against Leicestershire; 11 wickets against Nottinghamshire; 9 wickets against Cambridge University; 11 wickets against Oxford University; 8 wickets again against Kent; 11 wickets for MCC against Worcestershire; a mere 5 wickets against Sussex; and 13 wickets against Surrey. That brought him up to the events of 31 July, when he hit the ball from Monty Noble onto the back slope of the new Lord's pavilion roof and into the garden of Phil Need, the dressing room attendant: in some estimates, a carry of 130 yards. Trott finished that season with 1,175 first-class runs and 239 wickets. He also held 40 catches. Though obviously not beyond the reach of flattery, Trott struck his countless admirers as the most natural and unspoiled of men. 'Following this, he went to the top of the tree', *Wisden* said. 'Thanks to his bowling, his hard hitting, and brilliant fielding, and also his strong personality, he became for the time more popular at Lord's than any other professional.'

Yet Trott's fame did not spare him the periods of depression that accompanied him in retirement. He quickly became a man for whom every day was the same as the one before it and the one that would follow. Trott's business acumen was considered modest, and he had thrown money away when he had it. It seems somehow appropriate that he should have undermined his own finances in his benefit game. He umpired for a few seasons, but health and cash troubles multiplied, and the stories about him invariably touched on his taste for the bottle. In time, Trott became one of those victims of his own fame who accomplish all they can early in life and go downhill from there. The truth was that he had lost all interest in sport and all capacity for enjoyment. A profile in the *Daily Telegraph* said that 'a more pathetic figure of a man in later days than him it would be difficult to imagine'.

On 20 July 1914, Trott was admitted to St Mary's Hospital, Paddington, and put under the care of the royal physician Sir John Broadbent. He was complaining of insomnia, and had been suffering from headaches, swollen gums and a difficulty in swallowing. His voice had become increasingly hoarse. Nine days later, against medical advice, Trott discharged himself and took a taxi home to his lodgings. He was short of funds, so the hospital paid his fare to get him back to Willesden. On Thursday 30 July, he told his landlady, Mrs Crowhurst, that he could not go through another night like the last. In the early hours of the next morning, Albert Trott shot himself. It was the anniversary of his famous hit at Lord's. He was 41.

After twenty years of professional competition, Trott died with just £4 to his name. He had written out his will on the back of a laundry ticket, leaving his landlady his cricket flannels and England cap in lieu of rent. There were no obvious signs of mourning when, a few hours later, the Cheltenham and Haileybury school sides began a two-day match under heavy skies at Lord's, although MCC later took responsibility for Trott's funeral, a sparsely attended affair, held in the rain at Willesden New Cemetery.

6

BLOOD-RED SUNSET
OVER THE THAMES

It is part of the irony of the dark high summer of 1914 that few ordinary Britons had any inkling of an imminent threat of war that might directly involve themselves until almost the last moment, and that by the time they did so events had already conspired to transform Germany's idea for a lightning-fast attack on France from an option into an inevitability. The start of hostilities came as a far greater shock to London than it did to Berlin, St Petersburg, Vienna or Paris. Things began in earnest only on Friday 31 July, when the financial markets panicked. Over the bank holiday weekend, military personnel on leave were recalled to their units, the band of the Royal Irish Rifles received its immediate mobilisation orders while in the middle of a concert at Tunbridge Wells, and Edward Grey told the German ambassador that any violation of Belgium 'would make it difficult for the Government here to adopt an attitude of friendly neutrality'. Germany's failure to pledge that it would not enter Belgium, Grey had added, 'has caused an unfortunate impression'. The normally imperturbable Foreign Secretary spoke these words with some heat, it was later reported, 'taut and shrill with emotion, the Adam's apple dancing up and down his narrow neck'. On the fourth Sunday after the teenaged assassin had finally succeeded in firing two shots into the royal car at Sarajevo, German cavalry units began moving into Luxembourg to seize bridges and rail lines leading into both Belgium and France. In London, the paper-boys shouted 'War Special!' and sold large-scale maps of Europe, helpfully marking the 'contestant nations' in red and black. According to the *Daily Telegraph* journalist Philip Gibbs, soon to become a noted war correspondent, 'in Fleet Street, editors were emerging from little dark rooms with a new excitement in eyes that had grown tired with proof-correcting … it was a chance of seeing the greatest drama in life with real properties, real corpses, real blood, real horrors with a devilish thrill in them.'

On 31 July, the schools match at Lord's began in a steady drizzle in front of a crowd of over 5,000, perhaps an indication of how many people tried to cling to normality. Play was eventually abandoned owing to torrential rain on the second day. Cheltenham's opening bat Cyril Hillier managed to enlist in the infantry that winter; wounded in action in January 1915, he died the following month in a military hospital, incredibly still aged only 17. Eighteen months later, his team-mate Hubert Du Boulay, of the Wiltshire Regiment, was struck by German artillery fire directed on his position at the Somme. He had helped another man to safety before he succumbed to his wounds. He was 19. *Wisden* had said of him while at Cheltenham, 'for a boy of his age he is a batsman far above the ordinary, and it is not too much to say that with average luck he might develop into a great crick-eter'. Cheltenham's opening bowler Norman Birtwistle was turned down on the grounds of age when he first tried to join the army in September 1914. A year later he was commissioned in the Hussars, won the MC, but died in fighting around Amiens in 1918 at the age of 21.

For Haileybury, 17-year-old Gordon Thorne had carried off the batting honours at Lord's by scoring 123 runs for once out. Within a month he had vol-unteered for the army, and later spent the best part of two years fighting with the Cambridgeshire Regiment in the blood-soaked ground around Cambrai. Lieutenant Colonel Thorne survived the war and played his only first-class match for the Army against Oxford University at the Parks in 1927. In March 1942 he was listed as missing presumed dead while commanding his regiment at Singapore. It was his 45th birthday. Thorne's Haileybury teammate Geoffrey Butler, of the Lancashire Fusiliers, fell in action at Ypres in May 1917, aged 20.

While the young cricketers ran from the field in the rain at Lord's, ministers were now finally confronted with the accelerating pace of aggression in Europe. The new French premier René Viviani admitted he was in a state of 'frightful nervous tension' which, as his War Minister described it, 'became a permanent condition during the month of August'. The French naval secretary, a medical doctor with no previous government experience, appears to have had a nervous breakdown and had to be abruptly replaced. Viviani later remarked that the war seemed to him to have 'come like thunder out of a clear summer sky', and that until almost the last moment 'the French people and the newspapers they read were preoccupied' with other affairs. Just as in London there had been the Irish crisis, in Paris there was that defining example of 'what men mean when they speak of France's decadence and frivolity', the Caillaux scandal.

In early 1914, Joseph Caillaux, a former socialist premier and the current minister of finance, had launched a bid to become the head of government again. Among other things, he favoured the introduction of an income tax, and took a nuanced approach to his country's alliance with tsarist Russia, both 'not uncontroversial' subjects, he later noted. During the course of the campaign, Caillaux's first wife, whom he had divorced after he entered into an affair with her successor, made available to Gaston Calmette, the editor of the *Le Figaro* newspaper, letters her husband had sent her in 1901 when she was still his mistress. Though not especially salacious, they provided what Calmette called a 'comic interlude', and suggested that the man who again wished to govern France had at one time been an enthusiastic womaniser. Caillaux's present wife, Henriette, was not amused. On the afternoon of 16 March 1914 she put on her most elegant dress, went by chauffeured limousine to the offices of *Le Figaro*, withdrew a small pistol from her purse and fired six shots into Calmette's chest, killing him instantly. When the police arrived, Madame Caillaux surrendered her weapon, but declined to enter their waiting car. She preferred to travel with her own chauffeur, she said, an arrangement the police allowed. While the subsequent trial took many *bouleversements* (at one stage, two of the three presiding judges challenged each other to a duel), its central issue was whether Henriette Caillaux had committed pre-meditated murder, or if her 'uncontrollable female emotions', as the defence insisted, had resulted in a *crime passionel*. Joseph Caillaux resigned his ministerial office on the day following Calmette's death; since he went on to become the leader of the peace party in the French Assembly, and ultimately to be found guilty of treason for advocating a negotiated treaty with Germany, it is a reasonable counterfactual to ask what might have happened had he, and not the ineffectual Viviani, held power in August 1914. On 29 July, a chivalrous jury found the defendant not guilty. The next day, the Caillauxs had vanished from the newspapers, and the headlines suddenly announced that Europe was on the brink of war.

On 31 July, Prime Minister Viviani returned from a state visit to Russia to find Paris 'had awoken from a dream ... Everywhere the crowds were jostling and all at this dark and dangerous hour were shouting, "*Vive la France!*"' Later that night, a young man shot dead the pacifist leader Jean Jaures as he ate dinner in a Montmartre cafe. Had Joseph Caillaux come to office, he had announced his intention to make Jaures his foreign minister. As at Sarajevo, assassination blocked the better road. At 8 a.m. the next morning, France's army commander General Joseph Joffre came to the War Office to demand action from the government. 'Joffre looked like Santa Claus and gave an impression of benevolence and naiveté – two qualities not noticeably part of his character', it has been said. At 4 p.m. the same day the first mobilisation posters went up in the streets of Paris. Five minutes later Germany announced her own general mobilisation. None of this went down particularly well in Belgium, whose neutrality had been guaranteed by all the major powers since 1839.

In London, where the Cabinet met exceptionally on a Saturday, the First Lord of the Admiralty Winston Churchill wanted a full mobilisation of the fleet but was opposed by a group led by the Chancellor of the Exchequer, David Lloyd George. Running his finger over a map of Europe to trace a line he thought would be the German route through Belgium, Lloyd George remarked that it would only be a 'little violation'. That afternoon the German ambassador Lichnowsky cabled his government with assurances about British neutrality which he mistakenly believed Edward Grey had given him. At 6 p.m. that evening the Kaiser sent a 'Dear George' message to Buckingham Palace to confirm the arrangement. But, as the king wrote in his cabled reply, 'I think there must be some misunderstanding … no such position [has] ever been stated'. A day of crossed wires and diplomatic turmoil ended with Churchill entertaining a small group of friends including Max Aitken, the future Lord Beaverbrook, to dinner at the Admiralty. At around 10 p.m. the party was settling down to a hand of bridge when a government messenger brought in a large red official box. Churchill took out a key and opened it. It contained a single sheet of paper, on which was written: 'War declared by Germany on Russia.' Taking leave of his guests, Churchill changed out of his dinner jacket and walked across the road to Downing Street, 'looking like a man going to a well-accustomed job', Aitken remembered.

Perhaps unsurprisingly, the Cabinet was again in session the following morning. This time, Churchill was given full authority to mobilise the navy. This same force would intervene, Grey later announced, should Germany attack the undefended French Channel coast. At the same time, he stressed, 'that pledge does not bind us to go to war with Germany' and there was 'no question as yet' of sending land forces to the Continent. In the face of even this guarded response, two Liberal ministers resigned. Asquith believed that the dissolution of the government now had to be faced, and that 'a good three-quarters of our own party' in the Commons 'are for absolute non-interference at any price'. In Paris, the government enquired if Britain would consider sending over even two divisions for 'moral effect'. Grey, his under-taker persona again intact, replied that to do so 'would entail the maximum of risk to them and produce the minimum of good', and thus 'would not be entertained'. In Berlin the Foreign Office announced prematurely that France and Russia had already opened hostilities, and noted that French agents had been detained near Basel for sending carrier pigeons to Paris with details of German troop movements. Italy as yet declined to honour her treaty of alliance with Germany and Austria, as neither country was under attack. The Italian War Minister added that full mobi-lisation would be difficult to achieve in any event because his troops did not have enough uniforms. That evening in London Edward Grey had just settled down to dinner with friends when, once again, a messenger appeared with a red dispatch box. It contained a telegram which, Grey told his guests, warned that 'Germany was about to invade Belgium'. An 'intense silence' followed. While his party dispersed, Grey took a car to Downing Street, showed the cable to Asquith and recommended a full mobilisation. Asquith agreed.

III

As the Foreign Secretary addressed the House of Commons on the crisis the following afternoon, bank holiday Monday, a crowd of 8,650 sat in sweltering heat at Lord's to watch two more teams of schoolboys play cricket.

'It was curious,' Grey himself later wrote, 'how at this hour, the normal and unhurried poetry of English life went on.' The few official public remarks on the situation up until then, Churchill felt, could easily have come 'from the secretary of a firm of provincial lawyers reading the minutes of the last meeting'. To the schoolmaster and future cricket scholar Harry Altham:

> The outbreak of the war will always be associated in my mind with Lord's. I was up there watching the Lord's Schools v. The Rest match, and can remember buying an evening paper on the ground and reading in the stop-press column the opening sentences of the speech Grey was then making in the Commons, and subsequently travelling down from Waterloo to Esher, where I was staying with the Howell brothers, and seeing in the blood-red sunset over the Thames an omen of the years to come.

A case can be made for saying that that match at Lord's was as good a symbol as any of how some of Britain's most gifted, and seemingly privileged young athletes would be cut down in the spring of life. *The Times* later thought the game had 'the peculiar character of that summer written all over it'. It certainly personified the point about how the old men make the wars and the young ones fight them. While the politicians spoke of troop movements and ultimatums, it was said of the cricket that the gilded youth in flannels 'disported themselves in the sunshine', as a 'graceful throng of ladies, elegantly attired, added a picturesque brilliancy to the old ground'. Five of the boys who took part in the match lost their lives in the war. Angus Pearson, of St Paul's School, commissioned in the Royal Fusiliers, the winner of chestfuls of medals for athletics and said in his regimental history to have been 'as gifted in mind as in body', fell on the first day of the Somme offensive, aged 18. Dallas Veitch of Westminster headed his school's batting averages in

1914, when in the same week he scored 118 against Radley and 105 against the Free Foresters. He died in fighting around Ypres just over a year afterwards. Rex Sherwell, of Tonbridge, joined the Royal Flying Corps and was lost over the Salient in March 1918, aged 21. George Whitehead of Clifton, also in the Royal Flying Corps, died at Menin in October 1918, aged 23. In the last summer of peace he had scored an unbeaten innings of 259 against Liverpool and had a trial for Kent. An Old Cliftonian wrote of him in *Wisden* as:

> A perfect flower of the public schools. He was not limited to athletics only, great though he was in this respect. Intellectually he was far above the average and was as happy with a good book as when he was scoring centuries. His ideas were singularly high and though gentle and broad-minded, he always stood uncompromisingly for all that was clean ... Clifton has lost more than 500 of her sons in the war. She is proud of every one of them, but of none more than this very perfect gentleman.

Don Denton of Wellingborough also fought in the war. As we have seen, despite the loss of a leg he was later able to appear for Northants, batting with a runner. His teammate at Lord's, Geoffrey Eden, had three cricket-playing first cousins named Jack, Nicholas and Anthony. The first two of them died in the war and the third of them became prime minister. Shortly after leaving the ground, Harry Altham volunteered for service and survived nearly four years on the front with the 60th Rifles, winning the DSO and MC. One of his young hosts that weekend at Esher was John Howell, who had opened the batting for the Rest at Lord's, scoring 160 runs for once out. *Wisden* wrote of him while at Repton that it was 'not too much to say that he is potentially an England star'. At the end of August 1914, Howell also volunteered, and by Christmas was commissioned as a 2nd lieutenant in the King's Royal Corps. Neither Altham nor Howell's family ever saw him again. He was killed during a night patrol near Hooge in September 1915, aged 20.

On Monday 3 August, Kent began a significant county match with Sussex at Canterbury. On both sides of the boundary, it was a game of two halves. Reading the spectators' diaries and published accounts of the first day's play is a bit like looking through the pinhole of a scenic souvenir charm at some late Edwardian garden party. There is an innocence about the newspaper reports as archaic as the actual press facilities on the ground. There were 'marching bands and decorous applause … parasols and fans, and vendors selling straw boaters to strolling Kentish vicars', said the *Globe*. 'Not an inflamed crowd', as Colin Blythe described them. 'Nice.' Between innings, schoolboys set up stumps and knocked tennis balls to each other, and a black-suited salesman from the One and All Horticultural Company hawked packets of lawn sand, 'guaranteed to improve the colour and growth of fine grasses' at 6d each, or 2s for the 7lb bag. Temperatures were in the mid-eighties. No one mentioned the war. The first two days were 'exquisite', *Wisden* wrote. 'But, hostilities being declared on the Tuesday, the Canterbury Week was shorn of most of its social adornments.' Overnight, the brass bands vanished, along with both the military personnel and most other men between the ages of 18 and 40, and a gala performance by the Old Stagers at the Theatre Royal was cancelled. A grand summer ball to be held on 5 August was also called off 'due to the unfavourable international situation', as were the planned fireworks and 'electrical illuminations'. Dover became an armed camp, so Kent's games scheduled there the following week were transferred to Canterbury 'and both resulted in heavy financial loss'. 'It was like walking out into someone's funeral', Blythe said.

The actual cricket at Canterbury shared some of the same downhill trajectory as the ground's social functions. Sussex and Kent both scored heavily in the first innings. It rained on the third morning, immediately after the declaration of war, and to Robb Johnson, a London bank clerk, one of the few remaining male spectators in front of the pavilion, 'the place was so quiet you could hear the umpires' footsteps as they walked over the grass to survey the wicket'. When play resumed at 2.30 p.m., Blythe and Woolley took 4 wickets apiece and Sussex declared at 78-8. Kent were set 172 to win in just over two hours, and failed by 35 runs. We last saw Ken Woodroffe of Sussex playing for Cambridge at Lord's before joining the army. *Wisden* had said of him:

> He is really fast, and can make the ball turn from the off on nearly any wicket. His action is a high and easy one, and, being tall, he often makes the ball get up very quickly. Moreover, what is most important, missed chances do not appear to worry him unduly, and he keeps trying all the time.

The Kent match was to be Woodroffe's last. Commissioned into the Rifle Brigade in September 1914, he fell in action during a gas and artillery attack on the Ypres ramparts nine months later. Woodroffe's Sussex teammate George Street survived the war, but died in a motorcycle crash on his return home. By a morbid coincidence, a motorcycle also featured in a later tragedy involving the Sussex all-rounder Vallance Jupp, who scored a brisk 64 on the first morning's play against Kent at Canterbury. Jupp fought with gallantry in the war with both the Royal Engineers and the newly formed Royal Air Force, and eventually returned to play cricket for England. One winter night in 1935, his car was in collision with a motorcycle, killing the latter's pillion passenger. There was some talk, never fully substantiated, of one or both of the drivers being under the influence. *Wisden* and most of the cricket press discreetly passed over the fact, but Jupp was convicted of manslaughter and sentenced to nine months in prison.

The weather also played a major role in Derbyshire's home match that week against Essex. On the Monday, the visitors 'batted steadily, with very little enterprise, to score 238 for 7 wickets'. That night 'a thunderstorm of Biblical proportions fell over Derby', and on Tuesday the players went out 'bundled in sweaters, [in] dry but autumnal conditions'. The home team was dismissed twice in a little over four hours, and lost by an innings and 131 runs. Johnny Douglas took 9-62 in the match and Bert Tremlin 10-52, including a hat-trick. The Derbyshire side was to assume an 'increasingly novel' look during the rest of the season. 'Naturally,' *Wisden* said, 'in so sporting a county many of the cricketers enrolled themselves in different capacities for the War. Capt. Baggallay of course is with the 11th Hussars, and Chapman is assisting in the Government Remount Department. Curgenven, Hughes-Hallett, GL Jackson, Taylor, the secretary, Blacklidge, the coach, and two or three of the professionals are assisting in various units.' Lieutenant Colonel Richard Baggallay survived the fighting at the Somme, won the DSO and MC and returned to lead Derbyshire in three matches in the 1919 season, before being appointed Military Secretary to the Viceroy of Ireland. While in office, he survived at least four terrorist attempts on his life. At the time of his eventual death in 1975, aged 91, he was the last remaining pre-First World War county captain.

III

'What happens now?' Winston Churchill asked Edward Grey as they left the Commons together in the early evening of 3 August. 'Now,' said Grey, 'we shall send them a sharp note to stop the invasion of Belgium within twenty-four hours.' In fact, the British cable was delivered in Berlin only at 7 p.m. on 4 August, and gave Germany five hours in which to reply. She never did so, although her Chancellor, von Bethmann, expressed indignation at 'this hypocritical harping on Belgium, which was not the thing that had driven England into war … all for just a word – "neutrality" – just for a scrap of paper'. Unsurprisingly, there was a febrile mood on the streets of Berlin that night, where rumours followed one another in quick succession. At one point a large crowd gathered in front of the Japanese embassy, on the basis of a report that that country had declared war against Russia. A Reichstag deputy named Hans Peter Hanssen wrote: 'the mob rushed away carrying everybody with it and soon besieged the Embassy. "Long live Japan! Long live Japan!" people shouted impetuously until the Japanese ambassador finally appeared and, perplexed, stammered his thanks for this unexpected homage'. Two weeks later, Japan declared war on Germany. There were neither demonstrators nor reporters on hand the following morning at London's Victoria station when Germany's ambassador Lichnowsky and his staff took their leave on the boat-train. An English-born colleague named Evelyn Blucher was struck by the 'sadness and bitterness' of the party, who had 'no enthusiasm for the war forced upon them by their officials at home'.

In the midst of this cricket rumbled on, while the Germans pounded Liège and in Britain Churchill remarked that 'the rush to [mobilise] turned frenzied and profound'. The 64-year-old Lord Kitchener, hurriedly taken off a Channel steamer about to return to Egypt, where he was proconsul, stunned the Cabinet on his appointment as War Minister by announcing that the hostilities would last not three months, but at least three years. 'We must be prepared to put a professional army of several millions into the field', he concluded. Kitchener barely bothered to conceal his contempt for the fourteen divisions of Territorials, whom he regarded rather harshly as a lot of 'gentlemen cricketers' who were 'pleasant enough chaps [but] useless as soldiers'. On 7 August, the first of the famous 'Your Country Needs YOU' posters went up in the streets of London. By the end of the month, roughly a third of a million men had signed up to fight. In most parts of Britain, recruiting stations were crammed to overflowing for the rest of the summer. There was a ghastly pantomime in many of them, where young men, grinning, stood on tiptoe in order to appear taller and pass muster. One sub-office in St Martin's Lane, central London, was so crowded that cars could not pass by, and the noise of the 'milling hordes' at the door struck Robb Johnson as 'a lowing … as deep and uniform as that within an abattoir'. The Sportsman's Battalion of the Royal Fusiliers advertised in *The Times* for men, 'upper and middle-class only'; there was a non-refundable application fee of £2, and candidates were asked to present themselves at 'Lord's Cricket Ground, N.W., where there may subsequently be the prospect of a game'. So successful was the recruitment drive as a whole that early in September the War Office was obliged to raise the minimum height standard to 5ft 7in (though as military reverses followed, this was hurriedly reduced to 5ft 5in and ultimately to 5ft 3in). Adding to the air of drama of the first day of war, in a raging thunderstorm, the streets of London were also full of Americans ordered out of Germany and fleeing from the Continent generally, many of them standing in open-topped taxis that raced through the streets, waving handkerchiefs and shouting 'Good luck!' Other cars flew round Piccadilly, Robb Johnson wrote, 'with English and French colours fluttering and klaxons sounding. Large troops of young men marched here and there, singing and cheering. So deafening was the noise that it seemed the Kaiser could not fail to hear it in Berlin.'

In the round of Championship cricket matches that began on 3 August, a crowd of 15,000 saw Jack Hobbs hit his double hundred in even time for Surrey against Nottinghamshire at the Oval. On the second afternoon, a telegram recalling the visitors' young captain Arthur Carr to his regiment was taken out to him as he batted. 'I'll have one more over', he said, before slogging a ball to the outfield. There were similar call-ups elsewhere on the circuit. The scorebook for Leicestershire's second innings in their match at Northampton reads 'Mr AT Sharp ... absent ...o.' Perhaps as a result, the home team won the game by just 4 runs. On the morning of 5 August, 24-year-old Aubrey Sharp had packed his bags and returned to his Territorial unit. Commissioned into the Machine Gun Corps, Sharp survived three years service at the front and eventually died in a car accident, aged 83. At Edgbaston, Percy Jeeves took 7-52 and 2-7 for Warwickshire against Worcestershire, who on the last day lacked the services of Geoffrey and Neville Foster. Both brothers were to fight at the Somme, but returned to England after the war and lived to be 86 and 87 respectively.

At Old Trafford, Yorkshire won a rain-soaked Roses Match of low scores. Since the two sides had last met at Hull just nine days earlier, the prospect of a European war had gone from strangely improbable to inevitable. There was a 'Northern air of stoicism about the proceedings', it was reported. For the Yorkshire captain Sir Archibald White, the unexpected Austrian ultimatum was not a great deal worse than a mild impertinence. 'Like others, I underestimated the sense of rising tension and the dreadful tide of events that followed', he wrote. Following the Roses Match, Sir Archibald would not play another organised cricket game for six years. On the morning of 8 August, he joined his regiment at Colchester. Although he survived the fighting at Ypres and the Somme, White would appear just twice more for Yorkshire after the war.

Meanwhile, Lancashire's captain Albert Hornby had been summoned to the War Office early on the Monday morning of 3 August, and would go from organising army remounts to leading an infantry attack in the shambles of Ypres just two months later. Although Hornby lived for a further thirty-eight years, he never again played a first-class cricket match. His colleague Archie MacLaren enlisted in October 1914, aged 42, and spent most of the next four years recruiting around Manchester. The 43-year-old former Yorkshire and England captain Stanley Jackson, having served in the Boer War, now raised and commanded his own regiment. He survived both the war and later being shot at point-blank range by a disaffected student, and died in London, aged 76, following a road accident.

Perhaps one of the few cricketers as yet unaffected by the events of August 1914 was Jack Hobbs, who later wrote that he scored his bank holiday double hundred 'with never a thought of war'. If so, his detachment was to be short-lived. Later on that same Monday evening, Hobbs was one of the thousands of people who lined the Mall as the Lord Mayor's coach rattled by taking Asquith to Buckingham Palace for the meeting which sanctioned the proclamation of war, when *The Times* spoke of the 'many hurrahs shouted in the street', and Osbert Sitwell heard 'the great crowd roar for its own death'. Two days later, Hobbs was told that the army had requisitioned the Oval, and that his scheduled benefit game against Kent could either be postponed 'until normal affairs resume' or be transferred to Lord's. The fact that he chose the latter suggests he suspected the war might be prolonged. *Wisden* records that the Lord's match 'did not yield anything like the sum which could have been confidently expected in other circumstances'. Hobbs was then 31, and we will return to the contentious matter of how he occupied the next four years. The cold figures show that he scored sixty-five first-class centuries in his career before the war, and more than twice as many afterwards. Yet Hobbs himself wrote, 'I was never the same player after 1918 – I couldn't be, I couldn't play the strokes. I was too old.'

Hobbs was not alone in his nonchalance towards the events of Tuesday 4 August, which he saw primarily as a 'day of work'. The behaviour of several other cricketers, and many ordinary citizens, was similarly disengaged. On the evening that the Belgians began destroying the bridges over the Meuse and the Germans, crossing the river on pontoons, announced their arrival by the shooting not only of unarmed civilians but of Belgian priests, Percy Fender left the Oval and took a cab to his family's stationery and printing firm in Southwark, to discuss what it all meant. 'The air of unreality continued for some time,' Fender said; 'the prevailing mood was that life should continue normally as far as possible. Things might resolve themselves in a week or two.' A few miles away, Lionel Tennyson was enjoying three days' leave at his flat in Piccadilly and idly thinking about accepting an invitation to play for the Green Jackets XI that weekend, when the night-porter arrived with his recall papers. 'The very clear impression was that [the war] came as a sort of unexpected and on the whole quite interesting away match, which might last a few weeks.' Other military personnel playing golf or cricket over the period 4–5 August were summoned by telegraph boys on bicycles or the waving of white handkerchiefs. A maid named Hilda French went up from Surrey to Waterloo station on 5 August, which she found packed both with soldiers and those waiting to enlist. 'They all said, "Oh, let's go and join up and have a bit of fun. It won't last long".' Later in the week, she watched as 'girls handed bunches of flowers through a window' as a troop train began to roll away, the crowd cheered, and a band played 'God Save the King'. Twenty-year-old Harold Macmillan expressed a popular mood when he spoke of the 'trance-like atmosphere, combin[ing] detachment and excitement', among many young men. 'We thought it would be over by Christmas', he said.

For some, the war was a godsend. It clearly gave them a sense of purpose and, more than that, a sense of belonging. Regimental life was a substitute home, where food, clothing, accommodation and the comradeship of one's fellows were all provided. It was an attractive proposition even to many of those already in reasonably fulfilling work. After finishing the cricket season with match figures of 9–115 against Gloucestershire, Percy Fender talked it over again with his family, enlisted in the Inns of Court regiment, and was later gazetted a lieutenant in the Royal Fusiliers. He was not the only young man to find life in uniform at least initially 'on the whole preferable to the alternative. As one walked rifle on shoulder through the streets of London, men raised their hats and pretty girls smiled, or frequently paused to talk at length. It was a dreamlike but pleasant thing.'

The call to arms came not only in a heady atmosphere of patriotic fervour, but also as an opportunity for perhaps tens of thousands of older recruits whose options in life had narrowed. On the whole, these were men less in the thrall of emotional delirium, or who were elated by the prospect of war, but who saw the army as a fresh start, or somewhere to escape from a life of pointless labour. The authorities also soon appreciated that men would enlist more readily if they could be sure of serving with their friends, neighbours or teammates. A total of 172 such Pals Battalions of infantry were raised on that basis, plus eighty-four units of artillery and forty-eight of engineers – perhaps 250,000 men in all.

The arrangements for housing, feeding and drilling the nation's new soldiers were overstretched by the rush to the recruiting offices. Prior to August 1914, there was barracks accommodation in Great Britain for no more than 160,000 troops – clearly a shortfall at a time when men were joining up at the rate of 10,000 a day. Overnight, schools and other public buildings were commandeered, and in the week of 10 August the War Office began to send out notices under the Defence of the Realm Act to the authorities at several first-class cricket grounds. The Oval, as we have seen, was requisitioned just in time to play havoc with the arrangements for Hobbs's benefit match, although the army moved out again three weeks later. Elsewhere, cricket pavilions and spectator stands served as staff headquarters, housed wireless-instruction and small-arms training classes, and soon accommodated thousands of those invalided back from the front. The Essex committee used their ground at Leyton for a variety of patriotic causes, while in Kent 'the field at Canterbury [was to] be lent free of charge to soldiers stationed in the neighbourhood both for matches and practice'. Over the next four years there were regular military drills on the playing areas at Nottingham, Leicester, Bristol and Derby. At Lord's there were not only Territorial units to be found sleeping on iron cots without 'biscuits' – army slang for barrack mattresses – in the members' library and elsewhere in the pavilion, but the powerful aroma of military-cooking classes emanating from somewhere under the Long Room.

Perhaps typical of the crowd who stood in the streets of central London on the nights of 3 and 4 August, to feel themselves somehow nearer the heart of the drama (if eclipsing most of them at cricket) was a fair-haired 33-year-old named Henry Keigwin, a scholar-athlete of St Paul's School and Cambridge who had returned from a farm in Rhodesia just a few days earlier. While never of the very top flight as a first-class cricketer, Keigwin had been a student prodigy. Going in to open the batting with his brother Richard for Peterhouse College against Fitzwilliam at Cambridge in April 1904, he shared an unbeaten partnership of 318. Nine days later, the same pair added an unbeaten stand of 244. Henry Keigwin later played first-class cricket for Essex, the Gentlemen and Scotland, which he combined with a career as an organ scholar, composer and performer, an author of learned articles on everything from medieval choral styles to Highland salmon-fishing, and latterly as Master of Music at Trinity College, Glenalmond. A Cambridge contemporary named Keir Ramsey wrote of him:

> Sometimes nature runs riot in her gifts and produces a very king of men, who seems almost unfairly poised. The best judges who saw 'HK' in his brief prime rank him in the company of the great varsity athletes, a paragon of grace, and of intellect and character. There were no earthly attainments beyond his reach.

Immediately war was declared, Henry Keigwin applied for service and went to France as a 2nd lieutenant with the Lancashire Fusiliers. He was killed in September 1916, leading a charge on Thiepval near the Somme. *Wisden* lists the names of seventy-eight other active players who were lost in that month.

III

In Southampton, a match between Hampshire and Middlesex which had initially produced all the wet and tedious traits of most county cricket in early August 1914 finished with some combative hitting by Phil Mead of Hampshire and England. Having destroyed the game's apparently set course with a whirlwind, unbeaten 97, in the end Mead had to be content with a draw after monsoon rain settled in on the third afternoon. Immediately stumps were drawn, Middlesex's captain Pelham Warner reported back for duty with his regiment. By the end of the week, Warner's teammates Bill Robertson and Frank Mann had followed his example, and Middlesex were soon finding it hard to put a full XI into the field. 'The declaration of War quite upset the county's plans', *Wisden* noted. On the Saturday morning of 8 August, the Middlesex secretary cabled his opposite number in Yorkshire to cancel a game set to begin in Sheffield the following Monday. 'Later that day, however, it was found that a good side could be raised, so the original arrangement was adhered to', to quote *Wisden* again. The improvised Middlesex team arrived at the ground just twenty minutes before the scheduled start, but they put up a spirited fight – needing no more than 86 to win, Yorkshire got home with only 2 wickets in hand.

There was an even tighter finish at Bristol, in the game between Gloucestershire and Somerset – two sides of relatively modest pretensions who nevertheless provided a rich and often eccentric contest. Thirteen of the players were amateurs, and Gilbert Jessop arrived at the ground half an hour late for the start, still clad in a dinner jacket. Memory would recall him 'very ruffled-looking, his shoulders hunched, cap at a precarious angle … He eventually moved on to the field at a laconic pace and within minutes had taken a smart catch and come on to bowl'; he took 4-34 in the innings. Whether as a result of war fears, the rain or general apathy, the hoped-for bank holiday crowds never fully materialised. 'The support given by the public was very small', *Wisden* said of the Gloucestershire season as a whole. 'So far from helping the eleven in the hour of need, the good people of Bristol studiously kept away from the matches at Ashley Down … The gates during the season amounted to only £760 as compared with an average of £1,230 for the previous five years.' At the end of a low-scoring match, Gloucester were set just 77 to win, and characteristically came to the brink of self-destruction with a series of ill-fated slogs and run-outs. The Somerset keeper Harry Chidgey almost went berserk when, after bringing off a smart leg-side take and removing the bails, the umpires denied his prolonged appeal for both a catch and a stumping. By now the sparse but increasingly vocal crowd was 'not reluctant to give out a choice selection of verbal analysis', and the game ended in an atmosphere that became noticeably more tense and partisan after the home team's number eleven, Charlie Parker, had been struck by a bouncer. Gloucester finally got home by 1 wicket, to record their only Championship victory of the season.

On 6 August, the MCC issued a statement saying that 'no good purpose can be served at the moment by cancelling matches', and that 'aspects of normal life' should continue for as long and as far as possible. They already had fewer cricketers than just a few days before with whom to share these convictions. A total of 210 past or current first-class players would sign up for various forms of military duty, and the matches beginning on 10 August had a distinctly makeshift feel to them. Apart from Surrey's enforced move to Lord's, there was the unfamiliar look to Middlesex's side against Yorkshire, while at Hove Leicestershire called up 20-year-old Gordon Salmon and 19-year-old William Berridge for the tie against Sussex, among other expedients. Three years later, a grave would be dug for Salmon at a dressing-station near Arras, so severe were wounds he sustained to his chest and arm, but he returned to play first-class cricket after the war. As well as the gaps being left by recruitment, heavy rain continued to affect many matches played in the first half of August, and on 8 August – while the first units of the BEF were assembling for embarkation at Southampton – the temperature in the south-east reached only 58°F. At Lord's, an MCC *v*. London Clubs game was abandoned as a draw after rain fell incessantly on the second day. Watching this melancholy scene from the pavilion, MCC's acting secretary John Shuter would remember Lord Hawke's words: 'we shall throw the Germans back, we shall expel them from Belgium and France. We'll seal off the Channel from attack, we'll destroy any resistance that may occur with our cavalry …' For all the show of confidence, Shuter noticed that as a precaution all the paintings and trophies had been removed from the Lord's committee room.

Like many Englishmen, Lionel Tennyson of Hampshire took some convincing that the war would last until Christmas; more, in fact, than the politicians or the newspapers could supply. During the second week of August, Tennyson was back in barracks at Colchester and cheerfully jotting down his pre-embarkation duties in his diary almost as if preparing for a Continental holiday. On the day after war was declared Tennyson wrote to his solicitors advising them that the sum of £750 due to him from the North British & Mercantile insurance company was to pass to his father Hallam 'in the event I am unable to claim it', before turning to more prosaic matters. After 'packing up furniture, etc' in the officers mess, he was chiefly concerned about both his wardrobe and having the necessary inoculations before travelling abroad. On 11 August, Tennyson paid a visit to the Colchester firm of Griffin & Son to see about the storage of 'personal paintings, books, silver, etc' while he was away. On 14 August he noted that he had been in bed all day after reacting poorly to an anti-typhus shot. Later that evening, Tennyson was feeling well enough to join his parents for a long dinner at Colchester's Red Lion hotel. On Sunday 16 August there was an open-air service at the barracks for anyone who wished to attend, 'and a very impressive address by the Bishop'. On 18 August Tennyson's battalion drove over to a new depot in Harrow, and he wrote that he was 'terribly disappointed' at not immediately setting sail for France. If he had read of the early carnage in Belgium, or of the Germans' avoidance of the traditional cavalry charge in favour of machine-gun fire, he never mentioned it in his diary. The shooting of Belgian resisters and the burning down of whole villages does not seem to have crossed his mind; again, he never mentioned it. Like millions of other Britons,

Tennyson was under the impression that his services would be required for only a short time in order to restore matters on the Continent to their rightful order. As it turned out, the war changed the whole direction of his life. From it followed a long and varied series of experiences over four years, in Britain and abroad, that stretched his mind beyond anything he had known at Eton and Cambridge, or for that matter on the cricket fields and racecourses of England. 'My whole later career,' he once said, 'was based upon what happened in France.' Not only was Tennyson himself wounded three times, finding himself at the Somme amid 'dead faces looking at one everywhere out of the mud, while the smell was too overpowering and awful for words', but both his brothers were killed in action. 'Such things tend to affect one', he wrote with some understatement.

Lionel Tennyson and the thousands of other cricketers of all levels and backgrounds who went to the war may not always fit into the popular mythology which treats them collectively either as a sort of sporting harvest god to be devoured at summer's end by the furies, or as characters engaged in some tragicomic, indiscriminate acts of slaughter out of a scene in *Blackadder Goes Forth*. The motives in particular of those 210 first-class players who served their country were as mixed as any of the other young men who were eventually to fight four years of offensives and counter-offensives over nearly identical French soil. Many clearly saw it, like Tennyson, as an 'unexpected and on the whole quite interesting away match'. For at least the first few weeks, the experience of sailing off to France and being greeted on arrival there with cries of '*Vivent les Anglais!*' and offers of food, drink and other inducements 'wasn't the worst alternative', Tennyson noted, to life at home. A fellow cricketing soldier would remember that on embarkation, each man in his unit had been handed a printed notice signed by Lord Kitchener, warning the troops that they might expect to 'find temptations, both in wine and women' on their arrival. 'So far from dampening our spirits, this had rather the opposite effect.' Even after the war had turned into a protracted fiasco that taught Europe to accept a new form of barbarism, many more of those who set off to fight in August 1914 returned than perished. Similarly, the tensions and dangers of the home front were very real, as anyone who endured that era characterised by icy nights in gaslit rooms, often to the accompaniment of Zeppelin air raids, and on a subsistence diet of whale fat and tinned beef, would attest. For all that, there were those who in a variety of ways sat out the war in relative comfort, as one senior Surrey player said, its visual symbols 'bored soldiers and parked lorries along the coast, big guns usually silent except for token barrages'. The papers continued to publish sports scores and theatrical reviews, while on the day war was declared the social column of *The Times* contained the announcement that 'Mrs A Sassoon has arrived at Tulchan

Lodge, Elgin, where she will entertain a party for the shooting season'. For many of those too young to fight, the whole experience was a prolonged and visually intoxicating adventure. In just one case study that may be exceptional, but also relevant to the story, in September 1914 an 11-year-old boy went up to Portsmouth Grammar School, where he saw 'nothing urgent' on the horizon, but professed himself delighted to be in a town 'bustling with English soldiers and sailors, flags fluttering everywhere from buildings and cars, and pretty young girls lining the streets to kiss the troops', and with local facilities 'of the highest kind' for a 'God-given sport' he took to like a duck to water just as soon as he could. The sport was cricket; the boy was Walter Hammond.

III

To many other Britons, of course, it was not hard to be convinced that there was something urgent about the war. First-class cricket may have continued in August 1914, but events brought a swift close to the game elsewhere. *The Times* of 4 August carried the headline: 'To All Who Call Themselves English Gentlemen – Are You Drilled and Armed Ready to Defend Your Country?' A few columns on, Germans exiled in Britain were informed by the War Office that 'His Imperial and Royal Apostolic Majesty has ordered a General Mobilisation of all men liable to serve in the Army and Navy. They are instructed to proceed home at once to their respective depots for obtaining equipment.' The paper charged a shilling a line for this courtesy to impending enemies. In the next few days, cricket stopped dead in its tracks almost everywhere below first-class level. 'Very hard hit by the War, Buckinghamshire played only two matches, nearly all of the team joining the colours', *Wisden* notes.

> Lincolnshire had five of their ten matches upset by the War … Like most of the other teams, Surrey Second Eleven were affected by the War … Berkshire suffered severely from the War, getting only half-way through their programme, before having to cancel the rest … Dorset could play only two matches due to enlistments, and losing them both finished at the bottom of the table without a single point.

A notice pinned to the door of the club pavilion in Farnham, Surrey, read: 'It is regretted that the Ramblers are engaged with the Germans, which is more vital than cricket.'

As we have seen, the initial problem that summer wasn't so much in enlisting new soldiers as in accommodating and feeding the 10,000 or so men a day who joined up in the first weeks of hostilities. Much of their equipment also had an improvised, *Dad's Army* feel to it, with many of the new recruits parading around with brooms and cricket bats instead of rifles. Even at the front, the typical infantry soldier of August 1914 could almost have passed for a young man on a pleasant summer walking tour, with his soft cap, puttees and rucksack. It was to be twenty long months of combat characterised by a dawning appreciation of the impact of modern technology and firepower on the battlefield, and the consequent need to prepare the nation to accept high casualties ('wastage') before voluntary duty was replaced by conscription. While national service continued, so did the Military Service Tribunals with their raft of regulations enforceable in the courts. Sixteen Essex-based club and village cricketers would soon find themselves working long hours together at the Silvertown shell-filling plant in West Ham, where nine of them perished in a TNT explosion that killed a total of seventy-three assembly-line staff and injured 400 others.

With war looming in August 1914, it was not only English cricketers who rose to the occasion. Of the 330,000 Australians who put on a uniform during the conflict, some 59,000 died and 172,000 were wounded. Among them was Albert Cotter of the 12th Australian Light Horse regiment, holder of twenty-one Test caps, who was killed in October 1917, aged 33. Eighteen-year-old Norman Callaway made his first-class debut for New South Wales against Queensland in a timeless match at Sydney in February 1915. Coming in with the score at 17-3, he left again when it was 437-7, having hit 207 at fractionally under a run a minute. Callaway's first taste of state cricket was also to be his last. The Australian authorities brought a premature curtain down on the Sheffield Shield later that week. Private Callaway of the 19th Battalion (Infantry), having volunteered for duty, was killed in France in May 1917. He had just had his 21st birthday. As we've seen, the South African Test cricketers Gordon White, Reggie Schwarz, Claude Newberry, Arthur Ochse, Reginald Hands and Eric Lundie all fell in the war or, in the case of Major Schwarz, succumbed to the flu pandemic of 1918. Like most other walks of life, cricket was disrupted by the events of 1914–18 literally everywhere it was played. The MCC minutes of 10 August 1914 record the club's decision not to send teams to Holland and the West Indies later that year, due to the 'new circumstances' that now 'caused some concern' on the Continent. Professional or semi-professional matches in New Zealand, India and Ceylon were all scratched. *Wisden* reported that in August 1914 the annual derby game between the United States and Canada was cancelled 'owing to the military conditions in Canada'.

In the week of 3 August 1914, Britain with a few vocal exceptions was in a mood of high crusading confidence, and able-bodied men were expected to 'do their bit'. Under the circumstances, it was reasonable to ask – as many did – how the presiding genius of English sport and hero-material for tens of thousands of impressionable fans might respond to the challenge. Jack Hobbs was then a married man with four young children and a widowed mother to support. The exact figures are elusive, but the Surrey accounts books suggest that he was earning around £500 to £550 a year from all sources, which was better than many, but still only about what a provincial head master or a middling civil servant made. Hobbs was later to write of these circumstances and to add that he 'hadn't initially understood [the] gravity of the crisis' when choosing not to join his county colleagues like Andrew Sandham, Percy Fender, Neville Knox, Ernie Hayes and Bill Hitch in volunteering for duty. It should be said again that there was no legal obligation for Hobbs to do so, and that many other Britons later said that they, too, had failed to grasp the full enormity of events in August 1914, even as the war editions of newspapers began to fill with the lists of British casualties on the Marne – with 20,000 dead before the cricket season ended in early September – and the first convoys of the often hideously wounded began arriving back at Southampton.

Hobbs was no 'shirker', as the word came to be used by the military tribunals and others, but it was perhaps unfortunate that he placed himself, by association, in the company of those thought fit to receive the white feathers of cowardice. For the first year of the war, he remained on the staff at Surrey while also working in a London munitions factory, possibly as a clerk. This typically involved long hours spent in ill-paid, noisy and often dangerous conditions, and was not a comfortable way to see out the crisis. In March 1915, Hobbs took a part-time position as a games coach at Westminster School. Over the next two seasons, he was paid to play weekend cricket for Idle in the Bradford League, where he finished with the relatively modest batting averages of 36.63 and 52.60 in 1915 and 1916 respectively. In October 1916, Hobbs was conscripted into the Royal Flying Corps, where he was listed as a mechanic. His squadron remained stationed in the Home Counties, and he was able to play in a variety of charity matches during the final two summers of the war. On 31 August 1918 Hobbs opened the batting for Captain P.F. Warner's XI against Colonel F.S. Jackson's XI at Lord's. *Wisden* wrote that:

> The game proved a big attraction, the crowd being estimated at 8,000. Warner's XI [won] in the easiest fashion and only just missed a single innings victory. Those present had the pleasure of seeing Hobbs bat in his very best form. By general consent his 86 was the finest display of the season.

On 25 September of that year, Hobbs's squadron was deployed to France and undertook a number of aerial reconnaissance missions in the St Quentin sector, where British and American forces began a crushing four-day advance that finally led to the collapse of German fighting ability, amid scenes of revolutionary unrest in Berlin. The armistice was signed six weeks later.

In later years Hobbs rarely if ever spoke of his wartime experience, although several others did so on his behalf. Between May 1915 and June 1917, there had been a lively correspondence between MCC's *éminence grise* Lord Hawke and the organisers of the Bradford League, in which Hobbs was often mentioned by name, about the propriety of playing professional sport while thousands of young men were losing their lives every day at the Somme and elsewhere. In time there were some heated newspaper stories written on the subject. Sharp-eyed editors did not miss the opportunity to point out that Hobbs's primary team during this period was named Idle. More than once, that word appeared chalked up on the front wall of the player's home, along with other unappreciative remarks. Some of Hobbs's own family, including his brothers who served in the army, publicly resented what they saw as the favouritism of the War Office in allowing him to travel up and down the country more or less as he wished in order to play cricket. The accusation that 'the Master' was also somehow a coward was polemically effective but factually wrong. Although Hobbs seems never quite to have understood the depth of emotion stirred up by his League activities, he also presented himself for duty the moment the law required it and made no known attempt to evade overseas service thereafter. He acted entirely correctly, even if for Lord Hawke and others that was not quite enough. To them, he was Britain's least-loved hero.

TO ARMS

In keeping with many activities, cricket had no very clear idea in August 1914 of what to expect from the war, except that it would be brief. Winston Churchill was not alone in using the image of a 'short, sharp thunderstorm' to convey the general mood. Others, like Percy Fender, thought the whole thing would 'spark up and swiftly burn itself out' like a typical Jessop innings. Even then, the public euphoria was neither universal nor permanent. Observers such as Philip Gibbs noted the prevalence of support for the 1914 Defence of the Realm Act, which provided for press censorship and imprisonment without trial, and restricted pub-licensing hours, in the educated and professional classes, but detected 'little warmth among the workers'. The terms of the legislation soon became a subject for debate, and would be a major bone of contention during the first post-war general election campaign. It may be that truly popular war enthusiasm peaked in the first week of August 1914, and after that never quite recovered its original zeal. On the afternoon of 4 August, as ministers drove to and from parliament to draft the proclamation of war, they were roared on by what Asquith called 'cheering crowds of loafers and holiday makers'. Major-General (later Field Marshal) William Birdwood, soon to be the British commander-in-chief at Gallipoli, spoke for many when he said, 'what a real piece of luck this scrap with Germany is as regards Ireland – just averted a civil war'. He added, 'when it is over we may all be tired of fighting'.

On Wednesday 12 August, the Surrey Committee met and expressed regret that the 'tensions on the Continent' had 'quite upset' plans at the Oval, where several hundred Territorial army soldiers and their horses were currently billeted at the Vauxhall end. A number of other cricket authorities similarly noted the passing unpleasantness, but in general remained optimistic that the game would survive – after all, it was 'the fulfillment of the English way of life', to quote Lord Hawke. It was one of the things the nation was fighting to preserve. The irony for Hawke, as for other ambitious but innately conservative Britons, was that the very system that fuelled their romantic traditionalism and found its most perfect expression in cricket was itself on the point of dissolution. The First World War was the high-water mark of the world of duty, rank and sound patriotic values that seemed to carry over logically from the national sport into the armed forces. It gave numerous individual cricketers ample opportunity for acts of heroism. Several of them made the ultimate sacrifice. But the war also brought about the complete collapse of the society that had managed to preserve the core feudal structure of English cricket since the origins of the county system in 1839. It was the ignition point for the whole modernisation crisis that followed. In time, Hawke shared with many other Britons of the old school the sense of disorientation and frustration that ensued in the 1920s – 'an alteration not for the best', in his measured phrase.

Imagining the crowds cheering in the streets and queuing at recruitment offices in the early part of August 1914, Philip Larkin wrote of 'Those long uneven lines / Standing as patiently / As if they were stretched outside / The Oval or Villa Park', all of them grinning as if it were 'a Bank holiday lark'. Later research has suggested that war enthusiasm was more a product of the educated and business classes in British towns than of a monolithic, nationalistic bloc. The call to arms, while certainly impressively swift in its early stages, was not a universal success, nor did it always proceed in that 'spirit of sober and God-fearing nobility of soul' later cited by Lord Hawke. A young MCC player and Special Reserve officer named Cyril Drummond remembered his platoon being sent at short notice to Tipperary, where the regular garrison had already left for France:

> We marched right across Dublin, with old Irish women pushing bottles of whisky at us and shouting 'Kill the bloody Germans!'. At 7.30 in the morning [another officer] and his Reservists turned up. He had been marching them around the square to get them sober. Even then our troubles were not over. Directly opposite our ship was a pub. The head of the column of men marched up the gangway; the tail disappeared into the pub. We spent half an hour fetching them out one by one and pushing them on board … All the while the crowd on the quayside were singing their heads off – *Pack Up Your Troubles* and *Tipperary*. I never heard *Tipperary* sung in France while I was there.

Patriotism, escapism and, to some, an exciting prospect for travel and adventure all played their part in rallying young men to the colours. As well as the more than 200 county cricketers who went to war – divided about equally between amateurs who held commissions in the Territorial army and professionals who enlisted in the ranks – perhaps ten times as many lesser or part-time players joined up.

The honour board at Lord's lists the names of 331 members of MCC who died in combat between 1914 and 1918. Thirty-four first-class cricketers were killed. In time, every English county or club pavilion would have its own memorial to those who fell in the war. As August drew on, and the shocking news from Mons finally came to light at the nation's breakfast tables, even Lord Hawke acknowledged that much of Britain went from 'a mood of euphoria to one of acceptance and grim resolve', a pragmatism that saw private and commercial vehicles commandeered by the army, country homes pressed into service as hospitals and, in London's Regent Street, 'a German meat shop kicked into matchsticks' by a mob. Almost incredibly, the county cricket season continued, although on 18 August MCC was forced to admit that the war situation had not so far gone as hoped. 'Owing to events', it announced, all matches scheduled at Lord's in September had been cancelled.

On the Monday morning of 10 August, Somerset should have begun a three-day Championship match against Northamptonshire at Taunton. *Wisden* remarks merely that the fixture was 'abandoned owing to the War', and more specifically to five of the Somerset amateurs having rejoined their units and the county struggling to put a team in the field as a result. But cricket resumed as scheduled at Taunton on the following Thursday. Somerset hosted Worcestershire, a game notable not so much for its technical merits or its result (an easy away win), as for the fact that it marked the last appearance of the home opening batsman Dudley Rippon before he went off to war.

The tall and dark-eyed Rippon and his twin brother Sydney, then 22, had already quite often opened the innings for Somerset, where they made a lot of runs and caused confusion by their resemblance to each other. On 3 August, when they walked out together into the middle at Bristol, twirling their bats in unison, Gloucestershire's bowler Ted Dennett had taken one look and enquired, 'How are you meant to tell these buggers apart?' Since the brothers appeared under the names 'A.D.E.' and 'A.E.S.' Rippon, there was also a certain amount of confusion over the years among the county scorers. When Sydney Rippon lunched in the Northampton pavilion during the course of a Championship match that season, he was able to maintain the running joke that he was actually his brother. Each time the over-friendly waiter tried to resume the conversation of the day before, Sydney would say, perplexed, 'You must have been talking to my twin Dudley.' The waiter would protest, 'But didn't you tell me yesterday you were buying a car – ?' 'No, no,' Sydney would interrupt, straight-faced. 'That was Dudley.' The next day he became his twin again. 'Are you sure you're not confusing me with that swine Sydney?' The waiter would reel away, leaving Sydney and his table in gales of mirth. It is remembered in the yearbook that both brothers 'laughed a good deal, frequently at themselves'.

Dudley Rippon volunteered for duty promptly in August 1914, and saw action as a 2nd lieutenant with the Army Service Corps at Gallipoli, where he was badly wounded in the feet and legs. In the course of the war he also had three lorries blown up underneath him, picked up a Turkish grenade and threw it back a moment before it exploded, and shot down a low-flying enemy reconnaissance plane with his rifle. As a result of his injuries he was discharged with the Silver War Badge, but later obtained a new commission in the Royal Flying Corps. He played thirteen more times for Somerset in 1919 but only once in the 1920 season, his wounds finally taking their toll. Rippon's last match lists him as 'Run out, o' and 'Absent hurt' in the two Somerset innings. He finished his career with 1,043 runs at an average of 20, but statistics are absurd in such a man. Rippon's twin Sydney returned from the Western Front, also wounded, and took up a position with the Inland Revenue. In later years, he took the magnanimous view that while the war itself had been a 'malicious, gruesome mass assassination', a 'decent peace' would ensue if only the main European powers were 'tied together by the bonds of economic cooperation … in a community of trade, commerce and culture'.

In June 1919, both Rippon brothers appeared for Somerset against Gloucestershire at Taunton, although Sydney did so under the *nom de jeu* 'S. Trimnell'. None of the newspapers seem to have immediately made the connection, or to have known that Trimnell was his mother's maiden name. This unusual arrangement was made necessary because Rippon's employers had denied him permission to play in the match, and he had thus rung in sick before making his way to the county ground. Unfortunately, he then chose to score a career-best 92 in the Somerset first innings, which perhaps attracted more media interest in 'Trimnell' than the player himself might have wished. The *Western Daily Press* was left to remark that 'although the name is new, he is by no means a stranger to county cricket'. A very observant spectator might also have spotted that both Trimnell and Rippon shared the odd habit of gradually turning their caps around back-to-front on their heads, so that by the end of an innings they resembled a modern teenager. The record books were eventually modified, and Sydney continued to play county cricket on and off until 1937. His son was the Conservative politician Geoffrey Rippon, the man chiefly responsible for negotiating Britain's eventual entry into the Common Market.

III

As the war heightened, so did MCC's concern about the proper way to do their bit. At their second regular Monday meeting in August, Lord Hawke moved that the Club subscribe £230 to the Prince of Wales' National Relief Fund. 'Letters and

Telegrams on the question of closing Lord's were read out', although 'after discussion, it was decided to keep the ground open as long as possible; if an emergency arises, the Committee, if possible, should be convened; if not, discretion should be given to the Secretary and Acting Secretary'. It was noted elsewhere that such a crisis might constitute both possible commandeering by the home authorities, and not preclude an invasion by the Germans. Reflecting the fact that several players had made themselves unavailable 'due to overseas-duty commitments', proposed MCC tours of Devon and the south coast were cancelled. The club secretary was given discretionary powers 'as to allowing full or half wages to employees during enlistment'. A final melancholy entry records that the Committee discussed making a payment of £10 to Albert Trott's funeral expenses. 'This was approved', the minutes note, without further comment.

As we have seen, cricket was eventually suspended at Lord's, whose 15-acre site and maze of stands and buildings in a prime north London location proved irresistible to the War Office. During the few remaining games of the 1914 season, a local St John's Wood solicitor named Pipe reported that:

> The old ground was decorated with English and French colours flying over the roof, and there were notices everywhere about extinguishing unnecessary lights. All sorts of rumours were flying about that the Germans would land on the east coast. The paper-boy at the main gate was besieged by anxious customers on their way in and out. One saw sentries on duty at the recruiting office on Baker Street, where hundreds of men were pushing and shoving in their excitement to become civilian soldiers.

Other large open spaces in London such as White City had immediately become an army barracks or, like Alexandra Palace, a reception centre for Belgian refugees. For now, Lord's was able to carry on, although it was noticed by a naval doctor present named Holmes that in the Middlesex home tie with Surrey beginning on 22 August 'uniformed figures [had] passed solemnly among the crowd, extending Red Cross Fund collecting boxes "for the relief of our sick and wounded"'. The military authorities began to occupy Lord's in October 1914. Among the expedients that followed was the keeping of a chicken coop on the Nursery end boundary, although for some traditionalists the greater shock may have been the staging at Lord's in 1916 of a baseball game between London Americans and Canada to raise money for the widows and orphans of Canadians who had fallen in battle. *Wisden* reported that 'HRH Princess Louise (Duchess of Argyll) graciously gave her patronage to the undertakings and watched the game from the pavilion. The proceeds exceeded £100.'

In Birmingham there was an almost festive air around the New Street station, where there were reported to be 'large crowds of soldiers and civilians, young women to the fore, cheering, waving flags and blowing trumpets' during August 1914. There were Union flags flying on Pershore Road leading down to Edgbaston, where the outer wall was soon plastered with official notices about the commandeering of trains and buses and the desirability of 'Loyal Girls' to train as nurses. A regiment of Territorials had arrived nearby to find their new quarters not altogether attractive. For one thing, it was said 'there was no supply of underwear or winter clothes' as the cold autumn nights drew in, and sanitary facilities were 'low, even by military standards'. No one in the camp was allowed to smoke after dark 'as this could attract enemy fire', and there was a general suspicion that spies and saboteurs were at work in the area. In fact, during the first two weeks of their tenure, the local Territorials had just one bona fide emergency to deal with, and that came when some patriotic citizens took exception to a 'neighbourhood sausage shop, run by one Schmidt' and conveyed their displeasure by burning it down.

It was somehow peculiarly English that in the midst of all this county cricket was being played just a few hundred yards away, with a match at Edgbaston between Warwickshire and Kent beginning on 13 August. When the Warwickshire openers Kinneir and Charlesworth went out to bat the large crowd, enjoying a sunny Birmingham day after a patchy summer, may have expected to see plenty of runs. As it was, 30 wickets went down before 6 p.m. that evening. 'The batting, indeed, was unworthy of the teams engaged', said *Wisden*. 'Tich' Freeman with his legbreaks did the initial damage, with the notable figures of 7-25 in 10 overs. The Kent first innings, which lasted the exact same time as that of Warwickshire, also closed for the same score – 111. Percy Jeeves and Frank Foster each took 3-36. Almost incredibly, Warwickshire's batting got even worse in their second innings, which saw them jeered from the field after making just 78 runs (11 of them byes) off 29 overs. Kent won by 9 wickets early on the second morning, with five full sessions of play in hand. For Colin Blythe, it was the 435th match of a professional career that had begun at the tail end of the nineteenth century. He would make just four more appearances. Now 26 and rather belatedly launched on his twenty-two-year-long career, Freeman could finally be bracketed alongside his eminent predecessor for Kent and England. On the evening of 14 August Blythe took the train home to Tonbridge and enjoyed an unscheduled day off before the county's next home game against Lancashire. Twelve days after that, he went to a local recruiting depot and volunteered for a home-front service called the Kent Fortress Engineers. In September 1917, following the news of his brother Sidney's death, Blythe asked to be transferred to an active unit, and less than a week later found himself in the 12th Battalion, King's Own Yorkshire Light Infantry, on his way to Ypres.

While Kent were completing their rout of Warwickshire at Edgbaston, Hampshire's Lionel Tennyson continued his pre-embarkation exercises at brigade headquarters, which were once again in Colchester. On the whole these do not seem to have anticipated any possible imminent confrontation with the likes of hostile aircraft, flamethrowers or poison gas. In his diary Tennyson would list a daily routine dominated by the elaborate protocol of the officers' mess, the sound of bugles, the shouted orders and the grumbles of soldiers and all the animation that marked an 'endless series of parades', constant (and often pointless) polishing and cleaning, and various other petty rituals deemed to be 'tedious and futile'. Also not fully resolved by the middle of August 1914 was the role to be played by the troops in the face of withering enemy machine-gun fire. Less than a month later, in France, Tennyson recorded his first experience of it:

> We started marching again about 11 a.m. and went about twelve miles to a place called Maisoncelles. We got there just as it was getting dusk, when suddenly there was a great fusillade against the brigade that was in front of us by the Germans, or rather by their rearguard. Several Fusiliers were killed, and many came bolting back to our battalion as well as several Highlanders, saying their battalions had been scuppered.

By then the once unthinkable news had reached Britain that the Allied armies were in retreat, and beset on both flanks. It was an exceptionally hot and wet late summer, and Tennyson makes frequent reference in his diary to the challenge of long slogs with full equipment through marshland and the hedgerows of the *bocage* as well as the steep banks of the Marne itself. At this stage, the war was still a kaleidoscope of fast-moving events, and in general everything was novel and exciting – the language, the French people, the dinners in local cafes 'where everyone got up and sang the English, French and Russian national anthems, which was very fine', the standing ovations, the local claret, 'the little French girl of about six [who] rushed up and gave me a lovely bunch of flowers and asked me for a kiss'. Set against this, there was the first day of the Battle of the Marne, when Tennyson and his unit:

> Looked down on the fight going on beneath us from the top of a hill … We could see the German shells bursting amongst our troops advancing, and our shells bursting amongst the German cavalry as they were entering a wood on the opposite side of the river … When we pushed on a bit and halted outside

a house which was the dressing station, we saw some fellows brought in with ghastly wounds. [At night] the noise was simply deafening. It then rained as I have never seen it rain before, for about an hour, and we all got soaked … Nothing much more happened to us today.

Less than a month before he wrote these words, Lionel Tennyson had been at home in Piccadilly and wondering about playing a weekend game of cricket.

On 17 August, while Tennyson and a transport of 20,000 other troops were about to embark for France, the Middlesex committee held its scheduled monthly meeting at Lord's. Cricket's apparent official detachment from the war was seen in the minutes, which are concerned largely with playing matters, discipline and budgets. 'Correspondence was read by Mr Webbe,' we learn, 'from which it appeared that Tarrant had received an offer to remain in India at a salary of £600 a year. He was prepared, however, to forgo this sum and continue to play for Middlesex provided that the Middlesex Club were prepared to guarantee him £300 a year exclusive.' While noting that the player had rendered valuable service over some ten seasons (just the week before, he had taken 16 wickets in a game against Lancashire at Old Trafford) the committee was not minded to adjust his salary. 'It must be for Tarrant to decide if he will accept the offer from India or not', the minutes conclude. The tone elsewhere is of a club struggling to rein in expenses as players' wages soared to undreamed-of heights, with an 'annual commitment approaching £1,000' for the team's seven contracted professionals. However, 'it was agreed to grant £3-3-0 to Hobbs's benefit as a special case', the minutes add.

On that same August Monday morning, Frank Tarrant and Harry Lee went out to open the Middlesex batting against Nottinghamshire at Lord's. The ground was respectably full, and a French *tricoleur* flew above the Tavern; the weather was pleasantly breezy. The cricket that ensued was largely undistinguished for the first two days, although Hendren hit 88 (roughly 50,000 more first-class runs would come before he finally retired) in his last match before he went off to first get married and then join the Royal Engineers. In the Middlesex second innings, however, Lee scored 139 in just over three hours – 'a performance which included fourteen fours and showed delightful cricket'. Declaring at 375-7, Middlesex won by 239 runs.

Harry Lee, a greengrocer's son from north London, was then aged 23, and thus far had played only a few times for his county without any great luck. He had only come in to the Middlesex side in August because of the departure of Warner and most of the other amateurs to the army. Having seized his chance, Lee himself then selflessly signed up immediately Middlesex finished their season. He spent the winter of 1914–15 as a private with the 1/13th (County of London) Battalion on home duty, before shipping out to France the following spring in time to take part in the battles of Neuve Chapelle and Aubers Ridge. Of the 550 men in his unit deployed in an attack on 9 May 1915, there were 499 casualties. Lee was shot in the leg and lay for three days between the lines, having been given up for dead. Back in London, his parents organised a memorial service for him. 'I am glad to say this was premature', he later remarked. In fact, the Germans had eventually pulled Lee from the field and put him in a hastily commandeered cattle train bound for a hospital in Lille, itself a life-threatening ordeal for a man with a shattered femur and the first stages of gangrene. On embarkation, Lee found that, except for one carriage marked 'Officers Only', the remainder of the train consisted of closed railway wagons, each furnished with a pile of straw for the forty or so wounded Tommies packed in side by side, and a bucket which served as a communal toilet. During the two-day journey through occupied Belgium and France, which they completed without food, several of the soldiers died of their injuries. Lee then spent six weeks in hospital, at the end of which he was officially classified as unfit for combat and shipped home to England. When he was examined by the army doctors it was established that one of his legs would be permanently shorter than the other, and that he had suffered 'significant muscle death'. A prototype electro-shock machine meant to treat the injury may well have made it worse. Lee was told that he would never be able to fight or play cricket again. As it turned out this, too, proved wrong, and albeit with a marked crouch at the wicket and a tendency to score mainly on the leg side, he returned for fifteen further seasons and some 20,000 more runs.

Lee's wartime adventures were not quite over yet. Setting off in September 1918 for a season's appointment as the private cricket coach to the Maharajah of Cooch Behar, his passage was switched at the last moment from the SS *Nyanza* to the SS *Nagoya*: the *Nyanza* was torpedoed just out of Cardiff, and lost with all hands.

III

In Lionel Tennyson's unavoidable absence in the middle of August 1914, Hampshire took on Somerset at Southampton. Much too strong for the visitors, who included seven amateurs in their side, Hampshire won by an innings and 47 runs. One of the few Somerset successes was their number seven Cecil Banes-Walker, whose first innings score of 40 proved to be his highest in first-class cricket. A week later, Banes-Walker joined the army as a private, but was gazetted with the 3rd Battalion, Devonshire Regiment as a probationary 2nd lieutenant on 7 October 1914. The following May, he took part in the same Allied attack at Aubers Ridge in which Harry Lee was wounded. It is not known if any of the front-line troops in the action were aware of the large burial trench which a sanitary detail had prepared beforehand in an adjoining field. The battalion's war diary for 9 May records that as the first forces were moving up shortly after sunrise they 'came under heavy German artillery and machine-gun fire, [and that] between 6.45 and 7.30 2nd Lt. Banes-Walker was killed at the head of his men'. He was 26.

After playing Somerset, Hampshire were to have hosted Warwickshire at the United Services ground in Portsmouth. From the stream of army lorries, ambulances, wagons, commandeered bakers' vans, horse-boxes and even farm carts trundling in and out of the docks there that week, it soon became apparent that this was not the ideal setting for a three-day county cricket match, so the proceedings were hurriedly moved back to Southampton. The small crowd on hand made a sad sight, some of them already sporting improvised rubber gas masks around their necks and special constables walking among them to distribute notices about what to do in the event of an invasion. Nor was the mood jollied along by the pace of the cricket, which was sluggish for the first two days. With an average of only 30 overs bowled in each session, and those often in gloomy light, there was no indication that the match would produce such captivating theatre at the finish. Hampshire, set to make 189 in just over two hours, got home by 4 wickets with three minutes left. The crowd were not to know that some of the men they stood to cheer off would be among the casualties that devitalised English cricket: Frank Foster, who top-scored for Warwickshire with 92, injured in a motorcycle crash while on army duty and never to play again; his teammate Colin Langley, of Radley and Oxford, also lamed in the war, his first-class career over at the age of 25; Alister McLeod, who came into the Hampshire side in 1914 straight from rewriting the batting records at Felsted, and who returned from France so weak he could manage only six more appearances before retiring; Percy Jeeves, killed; Alban Arnold, killed; Arthur Jaques, killed. One of the two scorers that day at Southampton was the former Hampshire all-rounder Francis Bacon, who had played seventy-five matches for the county in the early years of the century. In October 1915 Bacon was serving on the Royal Yacht Squadron's steamer *Aries* when it was hit by a sea mine while on patrol near the South Goodwin Lightship and sank with all hands; he was 46. Hampshire's wicketkeeper Walter Livsey also went to war, but returned to play for another twelve seasons, a job he combined with that of butler to his county captain, Lionel Tennyson. He lived to be 84.

It would be hard to devise a more unequal professional cricket match than the one that took place late in August at Bristol between Gloucestershire and Yorkshire. Gloucester managed scores of just 94 and 84 and lost by an innings and 227 runs, with more than a day still left. Booth and Drake of Yorkshire bowled unchanged in both innings, with 12 and 8 wickets respectively. Roy Kilner scored 169, which was only 9 runs fewer than Gloucester managed in the whole match. It was a tribute either to Bristol's long-suffering cricket public or an indication, perhaps, of how so many of them still tried to cling to normality that there was a relatively good crowd on hand for both days' play. Among those in the pavilion seats was the 46-year-old Reverend Reginald Moss, the Rector of Icomb, himself a powerful, black-bearded cricket all-rounder, known as 'the bull' to teammates and opponents, because of both his size and his robust approach to the game. Moss had taken his Oxford blue in 1889, and played one professional match in 1893 for Liverpool & District against the Australians. His next first-class appearance was as a 57-year-old emergency recruit for Worcestershire against Gloucestershire in May 1925, when he took a wicket and 2 catches. The thirty-two-year gap between fixtures remains a record. During the tea interval, Moss accepted an invitation to go upstairs and bless both sets of players in the Bristol dining room.

Fresh from their easy win, the Yorkshire team continued their western tour of August 1914 with a Championship rout of Somerset at Weston-super-Mare. This time the home side managed scores of 44 and 90. Major Booth and Alonzo Drake again bowled unchanged in both innings. Drake had figures of 5-16 and 10-35. On the morning the match began, *The Sportsman* published the famous letter from W.G. Grace insisting that 'the time has arrived when the county cricket season should be closed, for it is not fitting at a time like the present that able-bodied men should play day after day and pleasure-seekers look on'. Alongside its cricket scores and race cards, the paper also carried news of 2,000 British war casualties. For the time being, the idyllic and the horrific would still co-exist. A full report had not yet come in of the previous day's 'holding action' at Le Cateau, widely judged a tactical success despite some 7,800 more Allied losses. Early the following week, Major Booth and Alonzo Drake would both make their final appearance in first-class cricket in the drawn match against Sussex at Hove. A subsequent game between Yorkshire and MCC at Scarborough was 'keenly anticipated, [but] abandoned owing to the War', *Wisden* said.

On the morning of 17 August, the five paid members of the Middlesex side selected to play Nottinghamshire at Lord's had found an envelope among the post waiting for them on the table in the professionals' dressing room. It contained a letter composed in red ink and apparently written in short bursts of manic energy around the edges of the paper, so that one had to turn the page through 360 degrees to read all of it. Distilled to the essence, it accused the players of 'rank cowardice' and 'funk' for preferring to play cricket instead of serve their country. The charge does not sit well – three of the men would go on to fight at the front and a fourth, Jack Hearne, was then 47 years old – but it expressed a view some people were beginning to take as the first units of the BEF advanced on the steaming slag-heaps around Mons for their inaugural meeting with the enemy. As noted, the two county captains, Warner of Middlesex and Carr of Notts, had already abandoned cricket and reported for military service. Other players up and down the country soon followed their lead, among them Charles Newcombe, late of Derbyshire, the Cambridge University and MCC wicketkeeper Walter Franklin, who enlisted on his 23rd birthday, and Douglas Carr of Kent and England. Newcombe was killed in December 1915, 'the top half of his body severed from the lower', while on duty in France with the King's Own Yorkshire Light Infantry; he was 24. Lancashire's 33-year-old opening bat Harry Makepeace, another who defied criticism, scored a typically busy 50 for his county against Hampshire in late August, and then vanished into 'the great game with the Hun'. Makepeace's physical appearance alone commanded respect: straight as an arrow and always immaculate in creased white flannels and a blazer, he had a rugged, chiseled face with piercing grey eyes, bone-crushing hands and big, blue-veined arms that, as a colleague said, 'seemed to have been built in a foundry'. In the course of a 46-year career with Lancashire as a player and coach he scored some 26,000 runs, appearing in four Tests, and still found time to turn out at right back for the England football side and win an FA Cup medal with Everton. Always a favourite with the crowds, from 1914 to 1918 Harry Makepeace was no longer the 'gay blade, a pair of boots slung over his shoulder, on his way to Goodison or Old Trafford'. He was more at home in the trenches. Makepeace survived the war, never speaking of his experiences at the front, and died aged 71.

Another early recruit was the terrifyingly fast bowler Neville Knox, of Surrey and England, who had once played alongside P.G. Wodehouse as a Dulwich school-boy and went on to take 12 wickets in a Gentlemen v. Players match deploying an 'entirely new kind of attack – the ball that never allows a batsman to feel entirely physically secure ... beginning his run in the vicinity of deep mid-off Knox generat[ed] pace and movement sufficient to trouble anyone not bold enough to go fully forward ... it was all a breathtaking sight'. Other than practising what to date was perhaps the fastest bowling ever seen in English county cricket, Knox's main ambition was to sing in the London music hall. Despite suffering from chronic shin strains, he joined the Royal Army Ordnance Corps as a 2nd lieutenant in August 1914, aged 29, and served on the Western Front for three of the next four years. After the war, Knox finally abandoned cricket, but continued his fitful career on the stage. He died in March 1935, aged 50.

The choice of whether or not to go to the war in August 1914 was clearly the vital one for cricketers and civilians alike. Those who joined up did so for a variety of reasons, and not always because they happened to be students of the great issues that divided Europe. Harry Makepeace, for one, said that he volunteered because 'it seemed obvious', and that he 'wasn't much interested in politics and such'. Most of those who enlisted returned, but, like cricket itself, few of them would ever be quite the same again.

Many of the generation of players who fought in the First World War simply felt unable to carry on when the first-class game eventually resumed. Whether through age or having lost the ability to find delight in life, 'nothing was as it had been', to quote Lieutenant Knox. 'Our world belonged to the past.' As Europe drifted onto the rocks in July 1914, the Gentlemen had defeated the Players in a thrilling match at Lord's, in large part due to the bowling of Johnny Douglas and Frank Foster. When they left the field time was called for both Foster and the likes of Jaques, Jessop, Fry and Barnes, none of whom would ever appear in the fixture again. The tall and slim Reggie Spooner, an aristocrat among batsmen, went out to serve in France at the age of 34. When he returned he graced only a dozen more games before retiring, though, like Percy Jeeves, he was to enjoy a literary afterlife when Harold Pinter gave his name to one of the characters in his play *No Man's Land*. The war also proved a watershed for the careers of men like Tom Hayward, Frank Tarrant, Albert Hornby, Jim Iremonger, Jack Hearne, and George Platt of Surrey. Thirty-year-old Ted Alletson of Nottinghamshire went off to fight with the Royal Artillery, and preferred to work in the mines on his return. In May 1911 Alletson had secured his place in cricket history when, coming in to bat at number nine, he scored 189 runs in just ninety minutes in a Championship tie against Sussex at Hove. The innings included eight sixes, and one shot that destroyed the pavilion clock. Alletson's 34 runs in a single over remained a record for first-class cricket for fifty-seven years, until it was broken by another Nottinghamshire batsman, named Sobers. The ferocious yet seemingly effortless power of the Hove innings was the more remarkable for the fact that in his career up to then the batsman had consistently managed to subordinate under a layer of discipline any latent stroke-making ability he may have had. A genuinely modest and charming man, Ted Alletson lived on, martyred by arthritis, until shortly after his 79th birthday.

The years 1914 to 1918 also brought an end to many careers that might have gone on to touch the heights of Test cricket. Prime among them was Gerard Anderson, 'Twiggy' to his friends and admirers, who left Eton to take a first in Greats at Oxford and a fellowship at All Souls. An Olympic hurdler and prodigiously quick rugby three-quarter, Anderson's batting was reported by *Young England* magazine to be 'in the gallant style, with a daring and brilliance of improvisation that dispatched all and sundry to distant parts of the field'. Commissioned into the Cheshire Regiment, he was killed leading a charge at Ypres in November 1914, aged 25.

In his day, Francis Grenfell of the 9th Lancers had been described as a 'keen if somewhat deliberate opening batsman' and 'truly gifted leg-spin bowler of classical technique' while in the eleven at Eton. Just two weeks after the declaration of war Grenfell rode with his regiment in a frontal charge against heavy German artillery fire at Mons. Severely wounded, he announced, 'I'm going back – the doctors must make what they like of it', and managed to crawl forward to help push the battery's guns out of the range of enemy fire, again being shot in the process. He was awarded the first VC of the war. Grenfell's twin brother Riversdale and two of his cousins were killed in action. The author John Buchan saw the newly decorated Captain Grenfell 'limping about London that Christmas with a drawn face and haggard eyes, looking like a man searching for something he could not find'. It was thought that both the brothers could have played either cricket or rugby to international level. Francis Grenfell returned to the front and was killed in action at the head of his men on 24 May 1915, aged 34.

We have touched on the fate of Arthur Collins, an orphan who in 1899 scored an undefeated innings of 628 or so (there's some doubt over the exact total, as the scorers were the same age as the players), batting at Clifton. Collins's side won the match by an innings and 688 runs. Only two years later, having just turned 16, he joined the army. Described as 'slim, fair and handsome in a soft-featured way', Collins represented the Royal Military Academy, Woolwich, at both football and rugby as well as cricket, and later twice appeared for the Royal Engineers at Lord's. He married Ethel Slater, an army officer's daughter, in April 1914, and in August of that year went with his unit to France. Captain 'Boy' Collins was hit by enemy machine-gun fire while standing in front of a trench signalling to his men in the misty early hours of 11 November 1914, during the First Battle of Ypres. A comrade dragged him to a dressing station at the rear, where he died some time later. The following day, an estimated 200 officers and other ranks of the battalion were committed to a hurriedly prepared mass grave, but due to the continued fighting in the area this was never found.

In England, the military authorities were not slow to see the advertising potential of the nation's top cricketers, and of the national sport as a whole. Beginning in September 1914, the far-away eyes of a young man under the legend 'THE GAME OF WAR' were to gaze out over Britons from a recruiting poster for the 23rd and 24th (Service) units of the Royal Fusiliers, better known as the Sportsmen's Battalions. The other slogans widely used in this particular campaign were 'Join Together, Train Together, Embark Together, Fight Together' (the note of camaradie and *esprit de corps* sometimes amended by an unknown hand to add 'Die Together') and, with a certain inevitability, the line 'Play Up, Play Up and Play The Game'. Cricket was used as a particular theme in cartoons depicting the 'Hun's unsportsmanlike attitude to war'. A popular Sunday newspaper strip called *The Kaiser's Cricket* depicted a spike-helmeted German soldier using a net to defend his wicket, tripping up an opposition batsman and assaulting an umpire, among other breaches of etiquette. The Essex all-rounder Edward Sewell later appeared in a series of public-service announcements warning British citizens to carry their gas masks. Other official attempts were made to promote the army's Number 15 round hand-grenade as the 'cricket-ball bomb', though the weapon proved unreliable in the damp and was withdrawn following the Second Battle of Ypres in May 1915.

III

On 27 and 28 August 1914, Middlesex played their final Championship match of the season, scoring a handsome win against Kent at Lord's. On a damp pitch, the visitors managed totals of just 116 and 67. The game lasted until the second evening only because of frequent interruptions for bad light and rain. Colin Blythe salvaged some pride by taking 5-77 and 2-48 in the two Middlesex innings – passing 2,500 first-class wickets in the process – allying grim determination to his supremely efficient technique without ever quite finding his best form. From Lord's, Kent went on to play Hampshire at Bournemouth, where they lost by an innings and 83 runs. Blythe himself missed this game as he was preparing to report for service with the Fortress Engineers, where his teammates Hutchings, Hardinge and Fairservice all joined him in the first week of September. 'It was a relief to all when the curtain was rung down on the season', Kent's official history notes.

On the afternoon of 27 August the Middlesex committee met at Lord's to visit again the troubling matter of Frank Tarrant and his request for a salary of £300 a year. According to the minutes, after a lengthy debate, 'it was decided it was impossible and undesirable to offer better terms'. As the authorities were discussing this, Tarrant himself was a few dozen yards away opening the Middlesex bowling against Kent. He took 3-47 off 28 overs, and then scored 40 opening the batting. It proved to be his last appearance for the county. In other business, the committee discussed the pressing need for repairs and renovations to some of the facilities at Lord's, which they would share with MCC, and voted 'to make a gift of 25 guineas to the Prince of Wales's Relief Fund ... it was hoped the Club will be in a position to make a further donation'. Despite these measures, and the publication that morning of Grace's open letter in the press, much of the day-to-day protocol of county cricket carried on as usual. At Lord's, the amateurs' dressing room attendant, somewhat past the age for military duty, continued to lay out the players' neatly pressed flannels at the start of play; continued to arrange symmetrically the freshly ironed morning newspapers on the polished side-table, and to supply a steady succession of cups of tea and other refreshments served on a crested silver tray. The professional players were not so fortunate, as was testified by the 'stink of socks and stale cigarette smoke' Tarrant noted of his working environment, in the course of a letter home announcing his decision to leave Lord's, on the whole without regret.

Grace's remarks asking that 'all first-class players set a good example and come to the help of their country without delay', though widely reported, still failed to bring an immediate end to the season. The matches set to begin on Monday 31 August went ahead as scheduled, with Surrey back in action at the Oval against Gloucestershire. Later that day, 81-year-old Earl Roberts, Colonel of the National Reserve, made a speech in the City of London praising a newly raised battalion of some 1,200 stockbrokers and bankers. 'How different is your action to that of the men who can still go on with their cricket and football as if the very existence of this country was not at stake', he said. Arthur Conan Doyle added in the *Evening Post*: 'if the cricketer has a straight eye, let him look along the barrel of a rifle. If a footballer has strength of limb, let him serve and march in the field of battle'. The following day's press drastically reduced its coverage of all sports fixtures. Some of the accompanying editorials, such as that in *The Times*, said divisive things, and clearly not everyone in authority agreed that the war effort was best served by discontinuing any aspect of normal life. Sydney Pardon, the venerable editor of *Wisden*, wrote: 'public feeling [against cricket] having been worked up to rather a high pitch, the Surrey committee at a special meeting decided to cancel the two remaining fixtures … it was in some ways a pity this drastic step should have been found necessary'. In a less than wholehearted statement, MCC would go on to announce the early end to the Scarborough festival 'as the continuation of cricket is seemingly hurtful to the feelings of a section of the public'. This was perhaps not quite the rousing call to arms Lord Roberts had in mind. In a piece of dreadful irony, the weather finally turned gloriously hot just as the season wound up, with a long Indian summer that extended into the middle of October. On 7 September the daytime high temperature in London was 28°C or 82°F. Coming back to Tonbridge after his final match for Kent at Lord's, Colin Blythe found 'oven-like heat, the sky cloudless, the Medway veiled in haze'. There was no measurable rainfall in southern England between 20 September and 12 October. When Somerset played their final Championship match of the season, against Essex at Weston-super-Mare, it was said there was a carnival-like atmosphere 'with a police band, and rock cake and lemonade stalls catering to a large crowd in shirt-sleeves. One rosy-cheeked gentleman strode the boundary in a smock decorated with stray tufts of straw and a rubber frog attached to his waistband as a spur to merriment.'

Among those basking in the sunshine at Dean Park, Bournemouth, to watch Hampshire beat Essex in the last days of August was an extravagantly mousta-chioed, 53-year-old man of military gait named Teddy Wynyard. Born on 1 April 1861, nature seemed to have cast him in a lifelong role as a prankster. Wynyard had been the Hampshire captain from 1896 to 1899, and was by no means the last of the eccentric characters to hold that position. In 1903, appearing in an army team for which W.G. Grace had promised to play but then dropped out, he cleverly disguised himself with make-up and false beard and passed himself off to the crowd as the great man, even down to successfully imitating Grace's batting style. Wynyard played three Tests for England, and in 1907/08 declined an invita-tion to captain MCC in Australia because of army duties. Also an accomplished figure-skater, tobogganist and bare-knuckle boxer, he was remembered by Gilbert Jessop as a man of 'many and varied enthusiasms in life, whose occasional dark moods often took the form of a violent tirade which left those who witnessed it, or heard it from afar, shaken and exhausted'; in one such case at around the turn of the century, he and Ranjitsinhji loudly fell out over the ownership of a bunch of grapes. Early in September 1914, Wynyard went up to London and persuaded the authorities to recall him to active duty as a major with the King's Regiment. Despite aggressive lobbying on his part, he failed to see action at the front and instead served as the commandant of a military prison in Aldershot. While there he formed a golf club open to all ranks to which he gave the self-explanatory name 'The Jokers'. Awarded the OBE, Wynyard continued to play club cricket after the war, 'making myself obnoxious to the opposition' with his underarm lobs, and heading the bowling averages on an MCC tour of North America. He died in October 1936, at the age of 75.

Making only the fourth of his twelve appearances for Hampshire in the game against Essex, 19-year-old Alister McLeod scored an imperious 87 – 'soon into his attractive stride, and driving the ball to all parts', it was said. Within a week of this innings, McLeod volunteered for army service and spent much of the next four years as a lieutenant with the 5th Battalion, Hampshire Regiment, stationed on the Western Front, where he was twice wounded. He played only a handful of more cricket matches but was later a long-serving county secretary, and lived to be 87.

Another character of Hampshire cricket, Lionel Tennyson, arrived with his reg-iment at Le Havre on 24 August 1914. After barracks life in Colchester, France initially seemed everything a *bon vivant* bachelor might have hoped: the wine and the sunshine, the women, the clatter and jangle of trams taking groups of officers off to dine. Tennyson was impressed by the local train which took his men and him down to their arrival camp at Amiens and which he compared favourably to the home issue – the only challenge was 'in keeping our fellows from climbing out [on to] the top of the carriage and taking fruit off the villagers'. The area around Rouen was especially lovely at that time of year, with a 'fine forest' to walk through, well-stocked shops and market stalls that showed no sign of being affected by the war, and marble-floored public baths, where Tennyson 'soaked luxuriously before din[ing] at the Brasserie de l'Opera ... Rouen is the most beautiful town by a long way we have seen out here so far'.

Perhaps inevitably, Tennyson's good cheer was soon to be tested by the darkening turn of events. On his third evening in France, an old woman appeared at the door of her house and remarked to the British troops walking by, '*Pauvres petits anglais, ils vont bientôt etre tués.*' Later that night, Tennyson was jerked awake when 'a private soldier in the Inniskillen Fusiliers had a nightmare, and jumped up yelling, "The Germans are on us!" Everyone jumped up, seized rifles, and there was tremendous excitement – I have never been so frightened in my life.' On the fourth day, 'a man came into the camp this morning wounded from the front. He told us Sam Rickman had been killed, many injured, and the whole battalion had been cut up.' Even then, Tennyson spent the afternoon shopping and met up with a Captain Davies, 'who had had his foot run over by an Army Service Corps wagon which was running away', before dining at the Café Victor and 'looking in at the Hotel de Ville, which was very fine'.

On the fifth day, 'Reveille was at 4 a.m. ... we struck camp directly after this [and] spent all day in the boiling sun. At 6 p.m. we got into a train en route to Le Mans. [Wherever] we have been, trainloads of refugees pass us coming down from the north, and also trainloads of wounded.' On the sixth day, Tennyson

... arrived at the French barracks at Le Mans – Read, Johnson and I were put into the French NCO's bedroom to sleep, and all simply got devoured by bed lice and fleas, and in the morning were in a terrible state ... Later I had to settle a row between our cooks and the French cooks in barracks, such a lot of talking as I have never heard amongst the Frenchmen, as our cooks had started cooking at their oven, but it all ended amicably and they shook hands.

On the seventh day, Tennyson wrote:

I paid the men, giving them 5 francs each. This was the first pay they have had since we left England. I dined at the Hotel de Paris and had a hot bath there ... The news came in that we were off at about midnight to the front which pleased us, as we had been hanging about for some time now ready to go.

On 31 August, the newspapers in Britain carried more details of the success-ful delaying action at Le Cateau, but omitted to add the remarks of the BEF's commander-in-chief, Field Marshal Sir John French, describing his main force as 'shattered' and questioning the fighting spirit of his Allies, whose 'present tactics', he wrote to Kitchener, 'are practically to fall back right and left of me, usually without notice'. When Kitchener finished reading this telegram, he departed, in full dress uniform, by special train from Charing Cross in order to confer urgently with his commander in the field. Wedded to an indecisive strategy, French's vola-tile personality and Kitchener's bristling indignation at this 'conservatism of tactics' were enough to ensure the subsequent meeting was a lively one. Meanwhile, the German army was in action against the British and French rearguards 30 miles from Paris. 65-year-old General Joseph Gallieni was brought out of retirement post-haste and appointed the city's military governor, and took a whirlwind series of meas-ures: engineers demolished houses and trees that Gallieni deemed to obstruct his artillery; food and medicine were stockpiled; and private vehicles commandeered, including the taxis soon to be made famous, when a fleet of them rushed 6,000 reinforcements to the front. In Britain, a small but increasingly strident minor-ity took the opportunity not only to question the likelihood of military victory, but even of serious negotiation toward a reasonable compromise; to men like Keir Hardie, the British role of global leadership in the early twentieth century was itself deeply flawed.

There was still no concerted anti-war movement in England in August 1914. The general mood of the country was resolute. But the first month of the fighting in Belgium and France cruelly dashed some of the fonder hopes for the war that would be 'over by Christmas'. Many of the young men who ran to their recruiting stations to enlist before it was all over need not have hurried. It is quite coinci-dental that Edward Elgar's mournful work *Sospiri* ('Sighs') had its London debut just as tens of thousands of British troops were crossing the Channel in order to desperately press their shoulders against a door being battered by the Germans. Not many people can have consciously decided to get in taxis or buses and drive out to Queen's Hall to listen to the piece because of its supposed allegorical insights into the era. But it would be fair to say that it later symbolised a general darkening of spirit, just as W.G. Grace's letter did.

Although Britain continued to bask in late summer sunshine, this was small con-solation compared to both the war news and the sense of gloom – of life closing down – that marks the end of any cricket season. The special circumstances of mobi-lisation further contributed to the strange, twilight atmosphere that characterised the few outstanding first-class fixtures. All sixteen county clubs offered incentives for their professional players to enlist, and some, like Essex, declared that 'No man eligible for army service was [to be] employed in any capacity' on their grounds. The result was the drafting in of amateur players either too old or too young for active duty, and the disappearance of others into the colours just as the remaining games were being eked out. Before their annual winter meetings, several county clubs would hold memorial services. Nineteen of the members of the Warwickshire and Kent sides who met at Edgbaston in the middle of August would see combat at some stage during the next four years, and three of them, Jeeves, Jennings and Blythe, were killed. In the return match at Gravesend, a fortnight later, Kent gave a game to their young amateur batsman George Whitehead, who as we have seen was just down from Clifton. An impeccably modest and at the same time quietly self-confident man, he was said to have worn his striped school blazer 'with an air of invisible precedence'. As an early recruit to the flying service, he witnessed the scenes of burning houses and the 'ranks of pathetic, blackened-faced refugees' fleeing the German advance in Belgium, and from that time on was an implacable fighter in the Allied cause. Lieutenant Whitehead died in action in October 1918, shortly after his 23rd birthday.

In the robust tradition of Hampshire cricketers, Robert Jesson, the leg-break bowler who had taken 5-42 on his county debut but then went on to a career in the law, enlisted in the Wiltshire Regiment promptly on the outbreak of war. He had just turned 28, was unmarried, and a ruggedly competitive hockey, football and rugby player as well as a supremely versatile cricketer. Several club sides around Southampton persuaded him to turn out for them in 1914, which he did with unfailing modesty and a certain all-round prowess: batting in the middle order in one weekend match at Petersfield, he executed an overhead tennis smash at a bouncer, sending it high over the head of the bowler into the pavilion seats for six. 'Lucky shot', he remarked, with no trace of irony.

In September 1914, Jesson's slightly younger Oxford and Hampshire colleague Alfred Evans elected to join the Royal Flying Corps. Part of a large cricketing dynasty, he made his county debut in August 1908 with a typically brisk 50 against Derbyshire, said to have shown 'courage, coolness of judgement and a proper degree of aggression'. Evans extended much the same qualities while in the air service. Shot down over enemy lines in July 1916, he was first sent to the notorious Clausthal prison camp, a fortified castle in the Colditz style set high up in the Harz mountains of northern Germany. Evans immediately escaped, but was captured again a few days later while trying to cross the Dutch border. Transferred to the 'Fort 9' camp at Ingolstadt in Bavaria, reserved for 'incorrigibles', he again escaped and this time made his way successfully to Switzerland. Following a brief period of recuperation at home, Evans was sent to Palestine early in 1918, where he was once more to be shot down, and had the added misfortune of being captured by the Turks. This was widely considered a fate as dire as anything the war had to offer. Although systematically starved and beaten while in custody, Evans, with a certain inevitability, escaped for a third time. Continuing to play for Kent, the Gentlemen and MCC after the war, he made one appearance for England against Australia at Lord's in 1921, but was not a success.

Guy Napier of Cambridge University, MCC and Middlesex had taken 365 first-class wickets in just eighty-one matches up to the outbreak of war. 'Bowling with a fairly high and very easy action he had great command of length and made the ball go with the arm', *Wisden* wrote, noting with understatement that 'he could be genuinely quick'. Tall and slim with dark, tousled hair, Napier reserved some of his best performances for Lord's. In August 1914, he wrote in a letter home that his successes there 'seem to have given me a name which I have done nothing whatever to deserve'. Napier volunteered for the army that month. He was killed at Loos while attached as a lieutenant to the 35th Sikhs Regiment in September 1915, aged 31.

Jack MacBryan of Somerset had come into the county side in 1911, and achieved the modest distinction of top-scoring with 20 in a total of 97 against Surrey at the Oval. In June 1914 he hit 61 in the home match against Gloucestershire, and showed more than a glimpse of true all-round potential: a small but sturdily built man who once nodded a fast ball off his head to the Taunton square leg boundary, he was neat, compact and utterly fearless. Less than a month after his final cricket match of the season, MacBryan was wounded in the shoulder at Le Cateau, leaving him with a permanently shortened right arm, and, as we have seen, spent the rest of the war as a German prisoner. Despite his handicap, he played a further 194 first-class matches, including one Test. 'A rich character', in *Wisden's* view, he continued to apply a certain military doctrine at the crease, frequently thumping the ball from his presence with an indignant, short-arm jab, and chastising teammates and opponents alike for any deficiencies in their turnout. MacBryan was also a first-class mimic when the occasion warranted. He never spoke about the war.

III

On Thursday 27 August 1914, the Warwickshire team went out to bat in their last Championship match of the season, against Surrey at Edgbaston. It would be the final appearance in an organised cricket game of five of the home side, Frank Foster, Septimus Kinneir, Colin Langley, Sydney Santall and Percy Jeeves, and of one of the visitors, Razor Smith. Somewhat against form, Warwickshire won by 80 runs.

Like other fixtures, the game was sparsely reported in the press, although one correspondent said, 'Surrey looked to hold the stronger position on Friday evening when, with seven wickets in hand, they required only 130 for victory.' Those 7 wickets fell in an hour on Saturday. Percy Jeeves was once again the life and soul of the attack. It may be that the likes of Skelding of Leicestershire and Hitch of Surrey are the names one thinks of in terms of pure muzzle velocity, and on his day Arthur Jaques at Hampshire could rattle any batsman by his habit of pitching it fast on the leg stump, with a clutch of fieldsmen crowded close in on that side. But time and again Jeeves proved capable of putting the ball down accurately for longer periods than anyone else, swinging it both ways, and in general becoming a master of English conditions. He was also one of the most personally unassuming of pace bowlers. To read the interview with him in a November 1913 issue of *Cricket* is to enter a world of almost archaic courtesy. 'How did it happen that you took to cricket as a profession?' the paper enquired. 'I was very keen on the game, and was always longing to play, so when my employer at the Goole club told me I was getting too old for the work he could find me to do off-season, I thought I might try my hand', Jeeves answered, in tones as unflappable as those of his fictional counterpart. 'In 1909 I answered an advertisement in the *Athletic News* for a professional at Hawes, which is distant only a few miles from the scene of the recent terrible railway catastrophe. To my great surprise I got the job.' Apologising for the bluntness of the question, the interviewer asks, 'How came you to qualify for Warwickshire?' 'It was in rather a curious way,' Jeeves allows:

> Mr Ryder, the secretary to the Club, was spending his holidays in Wensleydale during the autumn of 1910, and while playing a round of golf was introduced to Mr Crallan of the Hawes club. Naturally the conversation soon turned upon cricket, and Mr Crallan very generously recommended me as a likely man for Warwickshire. The result was that I was offered an engagement on the ground staff at Edgbaston for the season of 1911, and gladly accepted it.

At the time he signed papers for Warwickshire, Jeeves was 23 years old. He was initially paid a basic £62 a season, which was modest enough even by the standards of English domestic cricket before the war. The county secretary also wrote to assure him that the club 'shall arrange for you to play regularly for a league team on Saturday afternoons, but there will not be an extra fee for these matches'. Should the side require him for any 'special appearances' outside the normal fixture list, 'you will be paid the usual rate, viz 15/6, for these'. In all, it amounted to an annual salary of about £150, which was roughly on a par with the take-home wages of a manual labourer. Jeeves took 106 first-class wickets at an average of 20 in 1913. Eight of them came in his first Championship game at Edgbaston, against Leicestershire, in which he also made 46 and 23. 'A particularly gratifying feature of the match,' wrote *Wisden*, 'was the fine work with both bat and ball of Jeeves, one of the most promising of all the younger generation of cricketers.' Staring out from a popular cigarette card, he is a lean, distinguished-looking man with an intense stare, a slightly beaky nose, and an air of coiled energy. Jeeves still lived in a room in his parents' terraced home in Goole, and admitted he was 'quite satisfied' with his brief professional career to date, but 'in no way wish[ed] to swank about' the prospect of international recognition. Such things are unknowable, but it seems more than likely he would have played for England within a year or two in the normal course of events. Jeeves took 5-52 and 2-36 in the two innings he bowled against Surrey, bringing his career total to 199 wickets, at an average of 20.03, in just fifty matches.

On that same Saturday, Leicestershire began their last home fixture, and, as it proved, the concluding match of their season. It was the final game for Leicester's William Odell, and for Jim Iremonger of the visitors, Nottinghamshire. Notts were the better side throughout, and in the course of a convincing win their young number five 'Dodger' Whysall passed 1,000 career first-class runs – a further 20,000 or so would follow before he finally retired. Second Lieutenant Odell, MC, of the Sherwood Foresters, was reported as missing, presumed killed, at Passchendaele in October 1917. 'Bill did everything, and shone in them all', said a contemporary at King Edward VI Camp School in Birmingham. Tall and saturninely handsome, his thin face topped by a slick of black hair, Odell was remembered as a fine seam bowler who twice took 8 wickets in an innings, and, like Jeeves, was often mentioned as a future England player. He was 31 at the time of his death.

On 28 August, Lancashire also began the final match of their season, against Northamptonshire at Old Trafford. When they left the field it was the end of an era for Bill Huddleston, Ralph Whitehead, William Tyldesley and Harold Garnett of Lancashire, the last two of whom were killed, and William East and Thomas Askham of the visitors. Askham had come into the Northants side fresh from heading the batting averages at Wellingborough Grammar School, and was said to have typically hit the ball with 'a whip of the arms and hands, usually accompanied by a broad smile'. Although *Wisden* restricted itself to remarking 'his back play was very sound and he was an excellent field', others were convinced he too was an England man in the making. As 2nd Lieutenant Askham of the Suffolk Regiment, he fell in action at Thiepval in August 1916; he was 19. Askham's county teammate Claud Woolley was wounded in November 1917, in the same shell explosion that killed Colin Blythe, but emerged to play thirteen more seasons of first-class cricket.

The match at Old Trafford was drawn. 'Most of the batsmen played in very sedate fashion', wrote *Wisden*, although 27-year-old William Tyldesley made a 'faultless' 92, his highest score of the season. An early recruit to the Loyal North Lancashire Regiment, he did not survive the war.

In 1914, a contest between Surrey and Gloucestershire at the Oval would have been seen as akin to the one between David and Goliath, although in this case there was to be no surprise victory for the underdog. On the afternoon of 1 September, the top team in the Championship duly beat the bottom one by an innings and 36 runs, with more than a day's play in hand. Although no one there may have known it, it was to be the last time that Tom Hayward and Jack Hobbs went out to bat together for Surrey. At the age of 43, Hayward was now a tall, stout, bulbous-nosed, moustachioed man with very little of his wispy dark hair remaining, but still good enough to get his thousand runs or more a season. Although he remained on Surrey's books until December 1918, he would take the opportunity of the war to quietly announce his retirement. Hayward scored only 1 against Gloucester, but Hobbs put up 141 in less than three hours. Percy Fender had an analysis of 6-83 in the visitors' second innings and match figures of 9-115, both the best of his career at that point. Gloucester's chances were not improved when they arrived at the Oval with only ten men, their long-serving opening bat Alf Dipper having enlisted. Dipper, then 28, but known affectionately as 'Old Dip', was an almost stereotypical example of West Country cricket – it is said that he had the 'most inelegant stance anywhere in England, with a disdain for such niceties as the backlift, [and] whenever he could, would twist his sturdy, stained old bat and clout the ball to leg'. Ironically, in 1908 he had also made his county debut when the Gloucester team arrived a man short for a match at Tonbridge, where he had happened to be in the crowd. Dipper returned from the war and played for fourteen more seasons, making one appearance for England, at a rather threadbare time for the Test side's batting, in 1921. He scored 40 and 11, but was dropped.

On 31 August Sussex and Yorkshire also began the final match of their season, at Hove. It was to be the last appearance on a professional cricket field of the visitors' Ben Wilson, Alonzo Drake and Major Booth, the last of whom fell at the Somme while serving with the Leeds Pals. Roy Kilner had time to score 88 and 54 before going off to the war, where he was wounded in the same action that killed Lieutenant Booth. The opener Joe Vine hit 175 for Sussex. After three days the game evened out in a draw, both teams appeared for a final bow on the pavilion balcony, 'and a small but satisfied crowd rose in appreciation of those of the players already in khaki attire'. During the course of the match the Surrey committee announced they would forfeit their last two fixtures of the Championship, and the other counties soon followed suit. From then on, *Wisden's* capsule reviews of the season's few outstanding games would read, 'Cancelled due to the War.'

After that, it would remain only for the newspapers to note the names of the large number of cricketers who were killed, wounded or decorated for gallantry fighting for their country. Among the earliest of the medal-winners was Gordon Belcher, sometime of Cambridge University and Hampshire. The son of a vicar, he is remembered as a 'huge, amiable bear of a man [who had] rapidly concluded he would never be a top-class cricketer, and cheerfully learnt to soldier as an alternative'. As Captain Belcher of the 1st Battalion, Royal Berkshires, he won the MC in fighting around Soissons in February 1915 but died in action on the Western Front just three months later, aged 29. His county teammate Alexander Johnston, born in 1884, had come down from breaking most of the batting records at Winchester to enter the military college at Sandhurst. He also fitted in a year living as a cowboy in Colorado and New Mexico. Johnston spent three years in France as part of the original BEF, was wounded four times, Mentioned in Dispatches five times, and, like Captain Belcher, won the MC at Soissons.

But probably the first cricketer to be commended in the field was Basil Hitchcock, who had played two matches as a 19-year-old middle-order batsman for Hampshire in 1896. Even then he had cut an impressively military figure, lean and tall, with a bristling cavalryman's moustache. Awarded the DSO for his action in fighting on while wounded at the First Battle of Ypres in November 1914, he eventually rose to the rank of lieutenant-general. After the war, Hitchcock restricted himself to regimental cricket and was said to have been the 'best-dressed man on the park, moustache immaculately waxed, his flannels adorned with a carefully polished brass belt, a cravat adding just that thin film of superiority between himself and the rest of the human race', a vestige of what a certain kind of gentleman cricketer had looked like in 1914.

Meanwhile, Middlesex had also wound up their season with their two-day win against Kent at Lord's. The next county cricket match on the ground would not be until May 1919, fifty-seven months in the future. It was the last appearance for their counties of Frank Tarrant and Henry Weston of the home side, and Arthur Fielder, Fred Huish and George Whitehead of the visitors. We have noted the death in action of Lieutenant Whitehead, RFA, in October 1918, aged 23. Colin Blythe also played his final game at that level, having kept his promise to get 150 wickets in the season with one match to spare. He finished with a career total of 2,503 at the low average of 16.81. As the not-out batsman, Blythe happened to be in the middle when the game ended and as he walked in he lifted his cap to the crowd, 'a short, slim, pale-faced figure with a square jaw and dark, neatly pasted hair, who could have passed himself off as 25 instead of 35', said the *Globe*. Three days later, Blythe signed up for the army and paused proudly for a photograph before setting out, dressed in a tweedy three-piece suit and cloth cap, a mac thrown jauntily over his right shoulder. His whole demeanour is good-humoured, breezy and confident. He has a wide smile. Across the bottom of the picture, Blythe wrote, 'Off to enlist!'

III

In France that week, Lionel Tennyson continued his transition from a state of mild excitement and optimism into one of first wariness and then full-blown horror as he approached the front. After a long and hot day's train journey with his men:

> We finally arrived at Versailles … we had a great ovation as we steamed slowly along from the French people, who all seem to worship the English. At 4 a.m. we woke up to find ourselves only three miles from the fortifications of Paris, and looking out of the window saw about three searchlights sweeping the skies for aircraft, which was rather a fine sight. Later that day I saw Bernard Gordon-Lennox at the station, who told me MacDougall of the Grenadiers had been killed, and George Morris, an old Rifle Brigade man, had been killed also, as well as many others. I also saw Col. Marker, who commanded 2nd Bn. Coldstream. This was the last time I saw both these fellows, as they were both killed.
>
> On our march to Crecy we passed lots of English troops retreating, all seemingly terribly done in. I had a great deal of trouble in keeping the men up in the ranks and in stopping them throwing away their packs as they were all dead beat, and terribly footsore. We spent the most awful night. [Next day] we moved off again about 6 a.m. and marched about twelve miles. It was terribly hot, and the smell of all the dead horses by the side of the road [was] too awful. We looked down to the battle going on beneath us from the top of a hill, overlooking the River Marne.
>
> At 2.30 a.m. I was awakened to go and inform our Colonel that we were going to have an attack at dawn on the opposite side of the river. The General sent me down on a bicycle with a message to the Col. of the East Lancs who was down in the village. As I was bicycling down the hill the German machine-guns from the far side of the river opened fire on me, but I kept close under a wall and so was fairly safe. I delivered my message to him and had some breakfast at the chateau with him, when I returned to the General. One minute after I left the Col. of the East Lancs was no more. He was shot through the head by a German sniper.

'16 Dead Englishmen'

At the stroke of teatime on the sunny afternoon of Wednesday 2 September 1914, at Hove, Edgar Oldroyd of Yorkshire wafted almost absent-mindedly at a ball from George Cox of Sussex, which turned and lifted enough to hit the top of the batsman's off stump. At that the players and umpires walked off to the pavilion, and did not return. During the interval, the captains met in the Sussex amateurs' dressing room and agreed to abandon the match as a draw. 'There were some zoological noises from the ale tent' at the announcement, the *Argus* said, but only 'respectful and sustained applause met the players on their subsequent appearance at the pavilion rail'. It was the last first-class match to be completed of the 1914 season. 'The men's hearts were barely in the game', the periodical *Cricket* wrote at the time, which if so was hardly surprising as the afternoon editions of the papers on sale around the ground carried hair-raising reports of the Allied retreat towards the Marne and the heavy casualties that ensued. Fifteen of the players at Hove would see front-line duty at some point during the next four years, and one of them was killed. In September 1939, the final professional match played before the outbreak of the Second World War saw the same sides facing each other on the same ground; on that occasion, George Cox's son, also named George, scored 198 for Sussex. Cox senior was to have had a benefit match later that week, but in the event it was postponed for six more years. When the lights finally went out at Hove that evening, they did so in a torrential thunderstorm. The weather had the last sardonic laugh.

Although Surrey were six points, and 4.40 percentage figures, clear at the top of the table as it stood that night, *Wisden* reported 'it was argued by many that in deciding to cancel their remaining fixtures, the county had forfeited their position and that the Championship [should] remain in abeyance for the year'. The matter was settled only at a meeting of the MCC Committee on 9 November, which ruled that 'the order of the constituent county clubs would not be changed'. Speaking on behalf of the runners-up, Pelham Warner noted for the record that 'Middlesex has no objection to urge'.

Justly enough, Hobbs and Hearne led the batting with averages nearly 10 runs ahead of the next man, although further down the order there were some curiosities like Essex's 39-year-old Rev. Frank Gillingham, who finished above the likes of Albert Relf and C.B. Fry, or the young Hon. Henry Mulholland, whose exploits for Cambridge University and Ireland put him on a statistical par with Tom Hayward. Colin Blythe again led the bowling list, having carried the attack for Kent – 'adept on a dry wicket,' *Cricket* said, 'and on a sticky one, a terror to the greatest batsmen of the day' – through twenty-nine matches and 1,008 overs, roughly a third of which were maidens. He had taken more than 100 wickets in every season since 1901, and more than 150 on eight occasions. Of the twenty leading bowlers in the averages, six (Blythe, Drake, Booth, Jaques, Jeeves and John Burrough of Cambridge) would die either during the war or shortly afterwards. Among his other virtues as a cricketer, Blythe was not one for dwelling on personal records, any more than he was one for histrionics. If he missed the stumps by an inch, or saw a catch put down, he did not pause, or glare, or ruminate on the batsman's good fortune, technique or parentage. He just got on with it. 'At the age of 35', *Cricket* wrote, 'he did more work than any of the other county bowlers, got most wickets and until he joined the army in September never missed a day's play.'

Two years earlier, on a glorious summer's afternoon at Lord's, the Imperial Cricket Conference had met under the presidency of the Duke of Devonshire to determine the dates of future international tours. 'The inter-change of visits and [the] wider circulation of our Old Game' of which the Duke spoke so effusively suggested a golden future of uninterrupted sport between the mother country and those of her colonies fortunate enough to play organised cricket. As well as the matches themselves, the schedule would emphasise the traditional virtues of 'mutual respect, understanding, peace[ful] assembly, order, goodwill and the civilising aspect of an exchange of the game's highest values'. Now all that rich promise lay in ruins. The planned visit of the Australians to South Africa in the winter of 1914–15 was cancelled on the outbreak of war, and the Conference was soon forced to acknowledge that its schedule as a whole had been 'upset by the developments in Europe'. At their Christmas meeting, the Australian Board of Control voted unanimously that:

> With regard to the proposed visit of an English team to Australia in 1915–16, and the request of the South African Association that the Imperial programme should be [continued], the Board is of the opinion that, owing to the gravity of the situation abroad, the matter be left solely to the Marylebone Cricket Club, [and] the South Africans be informed that their request cannot be dealt with until the wishes of the MCC are conveyed here.

All professional cricket was then cancelled in Australia, New Zealand and South Africa, although the Bombay Quadrangular Tournament and various other state matches continued to be keenly fought in India.

By the middle of September 1914, the regular pounding of the heavy guns in France could clearly be heard some 70 miles away on the largely empty games fields of southern England. At night, 'the peaceful stars were shaken in their heavens', wrote the cricket-loving Arthur Conan Doyle from his home in Sussex:

> In every way, the earth quaked … I can never forget, and our descendants can never imagine, the strange effect upon the mind which was produced by seeing the whole fabric of life drifting to the edge of the chasm … military surprises, starvation, revolution, bankruptcy – no one knew what [the] episode would produce.

When, in October, MCC came to publish the official record of their team's first-class results, they did so with the formula: 'Matches 9 – Won 3, Lost 4, Drawn 1. Abandoned owing to the War 1.'

Nine days after the abrupt end of the English cricket season, the weekly *Graphic* printed the first set of pictures of officers reported killed or wounded at the Battle of the Marne. The following week's edition contained a larger supplement. By the issue of 3 October, four full pages were devoted to reporting the names and potted biographies of 'Fallen or Missing English and Scottish Officers' at the front. The action itself, often presented in terms of the near-miraculous, may not have been preceded by heavenly visions or luminous angels, but was at least enough to put an end to German hopes of a quick knock-out victory. From now on the fighting would come to adopt much of the static, attritional quality most people identify with the war.

A few miles away, Lieutenant Lionel Tennyson, of Hampshire and the Rifle Brigade, continued to move from what had been almost a holiday mood into the depth of war. The days of the hearty cricketer-warrior – noting in his diary the size and quality of his dinners – were well and truly past. After leaving the doomed Colonel of the East Lancashires, Tennyson:

> Went down to the square in the village with the General, and the German machine guns opened on us again. The General is a particularly brave man and while we were standing the bullets from these machine guns were hitting the wall behind us only just above our heads, but he didn't seem to notice them. I must say I was very pleased when he moved as I had to stand there with him.
>
> As a man, I do not like the General very much. Nor does anybody else. He is very fussy, [and] has the reputation of being rather incompetent … I forgot to

mention that the first thing I saw today before breakfast as we entered Laferte was one English officer and four private soldiers, a white horse, and a dead German lying on the road … It was a wonderful sight to see our guns all day shelling the snipers on the opposite bank of the river, and we set many houses and farms on fire with our Lyddite shells, thus driving the Germans out. About 5 p.m. the General sent me to the chateau garden to get hold of the gardener and get some fresh vegetables for his dinner. This I did, but coming back through a small wood I came upon 16 dead Englishmen including the Colonel of the East Lancs, Le Marchant by name, all lying side by side ready to be buried. There are awful sights like these one sees now, but one has to get used to them.

Time and again, Tennyson was to enjoy notable luck in terms of his own safety. While digging in at the Marne on the night of 13–14 September, he met 45-year-old Lieutenant Colonel Sir Evelyn Bradford, who had played eight matches as an all-rounder for Hampshire in the 1890s. Although Bradford's bowling action had raised eyebrows among several first-class umpires, the player himself was always indignant to have been called for throwing. 'The matter has implications of honour and prestige which loom far larger than any technical consideration', he said. A professional soldier since he was 18, Bradford was a quintessential British officer to look at, with his richly tinted cheeks and walrus moustache, his army great-coat habitually draped round his shoulders in a vaguely gangsterish pose. He was also imperturbably brave, and widely respected by his men in the 2nd Battalion, Seaforth Highlanders. As Bradford now unhurriedly returned to his trench, smiling, after chatting with Tennyson, a German shell burst a few feet away, killing him instantly. Tennyson was uninjured.

III

At home, towns like Portsmouth, Eastbourne and Gravesend were being rapidly converted from their holiday cricket-festival days into use as garrisons and troop-embarkation points. At Dover there was a constant bustle as commandeered cross-Channel ferries set off for France, 'the cheerful refrain of *Hullo, hullo! Who's your lady friend?* borne up on the breeze'. A force of two regular brigades and a volunteer battalion composed of 'actors, book-makers, sportsmen, engineers, poets, journalists, musicians and men about town' marched up and down around the castle, protecting the homeland from invasion. For want of rifles, some of them carried cricket bats or other sporting equipment tucked under their arms. Only a few weeks earlier, on 17 August, the Kent committee had voted 'to allow the usual payment of £16 to Dover towards the cost of advertising the cricket week there'. At the same meeting, it was minuted, 'a letter was read from Mr Marsham suggesting that the professionals should be encouraged to help the nation … it was decided to reply that to expect men, many of them married, earning £5 or thereabouts a week, to enlist for foreign service would be unreasonable'. It must have struck many people, both in Kent and elsewhere, how much things had changed in so short a time. They seemed to have lived far more than a month since the middle of August.

While every English county side suffered its own losses during the war, probably none was worse hit than Hampshire. No fewer than twenty-three of those who had played first-class cricket for the club over the years gave their lives. Apart from those mentioned, there were men like Harold Foster, a left-arm spinner who took 9-92 on his debut, and Herbert Rogers, to *Wisden* 'an unfailingly cheerful competitor', whose efforts were not met by statistical success, with just 69 runs and 1 wicket to show for his seven first team appearances from 1912 to 1914; killed in France, aged 39 and 23 respectively. There is a dreadful symmetry to the fact that the equivalent of two full teams of Hampshire cricketers, and a spare man, died in action. As we have seen, the county even lost their popular and long-serving secretary Francis Bacon, who died at sea. Many of these men, like Robert 'Wilf' Jesson, volunteered long before there was any obligation for them to do so. Most of their names are not in the history books. While it might not be true of all these 'golden lads' that they fought to preserve the future of Britain, or to make the world safe for democracy, by and large they reflect a group where idealism, dedication to a cause and a certain muscular Christian enthusiasm for the rights of the weak had not yet been tainted by the amusing satire of a *Blackadder*. 'Everyone seemed very cheery,' Jesson wrote on his eventual embarkation. 'Although one could not help wondering for a moment how many of this fine Battalion would return, these thoughts did not worry anyone. Excitement and the relief that after eight months training we were at last to see the real thing kept everyone in the best of spirits.'

The names of cricket's dead can be found scattered over the war memorials and honour boards at almost every county and club ground in Britain, some more prominently displayed than others. A total of 65,500 men served in the twenty-four battalions of the Yorkshire Regiment. There were local cricketers of every level stationed both in the 'Pals' units and elsewhere and, almost incredibly, a 'robustly keen', and necessarily limited-over, contest between Yorkshire officers and other ranks took place among the trenches at Vermelles in France in 1914, when a bird cage with a dead carrier pigeon inside was used as a wicket:

Amid the crash and roar of artillery and the fusillade of rifle shots 22 hardy northern men were able to give an unhurried but determined exhibition of the game's finer points. As the afternoon wore on, the wide expanse of the field was lit up by the fitful radiance of the flares and the red and white rockets which were signals for barrage fire a mile or two in the distance.

Here was the British genius for keeping calm and carrying on. Play was eventually abandoned only due to 'excessive' German machine-gun activity nearby.

During the war, nearly 9,000 of those who served in the Yorkshire Regiment were killed, and 24,000 were wounded. As we've seen, the county lost two of the finest all-round prospects in its first-class history, Major Booth and Alonzo Drake, aged 29 and 34 respectively. Lieutenant Booth was struck by enemy fire as he went over the top at the Somme. He died in the arms of 23-year-old Private Abe Waddington, of the West Yorkshires, who had been hit by shrapnel in the chest and legs a few moments earlier and was lying prone in no-man's-land. He remembered that his friend's eyes 'were white, and he walked towards me like a zombie'. Booth's body then remained in place until it could be recovered and buried nine months later. Waddington survived and transferred to the Royal Flying Corps for the remainder of the war. He went on to play as a fast bowler for Yorkshire and England in the 1920s, and even in that context was widely considered a plain-spoken character; he once fell into a noisy quarrel about the class system with a 'toffee-nosed twat' standing at the bar of his local golf club, and emptied a pint of beer over the man's head to illustrate his point. Not surprisingly, Waddington never forgot the experience of holding the mortally wounded Booth as he died in the shambles of the Somme.

We have touched on the career of Jack Wilson, who appeared as an amateur for Yorkshire in eleven matches in the 1912 and 1913 seasons, while riding as a steeplechase jockey in the winter. In August 1914 Wilson, who stood 5ft 4in tall, with centre-parted black hair and intensely pale eyes, was commissioned into the Royal Naval Air Service. This was not a branch of the forces for the faint-hearted. The standard British warplane of the day was essentially a series of rectangular boxes supported by bicycle wheels, held together with wire and glue, and the official Navy history records them 'appearing over the scene and thence engaging the enemy by pirouetting and looping and rolling in a colourful and macabre dance that at once enthralled the ground troops and was also supremely hazardous to the fliers' lives'. As the majority of these planes could reach a top speed of only some 70mph, their ability to evade ground fire was severely limited. In July 1915, the Admiralty announced that the king had been graciously pleased to award the DSC to Major Wilson and his co-pilot 'for their services on June 7, when after a long flight in darkness over hostile territory, they threw bombs on the Zeppelin shed at Evere near Brussels, and destroyed a Zeppelin which was inside. The two officers were exposed to heavy anti-aircraft fire during the attack.' Lord Hawke moved a special vote of thanks for 'this doughty Yorkshireman' at the next county annual general meeting. In 1925, Wilson won the Grand National on a horse called Double Chance at odds of 100-9. He died in the same month as Abe Waddington in 1959, aged 70.

At the other end of the country, Essex also played its full role in the war effort. Johnny Douglas, the boxing and footballing county captain, rejoined the Bedfordshire Regiment in August 1914. He served in France for three of the four war years, and came to enjoy much the same reputation for demanding the very best both of himself and his men as he did in his peacetime occupation. In later years he was always known as Colonel Douglas; it was thought the pride he obviously took in this name was not untainted by an implied, though unjustified, aspiration to senior-officer status. Douglas continued to dominate Essex cricket until 1928, when he left them acrimoniously after his 'autocratic methods had bred revolution in the club', so it was claimed at the subsequent AGM, and died at sea two years later. Although some thought Douglas's chief flaw was an inability to get on with other ranks, no one ever doubted his personal bravery. He was just 48 at the time of his death.

On 24 August 1914, the Essex cricket committee had voted that 'Members of the Staff volunteering in the war should have their places kept open for them'. A month later, the committee noted with satisfaction that 'all available members of the team (amateur and professional) and of the ground staff have now joined the army'. On 26 September of the next year, 22-year-old Geoffrey Davies became the first of the thirteen Essex players to die in action. He had scored his maiden first-class century just over twelve months earlier, taking eighty-one minutes and 'hit[ting] in brilliant style' after coming in at number nine against Northants at Leyton. Tall and slim, Davies was both physically energetic and socially laconic and detached, with a gift for telling poker-faced jokes. He had taken off his gas mask to give to a wounded British soldier. *Wisden* was not alone in believing that Davies would have gone on to play the game at the very highest level, 'and quite possibly developed into an England leader'.

In addition to Captain Davies, there was 2nd Lieutenant Ralf Robinson, a stockbroker's clerk from Stratford, who kept wicket for Essex before the war. Commissioned into the Royal Fusiliers, he won the Military Medal for his part at the Somme, transferred to the Rifle Brigade, and then fell in action at Ypres in August 1917, aged 32. Robinson left behind a pregnant widow, Daisy, who wrote to enquire whether she 'could have his County Cap for the sake of their son', who was born the following spring. The committee forwarded the cap with 'great pleasure' and 'warmest wishes for the boy's future', but he was also to be a casualty of war, killed in 1942 while serving with the Eighth Army in Egypt.

After coming down from Oxford, the London-born Frank Street taught English at the Forest School in Walthamstow while playing summer-holiday matches for Essex. Aged 44 when the war broke out, he passed himself off as 35 and was commissioned in the Royal Fusiliers. He was killed by a sniper's bullet on 7 July 1916, while serving at the Somme. The Bromley-born Douglas Tosetti was a champagne salesman who played six times as an all-rounder for the Essex Seconds. He was regarded as a 'stalwart and cheerful cricketer', though he met with little personal success. Commissioned into the 8th Royal Berkshires, Tosetti won the MC for his action in fighting on while badly wounded at Loos, and later saw service at the Somme and Passchendaele. Promoted to major, he was killed in the early hours of 21 March 1918, leading his men in a counter-attack through the fog and rain at Arras, on the first day of the German spring offensive. He was 40.

If Hampshire held the unenviable record of losing more men in the war than any other county, Essex almost certainly came in next on the list. On 26–27 August 1914, the county's Second XI played in their final game of the season, a heavy loss to Surrey Seconds at the Oval. No fewer than five of the Essex team – Cecil Thompson, James Hilleard, Edward Coleman, Edward Pallett and Harold Mead – and two of the Surrey side – Frank Gillespie and Edwin Myers – would be among the fatalities, meaning that all but a third of the young cricketers in the match would fall in action.

Throughout the war, there was to be a complicated but crucial connection between the cricket establishment's acknowledgement of the emergency and its inherent desire to keep calm and carry on. The moral imperative that Lord Hawke, W.G. Grace and others had invoked to persuade any undecided men to sign up co-existed with an official determination that 'cricket [would] step into the breach and prove to the world that England [was] not easily put off her game', as Hawke wrote in September 1914. On 15 September the Middlesex committee again met, not so much to discuss the implications of that week's action at the Marne and the widespread fears of enemy landings on the east coast, as to revisit the thorny matter of Frank Tarrant's pay demands. Of late these had grown to include his views on certain past financial matters, which differed significantly from those of the county. 'Dear Tarrant,' the club secretary wrote:

Though the Committee felt that you must decide for yourself about accepting the offer of the Maharajah of Patiala, I think there is very little chance of their consenting to your having the gate money taken at the Whit-Monday match [played for Tarrant's benefit]. I feel sure that the subscribers will be much annoyed and will probably say that they would not have subscribed if they had had any idea that you would leave us.

Nine days later, the Middlesex committee took the unusual step of formally writing to MCC (thus, to their own address) to 'discuss the proposal to afford facilities for placing a rifle range at Lord's', though in the end the plan was shelved 'pending future War developments'. In a gesture to the overall crisis, the county did, however, vote to donate £25 to the Red Cross.

At Kent, in late August, 'a two-day match between Merion CC of the USA and the Club and Ground side, to be played at Tonbridge, was approved, the young professionals to receive £1 a day'. As a goodwill exercise, this fixture can only be described as falling short of ideal. The game ended in some disarray when, with the American visitors wanting 2 runs to win with 2 balls remaining, the Kent bowler was instructed to roll these along the ground to prevent the batsman scoring off them. In other business, it was agreed that a letter of thanks be sent acknowledging 'the kindness and hospitality shown to the Second Eleven' on their recent southern tour. After some debate, the committee 'considered [it] no longer necessary to have a watchman sleeping in the Pavilion at Canterbury, but the dog was to be retained'. It was not specified if this was primarily seen as a precaution against the Germans or marauding suffragettes.

At Surrey, of prime concern was 'the curatorship of the Oval field ... the removal of Dandelions, Daisies, Plantains and other weeds' that had sprouted at the Vauxhall end following the tenure there of the troops and their horses, though there was satisfaction that 'so many of the Club [were] serving their country, if not engaged on active duty'. As we've seen, Jack Hobbs, Herbert Strudwick and Razor Smith initially all took up munitions work. Their amateur colleague Ernest Kirk, a left-arm seamer, went off to the war, a silk scarf tied nonchalantly around his neck, but returned a sadly diminished figure, to die aged 47.

Percy Fender of Surrey, an all-rounder of keen intelligence and unshakable application, if not always of textbook correctness (and with a pleasing facial resemblance to Groucho Marx), transferred to the Royal Flying Corps in December 1914. He caught some of the primitive flavour of this branch of the service when he later said:

> I was on the way home from patrol when I saw this Hun plane. I remember I was sitting on an empty sugar crate because my seat was too low. I had a rifle strapped to the fuselage outside because we had orders to be armed, but I had never used it. Looking back it was all rather a waste of time.

Before being posted to India in 1916, Fender and a friend threw a going-away party for themselves and 400 guests at the Café Royal. Legend insists that between them they had gone on to consume 'literally thousands' of bottles of champagne, although

Fender himself gave a more modest figure. 'It was 986', he once told me, precisely. Fender was eventually invalided home with a combination of dysentery and heart trouble. In August 1918, he appeared in an England XI against The Dominions at the Oval in what was the first game held on the ground since 1914. It was exactly four years since the fateful British note to Germany, and across London the Rest were beating Lord's Schools in a tight finish, just as they had been doing on the day war was declared. Fender showed some of his old form by coming in with the score at 75-6 and smashing 70 in forty-five minutes. He would play some 500 more first-class matches before his retirement in 1936, including thirteen Tests, becoming famous along the way as the best county captain never to lead England.

Alan Luther had played seventeen first-class matches as an amateur for Sussex and MCC before the war. A born administrator, he not only volunteered to organise the chaotic archives at Hove but was later both secretary of Berkshire and ground superintendent at the Oval. In late August 1914, Luther was 33 and serving as a major with the King's Own Yorkshire Light Infantry in the sector around Le Cateau. At dawn on 26 August the order came down for his unit to leave their position and advance. 'A "big one" exploded within a yard of me, blew me ahead about ten feet', Luther noted. 'God was with me, and [I] was not badly hurt.' After coming to, Luther realised that the Germans were fast approaching the area of no-man's-land where he lay dazed and bruised, but otherwise unhurt. He played dead. A hand reached in to remove his identity papers, and then a voice said to him in immaculate English: 'You are a fortunate man. I see you are a member of the MCC. You can go back to your lines.' In what must literally have been a one in a million chance, the German soldier had lived in England and fallen in love with cricket before the war. Alan Luther lived to be 80.

Many others were not so lucky. It still fills one with a sort of passive rage to think such lives could be extinguished, often before their 20th birthday, by the brute lottery of the battlefield. In the first month of the war alone there was John Manners, only a year or two earlier the batting star of the Eton side which beat Harrow at Lord's, killed in action on 1 September; Hunter Browning, a wiry, shock-haired Kent schoolboy whom even Grace had praised for his 'utmost felicity of timing off either foot' and, it was thought, a future England wicketkeeper, killed; Arthur Byng, of the Royal Fusiliers and Hampshire, killed; Fred Lowe, a promising young seamer at Kent, killed; Douglas Sewell, Wellingborough and the Buffs, killed; Charles Sills, captain of his Oakham School XI just eighteen months earlier, killed; R.F. Simson, of the Edinburgh Academy XI, killed; Archer Windsor-Clive, devastating left-arm seamer and indomitably optimistic bat of Glamorgan and the Guards, killed. Arthur Hughes-Onslow, a swashbuckling club cricketer and three-time winner of the

Grand Military Steeplechase, suffered a heart attack and died while riding his horse up the gangway to the troop ship waiting to take them to France.

III

Colin Blythe was still in training that autumn as an army engineer, and most of his war was waged in various home camps some distance from no-man's-land. The records are sketchy, but it seems that he was paid 2s a day while learning about such things as electric lighting and road-laying, and periodically touring the Medway towns on recruiting drives. It was reported in the pages of *The Pilgrim* that Blythe's rucksack was seen to 'bulge significantly with assorted sportswear', and that he found ample time while in the orderly room to practise the violin. 'This gave some reason for critical comment.' As well as regimental cricket, Blythe was still able to perform at close to Test level: on 14 July 1917 he would be back at Lord's, taking the modest figures of 1-16 for the Army against the Australian Imperial Forces. There was an intensity about him and his cricket that barracks life would not diminish. Percy Fender, who also played in the Lord's game, recalled how Blythe, on the same day, first marched smartly through the front gate of the ground as part of his unit, then later answered an invitation to go to the Committee Room and give his views to Lord Hawke and others on the structure of post-war county cricket, and finally was seen 'leading a band of violin, banjo and piano through a spirited and well-oiled knees-up' at the Coal Hole pub near Charing Cross station. It is a sure bet that he put his heart and soul into it on all three occasions.

For Blythe, then, life in the army was initially less harrowing than for many of those who embarked for France in 1914, and of whom he wrote home with such admiration and pity. Despite the routine and monotony, he described the three years he was with his unit in Kent as among the happiest times of his life, a fair amount of it spent on weekend leave at Tonbridge. But death was often close. In October 1915 a battalion of Blythe's friends in the Fortress Engineers shipped out to Gallipoli and were aboard the ferry HMS *Hythe* when it collided with another boat and sank off Cape Helles, with the loss of 155 lives. The company's commanding officer, a fellow Tonbridge man and cricketer named David Salomons, was among the casualties. Exactly a year later Sidney Blythe, the youngest of the family's six brothers, fell in action on the Somme with the Hampshire Regiment. He had lied about his age when he followed his brother to the recruiting office in 1914. Although the army records listed him as 21, Sidney was only 19 at the time of his death.

Colin Blythe was not alone among first-class cricketers in voluntarily giving up an agreeable, if not always lucrative, civilian life for the army. There was Frank Joy, for example, of the Europeans and Somerset, emphasising the aptness of his surname with a personality said to be 'square, strong, cheerful and eminently likeable', and a batting style that 'veered to the rustic'. Joy had come down from Oxford without winning his blue and appeared fitfully in first-class cricket while working as a schoolteacher and journalist. He married in the spring of 1914, and in the autumn his wife found she was pregnant. Joy took the occasion of his 34th birthday that September to volunteer for the army. Commissioned into the King's Own Scottish Borderers, he served in France for the next two years.

Of a particularly oppressive stay at Ypres, Joy wrote that while in the trenches he had 'showered daily in the dirt sift[ing] down from the edges of a square sheet of corrugated tin that, along with sandbags and a lump of brick, served as one's roof'. He had frequently woken from a light sleep in order to see rats 'tap-dancing across the wet floor', a plague added to that of 'the lice, which were everywhere – at night you pulled them out of your shirts and underwear and monotonously counted them; there were always more than a century in number'. Joy was also to record 'feel[ing] exhausted and quite faint with hunger for most of the time', among other privations that had nothing directly to do with the enemy facing him from across the mud only a few hundred yards away. Despite this, he is remembered as an 'unfailingly happy officer, [with] a coolness and gallantry under fire that were the admiration of all the men'. Once, at the Somme, he exchanged grenades with a unit of five Germans, who were sufficiently impressed by his skill to 'turn around and decline to pursue the matter further'. Although Joy never again played first-class cricket, his daughter Nancy, born in July 1915, went on to become a pioneer of the women's game. For years after the war, some people persisted in the belief that the typical British officer had been a cruel and effete, university-educated snob who disappeared the moment the firing began. Frank Joy defied this image.

After the initial euphoria of August and September, recruiting totals in Britain fell off sharply in the autumn. 'It's now forgotten that in the beginning many more of us held back than joined up', wrote Jack Horan, an MCC cricketer and future hero of the first massed tank attack at Cambrai, but at this early stage of the proceedings still working as an articled clerk in Holborn, central London. Horan's own epiphany came about not so much as a result of official fiat as of an incident when he was 'on a bus in civilian clothes and I heard talking and giggling behind me, and someone said, "Well, do it then." A girl walked up the aisle and handed me a white feather.'

Those who did volunteer in the early days of the war included a disproportionately large number of Britain's sportsmen in addition to her cricketers. The Scottish rugby union centre Ronald Simson died on 14 September 1914, while serving with the Royal Field Artillery at the Aisne, aged 24. Of sixty players to appear for the London Scottish club in 1914, forty-five were to be killed on active service overseas. The war took an appalling toll on rugby of both codes and at all levels. Ronnie Poulton-Palmer, the captain of the England XV and scorer of four tries against France at Paris in 1914, fell in action less than a year later. Tall and graceful, earnestly religious, and somehow always immaculately groomed, with a penchant for running full tilt at even the biggest opponent and then helping the man to his feet afterwards, he seemed to be the epitome of the muscular Christian. While never a respecter of sportsmen, the war was especially devastating to some of Britain's most gifted amateur athletes. Of the thirty players who appeared in that particular match in Paris, eleven would die in combat. Poulton-Palmer was cut down by a sniper's bullet while supervising trench work as a lieutenant with the Royal Berkshires in Flanders, just three weeks after arriving at the front. He was 25. By a morbid coincidence, the Rugby League (or 'Northern') season kicked off as scheduled on 5 September 1914, the same day as the opening of the Battle of the Marne. Huddersfield's 'team of all talents' would go on to win all four cups to be contested before fixtures were suspended for the duration of the war. Thirty-four of the club's players volunteered; thirteen never returned.

In athletics, there was the especially poignant case of Wyndham Halswelle. Born in 1882, as part of a colourful Anglo-Scots tapestry, Halswelle swept all running records before him at Charterhouse school and Sandhurst. After winning the 110, 220, 440 and 880 yards races in a single afternoon in 1906 at the Scottish championships, he went on to add a gold medal at the 1908 London Olympics in unique circumstances. In the final of the 440 yards Halswelle was elbowed aside by an American opponent, and the race was declared void. None of the other competitors would take part in the re-run two days later, so Halswelle ran the race by himself – the only athlete ever to win an Olympic title by a walkover. Soured by the experience, he never ran competitively again. On 31 March 1915, Captain Halswelle was killed by a sniper's bullet at the Battle of Neuve Chapelle, while rushing forward, burdened by sixty-six pounds of kit, in an attempt to rescue a British soldier who was lying injured in no-man's-land. He was 32.

Kenneth Powell, born in 1885, competed in the 100 yards hurdles in the same London Olympics, played tennis both there and at Wimbledon, and found time to write lyric poetry – 'his was a union of strength and grace', his army obituary says. Private Powell of the Honourable Artillery Company fell in action in February 1915, at Ypres, aged 29. Five of the eight Leander oarsmen who rowed in the final of the 1914 Grand Challenge Cup at Henley were dead within two years. As we have seen, entire professional football teams joined up on the outbreak of war. The

Clapton (later Leyton) Orient and Hearts sides both enlisted en masse, and suffered heavy casualties. William Angus, of Celtic and the Highland Light Infantry, became the first professional sportsman to be awarded the VC. His citation read:

> For most conspicuous gallantry and devotion to duty at Givenchy, on 12th June 1915, in voluntarily leaving his trench under heavy fire and rescuing an officer who was lying within a few yards of the enemy position. Lance Corporal Angus had no chance of escaping the enemy's fire when undertaking this very gallant action, and in effecting the rescue he sustained about 40 wounds from bombs, some of them being very serious.

Sandy Turnbull, who won the FA Cup with both Manchester City and Manchester United, later to be banned by the League in a match-fixing scandal, told friends he was joining the army to efface the blot on his reputation. He died fighting at Arras in May 1917, aged 32. Major Frank Buckley, of Derby County and England, kept a record of the men under his command in the Football Battalion. He later wrote that by 1920 over 500 of the force's original 600 officers and men were dead, 'either killed in action, or as a result of the awful consequences of injuries and disease'.

III

Meanwhile, Lionel Tennyson continued his strangely schizophrenic daily routine around the River Marne. Much of it involved the tedium and discomfort of marching back and forth for eight or nine hours at a time, to eat bad, cold food and to find shelter at night where he could, whether in an abandoned home or an improvised trench, digging and excavating and widening and laying claim to this small patch of France. Occasionally, however, Tennyson was able to enjoy some of the trappings of regimental life as he knew it in England. Even in the thick of battle, few nights went by without the 'very basic amenity' of several glasses of a good wine. After coming across the dead bodies of the sixteen British soldiers while on his way home with vegetables for dinner, Tennyson was forced to walk on by himself in the dark of night for a further 3 miles:

> All I met was a French labourer, who said goodnight. I wasn't sorry when I eventually found the Hampshires, though I was nearly shot by their sentries who were very much on the 'qui vive' when I got there. I had a little more dinner, and a good glass of claret, with the Hampshires and then showed them the way down the hill to Laferte to where the General was.

When we reached the General's chateau, the [Hampshires] were ordered to cross the Marne in four boats, as well as the East Lancs, during the night, which they did, though the Hampshires lost two men drowned in doing so.

On the following morning, Thursday 10 September, Tennyson was roused by his servant at 4.30 a.m. and told that the general wanted him at once. The subsequent interview lasted only a minute. The general ordered Tennyson to cross the Marne immediately by any means, which he did by the expedient of standing up on the seat of a small rowing boat and pulling on a rope suspended over the river. Halfway across he saw a British officer in the water, and altered course in order to collect him. Tennyson recognised the man as Jack Seely, 1st Baron Mottistone, an Old Harrovian, cricketer and former MP who had resigned his position as Secretary of State for War and, at the age of 46, gone to fight in France with the Cavalry Brigade. He expressed no particular emotion on his rescue. Tennyson writes:

I said to him immediately, 'You don't remember me, do you, the last time we met was playing golf.' He replied, 'I recall your face perfectly, but not your name.' I answered, 'My name is Tennyson.' He said, 'What Lionel, dear me, that is very interesting to think we should meet again here.' By this time we had got [to] the other side of the river, and having asked me if my revolver was loaded, as we might meet some Germans, we proceeded together. He informed me he had been sent by General French to find out how the situation lay, and this he informed everyone he passed, and asked most of the sentries we came across their opinion of the situation, but the men were unable to answer him much.

Seely and I walked together all through Laferte, which only the day before had been shelled to bits by our guns, and the damage done was terrific. We saw a few French townspeople about, who had been hiding all the days before in the cellars, and these informed us all the Germans had retreated, except a lot of wounded in some of the houses, and that late last night before they left, one of the Germans told them they had buried 700 dead.

Although Tennyson was capable of occasional exaggeration and drama, both the official regimental history and the testimony of other soldiers give no reason to question the accuracy of his diary. At this point, the English county cricket season had been over for just a week, and play was still continuing in many of the leagues and clubs.

'Seely and I mounted the hill on the other side of Laferte,' Tennyson writes:

Eventually, about a mile on, [we] reached the little village of Le Limon, where a lot of damage had also been done. Here the East Lancs had taken up a position and my battalion was supposed to be with them, but they had not heard of either of them since yesterday ... Having entirely disagreed with the Major now commanding the East Lancs in everything, and eaten two eggs of which there were only about six on the table, Seely said goodbye and pushed off, so he said, to report to General French.[*]

As Tennyson's tragicomic adventures continued across northern France, many of his fellow cricketers also served on the home front. Men like Gilbert Jessop, promoted to the rank of captain in the 14th Service Battalion, Manchester Regiment, toured Britain to help in the recruitment drive. Other players worked in munitions, volunteered for civil defence duty or lent their names to public service advertisements about enlisting ('Be A Sport – Join Today!'), food stocks or fuel restrictions. In Wyke Regis, near Weymouth, Wilfred Brownlee was serving with the 3rd Dorset Regiment in an effort to 'fortify the town, [as] it was expected a Hun raid would be made by sea to burn, murder and pillage' during the first weeks of the war. Brownlee had been the star all-rounder of the Clifton XI before going on to play first-class cricket for Gloucestershire. *The Times* felt 'all the gifts of the gods were his', among them tireless energy, intellect, Grecian good looks, 'a fundamental kindness and charity, [and] a Christian soul beyond his years'. It was said Brownlee's greatest challenge in life would be his future decision about whether to become captain of the England Test team or merely the prime minister. In a brother officer's view, 'he might equally have played either role, or possibly both, with distinction'. It was to be another case of tragically unfulfilled potential. Lieutenant Brownlee was stricken by meningitis while serving with his regiment and died on 12 October 1914, aged 24.

Walter Parke, a batting prodigy at Winchester and Dorset, was killed at Ypres in October, aged 23; Robert Pringle, another Winchester batsman, whose aggregate of 34 runs in a season perhaps testified to a style that was said to be 'full-blooded rustic, [as] cheerfully unvarnished as the man', also fell at Ypres, aged 28; Vere Boscawen, demon spinner for Eton and the Coldstream Guards, was killed in the same shambles, aged 24. John Gregory was born in April 1887 in Eckington, near

---

[*] Colonel Seely's set-piece debut as Secretary of State in September 1912 had been inglorious. At full-scale army manoeuvres held in Norfolk, his horse went lame and both George V and the Chief of the General Staff, among other senior officers, were kept waiting for him. A replacement was eventually found, only for this horse to seize the king's foot in its mouth. Seely resigned his office as a result of official criticism of his handling of the Curragh Mutiny in March 1914. He eventually rose to the rank of major general, winning numerous medals for gallantry in the field, and lived to be 79.

Chesterfield. From 1904 to 1914 he was a stalwart of Derbyshire league and club cricket, 'a purveyor of fine left-arm spin, a cheerful if numerically modest batsman, a splendid person and a very funny one whose practical jokes enlivened many a team dinner'. He played a single match for Hampshire, against Oxford University at Southampton, but was not judged a success. The figures aside, he rated his three wet days on the first-class field to have been the great moment of his life. Rifleman Gregory fell in action near Zonnebeke, Belgium, in November 1914, aged 27.

Some of the units who fought in the trenches left behind group photographs, typically showing a dozen or so men standing with a sort of muddied and grim cheerfulness, holding up cricket bats and balls, almost like a picture in a team annual. It is impossible to know exactly how many soldier-sportsmen of all levels fell in action. Death came for them all regardless of their status, and in every theatre of war. Bernhard Pratt-Barlow is not a name widely found in the cricket reference books. He played the game with more enthusiasm than distinction, though he once top-scored with 62 for a Combined Services side at Devonport 'and obtained his runs with equal facility all round the wicket'. When war broke out he was a Commander attached to the cruiser HMS *Hawke*. The ship was soon at work patrolling the North Sea against what was thought to be a likely German invasion. On the night of 14 October 1914, she was sailing in convoy in known U-boat waters some 50 miles off the coast of Aberdeen. A surviving diary records that the ships proceeded at slow speed, under a sky 'punctuated by the sharp glare of rockets periodically going up and showering in sparks to the sea'. Early in the morning of 15 October *Hawke* was hit by a single torpedo fired from a German submarine. In the official report, 'the impact ignited a magazine and caus[ed] a terrific explosion which ripped much of the ship apart. *Hawke* sank in ten minutes.' Despite the attempts of her sister ship *Theseus* to go to her rescue, only seventy of *Hawke*'s 594 crew survived. Commander Pratt-Barlow is remembered as having been blown into the water, horrifically injured, where he remained for a few minutes attempting to comfort a man who was floating beside him choking to death on oil fuel. Both figures were then seen to disappear as *Hawke* went down with a further explosion, her funnels collapsing inwards and a thick smoke obscuring the whole ghastly scene. A survivor wrote later that 'the Commander was worth a VC twice over'. Instead, there would be only an Admiralty telegram to the bereaved parents, and the formal notice in the *London Gazette* the following April that 'all creditors and other persons having any debts, claims or demands against the estate of Cdr. Bernhard Alexander Pratt-Barlow, RN, late of Devonport, are hereby required to send particulars, in writing, to me, the undersigned, as Solicitor to the executors'. This brave man's official record, and his life, ended there.

Six days after the death of Commander Pratt-Barlow, Harold Hippisley, of the 1st Gloucestershire Regiment, was killed in action near Ypres, aged 24. He had played county cricket as a 'classically refined middle-order man' for Somerset, 'seemed to have a great chance of becoming an England bat', and was married on the morning he embarked for France. Two days later, William Yalland, of the same regiment, fell in action. He had played his first and only professional match for Gloucestershire, and gone on to bat 'in a style always, and thus indiscriminately, robust, but otherwise singularly free from fault' for club and army sides. Lieutenant Yalland was 25 at the time of his death. Captain Otho Gilliat, of Eton, I Zingari and MCC – 'everything he put his hand to [was] touched by his quiet excellence', said *Wisden* – fell in action later that week, aged 32.

III

It is surely not the least of cricket's charms that it appears to combine a fine competitive edge with a stubborn refusal, until recently, to truckle to the accepted idea of a popular amusement. A certain eccentricity is not exactly a new concept in British entertainment, but for long stretches of its history the national sport has seemed to exist in almost total isolation from the events going on around it. In England, in 1914, the administration of the game was often richly idiosyncratic. On Wednesday 7 October, British newspapers carried reports of their armies' desperate 'race to the sea' and the subsequent digging in along a 50-mile front to begin a strategy then known as 'wearing-down', and now called attrition. Later that evening, news came in of the horrific scenes at Antwerp. The city was a 'spectacle of pity and terror ... the German bombardment opened upon a town without electric light, gas or water supplies ... throughout the night many conflagrations raged under a canopy of dense, black smoke emitted by the oil-tanks which the retreating Belgians had fired'. It was as if the whole area had gone to bed in a Constable painting and woken up in one by Hieronymus Bosch. About a quarter of a million people fled by way of sea, into Holland, or on foot towards France. There were an estimated 40,000 deaths among civilian men, women and children. Before settling down into their protracted and bloody stalemate, the Allied and German armies then met in the farm country around Ypres, the only remaining place where each belligerent could still hope to outflank the other. As a result, there would be a total of around 265,000 casualties, roughly a third of them British.

On the day battle was joined, Francis Lacey, the MCC secretary, wrote to a member who had enquired 'most assiduously' on the subject: 'We have not yet been asked to make any alteration in the usual procedure with regard to the County

Championship. I do not suppose, therefore, that Surrey's position will be disputed. Of course, it is open to the counties to make a request to the Marylebone club.' Lacey, who was recovering from illness, was among the most conscientious of cricket officials, but after 'many dozens' of subsequent hours discussing the issue, even he must have begun to wonder whether he could not have spent the time more profitably. A month later, a meeting of the full MCC Committee finally ratified the county table as it stood. There was a 'certain warmth of feeling about this,' *The Times* reported, 'and many individual members of the clubs argued that the Championship should remain open in 1914.' Surrey had last won the title as long ago as 1899. Lacey then reported that he remained 'personally sanguine' that some form of 'recognisable first-class cricket programme' would take place in 1915, 'any shortfall of teams or players made good by draftees from Minor County sides'. His optimism would be overtaken by events. The minute book of the MCC for May 1915 records simply: 'Agreed to cancel fixtures because of the War.'

Faced with the crisis, the sixteen first-class counties contributed to the war effort and struggled for their own financial survival as best they could. We have seen that the buildings at Lord's, Old Trafford and Trent Bridge were given over to accommodation for army units and military hospitals, while many of the county grounds of Derbyshire, Leicestershire and Yorkshire were pressed into service as tented camps or training centres. The lovely field at Sheffield Park near Uckfield, Sussex, set among rhododendron bushes, a bandstand and tiered seating for as many as 25,000 spectators, was ploughed up in order to grow vegetables. Balls Park in Hertford remained a hayfield until the mid-1920s. The University ground at Cambridge was commandeered by the War Office and prepared for use as an internment camp for enemy invaders. When these failed to materialise, the playing area was used to keep chickens and graze sheep. All of the first-class clubs encouraged their players to enlist, though this was achieved more readily at some than at others. At a meeting of the Kent committee on 16 December 1914:

> A letter was read out from Major D'Aeth calling attention to the fact that many of the professionals appeared to be avoiding service to the Country at this time. Mr McAlpine proposed that eight of the professionals of the right age for service should be informed that correspondence critical of their inaction had been received, and that they be asked to give their reasons for not enlisting, or, if they are doing anything to help the country to state in what capacity.

Not surprisingly, all the counties lost money during the war. Kent had only £447 on hand early in 1915, with pressing maintenance and salary bills of £900.

Fortunately, the Treasurer reported, 'our bank may be willing to advance the difference on receipt of a letter signed by the Chairman, Lord Harris'.

At schools up and down Britain, the declaration of war brought with it an almost delirious joy, at least among those who had no hope or intention of joining up and risking life and limb. In the years from 1908 to 1911 226 boys entered Hurstpierpoint College in Sussex. Of those 226, 185 are known to have served in the armed forces, and 39 were killed in action, a fatality rate of more than one in five. Of the Radley First XI of 1914, *Wisden* wrote, 'all of last year's [side] are still at the school, [and] the prospects are promising'. In fact, five of the eleven would be dead within four years. Since it was a buyer's market, the War Office instructions in August 1914 reminded recruiters that they were to 'select men on the basis of merit alone', and that the ideal candidate was to be 'physically fit, an individual of bearing [who] had already shown some sense of responsibility in civil life', a list that seemed to apply to a disproportionately large number of those who played public schools cricket.

The toll was particularly hard at Clifton, who lost a total of 578 old boys during the war. Arthur Collins was the school's most famous casualty, but there were many others. *Wisden* thought the batsman-wicketkeeper Alexander Leslie had 'heaps of shots [and] needed only time and experience to become a first-class star'. Leslie survived more than two years' duty on the Western Front, but came back a changed man, the lingering pain from a leg wound no doubt the source of his 'sometimes tetchy, even gruff' demeanour, and his anger that what he had seen in the flooding and mud and incessant barrage at Ypres was so underappreciated by a society that seemed to be embarrassed by its returning wounded. He never played competitive cricket again. Clifton not only provided a commander-in-chief (Douglas Haig) and an army commander (William Birdwood) – the senior officers on the Western Front and at Gallipoli – but twenty-three major-generals and fifty-two brigadier-generals. The school could also boast Henry Newbolt, whose *Vitai Lampada* famously bound up the spirit of cricket with a patriotic devotion to duty. It contained perhaps the most over-quoted lines of the war years. Richard Sandford played cricket at Clifton before joining the Royal Navy. At Zeebrugge, in April 1918, he successfully drove his dynamite-packed submarine into the harbour wall and, under heavy German fire, abandoned the ship moments before she exploded. Lieutenant Sandford survived the action and was awarded the VC. He died of typhoid fever in November 1918, twelve days after the signing of the armistice; he was 27.

It would be hard to credit as a work of fiction the strange and providential tale of Rev. Archibald 'Biffer' Fargus, whose obituary appears in the 1915 edition of *Wisden*. Born in 1878, in Bristol, Fargus was another Clifton boy who had gone on to play competitive cricket, in his case as an all-rounder for Cambridge University and Gloucestershire. His best figures came in his first County Championship match, against Middlesex in June 1900, at Lord's, when he took 5-32 in the first innings and 7-55 in the second – the best analysis by any player on his debut in the Championship at that time, and a record that would stand for 104 years. *Wisden* described Fargus as a 'stout hitter, a good hammer and tongs bowler, and a hard-working field'. The more you learn about the amateur cricketers in the early years of the twentieth century, the more you find (as well as dotty nicknames) the tendency to be good in more than one walk of life. By all accounts, Fargus was another of the Renaissance men of his generation, with 'boundless energy, clean looks and a nimble and often fantastical wit'. A very muscular Christian, he also boxed for Cambridge and played rugby for Devon. He was ordained in 1904, and joined the Royal Navy as a chaplain. In 1913, Fargus left the service to take up a ministry in Yorkshire, but rejoined immediately upon the outbreak of war.

On 21 August 1914, Fargus was officially posted to the armoured cruiser *Monmouth*, which set sail the following morning for the South Atlantic. In the week of 5 October, *Monmouth* and two other ships completed a rendezvous with the cruiser *Good Hope*, commanded by Admiral Christopher Craddock, at the Falkland Islands. On 22 October this squadron, better equipped for speed than it was for heavy gunnery, rounded Cape Horn and moved up the coast of Chile in pursuit of a German convoy. Late on the afternoon of 1 November the opposing forces met in stormy weather off the port of Coronel. The Germans opened the battle at the extreme range of Craddock's guns, and both *Good Hope* and *Monmouth* were quickly overwhelmed without being able to return significant fire. *Monmouth* was left drifting into the darkness, where her attackers followed at their leisure and struck her with seventy-five shells at close range. Both British ships sank, with a combined loss of 1,570 lives. There were no survivors. It was to be the first major Royal Navy defeat since Napoleonic days, and it understandably caused shock-waves at a time when the British public was still absorbing the daily casualty lists from Ypres. Among the many sombre reports of the battle was the stark notice in *Wisden* that Rev. Fargus had been 'temporary Acting-Chaplain to the *Monmouth*, on which he went down'.

In fact, Fargus had not been lost in the fearful carnage in the icy waters off Coronel. He was serving as an interim vicar at an Anglican parsonage outside of Bristol. On the afternoon of 21 August, Fargus had gone to Waterloo station, where he found a scene of 'almost abysmal chaos, every platform choked with people, men, women and children blowing whistles and horns [and] grinning soldiers climbing on the roofs of trains to wave wildly at their loved ones before moving off'. Under the circumstances, he had decided to postpone his journey south by a day, not realising that the *Monmouth* would sail from Portsmouth in the morning. Fargus spent the remainder of the war attached to a variety of civil and naval posts, and later became chancellor of St Paul's Anglican Cathedral in Malta. He lived until October 1963, when he was 84. Having reported his demise forty-nine years earlier, *Wisden* failed to note Fargus's actual death, and his obituary did not appear until the 1994 edition.

Other cricketers were not so lucky. Men who had graced the game from the splendours of Lord's down to the most rustic village track were being taken every day: Arnold Nesbitt, modestly gifted but supremely self-confident wicketkeeper for Bradfield College, the Army and Worcestershire – of whom Frank Chester once said, 'what fun county cricket was when men like that were in it' – was killed on 7 November 1914, aged 35. Charles Kennaway of Harrow, MCC and I Zingari died on 30 November, aged 34. In the course of a 'brief but enthusiastic' career, as *Wisden* delicately phrased it, 'he was described as "A slow right-hand bowler; varies his pace well. Only moderate field".' Cecil Wood, whose headmaster's leaving report at Tonbridge read in full, 'an excellent spin bowler (right arm), breaking both ways; keeps a good length and uses his head well; a fine hitter, but lacks defence, and should therefore play a forcing game', was killed at Ypres, aged 40. The Canadian-born Bill Holbech, a pugnacious middle-order bat for MCC and Warwickshire, who was said to treat the fastest bowling 'as if it were something served up to amuse him and the spectators', also fell in November, aged 32.

Charles Deane, who played for Somerset between 1909 and 1914, died in India while serving with the 5th Devon Territorials, aged 29; Philip Doll, of Charterhouse and MCC, fell at Ypres, aged 25; Hugh McArthur, hard-hitting bat for Winchester and MCC, fell under a train while embarking with his regiment for France, at Bristol Temple Meads station on 3 November 1914, aged 26. Second Lieutenant Carleton Tufnell, of the Grenadier Guards, had once been thought among the most gilded of youth even at Eton, 'where admirers seemed to spring up at his feet'. He was in the school XI in 1910 and 1911, top scoring in both the grudge matches with Harrow, and went on to captain the Sandhurst team. Co-existent with these activities, Tufnell won medals and prizes for athletics, football and rugby, and once when passing through London casually turned out for the Surrey Second XI. He founded two literary societies, raised money in the mess-hall for the relief of victims of Turkish aggression in present-day Albania and organised a public meeting in Whitehall on the same subject. Although precociously gifted in most walks of life, Tufnell was not obviously competitive. Watching him stroll out to bat at Lord's, *Cricket* thought him to be 'engaged in a pleasant ritual rather than a contest', and army colleagues spoke of the same kind of drowsy excellence. Flaxen-haired, slim and almost invariably cheerful, Tufnell had shipped out with the Guards in August 1914 convinced that 'it [would] be fine ... the fighting excitement vitalizes everything, it reinforces one's belief in God and the Old Flag and the Mother Country'. He never returned. Lieutenant Tufnell was killed in action at Ypres on 6 November 1914, at the age of 22.

A county cricket career that consists of nine matches as an all-rounder for Somerset and ends wicketless and with a batting average of 12 does not, perhaps, compel the word 'distinguished'. But what the cold facts fail to relate is the infectious good cheer and undying optimism of Lieutenant Ralph Hancock, of the Devon Regiment, said by no less a judge than Gilbert Jessop to have been 'held by a singularly wide range of men in an unusual degree of respect and affection'. Born in Wales in 1887, Hancock had gone on to play for the Rugby XI, and in 1906 top-scored with 64 in the school's annual tie against Marlborough at Lord's – 'batting admirably and hitting with freedom all round', *Wisden* said. His fitful first-class career began in 1907 and involved roughly one match a year over the next seven seasons, which he fitted in around his army duties. *Young England* magazine described Hancock as a 'compact and sturdy fellow with a determined set to his jaw, and a physique that suggested it had been hammered together in a blacksmith's forge'. As a personality, 'his quiet commitment to the job at hand never fail[ed] to communicate his simple belief that life was there to be lived with zest, honour, purpose and courage'. Although only modestly successful at that level, while batting against Sussex in late May 1914 Hancock flat-batted a six with sufficient clout to dislodge several tiles from the pavilion roof at the Recreation Ground, Bath. It was to prove to be his last first-class appearance. Ten weeks later, Lieutenant Hancock sailed for France with his regiment and was swiftly awarded the DSO for conspicuous gallantry at the Marne. He was killed in action on 29 October 1914, aged 26.

Perhaps wisely, the War Office initially did not allow reporters anywhere near the front, so the newspapers carried only partial reports of the retreat of the BEF at Mons and the subsequent bloody, protracted and almost stationary battles around the Marne and the Aisne. But while the accredited correspondents were necessarily slow off the mark, there was soon overwhelming human evidence of the losses – by the end of October, Eton had sixty-five old boys killed, Cheltenham sixty and Wellington forty-one. For the time being, several other schools, associations and clubs of one kind or another preferred to withhold their rolls of honour from the public domain. Nor was the slaughter limited to the perfect flower of public schools, or to other blazered young men with recent OTC experience. Thousands of potential scientists, teachers, engineers, doctors, artists and writers and tens of thousands more of instinctively patriotic ordinary Britons were among the casualties of the first three months of fighting. More than half the original BEF had been lost by Christmas.

1 & 2. An air of jollity comes through in this
pre-war crowd at Leyton, if not quite the same level
of exuberance as seen at Lord's for the 1914 Eton–
Harrow match. Although it was close, Eton won for
the fifth year running. Eight of the young players
at Lord's would go on to die in action. (*Top*: Peter
Edwards Museum and Library at Essex CCC)

3. Lionel Tennyson (*left*) and Phil Mead, two
Hampshire and England batting stalwarts who had
very different fortunes in the war. Nobody has made
more first-class runs for one team than Mead did
for his county. Tennyson, the poet's grandson, went
on to captain England briefly, but could devote only
so much time to cricket in a life largely dominated
by fast women and slow horses. (Hampshire CCC,
courtesy of Dave Allen)

4. The Hampshire side line up at the start of their last fixture of the 1914 season, against Kent at Bournemouth. By the time the picture was taken the war had already been on for three weeks. Hampshire's batsman Alban Arnold (*second from left*) was just down from Cambridge. Two years later, he died at the Somme, aged 23. The Shanghai-born bowler Arthur Jaques (*fourth from left*), who took 9-86 in the match, fell at the Battle of Loos in September 1915. He was 27, and his brother Joseph was killed in action on the same day. (Hampshire CCC, courtesy of Dave Allen)

5. The dashing double-international cricket and rugby captain Andrew Stoddart. He once stayed up all night dancing, and then strolled out and scored an innings of 485 in six hours. In failing health and depressed by events both at home and on the front, he shot himself in April 1915, aged 52. (E. Hawkins & Co., Brighton)

97.C.

HON. L. H. TENNYSON

6. Lionel Tennyson went straight from the games field to the front line, where he would be twice Mentioned in Dispatches and three times wounded, though to his chagrin never decorated. Two of his brothers died in the fighting. (Hampshire CCC, courtesy of Dave Allen)

7. Charles Fry: a prodigiously talented all-round sportsman, schoolteacher, politician, magazine editor, novelist and broadcaster, who made a comeback to cricket in 1914 at the age of 42. When hostilities broke out, Fry concentrated on training sea cadets on the River Hamble, where he could occasionally be seen sailing up and down on a tiny gunboat, flying an ensign of his own design showing crossed cricket bats.

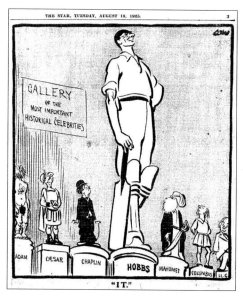

GALLERY OF THE MOST IMPORTANT HISTORICAL CELEBRITIES

ADAM   CÆSAR   CHAPLIN   HOBBS   MAHOMET   COLUMBUS   W.G.

"IT."

8 & 9. Like W.G. Grace before him, Jack Hobbs transcended cricket. He finished the 1914 season with 2,697 first-class runs at an average of just under 60, but faced criticism for initially failing to volunteer to fight. Hobbs later said he hadn't realised 'just how serious the war would be'.

10. Percy Jeeves of Warwickshire, who was as unflappable in real life as his fictional counterpart. After taking 199 wickets in his first fifty matches, he was described as 'a certain England bet' and 'one of the finest specimens of the clean-living young men that ever donned flannels'. Jeeves died at the Somme, aged 28. (Phil Britt, Museum Curator, Warwickshire CCC)

11. Edmund Blunden, soldier, poet and devoted cricketer.

OGDEN'S CIGARETTES.

MR. P. G. H. FENDER,
SURREY.

12. The national treasure Percy Fender (1892–1985), aviator, businessman, mercurially talented all-round cricketer and a fair ringer for Groucho Marx.

13. Dyson Williams, of Glamorgan. Awarded both the MC and DSO, he returned from the front mentally and physically scarred, took up gambling and lost most of his money in the process. He committed suicide at the age of 44. (Andrew Hignell, Glamorgan CCC)

14. Johnny Douglas, the boxing and footballing cricketer, who captained Essex and England. He served in France for three of the four war years, but later died at sea. (David Pracy)

15. Frank Gillingham (*left*) and 'Jack' Russell go out to bat for Essex. Ordained into the Church of England in 1899, Gillingham served as a chaplain to British troops on the front line. After the war he became canon to the king and, perhaps just as important, the BBC's first ball-by-ball commentator. Russell, a professional player, became the first English batsman to hit a century in each innings of a Test. (David Pracy)

16. The Yorkshire-born William 'Eddie' Bates was one of those cricketers who actually improved following the war, going on to a long second career at Glamorgan. (Andrew Hignell, Glamorgan CCC)

17. British troops arrive at Le Havre, where the initial state of mild excitement at being on a French summer holiday gave way to one of first weariness and then horror.

18. Lord Roberts. Aged 81 on the outbreak of war, he was an early rallying figure for British troops. 'How different is your action to that of the men who still go on with their cricket,' he said, while praising a volunteer battalion of bankers and stockbrokers. (Library of Congress)

19. Lord Kitchener in his famous poster. (Library of Congress)

20. The Marne.

21. Corporal Hitler (*seated left*). Was his view of Britain tainted by his experience of cricket in the Great War? (US National Archives)

22. Arthur 'Boy' Collins: an orphan, who scored an undefeated innings of 628 in a school match, he died at the First Battle of Ypres in November 1914, aged 29. Two of his brothers also fell in action. His old school, Clifton, lost a total of 578 former students in the war.

23. Colin Blythe of Kent and England, the supreme spin bowler of his era with 2,503 first-class wickets over fifteen seasons. In October 1917, after his brother's death, he asked to be moved up to the front line. The following month he was killed at Passchendaele, aged 38. (David Robertson, Kent CCC)

JOIN TOGETHER. TRAIN TOGETHER EMBARK TOGETHER FIGHT TOGETHER

SPORTS
THE MEDAL
OF MEDALS.

ENLIST
IN THE
SPORTSMEN'S
1000

PLAY UP PLAY UP & PLAY **THE** GAME

24 & 25. The military authorities weren't slow to see the advertising potential of the nation's top sportsmen. Among other promotional efforts was a campaign to extol the merits of the 'cricket ball grenade', though this was later dropped when the weapon proved unreliable in the field. (*Below*: Mary Evans Picture Library)

GERMANY: CRICKETERS ON ACTIVE SERVICE.

MR. A. T. SHARP,
Of the Leicestershire Team.

MR. J. CHAPMAN,
Captain of Derbyshire.

MR. G. N. FOSTER,
Of the Worcestershire Team.

MR. A. W. CARR,
Of the Notts Team.

CAPTAIN B. BAGGALLAY,
Of the Derbyshire Team.

LIEUTENANT HARRISON,
Of the Hampshire Team.

MR. P. F. WARNER,
Of the Middlesex Team.

MR. A. H. HORNBY,
Of the Lancashire Team.

The cricket field, like everything else, has been overshadowed by the war clouds; and though it was arranged that the County Championship matches should continue, the cricket season has naturally suffered. Some changes have been necessary in the county teams through members going on active service for a number of well-known amateur players have been called up for naval or military duty. In addition to those whose photographs are given on this page may be mentioned Mr. N. J. A. Foster, of Worcestershire. Several Cambridge cricket Blues, including Mr. J. H. Naumann, Mr. K. H. C. Woodruffe, and Mr. G. E. C. Wood, were among the 600 members of the University Officers' Training Corps who applied for Commissions as the Territorials or the Special Reserve.

Photographs by Sport and General (6), C.N. (1), and Hawkins (1).

26. The War Office began to occupy Lord's in October 1914. Among the expedients that followed was the keeping of chickens and geese in a coop on the Nursery End boundary, although for traditionalists the greater shock may have been the full-scale baseball game that followed in 1916. (Mary Evans Picture Library)

27. The Allied landings at Gallipoli eventually turned into another war of attrition, characterised by exhaustion, indecision and atrocious weather. The troops' evacuation from the area was probably the one part of the operation to go entirely to plan. As a diversionary tactic, some of the Australians staged a day-long cricket match on the beach while their comrades withdrew to the boats.

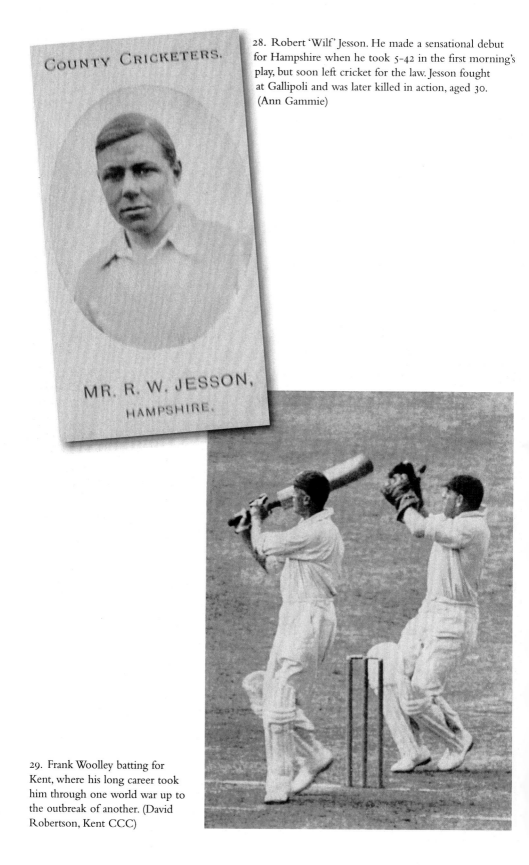

COUNTY CRICKETERS.

MR. R. W. JESSON,
HAMPSHIRE.

28. Robert 'Wilf' Jesson. He made a sensational debut for Hampshire when he took 5-42 in the first morning's play, but soon left cricket for the law. Jesson fought at Gallipoli and was later killed in action, aged 30. (Ann Gammie)

29. Frank Woolley batting for Kent, where his long career took him through one world war up to the outbreak of another. (David Robertson, Kent CCC)

30. In sheer staying power, 'Tich' Freeman of Kent ran Woolley neck and neck. Coming into the county side in 1914, he left it again in 1936, having taken 3,776 first-class wickets in the meantime. (David Robertson, Kent CCC)

31. Harry Lee, of Middlesex, who in May 1915 was shot in the leg while fighting in France and then lay for three days between the lines. He eventually recovered and returned both as a coach and a player. He made a single England appearance at the age of 40. (Mary Evans Picture Library)

32. Largely forgotten today, almost every long-serving English cricketer owes James Seymour of Kent a debt of gratitude for what he did on their behalf. (David Robertson, Kent CCC)

A. E. TROTT

1873 – 1914

A GREAT CRICKETER

AUSTRALIA

MIDDLESEX

AND

ENGLAND

33. The world's greatest all-round cricketer at around the turn of the twentieth century, Albert Trott was all but forgotten by the time he took his own life in July 1914. The war with Germany broke out just five days later. (John Price)

'Village cricketers, metropolitan club cricketers, county cricketers, cricketers from all corners of the Empire: they fell by the hundred of thousand in the filthy mud at Ypres, at Loos, at Arras, at the Somme, at Neuve Chapelle, at Mons, at Gallipoli', the author and historian David Frith wrote. Like their seniors, English cricket's Minor Counties brought their season to a premature end in August 1914. 'The War completely upset the doings of many of the teams,' *Wisden* reported; 'Staffordshire and Hertfordshire finished at the head of affairs, and in the ordinary course of events would have played a challenge match to decide the issue.' In the end Hertfordshire waived their right to a play-off and Staffordshire took the title, much like Middlesex and Surrey respectively in the Championship. There were twenty-one sides officially designated 'second-class' and a total of 429 players, the vast majority of them amateurs, appeared in the 122 matches held between 1 June and 27 August. Of those 429, ninety-three are known to have been killed or seriously wounded in the war, and at least twenty-two others succumbed to the flu pandemic that followed it. Most estimates agree that more than half of those who played competitively in the 1914 Minor Counties season would never do so again.

What was lost in human worth at the grass-roots of cricket, at clubs and villages throughout Britain, was just as appalling. Mirfield of the Yorkshire Council began their 1914 season in the rain and hill fog of early May and built up to a midsummer gala tie with Cleckheaton that included a weekend fete. The *Dewsbury Reporter* wrote that 'the Baptist Military Band played selections and dancing was indulged in. "Side attractions", in the shooting gallery etc, were provided and a jolly time was spent by a large number of people.' Cricket continued locally through the declaration of war, and the Council decided to carry on with a programme of friendlies the following season, 'with necessary adjustments made where enlistments [have] reduced to less than eleven the pool of players available'. On 1 May 1915 the *Dewsbury Reporter* said: 'the Mirfield team to meet Chickenley in their first match will include Reverend C.A. Bowden, a well-known Leicester County amateur, who is taking charge of the Parish Church during the illness of the vicar'. The club got through the season with the help both of Rev. Bowden and of Alonzo Drake, but 'attendances were off', it was said, and with increasing numbers of local women now employed in munitions, 'often the players were compelled to wait on themselves at teatimes'. The situation only worsened after Britain turned from a volunteer army to conscription in the spring of 1916. On 27 May, the Dewsbury paper reported the worst:

In consequence of enlistments, Mirfield cricket officials have been reluctantly compelled to cancel their 11 fixtures, and in consequence the summer game will not be seen at Park Bottom this season. South Kirkby should have visited the ground today, but a team could not be raised as several players have been called up during the last fortnight. The bowling and tennis teams will be run as formerly.

It would be thirty-six years before Mirfield next staged a league cricket match.

On 1 August 1914, the Chipping Sodbury club at Bristol recorded a famous win over arch-rivals Dyrham, who were bowled out for 48. Six days later, the club committee took the decision to cancel their remaining fixtures: 'sporting disputation suddenly has little interest for us', they wrote, anticipating the likes of W.G. Grace and Earl Roberts. At Little Marlow in Buckinghamshire, the widow of a local landowner named Bradish Ellames had just supplied the funds for a handsomely timbered new clubhouse. This was intended to provide 'a cricket pavilion and tea-room in the summer, [and] a meeting place for sober trade unionism and cookery classes in the winter'. In the event, it was primarily used over the next five years as a training centre for Territorials. At the Cregagh cricket club in suburban Belfast, 'play stopped dead immediately on the outbreak of hostilities', and resumed only in June 1920. Of the seventy-four players and members who volunteered for service, nine never returned. The pavilion was converted into a greenhouse for growing vegetables, and members of an Ulster volunteer battalion drilled in the outfield.

Thirty-nine-year-old Charlie Adamson was the star all-rounder at Durham, who over the previous twenty years had also found time to turn out as a rugby union full back for the British Isles. In 1899, he had gone to Australia on the first official Barbarians tour and played in all twenty matches, notching up 136 points in the process. Finding himself with three days off between fixtures, he arranged to play a Sheffield Shield game for Queensland. As a cricketer, Adamson is remembered as a brisk left-arm seamer and a batsman who generally preferred the bludgeon to the rapier. He once scored 146 in ninety minutes in a Minor Counties tie for Durham, 'and peppered the face of the old stand with straight hits'. On the evening of 4 August 1914, Adamson, who had just become engaged, left the field with Durham after narrowly losing their match with Northumberland at Chester-le-Street. Early the next morning he knocked on a door in the small hotel where some of the team were staying and told a colleague: 'we are at war with Germany and I haven't a penny to get home with'. The man lent Adamson enough money to get back to the equally modest family inn in the south of the county that he ran with his parents. There he recovered a suitcase and set off by bus to the recruiting station. The bus broke down on the way. A replacement was summoned and also broke down. Arriving to find the office closed, Adamson slept a night in a park and enlisted the following day, accepting their offer of a cup of tea as he did so. Commissioned into the 6th Battalion, Royal Scots Fusiliers, he rose to the rank of captain and fought at the head of his men both on the Western Front and at Gallipoli. Twice wounded, Adamson was Mentioned in Dispatches four times. On 17 September 1918, he was fatally shot at Salonika by a straggler of a Bulgarian army unit on its way to surrender. As comrades bore him away to die, Adamson made a grim jest about his likely prospects on the cricket field. He was buried in the military cemetery at Karasouli.

The Durham club were to lose four other members of their playing staff of seventeen before the war was over, a fatality rate of nearly one in three. Young men who, a short time before, had been enjoying a pint after stumps on a Saturday evening were squatting in hastily dug, rat-infested trenches or marching interminably down muddy French lanes, a tiny cog in a seemingly bewildered complex of military machinery. Durham's middle-order bat and captain-designate Jack Bennett was killed at Arras in May 1917, aged 26. In time the families of the county's George Breed, Reginald Callender and Alfred Maynard would all receive the telegram beginning 'The Secretary of State regrets to inform you ...' Even this mild courtesy was marred a day or two later when Maynard's family received a letter from him posted at Beaumont Hamel with the word 'Killed' scratched across the envelope.

Michael Falcon, born in 1888, had made his debut for Norfolk in the Minor Counties championship while still a 16-year-old schoolboy on his summer holiday from Harrow. In 1907 he went up to Pembroke College, Cambridge and graduated with a first-class LLB as the prelude to what seemed set to be a glittering career at the Bar. Falcon was actually on holiday in northern France in early August 1914. He returned to England, volunteered, and in due course found himself back at Boulogne with his Territorial unit. Exulting in the army, insisting that it suited his 'love of order and slightly stolid British sense of endurance', he fought at Ypres and the Somme. In 1918, Falcon was elected Conservative MP for East Norfolk, and held the seat until his defeat at the 1923 election. He was a lawyer, a combat veteran and a former Undersecretary of State, and he was still only 35. More pertinently, he played 89 first-class matches as an all-rounder for the likes of MCC, Free Foresters, Minor Counties and the Gentlemen of England, retiring from the game only on his 50th birthday. Ten years later, Falcon answered an emergency call to play for Norfolk in a Minor Counties knockout tie and, nearly immobile with gout, scored an even-time 70 on his comeback. He could be said to be typical of the sort of Briton who showed a natural courage and stoicism when under fire, and returned to civilian life apparently unshaken by the experience. Michael Falcon died in Norwich, the town where he had been born, in February 1976, aged 87.

Surely one of the most poignant sights of the war was that of the soldiers who would periodically leave the front and find themselves overnight temporarily at liberty in the middle of London or elsewhere. For many of them the experience was overwhelmingly intense, and in the face of the happy, mainly incurious civilians they encountered, most kept their stories to themselves. Over-burdening strangers with such things was bad form. Ernest Atkins, a cricket-loving private in the 16th Royal Rifles, spoke for many soldiers when he wrote of this sort of home-coming as a necessarily 'mixed [and] moody lot' as a result:

Arriving at Victoria, [I] changed my French money and out into Civvy Street. Catching sight of my bus I got on, cluttered with pack and rifle, and sat on a seat for three. The conductor says 'Where are you from, mate?' I say: 'Just behind Passchendaele'. Although I squeeze up in the corner as the bus fills, no one will sit next to me until a workman opposite comes across. 'Don't look so hurt, son,' he says. 'I for one am proud to sit next to you.' I said, 'I don't suppose you will catch anything, it's too bad even for THEM where we are.' It was a queer thing being on leave, you felt that you did not belong, it was a sort of lost feeling.

Continuing his activities that September around the River Marne, Lionel Tennyson recorded almost matter-of-factly how he and his men had come under 'rather intense' German bombardment. There had been many 'ghastly sights', Tennyson admitted, and the weather had turned overnight from high summer to the 'most wretched incessant rain'. The casualties would soon include his old commanding officer in Colchester, Captain Prittie. Even in these miserable conditions, though, there were still echoes of country-house life as he knew it in England. After parting at the breakfast table from Jack Seely, Tennyson:

Set off again in search of my battalion. I walked for some miles and saw a dead German major lying in the road, as well as several other Germans and dead horses, and eventually found the battalion, very comfortable, in a farm near the river. [They] had been there all night.

Tennyson and his men were soon to leave their cosy billet and embark on another route march while under fire from heavy German guns:

The battalion had a slight engagement crossing the river, but nothing much to speak of. In our march this afternoon we saw a British and German aeroplane having a terrific fight in the air, but neither, that we saw, came down. The dead horses now are becoming much more plentiful along the roads, and the smells are awful. Battle of Marne ended early this morning.

In England, the *Manchester Guardian* noted that a 'terrible bleakness' descended on county cricket grounds that autumn, 'quite different in intensity to the normal melancholy of the season'. George Cartland, the chairman of Warwickshire, wrote of shaking the hands of three of his professionals who had gone straight from Edgbaston to the recruiting station. Well before Christmas, he knew, 'these young men who had been such fine Christian athletes' were experiencing scenes that 'would literally have been unimaginable in their minds' a few weeks before. The first memorial service for fallen cricketers took place at Edgbaston on Sunday 18 October. Other clubs would soon follow suit. Many of those who might have gone on to play the game at the top level, like 20-year-old John Howell, were denied even the chance of a self-sacrifice brought on by their own deliberate actions. Their deaths were random, courtesy of a sniper's bullet, or by being blown to oblivion. Ronald Turner, born in Gillingham in 1885, was regarded as one of his generation's greatest all-round sportsmen: he is said to have played professional-grade tennis at a 'ferocious clip' as well as representing both Sussex and England at football and Gloucestershire at cricket. Turner volunteered immediately on the outbreak of war and, as a lieutenant in the Essex Regiment, fell in action at Gallipoli on 15 August 1915. He had just celebrated his 30th birthday, which he did largely by 'lying flat on the ground, alternately crawling forwards and rather futilely putting my hands over my head as one of the Turkish shells landed right beside me'. These were the sort of cricketers of all levels and nationalities whose memorial at Lord's calls them 'secure from change in their high-hearted ways'.

On 5 August 1914, 34-year-old John Isaac, of Worcestershire, took the train to the War Office in London and successfully applied to join his old battalion of the Rifle Brigade. As well as being a free-hitting middle-order bat for his county, he was well known as a gentleman jockey. In 1911 he had ridden the winner of the Cairo Grand National. Already a legendary figure in army and sporting circles, Captain Isaac was Mentioned in Dispatches for his 'persistent courage under fire' in September 1914, and for 'cheerfully sharing the splendours and travails' of the Marne campaign with men 'who will follow him anywhere'. Awarded the DSO in the field that Christmas, he fell in action in May 1915.

Edward Fitzherbert might have struggled as a full-time cricketer, and was by no means a boy prodigy at the game. He played just one first-class match, for the Army against Cambridge University, in which he scored 3 and 0, and was not called on to bowl. But like John Isaac, Fitzherbert was another outstanding example of 'the complete man', who appeared with equal ease for Corinthian Casuals at football and Harlequins at rugby, 'seem[ing] to excel naturally in all ball games, while over-exerting himself in none', it was said in his obituary. Captain Fitzherbert served for four full years on the Western Front, where, five times wounded, he won both the MC and DSO. He lived to be 93.

Norman Kilner, younger brother of the famous Roy, went out to France in one of the Leeds-based Sporting Battalions in September 1914, having just turned 19. Two years later, he was shot while going over the top at the Somme. The last rites were administered, so unlikely did it seem that he would survive his wounds, but instead of an early grave Private Kilner won an honourable discharge and the chance to play cricket for his native Yorkshire. After five years there he moved to Warwickshire, where he continued to star as what *Wisden* called 'an essentially correct [but] often violent hitter', and eventually club captain, until 1937. He lived for a further forty-two years.

III

While cricketers fought and died at the front, the game's administrators struggled with their own sometimes seemingly petty concerns at home in England. Meeting on 14 December in the library of the Junior Carlton Club, the MCC Committee noted that 'letters had been received from members on active service, with regard to payments of subscriptions. It was decided to consider the matter fully at a future meeting when cases of those temporarily embarrassed might also be dealt with.' There was some talk of drainage problems at Lord's, and that the secretary 'had been asked by the South Australian Association to try and secure a young and active cricket coach; but he could not be sanguine of success'. The club's tennis professional, for his part, had 'injured his knee [and] might not be able to resume for some time'. Among the housekeeping and maintenance issues it almost strikes a discordant note to read: 'a suggestion [has been] made that a Roll of Honour, containing the names of those members who have been killed in action, shall, if possible, be prepared'. In Bristol that month there had been a 'lamentable incident' when the county chairman Harry Beloe announced to a rowdy lunchtime forum of members, 'some of them over-lubricated', that there would be 'neither manpower nor funds' for any meaningful cricket schedule in 1915. Beloe, head of a large sporting family, and sometime president of Clifton rugby club, later complained that a pork pie that struck him still had a fork buried in it.

At Kent, whose managing committee also met in Christmas week 1914, though in more decorous circumstances, the focus was again on the financial consequences of the war. The minutes report that the King's School, Canterbury 'would not be able to pay the usual rent of £50 for the use of the Cricket Ground next summer … the Head Master asked on what terms they might have use of our pitch on their ordinary practice days'. The committee suggested a figure of £30. Writing in January 1915, Sydney Pardon, the editor of *Wisden*, worried that 'through lack of material, we may, a twelvemonth hence, have to return to the slender proportions of fifty years ago. In that case I hope readers will continue their support so that the *Almanack* may be itself again after the War.'

There was hardly a club, first-class or otherwise, that did not have a direct link with one or more of the seventy regiments of the army, or with the daily casualty rolls from France. Worcestershire's president Lord Dudley had already taken the initiative to commission a memorial plaque for the club pavilion. Initially honouring the side's wicketkeeper Arnold Nesbitt, who fell at Ypres, a further sixteen names would follow. Reviewing the 1914 season and ruing the 'likely absence of play' in the forseeable future, the Middlesex committee noted that two former players – Wilfred Bird, 6th Royal Rifles, and Guy Napier, 35th Sikhs – had already given their lives. Four other men had been wounded, and the former Eton, Norfolk and Middlesex batsman John Wormald been awarded the MC for his gallantry at Ypres. The committee added that '28 of the county's cricketers [are] serving with His Majesty's Forces', a role they distinguished from that of 'the three others working at home in munitions, etc.'. Signing off the minutes, the secretary wrote: 'we feel that the prompt manner in which these men joined the Army has been an example to the Country which cannot be too highly valued'.

In Kent, the general committee published the names of twenty-two current or former players who were under arms in December 1914. A final note to the list added: 'Lowe (killed in action), 1st Bath, The Buffs.' Two other players were said to be serving in an administrative capacity. The minutes conclude, 'the Committee regret that it is impossible at the present moment for them to foreshadow when County Cricket will be resumed.' Sydney Pardon at *Wisden* could only concur:

> Writing in the early days of the New Year it is impossible to take other than a gloomy view with regard to the immediate future of cricket. Never before has the game been in such a plight. Cricketers have made a splendid response to the call to the colours … after the War, whenever that may be, [we] will, no doubt, go on as before, but it will naturally take some time for the game to recover completely from the blow it has received.

Apart from the fearful toll taken by the war, the *Wisden* obituaries of the day suggest that cricket's golden age was fast running out of its own accord. Giants of the late Victorian era like Allan Steel, Reggie Foster and Arthur Jones, England captains all, died in 1914. The following year, the list included Victor Trumper and W.G. Grace, as well as Gervys Hazlitt, the Australian seamer who once took 7-25 in an innings against England at the Oval. At 42, Prince Ranjitsinhji was made an honorary major in the British army, but saw only a limited amount of combat at the front. In August 1915 he was struck by a stray salvo while taking part in a grouse-shoot on the Yorkshire moors, and subsequently lost the use of his right eye. Although he otherwise recovered, the inimitable Ranji spent the rest of the war years in India, and would return to play just three more English first-class matches, noticeably stouter than in his prime, before announcing his retirement. Another stalwart of the Victorian era, Edward Chandos Leigh, died in May 1915. *Wisden* reports that 'his passing followed very closely on that of his elder son, while his younger son had also earlier in the year met a soldier's death at the front'. Beginning in July 1914, *Wisden* also lists a small but steadily growing number of deaths given merely as 'by his own hand'. Amid the portentous events taking place in Europe, Albert Trott's suicide that month had passed largely unnoticed. The cricket world would be more shaken by the uniquely sorry fate that befell a former England Test captain nine months later. It is said that Lord Hawke wept when he heard the news. In 1914, even the jauntiest of sporting notices sometimes seemed to be an omen of loss. That year's *Wisden* carries a full-page endorsement signed by 'A.E. Relf, Sussex & All England XIs', extolling his 'Exceller' bat. 'This year [I] scored well over 2,000 runs with it. It is a real beauty, [and] looks good enough for another 2,000.' In fact, Albert Relf had already played the last of his thirteen Test matches. He managed just two more full seasons for Sussex after the war, and was rarely again at his best. He shot himself one stormy morning in March 1937, aged 62.

Over Christmas week 1914, the newspapers reported in a few lines the death of Lieutenant Bernard Shaw, of the West Yorkshire Regiment, at the age of 21. Just three years earlier he had been playing schoolboy cricket for Marlborough, before going on to captain the XI at Sandhurst. 'He was not naturally a combatant', said his father, the former Oxford University and Middlesex all-rounder Edward Shaw, who was now the Bishop of Buckingham. 'Like many others, he thought beyond his nation, to which he was nonetheless so keenly devoted.' Six days later, on Christmas Eve, the casualty lists included the name of Major Edmund Thomson, of the Royal Munster Fusiliers. He was another of those extravagantly gifted ball players, who had moved casually between cricket for Fettes and the MCC, football for Corinthians, and hockey and polo for the army in the days before the war – 'a seemingly indestructible sort', in the words of his obituary, 'who gave no thought to his personal safety while at the front'. Shortly before the end, Thomson had remarked in a letter to an old school colleague that he had 'scored a few hits, [but] more importantly made many fine sporting friendships' over the years – 'and for that reason I've been luckier than any other man'.

9

ENDGAME

There is to be no cricket season. As Captain Jessop, the idol of a thousand 'gates' has himself declared, we cannot play cricket this year because it would not be cricket. We applaud the abandonment, but we heave a sigh in passing, for what is summer bereft of Yorkshire triumphs and Surrey centuries?

The author Herbert Farjeon probably spoke for many ordinary Britons when he wrote these words in the *Globe* of January 1915. In fact, he may have understated his case. Nothing quite brought home what the same newspaper called the 'truly dreadful cost of the War to those of us going about our daily lives here' like the MCC's blunt statement that it would be 'improper' to 'entertain a first-class list of any sort' that year. Their announcement came in the same month as both the first concentrated Zeppelin raids over England, and the extension of the Defence of the Realm Act to specifically prohibit such things as flying a kite, lighting a bonfire or buying binoculars, as well as enforcing the watering-down of alcohol for sale in shops and pubs. The confluence of these three events was 'disheartening', the *Globe* admitted. Writers such as Arthur Conan Doyle, Siegfried Sassoon, Ernest Raymond and A.A. Milne all went into print deploring the necessary sacrifice of the summer game. Doyle's brother-in-law 'Willie' Hornung, creator of the cricketing thief Raffles, wrote in a collection entitled *Wooden Cross*:

No Lord's this year; no silken lawn on which
A dignified and dainty throng meanders.
The Schools take guard upon a fiercer pitch
Somewhere in Flanders.

Hornung lost his only child Oscar, an Eton and army cricketer, at Ypres in July 1915; he was 20.

It is not quite true, even so, to say that organised cricket stopped dead during the course of the war. It may sound paradoxical, but the worse the actual fighting became, the more many Britons clung to normal life. The Club Cricket Conference was founded in March 1915 specifically to 'maintain and improve [a] regular series of sub-senior fixtures' in London and the south, while the northern leagues operated much as before. There was still intense competition among private teams, army units, villages and schools, and writing in July 1916, the month of the Somme, the *Globe* 'consider[ed] it one of the most heartening aspects of the [British] landscape to see young or even older men in flannels at play in every park'.

At Headingley, a Leeds Pals XI including Roy Kilner, Arthur Dolphin and Major Booth took on a variety of local all-comers, and the *Globe* – always prone to superlatives, whether of praise or censure – thought these 'some of the finest matches ever played on the ground'. On Whit Monday, 23 June, W.G. Grace made his last known appearance at a cricket match when he walked around the crowd at Catford with a collecting box, in a tie played for the benefit of Belgian refugees. Just five days later, the cricket world lost Victor Trumper. He was 37, and in London the event was chalked on newspaper hoardings and flashed on cinema newsreels as 'Death of a Great Man'. Cricket also raised its head above the parapet in several well-attended Services matches that summer. Before long, the settings for these would move from the likes of Aldershot and Woolwich to Lord's and Old Trafford. Lieutenant Percy Fender emerged from a long period of convalescence from what was probably a tropical disease contracted on duty in India to top-score with a whirlwind 70 for an England XI against the Dominions, 'an innings worthy of Jessop at his best', as *Wisden* enthused.

Wartime cricket also continued in several more unorthodox circumstances and exotic locales. There may not be a single match quite as iconic as the Anglo-German football kickabout around Ypres on Christmas Day 1914, but some came close. Commander Charles Stow, RN, wrote in his ship's log of a fixture that winter between the Anglo-Australian crew of HMAS *Encounter* and a team of natives 'wearing local costume, and without shoes' at Nuku'alofa in the Tonga islands. It proved a chastening experience for the visitors. 'I was I regret to say the captain of our side,' Stow writes, 'and surely never was a leader so misinformed of the powers of his followers, or to put it another way, so surprised at the all-round excellence of his opponents.' After a long and hot day's play on a matting wicket 'of variable conduct', the scores read: Tonga 300-1 dec; *Encounter* 13 all out. Over a subsequent high tea, 'for which we were very grateful', served in a gabled pavilion replete with a portrait of Queen Victoria, Stow was left to reflect on cricket's particular genius for reaching out across barriers of culture or religion. 'I feel sure a touring Tonga side would add a much needed interest to the English summer and possibly be a financial success', he wrote.

The indomitable spirit of the game also surfaced in 1915 at Shell Green, Gallipoli, where to deflect attention from the gradual evacuation of their troops Allied commanders staged a day-long cricket match in full view of nearby Turkish artillery units. Caught unawares, the Turks awoke in the morning to find their enemy gone. Prior to that, Anzac soldiers more than once engaged in improvised single-wicket competitions while under shell fire on the Gallipoli beaches. The Imperial War Museum in London has a photograph of Private Cooke of the Bombay Section, Volunteer Machine Gunners, at bat 'during a match played with a coconut and a mealie-crusher while stationed at Umba camp' in the jungle of modern Burundi. A game pitting an English XI against an All-India team held at the Bombay Gymkhana in early 1915 for war relief attracted 55,600 paying spectators over three days. Following stumps, the local paper says 'there was a meditation over dinner on the nobility of trial by sport over armed conflict'.

Continuing its apparent detachment from outside events, the MCC Committee reported at the top of its business in March 1915: 'the wall behind the pavilion has been put back three feet and reduced in height, thus making the passage more comfortable for big occasions, and the surroundings brighter'. 'Disdaining any change to the rules' on club candidacy, it was also minuted, 'Mr M.J. Godby wished his name substituted in the [waiting] list for that of his son now abroad. It was decided that this could not be done.' Two years later, the MCC treasurer was able to report that 'owing to the fact that many members serving with the colours have not applied for a return of their subscriptions, the finances of the club are better than could have been anticipated'. By 1920, the committee was considering expansion and so:

Wrote to 5,100 candidates entered in the books between 1889 and 1896 in order to ascertain if they were still desirous of becoming members of the club. Of these 1,360 decided to take up their election, 268 asked for their election to be postponed, 158 desired to take up their election [but then] did not apply, while from 1,650 no replies were received. In the case of 760 the letters were returned by the Post Office.

It is recorded in the same spirit of statistical precision, 'the Committee are informed that 614 were killed in action or are deceased'.

At Kent, the committee sent letters in January 1915 to eight of their professionals 'asking them to state their reasons for not coming forward to [join] the army'. The replies ranged from those who pleaded that they were supporting their elderly parents or young children, down to the not unreasonable response of 'Tich' Freeman, 'who stated that he was below the standard height'. Even at the nadir of the fighting around Ypres and the first unleashing of gas attacks on British troops in April, the Kent board seemed to preserve its starchy sense of propriety. It was almost as if the war wasn't happening. 'Endeavours are being made to find places as "Coaches" for the professional staff members who are at home, and those who cannot find situations will be employed as bowlers on [other] cricket grounds', officials minuted. 'The ground at Canterbury will be got into order [in 1915] and the Manager has been authorised to purchase a horse. School cricket will be played there.'

For others, of course, the war was all too real. Jack Wilson of Yorkshire had now begun his daily flights over the front, initially for reconnaissance purposes but from around March 1915, as his log says, 'including trench-strafing, close air support, interdiction [and] bombing runs'. He was often accompanied on long and arduous sorties over enemy territory by Flight Lieutenant Jack Mills, who went on to enjoy success as a bowling all-rounder with Devon and MCC after the war. It would be pleasant to think that they sometimes passed the down time on their journeys by discussing their mutual trade as off-spinners. Percy Fender was then stationed at Hounslow, and went up on alternate nights to ward off Zeppelin attacks. 'We had one or two good cracks at them', he remarked, although at first it was an unequal struggle. Later in the spring Fender was able to enhance his plane's firepower significantly by strapping an automatic rifle to its nose and, after an alarming trial run, having the ground-crew fit the propeller with rubber tips to deflect any stray bullets that might hit the blades. Fender was able to make use of his improvised weapon in 'several quite invigorating spats' over the Home Counties, before his eventual posting abroad in 1916.

Meanwhile, Lionel Tennyson continued to enjoy mixed but on the whole worsening fortunes in the ground war. He had now been at the front for some three and a half months. In November 1914, Tennyson was shot in the leg while out digging a trench, an injury aggravated when he then fell into a large shell-hole, severely tearing his muscles and ligaments. On his subsequent way home on medical leave, he was able to share a bottle of champagne with Frank Gillingham, the cricketing vicar from Essex. Tennyson arrived in England to find that *The Times* of the day before had reported him dead. After rehabilitation, he was fit enough the following May to captain the 60th Infantry Brigade XI in a match played at the county ground in Southampton; he was back in France in July.

But perhaps nothing shocked both the cricket world and the wider public more than the loss that April of Andrew Stoddart at the age of 52. We last saw Stoddart as, following the early death of his brother, and with his finances at a low ebb, he had shut himself away in his north London home. To make matters worse, he was subject to violent mood swings, sometimes seemingly catatonic, on other occasions voluble and furious, 'possibly as a result of the wearing-down of his nerves due to pneumonia', it was said at the inquest. On the evening of Easter Saturday, Stoddart quietly informed his wife that 'life is not worth living', and went upstairs to his bedroom. It happened to be the week in which the professional players had been scheduled to report back to Lord's for the start of the 1915 season, and, like others, Stoddart was distraught at its cancellation. In those next few dark hours, did his mind drift back to the match when, after staying up all night playing poker, he scored 485 runs in a single day, or to the time when he had presented the young Arthur Collins with a bat for breaking his record? Now Collins himself was dead. Or could he have been thinking fondly of his old friend and rival Albert Trott? Perhaps it was just depression that led Stoddart to put an end to it all that Saturday night, lying alone in his room a few minutes' walk from Lord's. Going up later to check on him, his wife found him in bed, 'looking quite peaceful', the gun still clenched in his right hand.

With Stoddart's death the romance of cricket's golden age seemed to go sour. 'The tragedy has drawn a sigh from thousands', the *Pall Mall Gazette* wrote within black borders. 'Had his admirers but known of his difficulties would they not gladly have ended them? Something forbade it, perhaps pride. It is all too sad for words.' Although there was no official mention of Stoddart at the MCC Committee meeting six days later (though the minutes regret 'the passing of Mr Martin, secretary of the Junior Carlton Club, whose unfailing courtesy had always been appreciated'), they may have been the one body not to mourn him publicly. Later that spring, the Middlesex annual report wrote of 'the death of A.E. Stoddart [as] a great shock to the whole cricketing world. His loss was deplored in Australia, where he had endeared himself to everybody as much as in England.' The *Daily Telegraph* was rhapsodic:

> The votaries of the new Rugby game may say that the old was slow, but the crowds of witnesses never found football dull when Stoddart's black and red stockings were seen twinkling down the touch-line … and in summer how often, on the classic playing-grounds of England, [he] set every pulse beating faster round the ropes, divided between joy in the bright beauty of his cricket and anxiety lest he should make too many runs and win the match.

Stoddart's funeral took place at Golders Green on 7 April and attracted many of his Middlesex, Hampstead and England teammates, though there might have been a larger turnout but for the war. Several of the mourners, like Pelham Warner, were in khaki. Stoddart's biographer David Frith writes: 'on the stroke of four o'clock the open hearse came into sight, the coffin almost hidden beneath the flowers and wreaths, the most prominent being a sheaf of white lilac to "My darling Nello, from his wife". Four carriages followed with mourners.' Sydney Pardon, the unflappable editor of *Wisden*, wept openly.

III

County cricket journals, the few that survived, were meanwhile busy recording gallantries, decorations and casualties. In the foggy light of dawn on 27 September 1915, at Loos, Hampshire's Arthur Jaques, of the West Yorkshire Regiment, was killed in action. He was 27, and less than a year before *Wisden* had described him as a bowler 'who has developed his skill in most striking fashion'. Foreshadowing Bodyline by a generation:

> He usually pitched on the wicket or outside the leg stump and, with a bunch of fieldsmen crowded close in on the leg-side, he so cramped the batsmen that sooner or later he exhausted their patience and so secured many victims ... His enterprise will surely be rewarded by many more years' success.

Jaques's elder brother Joseph died in the same battle, on the same day. Both men were youthful-looking, with dark eyes and curly black hair, and 6ft 3in tall. Arthur was also remembered as quick-witted, good-natured and 'quite decisive' in his battlefield persona. *The Times* of 1 October filled a page and a half with the closely printed names and units of merely the first wave of casualties from Loos. Another county strike bowler, Percy Jeeves, arrived in France that month as a private with the Royal Warwickshires. As we've seen, he was single, the son of a guard with the Yorkshire Railway, and had been living with his parents in their terraced home in Goole, East Riding. Even in the trenches, Jeeves was known for his impeccable grooming, neatly packed kit and miraculously spotless uniform. He was also soft-spoken and well-read, 'full of kindness and shrewdness mixed'. The more you learn about this quietly efficient individual, the more you find a happy fit to his fictional namesake. A letter back to his parents remarked only that, as winter set in, he 'smoked more and slept less'.

The Zeppelin raids of 1915 hit south-eastern England hard. In July, the MCC Committee voted 'to insure the Lord's Pavilion, by the Government scheme, against hostile aircraft for £25,000'. The actual damage inflicted was slight compared to the Blitz a quarter of a century later, but was quite enough to cause widespread alarm in the civilian population. 'Many rumours were flying about and streams of cars fled the town in the morning', the *Globe* reported of one attack in Essex. On the night of 13 October a concentrated Zeppelin raid took place on south London and bombs fell close to W.G. Grace's home at Eltham. Already laid low by a stroke, Grace suffered a heart attack and died on 23 October; he was 67. Even at the time, it was widely mourned as the end of an era. It could be argued, for a whole variety of reasons, that the year from the autumn of 1914 to the autumn of 1915 was the most transitional, profound and in general traumatic one in England's history.

Robert Jesson, the slightly built Hampshire spin bowler who had been commissioned into the Wiltshire Regiment, left England on 1 July for what he called 'the Great Adventure'. There had initially been some difficulty in finding uniform and boots small enough to fit him. He had just turned 29, and recently qualified as a solicitor. Like Lionel Tennyson before him, Jesson's early experience of war was a curious mix of boredom, exhilaration and occasional terror, all of which he recorded with an unfailingly dry humour in his diary. After a week at sea, he writes:

> We reached Malta and at 8.30 a.m. entered the harbour of Valetta. Here was a scene, the strange white houses rising up from the Deep, the Mediterranean, blue, a deep blue sky, and there in the harbour countless pedlar boats with awnings rigged up to keep off the sun, lazily sculled by their owners. Suddenly the pedlars seem[ed] to spring to life and a battle ensued. Scurrying hither and thither they bombarded one another with tomatoes. The red fruit soon lay thick on the dark blue waters [an indelible image in light of the terrible scenes that would follow at Gallipoli] to be collected again later by the more thrifty and sold to the ignorant.

Arriving in Alexandria, Lieutenant Jesson and some brother officers 'drove to Nouzha Gardens and had tea and then later dined at the Majestic hotel ... then we went to the Moulin Rouge, but finding it extremely dull we left and went out to see the Native Quarter'.

The coaling of the regiment's ship the next morning was all part of what Jesson still excitedly foresaw as a 'wonderful escapade'. Looking down from the deck in his smartly ironed tropical kit, he watched as:

> Barges came alongside and planks were fixed to the fuel shoots, along these the coalers ran carrying baskets on their heads and deposited them into the shoot, throwing back the empty basket to be filled by others whilst they themselves ran back to get another one. All this was done at a great pace, with much clamour and incessant babbling. They were a villainous looking crew, and when some bones and pieces of meat were thrown into the barge they pounced upon them like a pack of dogs.

Later that day, Jesson's ship left Egypt, northward bound for a destination 'still not officially stated' but increasingly guessed at by its 988 passengers. 'It was during this time that ammunition was issued out, as things were approaching the real thing,' he writes; 'early on the 15th, we sailed into Mudros harbour.' From there Jesson transferred to 'the liner packet *Osmanieh*, which had once sailed on pleasure cruises on the Clyde', for the final four-hour trip into Gallipoli.

After dinner on board that night, Jesson stood on deck and 'realised quite abruptly' that his life had changed:

Away on the port side rose a mountain range and then we sighted Imbros and then the Cape, and heard the guns. It was getting dark and standing there we strained our eyes forward but a hospital ship brilliantly lit up and the dark outline of the land and an occasional star shell was all we could see. At this time a strange, and although faint yet perfectly beastly smell was wafted off the land. I remember it quite well, and not liking it I smoked a pipe until all lights had to be extinguished.

As the troops then disembarked:

A certain Private fell on the pier and from under his coat an empty whisky bottle rolled away. This fellow tried to embrace his company commander, who promptly put him under arrest and then marched off with the Company leaving me with the stragglers, servants, officers' kit and an intensely drunk soldier and his escort ... we had not gone far when my troublesome prisoner burst into song and at that moment a staff officer passed by [and] demanded: 'What Regiment is that?' He was told and then requested to see the officer in charge, and I went to him. He told me 'That man's drunk', I said I was painfully aware of the fact, and he next told me we were in a hostile country. I admitted I knew that also, then he told me to stop the man making the noise 'with a bayonet or something'. I promised to comply and passed on ... presently A Company came along and we marched forth with a guide, [and] as we got to the top of the cliff along which the path ran we could hear the rattle of musketry and saw a few star shells and a search light which the Turks were using from Achi Baba. It was a very hot dusty march and our packs seemed very heavy, and I remember I was carrying a periscope and a rifle. At about 2.30 a.m. we came upon the tail of B Company on the beach and halted and lay down and slept.

III

By January 1916, Sydney Pardon's worst misgivings about the immediate future both of *Wisden* and cricket in general had been fulfilled. For each of the next three years, the almanack contained less than half the usual number of pages. A large proportion of these consisted of obituaries: 396 for the calendar year 1915, of which 269, or more than two-thirds, were as a result of the war. They ranged alphabetically from 2nd Lieutenant Bernard Russell Abinger, Royal Berkshire Regiment, who was 'killed in France on Sept 26, aged 21, played much cricket in South America; he had been awarded the Military Cross nine days before his death' to Major Arthur Young, 10th Sherwood Foresters, 'killed in Flanders Sept 13, aged 47 – He was not in the XI whilst at Harrow, but played subsequently for the Derbyshire Friars. Was well known in the hunting-field'. The fast-rolling phrases, so compelling in their simplicity and repetition, could only hint at the individual scenes of horror and sacrifice: 'Died of wounds received in France ... Killed in Flanders ... Fell in action ... Died of wounds in the Dardanelles ... Perished in the trenches ... Previously reported missing, officially stated dead.' 'This edition of *Wisden's Almanack* is of necessity a rather mournful volume', Pardon wrote with some understatement:

> Its chief feature is a record of the cricketers who have fallen in the War ... At the time of writing the outlook for the game is as dark as possible, another blank season as regards first-class cricket being to all appearance certain. So far support-ers of the various county clubs have for the most part been very loyal, but this year some further falling off in subscriptions is almost inevitable.

While the war continued, so did the various official attempts to promote cricket-ers and sportsmen in general as role-models. The tone of much of the publicity seems ludicrous today: 'The British Empire! The Land of Beauty, Virtue, Valour, Truth. Oh! Who Would Not Play Up and Play The Game For Such A Land!' As we have seen, there was a brief but spirited campaign in 1915 to extol the merits of 'the British No. 15 time-fused weapon', known colloquially as the 'Ball grenade' or 'cricket ball grenade'. Like the device itself, this particular plan proved only fitfully successful, and was soon discontinued. There was some understandable excitement later that spring over the exploits of Sub-Lieutenant Reginald Warneford, Royal Naval Air Service, whose story stood out even in the galactic setting of the athlete-soldiers of the time. Educated in England, North America and India, Warneford shone as a classically correct but pugnacious schoolboy batsman, as well as a rugby three-quarter, hurdler and sprinter. In August 1914 he immediately sailed home from Canada and joined the 2nd Sportsman's Battalion, later transferring to the air service. Warneford's flying instructor was said to have remarked, 'this youngster will either do big things or kill himself'. On 7 June 1915, less than a month after arriving at the front, he chased and eventually dropped his bombs on a P-class Zeppelin flying at 6,000ft over the coast of Belgium. The subsequent explosion turned Warneford's Morane-Saulnier monoplane upside down, cutting out its engine. He had no option but to land in enemy-held territory. After thirty-five minutes spent on repairs, under constant small-arms fire, Warneford managed to take off again and return safely to base. It was soon determined that the Zeppelin he destroyed had been on its way to attack southern England. Within a week, Warneford was awarded both the VC and the Légion d'honneur for his action. An artist's sketch of his encounter with the German airship became a popular newspaper image in Britain and elsewhere. Posters depicting the scene were hurriedly mass-produced. While in Paris to collect his medal from the French War Minister, Warneford was handed a bunch of roses by a young female admirer – one of many – in a theatre. 'What joy there will be among the ladies when you go home to London,' she told him. He answered matter-of-factly: 'I have a strong feeling that I shall not get there.' The next day, he and his passenger were killed in a flying accident over Versailles. Reginald Warneford was 23 at the time of his death.

III

The protracted blood-bath in 1916 around the River Somme commands a wide literature. It is a frequently repeated fact that there were close to 60,000 British casualties on the first day of battle, a third of them killed, and that 140 more days of attritional fighting followed. Lieutenant Raymond Asquith of the Grenadier Guards, his battalion's star bat, and the prime minister's eldest son, died there in September; he was 37. Academically a star performer like his father, elected a fellow of All Souls at 23, Asquith also had a flair for subversive black humour. 'I am in the trenches & have been for three or four days now,' he wrote in one letter home:

> So far they are more uncomfortable and less dangerous than I had been led to expect. Waders are advisable as the mud and water are well above the knee and the cold is intense. An unpleasant feature is the vast number of rats which gnaw the dead bodies and then run about on one's face, making obscene noises and gestures.

The tall, austerely handsome Asquith shrank from facile acquaintance, disliked most physical contact, and would not have been an obvious candidate to follow his father into the political limelight. One contemporary appraisal of his gifts suggested that 'he would have continued to be a great forensic lawyer and a gentleman cricketer'.

We have noted the fate of Yorkshire's Major Booth, who was mortally injured when advancing through no-man's-land at the Somme in the early hours of 1 July 1916. He was 29, and had played his last organised match for Leeds Pals, at Masham, just a year earlier, when his swerve and pace off the pitch brought him 5-38 in the only innings. Booth died in the arms of a cricket-playing comrade from one of the eleven battalions involved in the assault on the heavily fortified German position at Serre ridge. It was a particularly cruel twist that his body could not be recovered until the following spring. It was only identified by an engraved cigarette case presented to him by MCC 'with gratitude and respect' for his part in the 1913/14 tour to South Africa. Booth's sister refused to accept the fact of her brother's loss, and kept a light burning in the window of his room at their Pudsey home until her own death in 1950. Lance-Corporal Kilner was wounded in the opening artillery barrage in the sector, and was eventually sent home to Yorkshire to convalesce. The Bradford and England footballer Evelyn Lintott, 32, fell in the same action. It has been estimated that of the 750 Leeds Pals who went over the top that first morning at the Somme, 680 were killed or wounded. Serre was not taken.

By the spring of 1916, cricketers of every stamp were being cut down on a daily basis. We've touched on the fate of 21-year-old Bernard Shaw, who fell in action with the West Yorkshires. Shaw's elder brother Edward appeared as that comparative rarity, a bespectacled wicketkeeper, in the Oxford University and Buckinghamshire sides before the war. Although credited by *The Times* for 'scuttl[ing] with a sharp, crablike gait to either side of the stumps' when the need arose in one minor counties game, his value to the team as a whole lay 'less in what he did than in the enjoyment and enthusiasm he showed in all his dealings'. Edward Shaw joined the 6th Battalion, Oxford and Bucks Light Infantry, on the outbreak of war, and went to France in October 1914. He was killed in action there two years later, aged 24. A third brother, Robert, born in 1900, saw action as a 16-year-old midshipman on board HMS *Hercules* at Jutland. He survived the war, played cricket for the Navy and the Combined Services, and died in his bed in England at the age of 95.

Not every wartime casualty came as a result of enemy action. There was the case of the thickly moustachioed Australian fast bowler of aboriginal descent, Jack Marsh, whose exploits the press turned into a hazy concoction of claims, denials, rumours and outright fabrications. Marsh's professional career began in 1900, when, appearing for a Colts XV in a trial match against New South Wales, he clean bowled the leading Test batsmen Victor Trumper and Monty Noble, only to be repeatedly called for throwing later in the innings. Over the following two Sheffield Shield seasons, opinion was sharply divided on whether Marsh's action was fair or if he was being targeted because of his race (and possibly his tendency to berate umpires, batsmen and teammates alike in a colourful native dialect). The debate escalated with a dramatic but entirely spurious statement in the Sydney press claiming that the MCC side of 1903/04 under Pelham Warner had refused to play against him 'because the black bugger cheats'. In the event, Marsh was never selected for Australia. His formal cricket career ended in 1905 and, after brief attempts to become a professional sprinter and a wrestler (a role he sometimes illustrated by donning a caveman's suit and a disheveled wig), he spent his remaining years travelling around Australia in a circus sideshow. In the early hours of 25 May 1916, Marsh died as a result of a brawl outside the pool room of the Royal Hotel in Orange, New South Wales. A local bookmaker and his assistant were charged with his manslaughter, but acquitted. *The Bulletin* wrote in Marsh's obituary that he was 'a darkly troubled man with manners which white brothers found impossible to put up with'. He is thought to have been 42 at the time of his death.

But surely the most truly pathetic cricketing victim of the war was Frederick 'Percy' Hardy, who played a hundred first-class matches as a professional for Somerset and MCC between 1902 and 1914. Although not thought likely to scale the absolute heights of the game, with as fidgety a manner at the crease as in civilian life, he showed more than a glimpse of all-round potential. In 1910, when Somerset lost fifteen of their eighteen matches and failed to secure a single point in the Championship, Hardy, who was described as 'gaunt, with tight-knit dark hair', led the county's batting averages with 700 runs, and a top score of 91 against the all-powerful Kent. He also managed to take 6-82 against Middlesex with what *Wisden* called his 'not wholly ineffective' right-arm swing bowling. He made his last county appearance in May 1914, against Kent at Taunton, when, called upon to open the innings, he scored 2 and 1, and failed to take a wicket. By all accounts, Hardy was a loner: married but childless, quietly patriotic, conservative, and known to take a drink by himself at the close of play. Early in August, he joined the 1/1st City of London Yeomanry as a private soldier. Hardy not only shared in the general mood of enthusiasm for the war, but may have felt a personal sense of liberation from a professional and domestic routine that had begun to lose its appeal for him. He was then 33 years old.

Relatively little is known of Hardy's subsequent war, except that his unit spent the winter of 1914–15 in training around North Walsham in Norfolk, before shipping out to Gallipoli the following July. They arrived there just in time to take part in the bloody and ultimately futile fighting at Suvla Bay, which the official history says took place 'among a tangled mass of barbed-wire, during boiling days [and] freezing nights, surrounded by inhospitable ravines, ledges and precipices', and under a rain of Turkish shell fire. By autumn, many of the Allied forces were suffering from dysentery, and in their weakened state 'the military objectives became almost [a] physical impossibility'. Several weeks of attritional trench warfare followed. A freak blizzard at the end of November caused further suffering among the troops, with some 15,000 men laid low by frostbite. These were not conditions widely envied even by those on the Western Front. Eventually, the War Cabinet in London recommended evacuation as the only reasonable course, and this was successfully achieved on the night of 18–19 December: the one part of the eight-month campaign to go entirely according to plan. The 'Rough Riders' of the City of London Yeomanry arrived home on 24 January 1916. After a period of leave, the division was broken up: one unit was to remain on home duty, another was to embark for Egypt, and a third was sent to France to take part in the planned summer offensive at the Somme.

On the morning of 9 March 1916, a railway porter found the body of Private Hardy lying on the floor of the men's lavatory at King's Cross station. 'His throat was cut and a blood-stained knife was by his side', said *Wisden*. There was no note, and Hardy's pockets were empty but for his military papers and 8*s* in coins, the equivalent of about a week's pay. He was thought to have been changing trains after receiving his orders to report for embarkation to France. Hardy's wife later told the inquest that he had been 'overwhelmed' by his experience of the war, was tormented by nightmares, and had increasingly 'consoled himself with drink' in recent days. A verdict of suicide was returned. The taciturn but gentle Hardy, of whom it was said 'by determination and courage and knowing his limitations, he made himself into a very useful cricketer', left £11 in his will.

In Gallipoli itself, Robert Jesson of the Wiltshires continued to weigh the sometimes comic, the often horrific and the almost always chaotic aspects of the campaign there. In some sectors, the combatants were dug in only about 40 yards, or two pitch lengths, apart. 'The trenches gave no shade,' Jesson wrote:

And from 9am–5pm it was exceedingly hot and the flies – well, I think they were the worst thing on the Peninsula. They were absolutely nauseating, and from 7am till nightfall their presence was an abomination. One readily sympathised with the Egyptians when they were treated to a plague of flies, and one saw that it was an ingenious punishment[.]

Another morning I was badly scared off – I was looking at the enemy trenches when I saw what I thought was a Turk, a splendid target, so disregarding correct military phraseology I said to a man next to me 'Give me your gun'. I took very careful aim and pulled the trigger and to my annoyance the rifle was not loaded, then smack a bullet struck a sand bag quite close and smattered me with sand. I imagine it was a trap to catch fools like myself – apparently a figure had been put up on the parapet and [a] sniper posted a short distance away to await the enemy.

The next morn we bathed from the pier, it was priceless, there was a cooling breeze, a dark blue sky and dark blue sea, Imbros lay ahead and in the channel between a cruiser, some destroyers and mine sweepers were carrying on the ceaseless vigil. Later, [at] Mudros Hill, I set out on a shopping expedition. There are only a few shops there and they are nearly all universal providers on a small scale, and we returned a few hours later laden with bread, sardines, chocolate and tinned fruit. The bread was splendid and I then understood why it is termed the staff of life, for on the Peninsula in those days bread was unknown.

After this brief interval of relative normality, Jesson and his men were brought up to take part in the offensive intended to seize the high ground overlooking Suvla Bay. Military historians have tended to find fault with the overall leadership and strategy of the campaign, and Jesson's account gives some backing to that judgement. 'At 4.30 p.m. on August 3rd we embarked on board HMT *Samia* and sailed on the great enterprise,' he writes:

We [disembarked] and left the gully at 8 p.m. that night and, entering another, passed the 39th Brigade and the Gurkhas who were sitting by the side of the track waiting for the hour when they were to be let loose at the hills beyond, and then we marched out down to the beach, passed the New Zealanders and the Maori contingent, and so along the beach. A spirited rifle fire was going on from the trenches which the Australians held beyond on our right. As we advanced further the search lights from a naval ship [were] playing on the cliffs above, and one couldn't help thinking that perchance they would drop the rays too low and show us up, and then we should have got it properly as the Turks were at that time in possession of the ground on our right. As it was an occasional star shell from the Turks endangered the secret of our move and a few bullets whizzed round and an occasional shrapnel burst overhead. In time, a few of these bullets found a mark for it was here that poor young Belcher fell, whilst Wigmore, Perry, one man in my platoon and some others were wounded. And now it was time for us to turn inland. We found the Gen. waiting for us and we deployed into artillery formations at short intervals and distances and carried on ...

The advance was my right and Capt Spencer was on the right with No. 5 Platoon. I was with No. 7. It was a very black night and the country unknown, and presently I found myself at the bottom of a Turkish trench which had been cleared a few minutes before by the Borderers, with two or three men on top of me. We struggled up the other side only to find the bushes and scrub so thick that we had to make a short detour to the left, and meanwhile had we lost touch with the platoon in the right? To my great relief I saw some men on the right and learnt they were No. 6, then presently my Company Commander's voice asking in no polite terms whether I was aware that the march was by the right and if so why wasn't I marching by that flank? I replied that I was aware and that I was. He contradicted the latter statement and then I discovered two things, first that his march had been over easy ground whilst my party was struggling through a trench and exceedingly thick and difficult country, and, secondly, that No. 6 Platoon had split in two, that one part was with him and the other was with me. We adjusted the error and proceeded. After a time they halted on the right and a message was sent down for me. I went up to the right and found Hill, who told me that Spencer had fallen into a trench with the bombers on top of him and had lost touch with 'A' Coy. Then I went back to the Company and found that Spencer had returned [so] I was able to show him the line, which I did with a pocket torch, and then we proceeded to dig in and sleep.

After a few hours of rest, it was decided that Jesson's platoon should proceed up a steep hill in full view of Turkish spotter units. As the sun was already coming up, they elected not to wait for the preliminary Allied artillery barrage that had been promised them:

Then I was sent for by the CO and was pointed out the area up which we had to advance. 'D' Company under Major Hern was to lead. I was to support him, followed by 'A' and 'C'. We were at the bottom of a gully, hills rose up almost sheer on both sides and ahead – apparently the end of the gully – rose the steep ridge, our objective. These hills were covered with scrub and brush wood, intensely thick, and wandering up this we found a path. It was now daylight when D Company led on out of the trench in which we had sheltered, and after much squashing and squeezing 'B' Coy. followed. Now we advanced in small parties and at each bend the men were warned to keep low and double. And each bend presented its own warning in the shape of a few who would not pass again.

It was getting hotter now, and the climb up the hill became rather a toil but I found the Company flag useful as a stick. When at last we reached the crest we halted there under cover. Then [the] C.O. blew a whistle and called up [our] unit and told us to prepare … bayonets were fixed and we crawled up in close formation beneath the crest. And now you could not hear yourself speak, the roar of the guns, the crack of the rifles, the rattle of machine guns, the whiz and screeching of bullets and shells created an absolute inferno. At about that time I went forward to the Gurkha machine gun emplacement to see Major Hern and to look at what lay over the crest. The machine gun I remember was firing at the small knoll beyond – our objective – at 500 yards. Having heard Major Hern's views on the situation, I went towards my left to see 'A' Company, but on the way I was hit by a rifle bullet in the thigh. I called Hinxman and told him and he and Sgt. Lintern bound up the leg. Then I wriggled to Bn. Hd Qtrs and reported to the C.O. and there saw Ricketts and was awfully glad to see that he had returned safe. Then, hanging on to my servant, Neeve's, neck, I started down the gully … and so we passed on down to the beach where we arrived at about 5 p.m., and here were hundreds of stretcher cases waiting for picket boats to convey them to the hospital ships lying beyond.

Although the scene was nothing less than a vision of hell, with the heavily churned beach strewn with burned-out vehicles and hideously wounded soldiers, Jesson was still able to see something noble about it all. 'I shall never forget the walk down that gully', he writes:

One thing that struck me more than most was a unique example of the greatness and unity of the British Empire. Here, [on] stretchers, lay side by side an Englishman, a New Zealander, an Australian, a Maori, a Gurkha! England had not called across the sea in vain, the young manhood of the colonies had heard the call and answered it with amazing devotion … Far-off subjects had been called and gladly gave of their best.

Gallipoli was bad enough. With every barn and dugout and trench already filled with wounded awaiting treatment, Robert Jesson was comparatively lucky to find his way down to the beach to be evacuated. Many of the new flood of patients could make it only as far as a crudely improvised dressing station, some crawling, some with rifles as crutches, others assisted by men nearly as crippled as themselves. That evening there was an 'apocalyptically hard' rain. The army surgeons at their lamp-lit amputation tables had a canvas rigged overhead for shelter, but everyone else, the treated and the untreated alike, was drenched. But for the presence of machine guns, it was a scene that could have been the aftermath of some Napoleonic slaughter. To Norman King-Wilson, a young Canadian international cricketer attached to the 88th Field Ambulance, it conveyed:

Almost medieval horror … the cold that night was bitter, and the mud was rapidly freezing. Dozens of old biscuit tins with holes knocked in them served as braziers in which we burned coke brought in sacks from the beach. At the relief stations hundreds of men were having their feet, swollen to double their size, blue and stone cold, rubbed in oil. The small aid posts in the trenches had some shocking cases brought in. Some frozen and unconscious, some quite drunk, for they had consumed large quantities of rum to keep warm. Some lying prone in the mud, dead. Oh God, it was pitiful.

Futile as it is to make the comparison, it is possible that conditions on the Western Front were even worse, at least as judged by the statistics. In the five months of attritional fighting from the start of the Somme offensive, the British suffered around 420,000 casualties and the French 195,000. They had advanced a maximum of 7 miles on a 16-mile front, none of it strategically key terrain. Clearly this was the next thing to a Pyrrhic victory. Since the Germans lost an estimated 600,000 casualties in the same period, it's possible to say that roughly two and a half men were killed or wounded for every inch of land.

At a meeting of the Kent general committee held at Canterbury on 5 December 1916, it was noted that thirty-two members of the county's First and Second XIs had joined the British forces. The officials expressed some pride in the example of the club's 1914 team captain, Lionel Troughton. 'It will doubtless seem to admirers of Kent cricket quite natural that the Captain of the Eleven should have led the men he now commands with such gallantry as has resulted in his receiving the distinction of the Military Cross.' However, a few lines later the minutes also record flatly that 'sympathy has been conveyed to the relatives of Lieut. K.L. Hutchings'. Regarded as the most graceful English batsman of his day, Ken Hutchings was said to combine some of the latent aggression and power of Jessop with the quick-footed smoothness and timing of Hobbs. Batting for England against Tibby Cotter and Australia on a fast track at Melbourne in January 1908, he reached 100 in fractionally over two hours, his second 50 taking just fifty-one minutes. In 207 first-class matches, Hutchings scored 10,054 runs at 33.62, though the figures hardly do justice to their style of execution. With his crisp black hair, lean face and habitually broad smile, he was the matinee idol of English county cricket in the years just before the war. Lieutenant Hutchings, King's Own Liverpool Regiment, was struck by a shell at Ginchy, by the Somme, on 3 September 1916. He was 33.

Not far away from these events, the newly promoted Captain Lionel Tennyson found himself more than once following up an initial Allied artillery barrage by going over the top into no-man's-land. One of the other officers in his platoon would later say that the experience was 'like dropping water on a hot stove, the [men] would disappear'. During the first few days of the Somme, Tennyson himself wrote that:

The unburied corpses of English, German and French soldiers were lying thick all over the countryside with the carcasses of dead horses and mules, while the stink was almost unendurable and all water in the area became undrinkable. In the midst of the various delays the weather set in wet, and the ground became nearly impassable for an attack.

Tennyson received a superficial wound in the same battle in which Ken Hutchings was killed, and for a second time was wrongly reported dead. Although he once again telegraphed home to correct the error, just three weeks later he was shot in the mouth and evacuated back to England. As well as his physical injury, he was suffering from shell shock: 'not fun', he noted with restraint. In the spring of 1917, Tennyson was well enough to appear in a series of regimental cricket matches, starting with an innings of 134 and ending with 'imperious' knocks of 170 and 47 for Aldershot Command against the Royal Military College. Less than a week later, he was back in the trenches in France.

By the beginning of that summer, every organised English cricket team had dispatched men to the front, and the domestic season was again cancelled 'from paucity of numbers', as MCC put it. The Yorkshire county club had fifty-one current or former players serving in some capacity in the armed forces, just three more than at Lancashire. In Essex, the secretary published a list which showed seven of their men killed in action, ten wounded, two severely wounded, and one – James Hilleard, who in fact had fallen eighteen months earlier, at Ypres – 'reported shot dead in action, now reported prisoner in Germany'. Kent lost a total of twelve players during the war. Between casualties and natural retirements, each first-class side would return in 1919 with an average of five men missing from its 1914 strength. In some village and club teams, only the grandfathers were left.

Like Lionel Tennyson, Colin Blythe played in several games of cricket in 1917. In his last first-class appearance, at Lord's on 18 August, for a services side against the combined Australians and South Africans, he took 1-54 and failed to score. Six days later, Blythe made out his will. He left his two violins and his cricket mementoes to his father and everything else – about £1,200 in shares and their small terraced home – to his wife. Neither she nor anyone else would be able to actually collect the funds for some time, since the Kent club still held most of them in escrow, it being thought imprudent for the player to manage them himself. It must have been a strange, bittersweet summer, which Blythe largely spent training in 'ludicrously comfortable' practice trenches at an army camp in Marlow-on-Thames. At some stage he made contact with the head of games at nearby Eton, and agreed to take on the coaching of the XI there after the war. On 25 September Blythe voluntarily transferred from the Fortress Engineers to the 12th Yorkshire Light Infantry. This was to exchange the agreeable and faintly comic *Dad's Army* routine of simulated battles, inspections and drills for the reality of the Western Front. On 1 October, Blythe's unit sailed for France. Two nights later, he was attempting to sleep under the roar of gunfire at Ypres.

Forty-two-year-old Captain Ernest English, at the head of around twenty men of the Shropshire Light Infantry, took off on a reconnaissance patrol to within a few yards of the enemy lines at Wulverghem, south of Ypres, on the night of 3 October. It was approaching dawn before they reached the banks of the River Douve, and at a critical junction in the dark the rear column took a right turn, prowling off to the north-east, the wrong direction. When asked by Captain English in 'hushed but quite distinct tones' where they were going, the 2nd lieutenant at fault replied that he had overheard a voice with what he thought was a 'Scotch accent' speaking a few yards away, and had been instinctively drawn to it. Just as he finished these remarks, the German soldier he had heard turned his machine gun on the patrol, killing the 2nd lieutenant and three other men. It took Captain English an 'exacting' forty-five minutes in the dark and under raking fire to collect his squad and return to base, where he was at least able to provide a detailed report of the enemy position. He was awarded the DSO and Croix de Guerre for his part in a subsequent action. In 1909, Ernest English had played a single first-class cricket match, for Gloucestershire against Middlesex at Lord's, in which he batted twice and scored a total of 2 runs. 'It was not an over-polished debut', *The Times* was forced to admit, though with his immaculate appearance, the light-hearted gleam in his eye and an exquisite show of manners to friends and strangers alike, 'the player won many admirers in the game's social functions over the years'. After leaving the army, Captain English became a stage and screen actor, making his film debut in the 1921 silent drama *The Rotters*, now lost to posterity. Although 'no longer a golden boy', he conceded, he continued to play competitive club cricket until the day of his death in August 1941, aged 66.

In the summer of 1917, 25-year-old Lieutenant Graham Mackay, a pre-war MCC batsman whose preferred technique was said to be 'unrestrained even [in] the worst crisis', found himself serving as Battery Athletics Officer with an artillery regiment outside Baghdad. Although campaigning in the area was difficult, especially when temperatures could reach 120°F for much of the day, he wrote home of the 'great solace' both of batting one evening 'under the relative cool of the palm trees' and of the mess entertainment that night: 'the Major has just got another lot of records for the gramophone – 30 in all arrived (19 all right and 11 cracked)'. Later in November, Lieutenant Mackay wrote of having had:

Quite a good dinner, with the Turks somewhere on the horizon ... we had soup, roast mutton, turnips and potatoes, fishcakes and pancakes, and just as we finished we heard the tractors approaching. They are the things with caterpillar wheels and make a fearful row pulling the big guns ... we stood to for an hour after sunset, manning the trenches and looking across the plain to the horizon, which was an absolute blank, although about 50 Arabs fired into the post during the night about a fortnight ago. I think [the] enemy is about finished, though. The deserters all tell the usual tales of woe, and say the Turks are getting more hopeless every day.

The rest of that month was a mixture of boredom, occasional skirmishes and more cricket, played beneath 'the blue and gold mosques, [or] out in the shimmering heat in sandy fields laid out between the orange groves'.

Lieutenant Mackay was not alone in his efforts to keep what he called 'England's one great gift to the world' alive while at the front. Although the initial buoyancy and keen sense of excitement had long since gone out of most of the young civilian soldiers to cross the Channel in 1914, they, too, managed occasional moments of relaxation. An elegantly printed programme dated 2 September 1917 hawks the '3rd Annual Sports held by the 3rd ASC Repair Shop, 358 Company, on the Union Sportive Ground, Somewhere in France'. As well as a full card of horse races, boxing and tennis, there was to be a gala cricket match staged over the course of two days, even though the unit's star fast bowler had 'recently absorbed an armful of shrapnel', and was therefore 'inoperative'. It was by no means the only organised fixture to be played in the midst of war. St George's Day 1918 was marked locally by various activities including cricket and a gymkhana, all accompanied by a regimental brass band. This was followed by an untypically 'good and full' dinner. It says something about the British genius for simply carrying on that, just a few miles away, the General HQ was sufficiently worried about the overall war situation to issue preliminary orders for the evacuation and demolition of Calais, and Field Marshal Haig's Order of the Day of 11 April read:

Many amongst us now are tired. With our backs to the wall and believing in the justice of our cause, each one of us must fight on to the end. The safety of our homes and the freedom of mankind alike depend on the conduct of each one of us at this critical moment.

Many of the sportsmen-soldiers fought without any outside encouragement to do so. Yorkshire-born Samuel Grimshaw had played league cricket for Farsley as long ago as the 1870s, before emigrating with his wife and young son to Canada. He went on to tear up most of the local batting records for the St Edmund's club in Toronto, with a technique 'far beyond mere occupation of the crease – if the ball [was] there, he hit it with opened shoulders and a swirling bat'. In the summer of 1916, Grimshaw was 62, and recently retired from a clerical job on the Ontario railway. He was not fully informed of the recent horrors of the Somme, but he knew things were going badly and he wanted to do his bit. Claiming to be 46, he enlisted that August in the Canada Expeditionary Force. Sapper Grimshaw was wounded on the Western Front the following June; trapped in no-man's-land, he took an agonising day and a night to die. On 31 July, Henry Willders-Lewis, 10th Battalion, Royal West Surrey Regiment, fell in action at Ypres. He had just come down from the University of London, and played club cricket as an opening batsman good enough for a trial at the Oval. 'He loved everyone, and everyone loved him', a Croydon Grammar School friend named Hugh Gunner said. 'There was something about him that just exuded the joy of life.' Willders-Lewis died on his 21st birthday. Eric Lundie of South Africa, a right-arm fast bowler 'who had no pretensions as to his batting ability', was killed that September at Passchendaele, aged 29. At Beersheba, seven weeks later, Tibby Cotter spoke to a friend of his presentiment that he was about to die, and then was cut down by a sniper's bullet.

Colin Blythe arrived at Ypres at a time when the scale of British casualties in relation to ground gained was worse than that of the first day at the Somme. He spent most of October 1917 on maintenance duty on the tangle of railway lines around Langemark and Zonnebeke, to the north of the salient and just across the front line from Passchendaele. It was hard and clearly dangerous work, and much of it went on at night to avoid German attacks. Despite these precautions, fourteen of Blythe's battalion were killed or wounded by enemy shell fire on 29 October. The historian Charles Crutwell, who fought on the front, described the conditions as:

> The culmination of horror. German writers have called it 'the supreme martyrdom of the War.' The rain was pitiless, the ubiquitous mud speedily engulfed man and beast if a step was taken astray from the narrow duckboards, upon which descended a perpetual storm of shells and gas.

While the Allies eventually deepened the Ypres salient by some 5 miles, they suffered around 300,000 casualties in doing so. More than 90,000 men were listed as missing in action, and 40,000 were never found – their bodies were pulverised, or simply disappeared into the mud. On the evening of 8 November, the Third Battle of Ypres, as it was officially known and seldom called – the soldiers used the familiar name Passchendaele – was coming to its temporary end (all the Allied gains were lost again in the German offensive the following spring). A burst of shrapnel from the retreating enemy was reported to have fallen 'quite at random, and slightly behind British lines' at around 8 p.m., just as many of the battle-weary men were attempting to dig in for the night. According to the 12th Battalion war diary, 'three other ranks [were] killed, 6 wounded, 1 missing – B Company' as a result. One of the dead was Colin Blythe, aged 38.

Twelve days later, the Infantry Record Office wrote to Gertrude Blythe in Tunbridge Wells 'with the painful duty to inform you that a report has been received from the War Office, notifying the death of your husband. I enclose a message of sympathy from the King and Queen ... Details of his interment will be sent in due course.' Blythe was buried in a military cemetery close to where he fell. A bat and a worn cricket ball are periodically laid on his grave, stolen and then replaced again. Blythe's shrapnel-damaged wallet was passed to his widow, and eventually presented to the Kent county club for their museum. Gertrude died in 1977, aged 89. Blythe's father Walter lived to see four of his sons predecease him; he committed suicide in 1932.

III

After five weeks' leave, the now Captain Jesson and his servant Neeve were once again back on the Gallipoli Peninsula. During their absence, the Allied campaign had become disturbingly like that on the Western Front, conducted from a maze of narrow, irregular ditches, with holes cut in the sides for shelter, which brought some immunity from enemy fire but increasing exposure to rain, mud and vermin, and all the other paraphernalia of trench-warfare. Jesson writes of his annoyance at being initially held back at a base camp some miles behind the front, and of his impatience to rejoin the fight. To pass the time, he was even able to take a ferry down the Aegean to the coast of Palestine and climb the 1,800ft Mount Elijah, smoking his pipe as he did so, to all visual intents and purposes the epitome of the public-school patriot who remained the same, essentially unflappable character in war as in peace. Reaching the summit of the mountain, Jesson writes, 'I found a small chapel or shrine dedicated to the Prophet, and inside was an old picture representing his ascent to Heaven in his chariot'. The view downhill to the lush and peaceful Jezreel Valley made another 'interesting con-trast' to the Turkish front. About three weeks after this interlude, there was a general call for all reserve units to return to Gallipoli. 'I was very glad', Jesson says.

Between the lines of the diary, one can sense that Captain Jesson now saw how much the strategic position had changed. 'We were on the back foot', he remarks at one point. Describing his new billet, he notes that:

The Turks now held all the higher ridges, and as our line was drawn back on the left we were not only subject to enfilade but almost reverse fire. As for reserves, I was informed there were none save for a handful on Lala Baba. It was obvious then that all idea of a great push had been abandoned.

At this point, the only meaningful, if not effective, form of attack came from two British destroyers at anchor in the bay. But even this attempt at inter-service cooperation fell some way short of ideal. 'The ships' guns used to pump lyddite into the Turks', Jesson writes:

How anybody or anything remained within 100 yards of where these shells pitched I have never understood. But whether they actually did much damage I do not know, and I'm inclined to think that their greatest achievement was to create a fearful noise, for after they had plastered a spot where we thought there was a gun we still suffered from the little brute the next day.

By this stage Jesson had no very high opinion of most of his superior officers, or of the strategic direction the campaign as a whole seemed to be taking. In the face of what was fast becoming another war of attrition, there was a certain 'wonderfully British' sense of fatalism among the troops, whose mood he summarises as "'I really don't know, but I suppose [we'll] be all right, and if not, well why worry?" That I think was the view of most people – anyhow, it was mine.'

Jesson devotes relatively little space to the daily hardships of war, but mentions almost in passing that there were two drawbacks to his new billet in the hills above Suvla Bay. The first was the physical discomfort:

The second was that the Turks seemed to think it an excellent place to send their shells. They frequently showered their favours on us, and usually when we were at lunch and tea … it was particularly annoying as they were what we called 'whiz bangs', because the report and explosion were almost simultaneous so there was no dodging them. One day I was talking to Inman and one of these beastly things came along and strik[ing] sandbags all round us threw dust in our faces, and afterwards we found four shrapnel bullets in the courtyard; one had gone through my canvas water bucket, one had torn one of the servants' shoulder straps, whilst others had buried themselves in the sandbags.

And still there were the flies. They were the emblematic scourge of Gallipoli, along with the lice. 'Whenever one passed down the support trenches one saw the men not on duty with their shirts off emulating the monkeys at the zoo. It was a quaint spectacle! Let it be whispered that the officers were not immune from the predatory visitations of these monsters.' Although an enemy aeroplane occasionally appeared over the bay, Jesson reports that 'we never hit one – nor did we have any more luck with the flocks of geese' that periodically flew out of the hills into the cold bright sky.

Like many others, over time Jesson grew increasingly disenchanted with military officialdom at Gallipoli, whose strategy he thought based on equal parts over-optimism and ignorance. 'Towards the end of my stay on the Peninsula we had a new CO and somehow or other we did not see eye to eye,' he admits:

It was most unfortunate, as I can faithfully say I enjoyed the life before he came. There [had been] much to entertain and amuse, but from then on there was constant friction. I will say no more [on] this score and only mention it as an introduction to stating my mental frame whilst on my [second tour] of the Peninsula.

Although an impasse seemed to have been reached in the actual fighting, the Allied troops were soon to face an even more daunting obstacle than the Turks. 'On November 26th,' Jesson notes:

My company went back into the reserve trenches of the Bn, which, although they were but 50 yards or so behind the fire trenches, meant no night watches. Inman and I were delighted at the prospect of a good meal and sleep, although it was not to be … we got comfortably settled in our new quarters and at about 7 p.m. I collected a working party and was taking them off when the rain, which had been coming down steadily for an hour or so, simply dropped from the heavens with all the fury of a tropical storm. Soon the night was made more hideous by blinding lightning flashes, and it was one of these I imagine which caused the men who were following me to lose communication, [for] when I found Greany a minute or two later half my men were missing … when I returned to my Hd Qtrs for dinner it must have been well after nine, and there I found a most depressing spectacle – the place was 3ft under water and the trenches themselves in almost as bad a condition … at dawn the next morning we found in many places the water had rushed down the slope, carving away the sand bags in the parapet and washing away parts of the traverses. The rain [and] mud filled up every form of dug-out. We improvised shelters … be it understood that we were not equipped for this weather, there was no such thing as trench boots or waders … The whole of that day was spent in trying to drain the trenches, but the rain came on again and it was becoming very cold …

That night it first froze and then snowed, for when I went out at dawn the ground was quite white. The first thing I did that morn was to rout out my CSM and CQMS and [send] them to collect parties for fuel and rum and then issue a ration of rum round the trenches. During that night and day we walked men up and down trying to keep up the circulation but a few died from exposure.

Now suffering from frostbite, Robert Jesson was again evacuated from the front and eventually transported by hospital ship to his home town of Southampton. After several weeks' convalescence, he asked to return to active duty. Promoted to Major, he arrived in Mesopotamia in time to take part in the Anglo-Indian counter-attack on the Turkish fortifications at Kut – 'the most insanitary place the Allied forces ever encountered', as it was called, and the scene of a protracted, Somme-like siege several months earlier. On 22 February 1917, Robert Jesson's battalion undertook a successful feinting manoeuvre in order to draw the Turks out onto the banks of the nearby River Tigris. According to the official war diary:

That [day], splashing noises were made at the water's edge. From information received from Corps, the enemy was entirely deceived and brought down 1 Battn, several machine guns, wire, field guns, etc, to repel any attack that may have been launched from the Licorice Factory. During afternoon 22 Feb, Major Jesson was killed by a sniper. His loss was deeply felt by all ranks.

He was 30.

III

At around midnight on 16 February 1918, 24-year-old Lieutenant Augustine Kelly, Royal Flying Corps, suffered a lacerated scalp, dislocated shoulder, two sprained ankles and what were described as 'other superficial wounds' when the stick-and-string plane he was flying in as a rear machine-gunner hit a tree and crash-landed in a field just west of Amiens. Despite the mishap, Kelly and his pilot were able to bring back valuable details of enemy troop movements on a roughly 70-mile line stretched behind the Somme, the preliminary to the German spring offensive that began five weeks later. Both men were awarded the MC for their gallantry in the face of 'sustained artillery and small-arms fire [while] operating in particularly hazardous conditions'. Lieutenant Kelly had twice been wounded on previous reconnaissance missions. Born in Dublin on New Year's Day 1894, he had played university and club cricket as a wicketkeeper-batsman before the war while qualifying as a barrister. After four years of combat duty at a time when aviators were as much at the mercy of the elements and their primitive, flimsy technology as of enemy gunfire, Kelly returned quietly to complete his degree. He was a mainstay of Irish cricket during the 1920s, where he not surprisingly proved utterly fearless in the face of even the fastest bowling. Batting at College Park, Dublin, in 1923, Kelly was struck in the face by the West Indian paceman George Francis. The crack as two of his lower teeth were shattered could be heard by colleagues in the pavilion. In the second innings, Kelly scored 36 in fifteen minutes, driving Francis out of the attack. 'I'll teach the bugger to hit me', he's said to have lisped on his return to the dressing room.

Another font of wartime leadership – and of disproportionate sacrifice – was South African cricket. As well as her other losses, there was Arthur Ochse, who, in March 1889, on the day after his 19th birthday, made his first-class debut in South Africa's own first Test, played against England at Port Elizabeth. Killed while fighting at Messines Ridge on 11 April 1918, aged 48, Corporal Ochse was not graced by a *Wisden* obituary. Nine days later, the South African Test cricketer and England rugby flanker Captain Reginald Hands died as a result of injuries sustained on the Western Front, aged just 29. A brilliant conversationalist, described by *Punch* as having 'a humour so elusive, a wit so dashing and a mind so agile [as] to make him an intellectual flying squirrel – before you grasped one pungent thought he was off another limb, whistling for you to follow' – the Princess of Wales is said to have swooned when seeing him once come down the clubhouse steps at Iffley Road, Oxford, dressed in his rugby shorts. Frederick Cook, a batsman from Eastern Province who won a single Test cap in 1895, fell to a sniper's bullet at Gallipoli shortly after his 45th birthday. South Africa's leg-spinning all-rounder Gordon White died of wounds suffered in the final campaign in Palestine in October 1918; ten years earlier, he had scored 147 in a Test against England at Johannesburg. The googly-bowling Reggie Schwarz left all his worldly possessions to his friend Bernard Bosanquet, who probably invented the googly in the first place before drifting out of the game to take Holy Orders. Bosanquet in turn named his son Reginald, born in 1932 – the future ITN newscaster – in Schwarz's honour. Not only did South Africa lose some of her finest sportsmen during the war, a combination of human and financial losses nearly closed down her programme of first-class cricket for good. In January 1920, the Secretary of Western Province was forced to apply for an emergency loan of £250 to pay the lease on the club's Newlands ground, which then conspicuously lacked some of its later charm. The paperwork describes the pavilion as 'offer[ing] sanctuary to an imposingly wide array of vermin', while 'assorted fowl gather daily on the pond in front of the scoreboard'.

After being wounded for a third time in November 1917, Lionel Tennyson was once again evacuated and spent the rest of the war on home duty. It was not quite the end of his ordeal, however. Having lost one brother, Harold, in action in 1916, he lost another one, Aubrey, in 1918. Although Tennyson understandably set out to live his post-war life to the full, personal happiness eluded him. In March 1918 he married an earl's daughter named Clarissa Tennant, whose first marriage had broken up after she and Tennyson 'frequently committed adultery [at] the Beacon Hotel, Crowborough ... and the Queens Hotel, Brighton', to quote the petition. Many of his society friends never quite forgave this public lapse of etiquette. Ten years later, the couple divorced after Clarissa had fallen in love with an American tycoon. Tennyson would continue to play first-class cricket into his late forties, by which time he tended to lumber while in the field. He became the 3rd Baron on his father's death in 1928, and sometime afterwards married a wealthy and attractive widow in California. This union also ended in the divorce court. Sitting down for a game of backgammon at White's Club one evening in September 1939, Tennyson lost £3,700 by the time he stood up again forty-five minutes later. He later sold the family's ancestral home on the Isle of Wight, though he retained the wine supply. On Tennyson's death in 1951, his material effects consisted of two Cartier cigarette cases, a gold watch and the royalties from his book *Sticky Wickets*, an engagingly written and rather wistful memoir that caused a brief stir in the press before going on to a long and peaceful retirement on the discount shelves.

Cricket tentatively returned to England in 1918, with an MCC minute noting that 'aspects of pre-war life' might now safely be resumed. There was a reasonably full programme of schools and regimental matches that summer, even if first enlistment and then conscription had 'necessarily thinned the ranks of many sides' as the *Globe* euphemistically put it. Representative cricket was staged on southern Test match grounds later that season. At Lord's on 6 July a crowd of 8,000 watched one of those wartime fixtures that seemed to revel in their unpredictably comic eccentricity. A young but close to full-power Australian XI met with defeat in a limited-overs clash with the Church. Batting first, the clergy managed just 67 off 22 overs. It would have been stretching it to say that the result seemed a foregone conclusion, but there was some evidence to that effect in the lunchtime stop-press of the London *Evening News* which read: '"Miracle Needed" at Lord's'. In the event the Australians were shot out for 62, largely thanks to the fast bowling of a young Barnet divinity student named Wilfrid Lord. He was never heard of as a cricketer again. A hastily arranged second innings to the match suggested that normal service was being restored: this time the Church made just 50 all out, and Australia finished the day at 56-1. On 5 August, the Lord's Schools lost to the Rest, just as they had in that fateful week four years earlier. On 7 August, Pelham Warner's XI took on the Public Schools at Lord's; Lord Harris took part, aged 67, and scored 11 before being run out. On 8 August, the Germans lost some 7 miles of land and 30,000 casualties on the Western Front – the 'Black Day' when their military leadership finally realised they could no longer win the war. When the full County Championship resumed in 1919, there was a sadly unfamiliar look both to the composition of the teams and the playing conditions. MCC had taken the opportunity to try out a series of two-day matches, with the hours of play extended from 10.30 a.m. until 7.30 p.m. Quickly withdrawn, it was not the last unsuccessful experiment by the authorities in their attempts at 'brighter cricket'.

Of course, despite the reassuring return of the summer game, the war changed everything, from the balance of world power down to the gradual but steady erosion of the age-old deference of one class of Englishmen to another. The social assumptions at the heart of cricket's amateur-professional divide were by no means dead, and would survive in name for another forty-four years. But they were already mortally wounded. Lieutenant Graham Mackay, the Sports Officer last seen organising matches for his artillery battalion under the palm trees of Baghdad, surely captured a mood when he wrote to his family in February 1918:

I am afraid [the] wise men at home are very wide of the mark if they think the troops will care to go back to the 'narrow life' in England, as they call it. The vast majority have had enough of pandering, [and] will go back to England by the million and will be the only people who will count. They will make the strongest and biggest 'Trade Union' in Great Britain, and will have very little use for all the little cliques and busybodies who are so prominent now with no-one to say them nay.

This was a prescient glimpse, as would become clear in the course of the next three or four decades, of a class structure that became steadily more disreputable. Young men like Lieutenant Mackay, whose only experience of life hitherto had been of 'bark[ing] at one's inferiors while grovel[ling] to the higher-ups', now increasingly felt the need to close the gap between the 'two nations' and 'kick away some [of] the rotten and foul-smelling traces of Britain's caste system'.

It's no more than commonplace, but still true, to say that none of this took place overnight, and cricket, in particular, retained some of its essentially Edwardian languor long enough to co-exist with an escalating satire boom, while the master-servant composition of most first-class teams survived to see the advent of the Rolling Stones, the hydrogen bomb and the space age. To the end of his playing days Lionel Tennyson, who admittedly revelled in certain *ancien régime* mannerisms, remained fond of communicating with his batsmen in the middle by telegram. If something about the current scoring rate displeased him, Tennyson's practice was to summon a messenger-boy to the captain's dressing room and dictate a wire that might read: 'Too slow. Run self out', or, alternatively: 'No more boundaries. Restrain urge at once.' The messenger would then take the slip to the nearest post office, where it would be transcribed into a cable and in turn brought back to the ground to be ceremonially presented in between overs to the offending player, while Tennyson himself continued to watch the proceedings with what was called 'an air of patrician and world-weary contempt – glancing up with pouchy eyes from his perusal of the sporting pages, his cheeks richly tinted, mouth slightly turned down over a heavy chin' to ensure his order had been promptly obeyed. It should be added that Tennyson could also be a charming and popular skipper when the mood took him, and was in the habit of leading both his professional and amateur colleagues onto the field from the same pavilion gate, thirty years before this became the standard practice. Perhaps it would be fair to say simply that the war brought an end to a widespread sense of security in society, for better or worse, and that even cricket gradually succumbed to the times.

It's also no more than commonplace to say that cricket has always offered a shared ground between the classes, and that even in the war it sometimes brought about surprising results. At La Marraine in June 1918, the officers and men of the 12th Lancashire Fusiliers paused in their defence of the enemy's final offensive long enough to stage a weekend tournament of limited-overs matches. After the Other Ranks easily won the first game, something of a social experiment took place, 'with the players swapping themselves around between sides without distinction, and a private soldier who had played in the Leagues solemnly writing out the batting order for the Lieutenants and Colonels now under his command'. It would be a stretch to say that this one case of enlisted men playing on level, or superior, terms with officers set a long-term precedent, but it demonstrates how the intensity of war sometimes forged a spirit of mutual comradeship not conspicuously available in peacetime.

But by far the strangest association between cricket and the war came about not in the trenches, but in a dressing station situated in a field south of Wervick, part of the southern front near Ypres, in the middle of October 1918. Mustard gas was now in extensive use by all the belligerents, and was deployed during a British attack, undertaken in shifting wind, launched in the early hours of 14 October. In the ensuing chaos, both German and Allied victims were taken back to a common area for first aid treatment before ultimately being evacuated behind their respective lines. According to a Conservative MP and Machine Gun Corps officer named Oliver Locker-Lampson, one of the enemy combatants in the dressing station was none other than 29-year-old Corporal Adolf Hitler. 'While he was recovering, he came to us and asked whether he might watch an eleven of cricket at play, so as to become initiated into the mysteries of our summer game. We welcomed him, of course.' But when himself invited to play in a friendly match, 'he proposed altering the laws of cricket, which he considered good enough for the pleasure-loving English, but not for the serious-minded Teuton'. Among other innovations, says Locker-Lampson, Hitler 'advocated the withdrawal of the use of pads. These artificial "bolsters" he dismissed as unmanly and un-German … in the end he also recommended a bigger and harder ball'. A day or two later, the future dictator was sent on to a military hospital near Stettin, thus ending his active involvement in England's national sport. Although there are some implausible points of the story – none of Hitler's many biographers mentions it, and Locker-Lampson also claimed to have taken a key personal role in the Russian Revolution – it conjures up an intriguing picture of a physically bold but not over-imaginative young German soldier grappling with the intricacies of googlies, sticky dogs and the LBW law. 'He finally gave the game up, exasperated,' said Locker-Lampson, 'but not before giving it a new motto, "*Ohne Hast, ohne Rast*" – which roughly translates as "Unhasting, unending".'

III

On 6 July 1914, a 25-year-old soldier-cricketer named Hugh Jones went out to bat for Gloucestershire on the first afternoon of their away fixture with Worcestershire. It was to be his only first-class appearance and, it has to be said, not a statistically distinguished one: he scored 11 and 0, and dropped an apparently easy catch in the outfield as drizzle began to fall on the third day. But this freckled, sturdily built character with a thatch of straw-coloured hair had what he called the 'real prize' in life; he had played in a county cricket match – briefly batting alongside Jessop – and his name would recur in *Wisden* as a result. After that, Jones was content to drop down to regimental level, where over time he enjoyed a reputation as what was called 'a fiercely aggressive attacker of all kinds of bowling, [and] an ever willing would-be leg spinner who, alas, rarely caught his captain's eye'.

Six weeks after playing his one and only Championship match, Lieutenant Jones was fighting with the 13th Battalion, Gloucestershire Regiment, at Mons. In 1916 he was awarded the MC for his gallantry at the Somme and promoted to captain. No one seems to have had a bad word to say about this solid West Country character, with a 'rich and beefy' complexion, 'unanimously loved' by virtue of his 'joyous ebullitions of excited mirth [even] in battle', which he called 'the great testing-ground' of men. In October 1918, however, Captain Jones, twice wounded and weakened after nearly four years of trench warfare, was struck down with pneumonia. The army evacuated him to a military hospital in Kent, where he arrived on 2 November. On the evening of 10 November, after insisting that he would soon be fit enough to return to the front, Jones died peacefully in his sleep, aged 29. He was chronologically the last first-class cricketer to be a victim of the 'great testing-ground'. The following morning, the war ended.

As we have seen, cricketers paid a full price. The annual obituary sections of *Wisden* continued to print the names of players and officials of all standards who died in service until well into the mid-1920s, as the lingering effects of wounds and disease took their toll. The First World War roll of honour at Lord's has the equivalent of thirty teams' worth of players and members who fell in action, from Lieutenant C.H. Abercrombie to Lieutenant C.F. Younger. In July 1919, *The Field* listed the names of 701 'cricketers sacrificed who played for school, college, university or county. There were 34 deaths among first-class men, 11 of them internationals [and] 32 who were Blues', eighteen from Cambridge and fourteen from Oxford. Whether or not they had originally supported it, the committee of very nearly every organised cricket side in Britain erected a memorial to the war, and more specifically their own victims of it. No county club lost fewer than ten men. At Kent, an obelisk was unveiled by the gates of the Canterbury ground in August 1919 to Colin Blythe 'and also to his comrades who fell in the service of their country'. A sadly fitting eleven names followed.

After the County Championship's failed attempt to embrace speed cricket in 1919, the domestic game settled down again the following season. Three-day play returned, it rained during much of the summer, and in early September Middlesex were vying at the top of the table with Surrey and Lancashire. Yet for all the reassuring sense of cohesion, if not of permanence, the wounds of the First World War would come to shape the everyday lives of all Britons, including those of her first-class cricketers. For nearly two generations, since the organisation of the Championship, both England's national sport and, broadly speaking, the nation as a whole had remained serenely in a state that reflected the social conventions of the early nineteenth century more than it anticipated those of the early twentieth. All this was quickly changing. Britons, in a phrase Lionel Tennyson used about himself, had found their old ideals 'eaten away by facts no one had cared to face'. The Victorian etiquette of gentlemen and players, separate dining areas, imperious telegrams and the like could not go on forever; 'and', Tennyson noted, 'a lot of people would like to see it stop now'. As he increasingly and sometimes bitterly came to recognise, this Regency character, with an insatiable appetite for the good things of life, slipped gradually from his special niche as an officially tolerated eccentric into a full-blown anachronism. 'I have become a waxwork,' he remarked in 1950. Tennyson died one morning at the age of 61, sitting up in bed at a seaside hotel, smoking a cigar over the racing page of *The Times*, while a valet ran his bath; 'passing away like an English gentleman', as his obituary said.

If some cricketers emerged from the trenches, like many thousands of other combatants, understandably traumatised (at least one of the names on the war memorial at Kent had succumbed to shell shock), others came home determined in their different ways to put an end to what Graham Mackay called the 'little cliques and busybodies' dominant in British life. The odd mixture of restoring traditional national assets like cricket while creating new personal opportunities, prospects and benefits formed the mythic core of the generally more socially free-swinging 1920s. One of those returning sportsmen-warriors determined to live life to the full was Percy Fender of Surrey and England, whose playing career would last long enough to see the Kaiser replaced by Hitler as the latest threat to peace. Britain, in the half-remembered, half-invented rendering Fender seemed to embody, was a simpler place, where the classes instinctively and cheerfully gravitated to their own level in society, and the haves kept a benign eye out for the have-nots – where everyone, in fact, was one big happy family. It was a land before a time of general strikes, unemployment and monarchs who abdicated or spoke of the country's malaise. Fender, possibly the best Test captain England never had, was clearly one of those who came home from the war determined to compensate for the delay, a rugged, competitive individual, willing to brave fortune in chancy ventures – yet one, Neville Cardus said, 'one could never quite see without expecting a chorus-line of girls to suddenly appear and start dancing around behind him'. At the time of his death, at 92, he was the last survivor of those who played county cricket regularly before the First World War.

The resumption of cricket in 1919 was also an opportunity for some to fill the playing ranks tragically thinned by the wastage of the last five years. Maurice Leyland, born in 1900, was what was called 'almost the Creator's original sketch for a Yorkshireman' and, nearly as crucial, among the most prolific English batsmen of his day. Demobilised from the army in 1919, Leyland went on to score 33,660 first-class runs over the next twenty-odd years, with a Test batting average of 46, and, along with his county colleague Herbert Sutcliffe, provides a welcome human link between the wars. The career of Elias 'Patsy' Hendren, born in 1889, has some of the same sense of continuity to it. In 1914 Hendren did not have a very happy time playing for Middlesex, at least until the first week of August. Starting in the match against Hampshire at Southampton, coinciding with the outbreak of war, he then scored a sequence of 59 not out, 51, 8, 121, 22, 88, 133 not out, 124 and 40, making a flurry of 646 runs at an average of 92 in just over a fortnight. Since Hendren also managed both to get married and to join the army in the same period, it's tempting to speculate that he simply decided to fling the bat at life while he could. He, too, continued to play very nearly up until the Second World War, scoring 57,611 first-class runs and 170 centuries in the process. It's somehow not entirely inapt that this stalwart professional cricketer, a firm believer in mucking-in between the classes, should have died on the same day in 1962 that an MCC Committee recommended the abolition of Gentleman and Player status. Hendren's era was also enlivened by the schoolboy who had excitedly watched the troop mobilisations in 1914 around Portsmouth harbour: Walter Hammond.

Perhaps the final lesson of 1914–18 is of man's continued capacity both for homicidal destruction and higher functions like cricket, and that, thankfully, the game itself still tends to be regularly renewed even in the direst circumstances. In May 1918, while the Germans battered away at the thin Allied line in France and the whole outcome of the war remained in flux, a boy was born in the more placid surroundings of Hendon, Middlesex. He has been described as 'seeming to have been endowed by fortune with a double charge of life, and with a double dose of human nature', and as a 'one-man miracle cure for the gloomy shabbiness of the time'. His name was Denis Compton, and apart from his uplifting role as a national stimulant he could bat a bit, too.

APPENDIX

A select list of those cricketers who fell in the war. There are differing interpretations of what constituted a 'first-class' player of the time, and no slight is intended on any individual omitted. The publisher would be glad to hear of any names to be included in future editions of the book.

Test Cricketers

Name	Test team	Date of death	Place of death
Colin Blythe	England	8 November 1917	near Passchendaele, Belgium
Major Booth	England	1 July 1916	near La Signy Farm, France
Frederick Cook	South Africa	30 November 1915	Cape Helles, Gallipoli Peninsula, Ottoman Empire
Tibby Cotter	Australia	31 October 1917	near Beersheba, Palestine
Reginald Hands	South Africa	20 April 1918	Boulogne, France
Kenneth Hutchings	England	3 September 1916	Ginchy, France
Eric Balfour 'Bill' Lundie	South Africa	12 September 1917	near Passchendaele, Belgium
Leonard Moon	England	23 November 1916	near Karasouli, Salonica, Greece
Claude Newberry	South Africa	1 August 1916	France
Arthur Edward Ochse	South Africa	11 April 1918	Middle Farm, Petit Puits, Messines Ridge, France
Reggie Schwarz	South Africa	18 November 1918	Étaples, France
Gordon White	South Africa	17 October 1918	Gaza, Palestine

First-class Cricketers

Name	Main first-class team	Date of death	Place of death
Cecil Abercrombie	Hampshire	31 May 1916	at sea, naval action off Jutland (HMS *Defence*)
Frederick Abraham	British Guiana	2 October 1918	Joncourt, France
Lestock Adams	Cambridge University	22 April 1918	Placaut Wood, France
Charlie Adamson	Queensland	17 September 1918	Salonica, Greece
Ernest Alderwick	Gloucestershire	26 August 1917	Péronne, France
Henry Anderson	Europeans (India)	29 October 1914	near La Gorgue, France
Alban Arnold	Hampshire	7 July 1916	Ovillers-la-Boisselle, France
Thomas Askham	Northamptonshire	21 August 1916	Maillet Wood, Sheepal, France
Charles Backman	South Australia	25 April 1915	Gallipoli, Ottoman Empire
Harold Bache	Worcestershire	15 February 1916	Comines Canal Bank, Ypres, Belgium
Francis Bacon	Hampshire	31 October 1915	at sea, on Yacht *Aries* off the coast of Belgium
Herbert Bailey	Barbados	31 July 1917	Hollebeke, France
James Balfour-Melville	Scotland	25 September 1915	Loos-en-Gohelle, France
Cecil Banes-Walker	Somerset	9 May 1915	Ypres, Belgium
Percy Banks	Somerset	26 April 1915	La Bricque, Ypres, Belgium
James Bannerman	Southland	23 December 1917	near Ypres, Belgium
Arthur Bateman	Ireland	28 March 1918	near Arras, France
Samuel Bates	Warwickshire	28 August 1916	near Hardecourt, France
Gordon Belcher	Hampshire	16 May 1915	near Richebourg, Belgium
William Benton	Middlesex	17 August 1916	near Méricourt-l'Abbé, France
Harry Biedermann	Argentina	10 August 1917	France

Frank Bingham	Derbyshire	22 May 1915	Sanctuary Wood, Ypres, Belgium
Wilfred Bird	Oxford University	9 May 1915	Richebourg St Vaast, France
Henry Blacklidge	Surrey	23 May 1917	Amarah, Mesopotamia
Cecil Bodington	Hampshire	11 April 1917	near Arras, France
William Boswell	Oxford University	28 July 1916	Thiepval, France
Evelyn Bradford	Hampshire	14 September 1914	near Bucy-le-Long, Soissons, France
Druce Brandt	Oxford University	6 July 1915	Boesinghe, Belgium
Bernard Brodhurst	Hampshire	27 April 1915	near Canadian Farm, St Julien, Ypres, Belgium
James Bryden	Otago	12 October 1917	Ypres, Belgium
William Burns	MCC	7 July 1916	Contalmaison, France
Frederick Burr	Worcestershire	12 March 1915	Kemmel, Belgium
Brian Butler	MCC	18 August 1916	Longueval, France
Leo Butler	Tasmania	23 August 1916	Puchevillers, France
Arthur Byng	Jamaica	14 September 1914	Vailly, France
William Cadogan	Europeans (India)	12 November 1914	Ypres, Belgium
Norman Callaway	New South Wales	3 May 1917	Second Battle of Bullecourt, France
John Campbell	Argentina	2 December 1917	Honnechy, France
William Carlsson	Western Province	14 July 1916	Delville Wood, France
Hugo Charteris	Gloucestershire	23 April 1916	Katia, Egypt
Esmé Chinnery	Surrey	18 January 1915	Issy, Paris, France
Harry Chinnery	Surrey	28 May 1916	Monchy-le-Preux, France
Gother Clarke	New South Wales	12 October 1917	Zonnebeke, Belgium
Leonard Colbeck	Cambridge University	3 January 1918	at sea, off the Cape of Good Hope in HMS *Ormonde*
Edward Coleman	Essex	2 April 1917	Salonica, Greece
Christopher Collier	Worcestershire	25 August 1916	near Mametz, France
Alexander Cowie	Cambridge University	7 April 1916	Amarah, Mesopotamia

Maurice Coxhead	Oxford University	3 May 1917	near Monchy-le-Preux, France
Alexander Crawford	Nottinghamshire	10 May 1916	Laventie, Richebourg-l'Avoué, France
Eustace Crawley	Cambridge University	2 November 1914	Wytschaete, Hollebeke, Belgium
Ernest Crawshaw	Canterbury	9 October 1918	Le Cateau, France
William Crozier	Dublin University	1 July 1916	Thiepval, France
Foster Cunliffe	Oxford University	10 July 1916	Ovillers-la-Boisselle, France
Wilfred Curwen	MCC	9 May 1915	near Poperinghe, Belgium
Edward Cuthbertson	Cambridge University	24 July 1917	Amarah, Mesopotamia
Leslie Davidson	MCC	3 August 1915	Rouen, France
Geoffrey Davies	Essex	26 September 1915	Hulluch, France
Arthur Davis	Leicestershire	4 November 1916	near Albert, France
Archibald Difford	Western Province	20 September 1918	Palestine
Ossie Douglas	Tasmania	24 April 1918	Dermancourt, near Albert, France
Sholto Douglas	Middlesex	28 January 1916	Cambrin, Arras, France
Geoffrey Dowling	Sussex	30 July 1915	Hooge, Belgium
Frank Dredge	Wellington	22 August 1916	Somme, France
G.E. Driver	Griqualand West	7 September 1916	East Africa
William Drysdale	Europeans (India)	29 September 1916	Gueudecourt, France
Arthur du Boulay	Kent	25 October 1918	Fillières, France
Arthur Edwards	Europeans (India)	25 September 1915	Loos-en-Gohelle, France
Keith Eltham	Tasmania	31 December 1916	near Lesboeufs, France
Charles Eyre	Cambridge University	25 September 1915	near Loos-en-Gohelle, France
Charles Fisher	Sussex	31 May 1916	at sea, aboard HMS *Invincible* at Jutland
Harold Forster	Hampshire	29 May 1918	Bouleuse Ridge, near Ventalay, France
Theodore Fowler	Gloucestershire	17 August 1915	London County Hospital, Epsom, Surrey, England

Harold Garnett	Lancashire	3 December 1917	Marcoing, Cambrai, France
Hugh Garrett	Somerset	4 June 1915	near Achi Baba, Gallipoli, Ottoman Empire
Laurence Gatenby	Tasmania	14 January 1917	Armentières, France
Fairfax Gill	Yorkshire	1 November 1917	Wimereux, Boulogne, France
Francis Gillespie	Surrey	18 June 1916	Ypres, Belgium
George Gilroy	Oxford University	15 July 1916	Corbie-sur-Somme, France
Cecil Gold	Middlesex	3 July 1916	Ovillers-la-Boisselle, France
Harold Goodwin	Cambridge University	24 April 1917	Arras, France
Steuart Gordon	Europeans (India)	31 October 1914	Messines, France
Lord Bernard Gordon-Lennox	Middlesex	10 November 1914	Kleinzillebeke, Belgium
Eric Gore-Browne	Europeans (India)	3 July 1918	Namacurra, Portuguese East Africa
Francis Gould	Europeans (India)	6 June 1915	Armentières, France
Tom Grace	Wellington	8 August 1915	Monash Valley, Gallipoli, Ottoman Empire
William Grant	Gloucestershire	26 September 1918	near Passchendaele, Belgium
Herbert Green	Europeans (India)	31 December 1918	Rouen, France
John Gregory	Hampshire	27 November 1914	near Zonnebeke, Belgium
Robert Gregory	Ireland	23 January 1918	near Grossa, Padua, Italy
Walter Greive	Scotland	1 April 1917	France
William Greive	Scotland	17 July 1916	Siege Farm, Kemmel, France
Neville Grell	Trinidad	5 June 1918	Trinidad
John Gunner	Hampshire	9 August 1918	Kemmel, Belgium
Ralph Hancock	Somerset	29 October 1914	Festubert, near La Bassée, France
Charles Handfield	Transvaal	6 May 1915	Gibeon, South-West Africa
Alfred Hartley	Lancashire	9 October 1918	near Maissemy, France

Eric Hatfeild	Kent	21 September 1918	Hargicourt, Cambrai, France
Percy Heath	Europeans (India)	14 July 1917	Baghdad, Mesopotamia
John Hellard	Somerset	2 July 1916	near Beaumont Hamel, France
Ralph Hemmingway	Nottinghamshire	15 October 1915	Hohenzollern Redoubt, near Vermelles, France
Rupert Hickmott	Canterbury	16 September 1916	Somme, France
Charles Higginbotham	Army	11 March 1915	near Neuve Chapelle, France
Harold Hippisley	Somerset	23 October 1914	Langemarck, Belgium
Harold Hodges	Nottinghamshire	22 March 1918	Ham, France
Bernard Holloway	MCC	27 September 1915	Loos-en-Gohelle, France
Gerald Howard-Smith	Cambridge University	29 March 1916	Merville St Vaast, France
Gilbert Howe	Wellington	10 January 1917	Messines, Belgium
John Hunt	Middlesex	16 September 1916	near Ginchy, France
de Courcy Ireland	Europeans (India)	28 January 1915	Hong Kong
Arthur Isaac	Worcestershire	7 July 1916	Contalmaison, France
John Isaac	Worcestershire	9 May 1915	Rouge Bancs, Fromelles Ridge, Armentières, France
Geoffrey Jackson	Derbyshire	9 April 1917	Faimpoux, Arras, Belgium
Arthur Jaques	Hampshire	27 September 1915	Bois Hugo, Loos-en-Gohelle, France
Burnet James	Gloucestershire	26 September 1915	Langemark, Belgium
Percy Jeeves	Warwickshire	22 July 1916	High Wood, Montauban-de-Picardie, France
David Jennings	Kent	6 August 1918	Tunbridge Wells, Kent, England
Robert Jesson	Hampshire	22 February 1917	near Kut, Mesopotamia
Donald Johnston	Oxford University	13 September 1918	Beugneux, France
Hugh Jones	Gloucestershire	10 November 1918	Chatham, Kent
Vivian Kavanagh	Auckland	9 August 1917	Ypres, Belgium
Henry Keigwin	Essex	20 September 1916	near Thiepval, France

David Kennedy	Scotland	1 July 1916	Somme, France
James Kinvig	Wellington	31 July 1917	Ploegsteert Wood, near Ypres, Belgium
Ronald Lagden	Oxford University	1 March 1915	St Eloi, Belgium
Arthur Lang	Sussex	25 January 1915	Cuinchy, France
Edwin Leat	Somerset	8 June 1918	near Beaumont Hamel, France
Lawrence Le Fleming	Kent	21 March 1918	Maissemy, France
Logie Leggat	Cambridge University	31 July 1917	Pilckem Ridge, Belgium
Richard Lewis	Oxford University	7 September 1917	Ypres, Belgium
Frank Lugton	Victoria	29 July 1916	near Villers-Bretonneux, France
Joseph Lynch	Gentlemen of Ireland	25 September 1915	Loos-en-Gohelle, France
Claude Mackay	Gloucestershire	7 June 1915	Boulogne, France
Mark McKenzie	Oxford University	25 September 1914	Soupir-sur-Aisne, Soissons, France
Meredith Magniac	South African Army	25 April 1917	France
Walter Malcolm	Otago	23 December 1917	Poelcapelle, Belgium
William Malraison	Transvaal	31 May 1916	East Africa
Bruce Manson	Europeans (India)	4 November 1914	Tanga, Tanganyika, German East Africa
Alan Marshall	Surrey	23 July 1915	Imtarfa, Malta
Edward Marvin	Transvaal	24 March 1918	Marrieres Wood, France
Arthur Marsden	Derbyshire	31 July 1916	St Pancras, London, England
Kenelm McCloughin	Free Foresters	26 September 1915	Hohenzollern Redoubt, near Cambrin, France
Stanley McKenzie	Tasmania	8 December 1915	Alexandria, Egypt
Ralph Melville	Gentlemen of Philadelphia	4 March 1919	Wimereux, France
Charles Minnaar	Western Province	16 November 1916	near Beaumont Hamel, France
Jacky Morkel	Transvaal	15 May 1916	East Africa
Claude Mulcahy	Natal	11 July 1916	Corbie-sur-Somme, France

John Murray	Scotland	23 September 1917	near Poelcappelle, Belgium
Guy Napier	Cambridge University	25 September 1915	Loos-en-Gohelle, France
George Neale	MCC	28 September 1915	near Loos-en-Gohelle, France
John Nelson	Lancashire	12 August 1917	near Pilckem, France
Arnold Nesbitt	Worcestershire	7 November 1914	Ploegsteert Wood, Belgium
Bernard Nevile	Worcestershire	11 February 1916	near Ypres, Belgium
Charles Newcombe	Derbyshire	27 December 1915	Fleurbaix, France
William Odell	Leicestershire	4 October 1917	near Passchendaele, Belgium
Cecil Palmer	Hampshire	26 July 1915	near Hill Q, Gallipoli, Ottoman Empire
Ernest Parker	Western Australia	2 May 1918	Caëstre, France
William Parker	MCC	30 July 1915	Hooge, Belgium
Eric Penn	Cambridge University	18 October 1915	Hohenzollern, near Loos-en-Gohelle, France
Charles Pepper	Nottinghamshire	13 September 1917	near La Clytte, Belgium
Henry Persse	Hampshire	28 June 1918	near Saint-Omer, France
Edward Phillips	Cambridge University	8 May 1915	near Ypres, Belgium
George Poeppel	Queensland	2 February 1917	German POW camp, Germany
Albert Pratt	Auckland	19 July 1916	Pozières, France
Reggie Pridmore	Warwickshire	13 March 1918	near Piave River, north of Venice, Italy
Donald Priestley	Gloucestershire	30 October 1917	Passchendale, Belgium
Richard Rail	Western Province	9 October 1917	Houthulst Forest, Passchendale, Belgium
John Raphael	Surrey	11 June 1917	Remy, Belgium
Cyril Rattigan	Cambridge University	13 November 1916	near Beaucourt, France
Rowland Raw	Gentlemen of England	7 August 1915	Suvla Bay, Gallipoli Peninsula, Ottoman Empire
Wilfrid Reay	Gentlemen of England	8 October 1915	near Thiepval, France

William Riley	Nottinghamshire	9 August 1917	near Coxyde, Belgium
Francis Roberts	Gloucestershire	8 February 1916	St Julien, Ypres, Belgium
Herbert Rogers	Hampshire	12 October 1916	Somme, France
Henry Rosher	J.G. Greig's XI	14 April 1915	Shaibah, Mesopotamia
James Ryan	Northamptonshire	25 September 1915	Loos-en-Gohelle, France
Oswald Samson	Somerset	7 September 1918	near Péronne, France
George Sandeman	Hampshire	26 April 1915	Zonnebeke, Belgium
Clifford Saville	Middlesex	8 November 1917	Fresnoy-le-Grand, Aisne, France
Herbert Sharp	Hawke's Bay	1 September 1918	France
Edward Shaw	Oxford University	7 October 1916	Le Sars, France
Ernest Shorrocks	Somerset	20 July 1916	Thiepval, France
Karl Siedle	Natal	30 May 1918	Doullens, Picardy, France
Ernest Simpson	Kent	2 October 1917	Saint-Omer, France
Leonard Slater	Gentlemen of the South	14 September 1914	Aisne, France
Hubert Selwyn-Smith	Queensland	7 June 1917	Messines, France
Allan Ivo Steel	MCC	8 October 1917	Langemark, Belgium
Frank Street	Essex	7 July 1916	Ovillers-la-Boisselle, France
William Stuart	Scotland	23 April 1917	Arras, France
Harvey Staunton	Nottinghamshire	14 January 1918	Arzizieh, Mesopotamia
Henry Stricker	Transvaal	15 February 1917	Dodoma, Tanganyika, German East Africa
James Sutcliffe	Hampshire	14 July 1915	Cape Helles, Gallipoli Peninsula, Ottoman Empire
Leonard Sutton	Somerset	3 June 1916	Zillebeke, France
Theodore Tapp	London County	21 October 1917	near Dozingham, Belgium
Edmund Thomson	MCC	21 December 1914	Festubert, near La Bassée, France
Charles Tomblin	Northamptonshire	1 June 1916	near Sissonne, France
Francis Townend	Europeans (India)	29 March 1915	Béthune, France

Geoffrey Toynbee	Hampshire	15 November 1914	Ploegsteert, Armentières, France
Thomas Truman	Gloucestershire	14 September 1918	near Étrun, France
Frederick Trumble	Royal Navy	10 May 1918	at sea, on board HMS *Warwick*
Hervey Tudway	Somerset	18 November 1914	Boulogne, France
Frank Tuff	Oxford University	5 November 1915	Imtarfa, Malta
Hugh Tuke	Hawke's Bay	7 June 1915	at sea, off Gallipoli, Ottoman Empire
Frederick Turner	Oxford University	10 January 1915	near Kemmel, Belgium
Ronald Turner	Gloucestershire	15 August 1915	Suvla Bay, Gallipoli Peninsula, Ottoman Empire
William Tyldesley	Lancashire	26 April 1918	Kemmel, Belgium
James Valiant	Essex	28 October 1917	Gaza, Palestine
Alan Wallace	Auckland	10 May 1915	at sea, off Gallipoli, Ottoman Empire
Gerald Ward	MCC	30 October 1914	Zandvoorde, Belgium
George Whatford	Sussex	22 November 1915	Ctesiphon, Ottoman Empire
George Whitehead	Kent	17 October 1918	Lanwe, near Menen, Belgium
Tony Wilding	Canterbury	9 May 1915	Neuve Chapelle, France
Joseph Williams	MCC	10 July 1916	Thiepval, France
Arthur Willmer	Oxford University	20 September 1916	Rouen, France
Francis Wilson	Jamaica	24 May 1915	Cape Helles, Gallipoli Peninsula, Ottoman Empire
George Wilson	Canterbury	14 December 1917	Belgium
Guy Wilson	Derbyshire	30 November 1917	Cambrai, France
Archer Windsor-Clive	Cambridge University	25 August 1914	Landrecies, France
John Winnington	Worcestershire	22 September 1918	near Kefar Kassin, Ramle, Palestine
Geoffrey Wood	Oxford University	13 October 1915	Hohenzollern, near Loos-en-Gohelle, France

Maxmillian Wood	Europeans (India)	22 August 1915	near Ismail Oglu Tepe, Gallipoli, Ottoman Empire
Kenneth Woodroffe	Cambridge University	13 May 1915	near Neuve Chapelle, France
Richard Worsley	Orange Free State	4 May 1917	at sea, off Gulf of Genoa, Italy
Oswald Wreford-Brown	Gloucestershire	7 July 1916	near Corbie, France
Egerton Wright	Oxford University	11 May 1918	Barly, France
Harold Wright	Leicestershire	14 September 1915	Marylebone, London, England
Charles Yaldren	Hampshire	23 October 1916	Thiepval, France
William Yalland	Gloucestershire	23 October 1914	Ypres, Belgium
Charles Younger	Scotland	21 March 1917	St Leger, near Aveluy, France

BIBLIOGRAPHY

Allen, David Rayvern, *Cricket's Silver Lining 1864–1914* (London: Willow Books, 1987)

Cruttwell, C.R.M.F., *A History of the Great War* (Chicago: Academy Publishers, 1991; orig. 1934)

David, Daniel, *The 1914 Campaign* (New York: Wieser and Wieser, 1987)

Edwards, Alan, *Lionel Tennyson: Regency Buck* (London: Robson Books, 2001)

Frith, David, *'My Dear Victorious Stod'* (Guildford: Lutterworth Press, 1977)

Frith, David, *The Golden Age of Cricket, 1890–1914* (Guildford: Lutterworth Press, 1978)

Fromkin, David, *Europe's Last Summer* (New York: Alfred A. Knopf, 2004)

Hudson, Roger, *The Jubilee Years* (London: Folio Society, 1996)

Keegan, John, *Opening Moves* (New York: Ballantine Books, 1971)

Kynaston, David, *W.G.'s Birthday Party* (London: Chatto & Windus, 1990)

McLeod, Kirsty, *The Last Summer* (London: William Collins, 1983)

Moynihan, Michael, ed., *People at War 1914–1918* (Newton Abbot: David & Charles, 1973)

Pardon, Sydney, ed., *Wisden's Cricketers' Almanack 1915* (London: John Wisden, 1915)

Pound, Reginald, *The Lost Generation of 1914* (New York: Coward-McCann, 1965)

Press Association, *100 Years of Cricket* (Lewes: Ammonite Press, 2008)

Rae, Simon, *W.G. Grace* (London: Faber and Faber, 1998)

Smart, John Blythe, *The Real Colin Blythe* (Kingsbridge: Blythe Smart Publications, 2009)

Streeton, Richard, *P.G.H. Fender* (London: Michael Joseph, 1981)

Telfer, Kevin, *Peter Pan's First XI* (London: Sceptre, 2010)

Thomas, W. Beach, *The English Year: Summer 1914* (London: T.C. and E.C. Jack; repr. Whitefish, Montana: Kessinger Publishing, 2007)

Tuchman, Barbara, *August 1914* (London: Constable, 1962)

Tucker, Spencer C., *The Great War 1914–18* (Bloomington: Indiana University Press, 1998)

SOURCES AND CHAPTER NOTES

The following pages show at least the formal interviews, published works, and/or primary archive material used in the preparation of the book. Although it necessarily lacks the direct input of any sportsmen-combatants of the First World War, bar that of the late Percy Fender, a number of their relatives, particularly those of Robert Jesson, kindly put their ancestors' diaries or other material at my disposal. A warm thanks to all the individuals and clubs listed, who should find their names in the acknowledgements at the front of the book.

Chapter 1

A good social overview of the English summer of 1914 can be found in Kirsty McLeod's *The Last Summer*, as cited in the bibliography. One or two of the direct quotes contained in this chapter first appeared in her book. The quote attributed to David Frith speaking of the 'soft, romantic shafts of museum lighting' appears in his peerless *The Golden Age of Cricket 1890–1914*. Other brief quotes here are excerpted from the same book. Primary source material included the private papers of Major Lord (Lionel) Tennyson, held at the Imperial War Museum. The UK National Archives provided details of UK Cabinet discussions and other ministerial actions (PREM 11 files) during the period. I should also particularly acknowledge and thank the staff at the Cambridge University Library, and the library of the RN Officers Club, Portsmouth.

Chapter 2

The quote beginning, '[We] stood up ...' appears in *Douglas Haig: Architect of Victory* by Walter Reid (Birlinn, 2006). Ronald Mason's quote beginning, 'The dry bright spring [sic] of 1914 is compact ...' appears in his biography *Jack Hobbs* (reprinted by Pavilion Books, 1988); I also re-read Mason's book *Sing All a Green Willow* (Epworth Press, 1967), and am delighted to have the opportunity of expressing my thanks to this particular author, whose cricket writing was the treat of an otherwise healthily austere childhood. Michael Moynihan's quote beginning, 'Marching on church parade ...' appears in his book *People at War 1914–1918*, cited in the bibliography.

Some of the historical context of this chapter comes from a reading of C.R.M.F. Cruttwell's *A History of the Great War*, and some from Spencer Tucker's *The Great War 1914–18*, both as cited in the bibliography. Cruttwell himself fought with bravery and distinction in the war before taking a position at Hertford College, Oxford, where his charges included the undergraduate Evelyn Waugh. The two do not seem to have hit it off. In time Waugh wrote a profile of Cruttwell in the student magazine *The Isis*, portraying him as 'a badger-like figure, clad in ancient tail-coat and lop-sided white tie', a relatively benign satire compared to the fictional treatments that followed at regular intervals over the next twenty years. Although Cruttwell appears not to have made an immediately sympathetic figure in some of his attitudes either to students in general ('Silly little suburban sods') or women in particular ('Drabs' or 'Breast-heavers') his published works make an important contribution to the history of the war. He died insane at the age of 54.

Other material in this chapter was made available by the staff or friends of Essex County Cricket Club, Hampshire County Cricket Club, Kent County Cricket Club and MCC, where I should particularly thank Neil Robinson and his colleagues. I consulted the Cabinet papers (PREM 11) held by the National Archives; the diaries of Lionel Tennyson and other combatants at the Imperial War Museum; and the archive libraries of *The Times*, the *New York Times* and the *New York World*, among others. It's also a pleasure to acknowledge the US Library of Congress who, if light on cricket, boast an impressive collection of diaries and other primary-source material on the England of 1914–18. My thanks also to the UK Family Records Centre, and the FBI – Freedom of Information Division.

Chapter 3

The quote by Michael Neiberg beginning, 'Neither Britain nor France ...' appears in his book *Fighting the Great War* (Harvard University Press, 2005). A number of brief quotes here first appeared in Kirsty McLeod's *The Last Summer*, or in Michael Moynihan's *People at War 1914–1918*, both as previously cited.

Primary source material again came from the Lionel Tennyson and other bequests at the Imperial War Museum; from the Cabinet papers (PREM 11) at the National Archives; from the MCC library at Lord's; and the US Library of Congress. I should again thank the staff both of the British Library and the UK Family Records Centre.

Printed sources included *The Times*, the *Daily Telegraph*, the *Morning Post*, the *Globe*, the *Hampshire Chronicle* and the *Birmingham Gazette*, as well as the back pages of *Cricket*. I'm grateful to the British Newspaper Library. Lionel Tennyson's book *Sticky Wickets* (Christopher Johnson, 1950) is a gripping account of that player's life and times, if not one that labours under any false modesty. I should also acknowledge Peter Wynne-Thomas's *The History of Hampshire County Cricket Club* (Christopher Helm, 1988), a title for authorship of which my own hat was briefly in the ring. The better man won.

Chapter 4

It's a pleasure to again acknowledge both Michael Neiberg's *Fighting the Great War* and other published sources including W.M.A. Beaverbrook, *Politicians and the War 1914–16*

(London: Thornton Butterworth, 1928); John Keegan, *The First World War* (London: Hutchinson, 1998); Barrie Pitt, *1918, The Last Act* (London: Cassell, 1962), Kirsty McLeod's *The Last Summer*, and others as cited in the bibliography. I should also particularly acknowledge the help, resources and kindness of David Pracy at Essex CCC, Dave Allen at Hampshire CCC, David Robertson at Kent CCC, and Andrew Hignell for his peerless knowledge of English and more particularly Welsh cricket of the period. The principal newspapers consulted were the *Daily Telegraph*, *Manchester Guardian*, *The Times*, the *Globe* and the *New York Times*; the journals consulted included *Bailey's Magazine*, *Cricket*, *The Cricketer*, and of course *Wisden Cricketer's Almanack*.

I'm again grateful to the Imperial War Museum, and particularly to their archivist Jane Rosen; to the archives of both the Cambridge University and British Libraries; and to the Harry Ransom Center, the University of Texas at Austin. Unlikely as it seems to connect the US National Security Archives with a book touching on historical English cricket, that institution very kindly put diaries and letters covering the years 1914–18 at my disposal. I should also thank my great friend the late but still inimitable Godfrey Evans: too young to have remembered the First World War, but an indefatigable fund of stories and scrapbooks covering the county cricket scene in the years immediately following it. He is much missed.

Some of the material in this chapter comes from the Private Papers of Major Lord Tennyson (file 13441) and some from the Private Papers of Commander C.F. Stow, RN (file 7241), both held by the Imperial War Museum. Other contemporary journals, diaries and oral accounts were supplied by the UK National Archives (formerly Public Record Office), the UK Family Records Centre and the National Archives and Record Service, Washington DC. I again consulted the previously listed newspapers and cricket journals. It is a great pleasure to acknowledge the help of Surrey County Council, who currently hold much of their county cricket club's archive material, including the committee minutes of the years 1914–18. My thanks, too, to my friends John Murray, Alastair Hignell and Imran Khan for their contacts. The South Africa Cricket Association very kindly supplied me with details of their cricketers' involvement in the war, which took such a heavy toll on both men and resources. I should also thank Wendy Adams of the Temple Reading Room, who kindly let me know of the part Rugby School and her cricketers played in the war. Grotesque as it is to think of it as a league table of some sort, perhaps the worst affected of all schoolboy elevens of the time was that at Radley, who lost close to half their 1914 side to one or another form of combat or disease. It is a melancholy record.

Chapter 5

The quote by Bessie Ellis beginning, 'They came for two or three weeks …' appears in Kirsty McLeod's *The Last Summer*. I should also particularly acknowledge published material including Daniel David's *The 1914 Campaign*, David Fromkin's *Europe's Last Summer* and Barbara Tuchman's *August 1914*, all as cited in the bibliography. I remember an interesting lecture by the late E.W. Swanton which touched particularly on that great cricketing polymath Harry Altham. My friend Peter Perchard, former benevolent tsar of *The Cricketer International*, very kindly put a number of contacts at my disposal. Generally reliable accounts of scores, if not necessarily of the individual players involved, can be found both in *Wisden Cricketer's Almanack* and on the *Cricket Archive* website. I'm again grateful for archive material including unpublished diaries, letters and scrapbooks to the Cambridge University Library and the Imperial War Museum, as cited.

For secondary sources I should credit *Chronicles*, *CricInfo*, the *Wisden Cricketer*, and the libraries of the *Observer*, the *Daily Telegraph*, *The Times* and the *New York Times*. Medical insight into the nature of the most common battlefield injuries – mental and physical – came from the initially elusive but eventually welcoming Dr Wallace Hodges; I'm grateful. I should also note the source, anonymous but then well placed, at the UK Ministry of Defence. The late John Arlott, while not one to exude millions of volts of synthetic charm, was at one time a kind, generous, slightly papal senior colleague who enlightened me on the whole subject of the golden age of cricket. I also remember a dinner with the elderly Gubby Allen in June 1989 which thrillingly evoked the period. I made further use of previously published articles in *The Sportsman* and *Cricket Lore*, and read John Major's very thorough *More Than a Game* (HarperCollins, 2007); the last, albeit perhaps labouring under its author's note of rampant nostalgia, is particularly good.

Chapter 6

The quote by Philip Gibbs beginning 'In Fleet Street, editors were emerging ...' appears in Kirsty McLeod's *The Last Summer*; the quote insisting General Joffre 'looked like Santa Claus and gave an impression ...' appears in Barbara Tuchman's *August 1914*. Other published sources included the *Daily Telegraph*, *The Times*, *Today*, *Wisden* and the *Wisden Cricketer*.

As well as the above, I again consulted the files of the Imperial War Museum, which contain journals and scrapbooks of sportsman-combatants in the war; the Cabinet papers (PREM 11) of the UK National Archive; and the correspondence files 1914–18 of the National Archives and Record Service, Washington DC. It's a great pleasure to acknowledge the help given by the Secretaries or staff of Lancashire CCC, Middlesex CCC, Sussex CCC and Worcestershire CCC. It was a particular pleasure to revisit the County ground, Hove (my thanks to Hugh Griffiths), where I first watched county cricket while incarcerated at a local prep school forty-odd years ago.

Other source material came from the British Library, *CricInfo*, the *Cricket Archive* site, the Public Record Office and HM Coroner's Office for West Sussex. I should again acknowledge the help of the RN Officers Club, Portsmouth, and of the National Army Museum in London.

Chapter 7

The quote by Cyril Drummond beginning, 'We marched right across Dublin ...' appears in Kirsty McLeod's *The Last Summer*. Other published sources for this chapter included Michael Moynihan, *People at War 1914–1918*; Reginald Pound, *The Lost Generation of 1914*, John Blythe Smart, *The Real Colin Blythe* and Richard Streeton, *P.G.H. Fender*, all as cited in the bibliography.

It's a pleasure to acknowledge again the resources of the Manuscripts Reading Room of the Cambridge University Library, where I recently spent rather longer in the course of a week than in my three years as a Cambridge undergraduate, and of the Rare Books Room of the British Library. Between them they provided the majority of the correspondence and the other private papers quoted here. I should also again credit the UK National Archives, and in particular their Cabinet papers of the period 1914–18. Newspaper archives consulted included *Collier's Weekly*, the *Daily Telegraph*, the *Globe*, the *Morning Post*, the *New York Times* and *The Times*. The US Library of Congress supplied other manuscript scrapbooks and diaries of the period.

For the long excerpts from Robert Jesson's diary I'm particularly grateful to Ann Gammie, who also kindly supplied personal details on Jesson's life and times. There are also various military websites, such as the Wiltshire Regiment archive, with details of this brave individual's career. Other documentary material was made available by the National Archives and Record Service, Washington DC; the Harry Ransom Center of the University of Texas at Austin; and the Imperial War Museum, all as previously cited. For oral history and reminiscences, I should again thank the late Gubby Allen, the late Godfrey Evans and the late Percy Fender, the last of whom would surely have made a bold and very likely successful choice as England Test captain. Although very far from the P.G. Wodehouse character sometimes portrayed, Fender somehow always gave contemporaries the impression that cricket, like life, was there to be enjoyed. It is a pity that he and Evans never quite overlapped in the same team.

Chapter 8

The quote by Arthur Conan Doyle beginning, 'I can never forget, and our descendants can never imagine ...' appears in his book *Memories and Adventures* (Boston: Little, Brown, 1924). It's a pleasure to again acknowledge the primary source material on Doyle made available both by the Rare Books Room of the British Library and by the Arthur Conan Doyle Collection (Richard Lancelyn Green Bequest) of Portsmouth City Council. The quote by Corporal B.J. Denore, Royal Berkshires, beginning, 'We marched, staggering about the road ...' appears in Reginald Pound's *The Lost Generation of 1914*. The specific description of the Dover of September 1914 as in the phrase 'The cheerful refrain of ...' appears in the same book. Percy Fender's quote beginning, 'I was on the way home ...' appears in Richard Streeton's very full *P.G. H. Fender: A Biography*. The description of Antwerp as 'a spectacle of pity and terror ...' appears in C.R.M.F. Cruttwell's *A History of the Great War*; David Frith's words beginning, 'Village cricketers, metropolitan club cricketers ...' appear in his book *The Golden Age of Cricket, 1890–1914*, as cited in the biography. The quote by Pt. Ernest Atkins beginning, 'Arriving at Victoria ...' appears in Michael Moynihan's *People at War 1914–1918*.

Primary source material came from the diaries of Lionel Tennyson, Commander C.F. Stow and others as named, which were kindly made available by Jane Rosen and her colleagues at the Imperial War Museum. I also again consulted the UK National Archives (PREM 11); the UK Family Records Centre; and the National Archives and Record Service, Washington DC. I'm grateful to Neil Robinson and his colleagues at the MCC Library for supplying minutes of MCC and other committee meetings of 1914–18. A source uniquely familiar with Lionel Tennyson's thoughts put Tennyson's views on his immediate post-war life, both as a soldier and cricketer, at my disposal.

Other published sources included David Kynaston, *W.G.'s Birthday Party* and Simon Rae's *W.G. Grace*, both as cited in the bibliography; Gerald Brodribb, *The Croucher – A Biography of Gilbert Jessop* (London Magazine Editions, 1974); C.B. Fry, *Life Worth Living* (reprinted by Pavilion Books, 1986); and Michael Marshall, *Gentleman and Players* (Grafton, 1987). I am grateful for the help of the R.N. Officers Club, Portsmouth, in tracing at least the nautical portion of Fry's long and enigmatic career.

Chapter 9

The quote by Herbert Farjeon beginning, 'There is to be no cricket season ...' is from his book *Herbert Farjeon's Cricket Bag* (Macdonald & Company, 1946). I'm surely not alone in thinking that a mistake has been made in allowing this Renaissance man of sport, literature and the theatre, at his best a comic turn to rival P.G. Wodehouse, to fall into relative obscurity. Farjeon richly deserves a biography, and if called upon by a publisher I will serve. The lines on A.E. Stoddart's funeral beginning, 'On the stroke of four o'clock the open hearse ...' appear in David Frith's *My Dear Victorious Stod*, as cited in the bibliography. The quote by Norman King-Wilson beginning, 'Dozens of old biscuit tins ...' appears in Michael Moynihan, *People at War*. The quote describing the Belgian front of 1914 as 'The culmination of horror ...' appears in C.R.M.F. Cruttwell's *A History of the Great War*. The quote by Oliver Locker-Lampson insisting, '[Hitler] asked whether he might watch ...' first appeared in an article by Locker-Lampson called 'Adolf Hitler as I Knew Him'. Originally published in the *Daily Mirror* of July 1930, it was revisited by the *Daily Mail* of 19 March 2010.

Documentary material on Lionel Tennyson came from the Imperial War Museum and the Isle of Wight Record Office (file JER/LTF/188); Other material was provided by David Robertson and the committee of Kent CCC; by the staff or committee at Essex CCC and Middlesex CCC; and the unpublished diary of Robert Jesson came from Ann Gammie. The details of Colin Blythe's war service can largely be found in the Lewisham Record Office and the Greenwich Record Office; some of the facts of his early life are held in the Metropolitan Archives, Clerkenwell. I also consulted the UK National Archives; the Clydesdale Cricket Club papers, Mitchell Library, Glasgow; and the National Archives and Record Service, Washington DC.

Among the secondary sources were the libraries of *Bailey's Magazine*, *Cricket Field*, *Cricket Lore*, the *Daily Telegraph*, *Essex Times*, *Sporting Life*, *Sportsman*, *The Times* and *Weekly Sun*. I would like to again acknowledge the help and encouragement of the various English county cricket clubs listed above, in particular of David Pracy at Essex CCC, Dave Allen at Hampshire CCC and David Robertson at Kent CCC; as well as the help of Ann Gammie and Andrew Hignell; and of my great and much missed friend Ted Stanley.

I can never repay the debt to my father Sefton Sandford.

INDEX

Service ranks have not been given, as they changed over time.

1st Battalion, Royal Berkshire Regiment 168
2nd Battalion, Northamptonshire Regiment 72
2nd Battalion, Seaforth Highlanders 173
2nd Dragoon Guards 94
3rd Battalion, Devonshire Regiment 152
4th Rifle Corps 48
5th Battalion, Hampshire Regiment 160
5th Battalion, Wiltshire Regiment 65
6th Battalion, Oxford and Bucks Light Infantry 211
6th Battalion, Loyal North Lancashire Regiment 19
8th Battalion, Rifle Brigade 97, 104
8th Battalion, Royal Berkshire Regiment 177
10th Battalion, Royal West Surrey Regiment 221
13th Battalion, Gloucestershire Regiment 230
15th Battalion, Royal Warwickshire Regiment 57
15th Battalion, West Yorkshire Regiment 41
35th Sikhs Regiment 164, 199

Abercrombie, Cecil 26–8, 231
Adamson, Charlie 194–5

Aisne 182, 192
Albert of Schleswig-Holstein, Prince 95
Allahakberries 20
Alletson, Ted 156
Altham, Harry 128, 129
Anderson, Gerard 156
Arnold, Alban 104, 118–19, 153
Askham, Thomas 166
Asquith, PM Herbert 40, 59, 127–8, 134, 144
Asquith, Raymond 210
Aubers Ridge 152
Auckinleck, Daniel G.H. 31
Australia 11, 15, 21, 23–5, 30, 38–9, 43–4, 48–9, 51–2, 55, 58, 63, 70, 81–2, 97, 106, 110, 115, 118, 121, 141, 154, 160, 164, 171–2, 180, 194, 198, 200, 202, 205, 211–8 passim, 227

Baggallay, Richard 131
Banes-Walker, Cecil 152–3
Barlow, Richard G. ('Dick') 106
Barnes, Sydney 12, 23, 109, 156
Barratt, Fred 79–80
Barrie, James 19–20, 23
Bateman, Arthur 111
Beck, Jack 35
Bedfordshire Regiment 176
Belcher, Gordon 168, 214
Benson, Hugh 94
Bird, Morice 11–12, 40

Birtwistle, Norman 125
Black Hand, the 98–9
Blofeld, Henry 105
Blunden, Edmund 85, 96
Blythe, Colin ('Charlie') 17–26 passim, 34, 39–40, 42, 53–6 passim, 80, 87–9, 99, 105, 107–8, 113, 117–8, 129–30, 149, 158–9, 163, 166, 168–71, 180, 218, 221–2, 231
Blythe, Sidney 17, 180
Booth, Major 11, 13–14, 25, 34, 40–1, 67, 92, 105, 153–4, 167, 171, 175, 202, 211
Bosanquet, Bernard 37, 226
Boswell, William 36–7, 104
Botha, Prime Minister Louis 12
Bradford, Sir Evelyn 173
Bradman, Donald 59
Brearley, Mike 17, 39
Brinton, Walter C. 84
Brooke, Rupert 47, 73, 101
Brookes, Norman 21
Browning, Hunter 179
Brownlee, Wilfred 185
Buckley, Frank 183

Caillaux, Joseph 125–6
Callaway, Norman 141
Calthorpe, Freddie 104–5
Cambrai 55, 82, 108, 120, 125, 181
Cambridge 23, 26, 32, 34, 37, 41, 48, 51–4, 71–2, 78–83 passim, 89–91, 96, 104–5,

118, 122, 130, 136, 139, 155, 164, 168, 171, 188, 190, 195, 197, 231
Cameron Highlanders 111, 114
Canada 141, 148, 209, 220–1
Carr, Arthur 23, 133, 155
Carr, Douglas 118, 155
Champion, Eric 47–8
Chaplin, Herbert 28
Cheshire Regiment 156
Chidson, Laurence 85
Churchill, Winston 127–8, 131–2, 144
Clarke, Sydney 48
Clifton College 85, 112, 129, 157, 163, 185, 189
Cody, Samuel 30
Coldstream Guards 70, 83, 106, 169, 185
Collins, Arthur 112, 157, 189, 205
Compton, Denis 49, 233
Coronel 190
Cotter, Albert ('Tibby') 141, 217, 221
Crisp, Francis F. 94
Cunliffe, Robert 97
Cuthbertson, Edward ('Ted') 78

Davies, Geoffrey 89–90, 176
Davies, George Llewelyn 20
Davies, Peter Llewelyn 20
Defence, HMS 26
Denton, Arthur D. ('Don') 72–3, 121, 129
Derbyshire CCC 69, 92–3, 100–1, 106–7, 131, 155, 163, 188
Dipper, Alf ('Old Dip') 58, 99, 167
Dolphin, Arthur 41–2, 202
Douglas, Johnny 11, 13, 34, 40, 68, 75, 95, 117, 131, 156, 176
Doyle, Arthur Conan 8, 20, 26, 159, 172, 201
Drake, Alonzo 41–2, 92, 112, 153–4, 167, 171, 175, 193
Ducat, Andrew 57–8, 92, 112, 115
du Boulay, Hubert 125
du Maurier, Guy 20

East Kent Regiment 22, 107
East Lancashire Regiment 169, 172–3, 184–5
Eden, Geoffrey 129

Edgbaston 92, 105–6, 133, 149–50, 163–6, 197
Egerton, Frederick G. 29
Egypt 77–9, 98, 132, 176, 208, 213
Ellis, Basil 84
English, Ernest 219
Essex CCC 11, 13, 51, 58, 67–9, 75, 85, 89–90, 96, 107–9, 117–19, 131, 135–6, 141, 158–60, 163, 176–7, 218
Essex Regiment 197
Eton College 11, 31, 61, 63, 77, 83, 85, 106–9, 139, 156–7, 179, 185, 187, 191–2, 199, 201, 218
Evans, Alfred 163–4
Evans, W.H.B. ('Bill') 30

Fagan, Niel 185
Falcon, Michael 195
Fargus, Reverend Archibald ('Biffer') 189–91
Fender, Percy 13, 27–8, 39–40, 57, 92, 112, 134–5, 142, 144, 167, 178–80, 202, 204, 232
Fitzherbert, Edward 197
Foster, Frank 86, 149, 153, 156, 164
Foster, Harold K. 96, 174
Foster, Reginald ('Tip') 70, 82, 199
Franklin, Walter 155
Freeman, Alfred P. ('Tich') 54–5, 149, 204
French, Field Marshal Sir John 162
Frith, David 24, 44, 193, 205
Froitzheim, Otto 22
Fry, Charles B. 17, 19, 44, 65–7, 70, 80–1, 89, 95, 97, 114, 156, 171

Gallipoli 8, 19, 65, 144, 147, 180, 189, 193, 195, 197, 203, 207–8, 212–3, 216, 222–4
Garnett, Harold 82, 99, 120, 166
George V, King 33–4, 60, 69, 97, 108, 127, 175, 222
Gilliat, Otho 187
Gillingham, Reverend Frank 68–9, 171, 204
Glamorgan CCC 54, 80, 94, 103, 179
Gloucestershire CCC 51–2, 57, 66, 79, 99, 113, 119 135,

137, 147, 153–4, 159, 164, 167, 185, 187, 190, 197, 219, 230
Gloucestershire Regiment 187, 230
Goggins, Peter 120
Gordon-Lennox, Lord Bernard 78–9, 169
Grace, William G. 23–4, 32, 35, 38, 45, 53, 59, 82–3, 96, 116–7, 122, 154, 160, 177, 179, 194, 199, 202, 207
Grant, William St Clair 114
Gray, Maurice 94
Green, Charles 96, 119
Grenadier Guards 79, 94, 191, 210
Grenfell, Francis 157
Grey, Sir Edward 77, 106, 113, 124, 127–8, 131
Grimshaw, Samuel 220–1
Guggisberg, Gordon 93–4
Gunn, George 22, 34, 81

Haig, Captain Nigel 42, 62–3
Haig, Field Marshal Douglas 20, 42, 189
Halswelle, Wyndham 182
Hammond, Walter 23, 59, 140, 233
Hampshire CCC 13, 19, 26–8, 30, 34, 53, 55, 58–66, 74, 77, 80–1, 88–92, 99, 103–5, 114, 115, 117–18, 121, 136, 138, 152–3, 155, 158, 160, 163, 165, 168, 172–4, 179, 186
Hampshire Regiment 160, 180
Hancock, Ralph 192
Hands, Reginald 12, 15, 26, 141, 226
Hardie, Keir 61, 162
Hardinge, Harold ('Wally') 54–5, 58, 74, 158
Hardy, Frederick ('Percy') 212–3
Harris, Lord George 42, 46, 96, 189, 227
Harrow School 11–12, 61, 79, 85, 92, 106–7, 109, 138, 179, 191, 195, 209
Hartley, Alfred 75, 120
Hatfeild, Eric 107–8
Havelock-Davies, Philip 54–5
Haverford College, Philadelphia 83–4

Hawke, HMS 186
Hawke, Lord Martin B. 34, 49, 76, 95–6, 143–7, 175, 177, 180, 200
Hay, Ian 15
Hayes, Ernest ('Ernie') 102, 142
Hayward, Tom 34, 92, 112, 118, 156, 167, 171
Hazlitt, Gervys 200
Heal, Cecil 48
Hearne, John W. ('Young Jack') 11–12, 34, 63, 67, 74, 92, 155, 156, 171
Hendren, Elias ('Patsy') 232
Hillier, Cyril 125
Hippisley, Harold 187
Hirst, George 25
Hitch, John W. ('Bill') 34, 58, 64, 112, 118, 142, 165
Hitchcock, Basil 168
Hitler, Adolf 229–30, 232
Hobbs, Jack 12, 22–3, 34, 36, 38, 45, 55, 57–62, 80, 92, 102, 104, 112, 115, 118, 133–4, 142–3, 167, 171, 178, 217
Hobhouse, Emily 61
Holbech, Bill 191
Honourable Artillery Company 182
Horan, Jack 181
Hornby, Albert H. 22, 26, 102, 108, 116, 133, 156
Horsley, Jim 107
Howell, John 85, 128–9, 197
Howell, Miles 36, 54, 128
Huddleston, William ('Bill') 102, 115, 116
Humphreys, Edward ('Punter') 61
Hurstpierpoint College 189
Hutchings, Kenneth L. 217–18

India 42, 63, 86, 141, 151, 172, 178, 191, 200, 202–3, 209
Ireland 70, 83–4, 111, 131, 144, 171
Iremonger, James ('Jim') 58–9, 156, 166
Isaac, John 197

Jackson, Geoffrey 92–3, 100
Jackson, Stanley 133
Jaques, Arthur 19, 28, 63, 81, 92, 106, 108, 153, 156, 165, 171, 206

Jaques, Joseph 206
Jeeves, Percy 57–8, 92, 106, 115, 133, 149, 153, 156, 163, 164–6, 171, 206
Jesson, Robert W. ('Wilf') 64–5, 91–2, 163, 174, 207–8, 213–4, 216, 222–5, 239, 246, 253
Jessop, Gilbert 25, 51–4, 79, 99, 114–15, 137, 144, 156, 160, 185, 192, 201–2, 217, 230
Johnston, Alexander 168
Johnston, Donald 37
Jones, Arthur 81–2, 199
Jones, Hugh 230–1
Joy, Frank 180–1
Jupp, Vallance 27, 130–1

Keigwin, Henry 136
Kelly, Augustine 225–6
Kelly, Frederick 21
Kennington Oval 22, 25, 38–9, 51, 56–60, 69, 86, 92, 96, 104, 108, 112, 118, 133–5, 144–5, 159, 164, 167, 177–9, 200, 221
Kent CCC 17–18, 22, 25, 30, 34, 38, 40, 41, 54–61 passim, 69–70, 75, 78, 80, 87–9, 99, 105, 107, 117–18, 122, 129–30, 134–5, 149–50, 155, 158–9, 163–4, 168, 171, 173, 178–80, 188, 198–9, 203–4, 212, 217–8, 222, 231–2
Kilner, Norman 198
Kilner, Roy 41–2, 154, 167
King's Own Liverpool Regiment 217
King's Own Scottish Borderers 181
King's Own Yorkshire Light Infantry 150, 155, 179
King's Royal Rifle Corps 15, 78
King's Shropshire Light Infantry 83
King-Wilson, Norman 216
Kinneir, Septimus 115, 149, 164
Kitchener, Earl Herbert 61, 132, 139, 162
Knight, Donald 35–6, 54
Knox, Neville 142, 155–6

Lancashire CCC 22, 32, 58–60, 72, 75, 82, 92, 98–9,

102, 106, 108, 112, 115–20 passim, 149, 151, 155, 166, 21, 231
Lancashire Fusiliers 120, 125, 136, 229
Lang, Arthur 28, 37
Larwood, Harold 26
Le Cateau 154, 162, 164, 179
Lee, Harry 151–2
Leicestershire CCC 19, 56, 69, 72, 75, 99, 103, 115, 119, 122, 138, 165–6, 188
Lewis, Wyndham 16
Leyland, Maurice 232
Lincolnshire CCC 140
Lincolnshire Regiment 23, 52
Littlejohn, Dr Arthur 62–3
Loos 19, 37, 164, 177, 193, 206
Lord, Wilfrid 227
Loyal North Lancashire Regiment 19, 99, 106, 167
Lundie, Eric ('Bill') 15, 141, 221
Luther, Alan 179

MacBryan, Jack 36–9, 164
Machine Gun Corps 133, 229
Mackay, Graham 219–20, 228, 232
Mackereth, Gilbert 120
Macmillan, Harold 74, 134
Makepeace, Harold 155–6
Makinson, Joseph 32–3
Malvern College 36, 78–9, 85, 104
Manners, John 179
Marlborough College 16, 47–8, 82, 192, 200
Marne, Battles of 78, 108, 112, 142, 150, 169–70, 172–3, 177, 182–4, 192, 196–7
Marsden-Smedley, George 85
Marsh, Jack 211–2
Mason, Ronald 45, 51, 59
McCloughlin, Kenelm 36–7
McIver, Colin 118–9
McKenzie, Mark K. 78
McLeod, Alister 153, 160
Mead, Charles P. ('Phil') 11–12, 27, 34–5, 81, 88, 136
Mead, Harold 119, 177
Mead, Walter 119
Melle, Basil 36
Messines 37, 48, 226, 234
Middlesex CCC 23, 30, 34, 36, 43, 49–50, 58, 62–8, 74–5, 77–80, 83, 92, 96, 99,

109, 117–18, 121–2, 136–7,
148, 151, 154–5, 158, 164,
168, 170, 177–8, 190, 193,
199–200, 205, 212, 219,
231–3
Mill Hill School 19
Mitchell, Frank 26
Molony, Trevor 72
Monmouth, HMS 190–1
Mons 13, 23, 90, 146, 155, 157,
192–3, 230
More, Richard 77
Moss, Reverend Reginald
154
Mulholland, Henry 171

Napier, Guy 164, 199
Nason, John 99
Neuve Chapelle 20, 22, 45,
90, 152, 182, 193
Newberry, Claude 15, 141
Newbolt, Henry 189
New Zealand 21, 69, 121, 141,
172, 214, 216
Northamptonshire CCC 41,
60, 72, 103, 121, 146, 166
Nottinghamshire CCC 22,
34, 58, 72, 80–2, 112–14,
122, 133, 151, 154, 156, 166

O'Brien, Sir Timothy 36–7
Onslow, Tom 83–4
Ochse, Arthur 141, 226
Odell, William 166
Old Trafford 22, 38, 75, 102,
116, 117, 119–20, 133, 151,
155, 166–7, 188, 202
Oxford 23, 30, 34–7, 51–2,
54–6, 64–5, 70, 77–8, 90,
92, 96, 100, 103–4, 107,
122, 125, 153, 154, 156, 163,
177, 181, 186, 200, 211,
226, 231

Pals Battalions 41, 120, 135,
167, 174, 202, 211
Pardon, Sydney 159, 199, 206,
209
Parker, William 97
Parkin, Cecil ('Ciss') 119
Parsons, John H. 85–6
Passchendaele 15, 17, 62, 114,
166, 177, 196, 221
Paul, Ernest 47–8
Pearson, Angus 128
Perrin, Percy ('Peter') 75
Poole, John 47–8

Poore, Robert M. 26
Poulton-Palmer, Ronnie 182
Powell, Kenneth 182
Pratt-Barlow, Bernhard 186–7
Priestley, John B. 16, 29
Prince Albert's Light Infantry
38
Princip, Gavrilo 44, 100–1

Queen's West Surrey
Regiment 118

Radley College 85, 129, 153,
189
Ranjitsinhji, Maharajah Jam
Sahib of Nawanagar 23,
66, 96, 160, 200
Relf, Albert 11, 13–14, 27, 34,
171, 200
Repton School 65, 72, 85,
129
Rhodes, Wilfred 11–12, 34,
116, 116
Richardson, Mary 32
Rifle Brigade 20, 62, 85, 92,
97, 104, 130, 169, 172, 176,
197
Rippon, Dudley 146–7
Rippon, Sydney 146–7
Roberts, Earl Frederick 159,
194
Robinson, Lionel 36–7
Robinson, Ralph 176
Rogers, Herbert 92, 174
Royal Army Medical Corps
68, 111
Royal Army Ordnance Corps
155
Royal Engineers 93, 112, 121,
130, 151, 157
Royal Field Artillery 63, 100,
182
Royal Flying Corps 72, 85,
99, 104, 129, 142, 147, 163,
175, 178, 225
Royal Fusiliers 104, 120, 128,
132, 135, 157, 176, 177, 179
Royal Irish Rifles 124
Royal Naval Air Service 67,
175, 209
Royal Scots Fusiliers 195
Royal Warwickshire
Regiment 57, 78, 206
Rugby School 47–8, 85, 106,
192, 249
Russia 46, 73, 77, 108, 110,
113, 126–7, 131, 150, 230

Salmon, Gordon 138
Sandford, Richard 189
Sassoon, Siegfried 30
Schwarz, Reginald ('Reggie')
15, 26, 37, 141, 226
Seely, Jack, 1st Baron
Mottistone 184–5, 196
Sewell, Edward 79, 158
Seymour, James 54–5, 69, 88
Sharp, Aubrey 121, 133
Shaw, Bernard 200, 211
Shaw, Edward 37, 104, 200
Sherwell, Rex 129
Sherwood Foresters 166, 209
Sitwell, Osbert 29, 134
Skelding, Alec 99–100, 115, 165
Smith, Razor 64, 164, 178
Smith, Sydney 121
Somerset CCC 50, 60, 69, 75,
79, 90, 92, 100, 137, 146–7,
152–4, 159, 164, 181, 187,
191–2, 212
Somme, the 13–15, 17, 20–1,
37, 42, 57, 63, 67 75, 85–6,
90, 93–4, 102, 104, 111,
119–20, 125, 128, 131, 133,
136, 139, 143, 167, 175–7,
180–1, 193, 195, 198, 202,
210–1, 213, 217, 221, 225,
230
South Africa 11–15, 23, 26,
32, 34, 36, 38–40, 60, 65–6,
109, 141, 171–2, 211, 218,
221, 226
South Wales Borderers 82
Spooner, Reginald 22–3, 96,
156
Sportsman's Battalion 102,
132
Staffordshire CCC 193
Steel, Allan G. 82–3, 199
Steel, Alan I. 83
Stoddart, Andrew E. 8, 24,
26, 43–5, 49–50, 109–10,
204–5
Stow, Charles 202
Strudwick, Herbert 11–12,
178
Suffragette movement 178
Surrey CCC 11, 13, 22, 27, 34,
36, 38–9, 54, 56–9, 64–5,
68–9, 72, 75, 80, 92, 96, 99,
102, 104, 112, 115, 117–18,
133, 137, 139–42, 144, 148,
155–6, 159, 164–7, 170,
177–8, 188, 191, 193, 201,
231–2

Sussex CCC 11, 13, 22, 24, 27–8, 37, 51, 54, 60, 65–6, 72–5, 99, 104, 114, 117, 121–2, 129–30, 138, 154, 156, 167, 170, 172, 179, 192, 197, 200

Tarrant, Frank 30, 63, 67, 109, 151, 156, 158–9, 168, 177
Tennyson, Lionel 27, 40–1, 62–3, 89–92, 114–15, 138–9, 150–3, 160–1, 172–3, 183–5, 196, 204, 218, 227–9, 231, passim
Thiepval 104, 136, 166
Thomson, Edmund 200
Thorne, Gordon 125
Tosetti, Douglas 177
Tremlin, Albert 68, 131
Trent Bridge 72, 80, 82, 113, 188
Trott, Albert 48–51, 121–3, 148, 200, 205
Trumble, Fred 97
Trumper, Victor 23, 45, 97, 199, 202, 211
Tufnell, Carleton 191–2
Tufnell, Neville 41–2
Turner, Ronald 197
Turner, Walter 89
Tyldesley, William 72, 99, 120, 166–7

Vardon, Harry 21
Verdun 129

Veitch, Dallas 128
Vine, Joe 27–8, 167

Waddington, Abe 175–6
Warner, Pelham 23, 42, 47–8, 58, 60, 62, 69, 74, 121, 136, 142, 151, 155, 170, 206, 212, 227
Warneford, Reginald 209–10
Warwickshire CCC 56–8, 64, 78, 80, 85–6, 92, 106, 109, 115, 117, 121, 133, 149–50, 153, 163–5, 191, 197–8, 206
Wellington College 14, 84, 192
Welsh Regiment 103
Westminster School 128, 142
West Surrey Regiment 221
West Yorkshire Regiment 13, 41, 63, 175, 200, 206, 211
White, Sir Archibald 22, 105, 108, 133
White, Gordon 141
Whitehead, George 85, 129, 163, 168
Whitehead, Ralph 116, 166
Willcocks, Harold 112–13
Wilhelm II, Kaiser 27, 46, 62, 73, 95, 127, 132, 232
Wilkinson, Cyril A. 39
Wilkinson, William A.C. 70–2
Willders-Lewis, Henry 221
Williams, Dyson 103
Wilson, Benjamin 67, 167
Wilson, Jack 175

Wilson, President Woodrow 77
Wiltshire Regiment 65, 115, 125, 163, 207
Wodehouse, Pelham G. 18, 20, 57, 155
Woodroffe, Kenneth 104, 130
Woodroffe, Sidney 17
Woolley, Frank E. 11–12, 23, 34, 42, 80, 88–9, 99, 105, 130
Worcestershire CCC 30, 50, 69–70, 86, 89, 99–100, 122, 133, 146, 154, 191, 197, 230
Wormald, John 199
Wright, Harold 8, 19
Wynyard, Edward ('Teddy') 160

Yorkshire CCC 22, 25, 34, 40–2, 49–51, 57, 67, 70, 75, 86, 89, 92, 94, 99, 105, 108, 112, 115–16, 119, 133, 137–8, 153–4, 167, 170, 175, 188, 190, 201, 204, 218
Yorkshire Light Infantry 150, 155, 179, 219
Ypres 48, 68, 70, 79, 90, 92, 94, 99, 104, 112, 119, 125, 129–30, 133, 150, 156–8, 168, 176, 181–2, 185, 187, 189–93, 195, 199, 201–2, 204, 218–9, 221, 229

Zeppelins 32, 45, 105, 139, 201, 204, 206–7, 210

Visit our website and discover thousands of other History Press books.

www.thehistorypress.co.uk